Structured Credit Products

Structured Credit Products

Pricing, Rating, Risk Management and Basel II

Edited by William Perraudin

RISK
BOOKS

Published by Risk Books, a Division of Incisive Financial Publishing Ltd

Haymarket House
28–29 Haymarket
London SW1Y 4RX
Tel: +44 (0)20 7484 9700
Fax: +44 (0)20 7484 9800
E-mail: books@riskwaters.com
Sites: www.riskbooks.com
www.riskwaters.com

ISBN 1 904339 26 3
ISBN 978 1 904339 26 3

British Library Cataloguing in Publication Data
A catalogue record for this book is available from the British Library

Managing Editor: Sarah Jenkins
Project Editor: Vasuki Balasubramaniam

Typeset by Mizpah Publishing Services, Chennai, India

Printed and bound in Spain by Espacegrafic, Pamplona, Navarra

Contents

SECTION 3: RISK MANAGEMENT

SECTION 4: BASEL II

List of Contributors

John Ammer is a senior economist in the International Finance Division at the Federal Reserve Board in Washington. He has broad research interests in finance and his work has appeared in *The Journal of Finance, Journal of Economics and Business, Journal of International Financial Markets Institutions and Money, European Financial Management,* and *The Journal of Fixed Income.* He earned a PhD in economics from Princeton University in 1992 and a BA (*magna cum laude*) in economics and mathematics from Yale University in 1984.

Alexander Batchvarov has served as Merrill Lynch's managing director of international structured credit research since 1998. This team is based both in London and Tokyo. It provides research on the traditional asset-backed securities (ABS) and mortgage-backed securities (MBS), market developments and on new market segments such as alternative asset classes, CDOs, CMBS, synthetic securitisation in Europe and Asia. The team regularly publishes *International Structured Credit Monthly* and *Japanese ABS Monthly* to provide in-depth analysis of market developments and suggest relative value opportunities. Alexander and members of his team have consistently been ranked top research analysts in numerous investors' surveys in Europe and Asia. Previously, he worked as a structured finance analyst in the Securitisation Group, and as a sovereign analyst in the Sovereign Risk Unit of Moody's Investors Service in London and New York. Prior to that, he was a manager in the emerging markets financial institutions group of Citibank in New York and worked in academia in Canada and Bulgaria. Alexander holds a PhD in international economics from the National Academy of Sciences in Bulgaria and an MBA in finance from the University of Alberta, Canada. He is a CFA Charterholder and a member of AIMR and NYSSA.

Nathanael Clinton is a research assistant in the International Finance Division at the Federal Reserve Board in Washington. His research interests include a variety of topics in finance and international economics. He earned a BA in economics and mathematics from Macalester College (St. Paul, Minnesota) in 2002.

Tom Dewyspelaere is a quantitative analyst in the credit methodology team at Dexia Group in Brussels. His current interests include developing models (in VB, Excel and MatLab) for structured products (CDOs and

MBS/ABS), credit derivatives, and credit risk. Prior to this position he worked as a risk analyst, specialising in structured products, at the Market Risk Group of Artesia Banking Corporation in Belgium. Before joining Artesia BC, he worked as a research and teaching assistant at the Department of Finance and at the MBA program at the Catholic University of Leuven (Belgium). He holds a BSc in commercial engineering, specialising in finance, from the Catholic University at Leuven.

João B.C. Garcia is a senior quantitative analyst in the credit methodology team at Dexia Group in Brussels. His current interests include credit derivatives, structured products and credit risk models for determining economic capital. Prior to this, he worked as a quantitative analyst at Artesia Banking Corporation in Brussels, modelling exotic interest rate derivatives. He holds a degree in electronic engineering from the Instituto Tecnologico de Aeronautica (ITA-Brazil), an MSc in physics from the UFPe-Brazil and a PhD in physics from the University of Antwerpen (UIA-Belgium). During his MSc he worked on neural networks and the dynamics of complex systems, and during his PhD he worked on information theory for pattern recognition in image processing, the modelling of proximity correction effects using neural networks for (mask building in) ebeam lithography (nanotechnology) and the pricing of equity derivatives.

Kai Gilkes is a director with Standard & Poor's in the European Structured Finance Group, based in Canary Wharf, London. Kai joined Standard & Poor's in 1998 as a rating analyst. He is currently head of the European structured finance analytics team, which is responsible for quantitative analysis, credit risk and cash flow modelling across the structured finance market, which includes RMBS, consumer ABS, CDOs and CMBS. Prior to joining Standard & Poor's, Kai lectured in physics and conducted research in condensed matter physics. Kai holds a BSc (Hons) in physics and computing from the University of Kent at Canterbury and a PhD in condensed matter physics from Clare Hall, University of Cambridge.

Michael B. Gordy is a senior economist in the research and statistics division of the Federal Reserve Board. His current research focuses on the design, calibration, computation and validation of models of portfolio credit risk, and on the adaptation of these models to setting regulatory capital requirements. He serves as an associate editor of the *Journal of Banking & Finance*. Michael was named *Risk* magazine's Quant of the Year for 2004 and GARP's 2003 Financial Risk Manager of the Year. He received his PhD in economics from MIT in 1994 and a BA in mathematics and philosophy from Yale University in 1985.

Peter-Paul Hoogbruin is the head of credit risk quantification at ING Corporate Credit Risk Management in Amsterdam. He is responsible for credit risk research, loan pricing and portfolio modelling. Prior to his current position, he worked for the portfolio management department of Group Credit Risk Management at Deutsche Bank in Frankfurt. His thinking on the topic of credit risk measurement and management can be found in *Euromarket Decisions*, *Finance Director Europe* and *Risk* Magazine. He holds a masters degree in econometrics from the Erasmus University in Rotterdam.

Richard V. Hrvatin is a managing director in the credit products group at Fitch Ratings. Richard is responsible for the analysis, structuring, and rating of cashflow, market value, and synthetic CDOs backed by a variety of asset classes, including alternative investments, asset-backed securities, and corporate debt, as well as developing rating criteria and cashflow models. In 2003, Richard led the project to update Fitch's CDO rating criteria, the centrepiece of which was the development of a new multi-step Monte Carlo simulation model, the Fitch Default VECTOR Model. Prior to joining Fitch, Richard was at Financial Security Assurance (FSA), where he structured and analysed transactions involving CDOs, trade receivables, other commercial assets, and perpetual bond repackagings. Prior to FSA, he was part of the structured finance group of Sakura Bank. In addition to being a CFA charterholder, Richard earned an MBA in international finance from St. John's University, New York, and a BS in manufacturing engineering from Rochester Institute of Technology. Richard has also lectured on various finance topics at St. John's University and the New York Institute of Finance.

Jian Hu is a vice president and senior analyst in credit policy research at Moody's Investors Service, New York. His main responsibilities are to lead research on defaults, losses and rating transitions among global structured finance securities. Previously, Jian was a senior financial economist within the Credit Portfolio Analytics Division of Fannie Mae in Washington, DC. Here, he developed and implemented measures of Fannie Mae's mortgage credit portfolio concentration risk, and developed and implemented counterparty risk pricing models for various types of Fannie Mae's credit guarantee business. He has co-authored a paper, with John Boyd and Ravi Jagannathan, entitled "The Stock Market's Reaction to Unemployment News: Why Bad News is Usually Good for Stocks", which is forthcoming in the *Journal of Finance*. Jian holds a PhD in finance from the Carlson School of Management, University of Minnesota, and an MA from the department of economics, State University of New York (SUNY) at Buffalo, USA. His BA was obtained from the School of Economics and Management, Tsinghua University, Beijing, China.

Norbert Jobst is an associate director at Standard & Poor's in the firm's European Structured Finance Ratings Group in London. He works in the group's analytics team, which is involved in the development of credit and cashflow models for all asset classes. Norbert's work focuses on quantitative credit risk models for CDOs and credit derivatives, as well as equity derivative products. Prior to joining Standard & Poor's, Norbert conducted research into credit risk modelling and optimisation under uncertainty, which was funded by Fidelity Investments. Norbert holds a degree in mathematics from Regensburg, Germany, and a PhD in mathematical sciences, Brunel University, UK.

Rüdiger Kiesel is a professor of financial mathematics at the University of Ulm. Previously he has been a lecturer and reader, for actuarial science and financial mathematics, at Birkbeck College, University of London and at the London School of Economics, where he is still a visiting professor. His main research areas are currently design and analysis of credit risk models, valuation and hedging of credit derivatives, methods of risk transfer and structuring of risk (securitisation) and the stochastic modelling of financial markets using Lévy-type processes. He is co-author of the *Springer Finance monograph Risk-Neutral Valuation* (now in its second edition) and has written more than twenty published research papers. He is a frequent speaker at international conferences and has organised several practitioner seminars. Rüdiger also consults for financial institutions and regulators on credit risk management and pricing models.

David Lando is a professor of finance at the Copenhagen Business School's Department of Finance. He holds a masters degree from the joint mathematics – economics program at the University of Copenhagen and a PhD in statistics from Cornell University. His main area of research in finance is credit risk modelling and risk management. He has been a visiting scholar at the Federal Reserve Board in Washington and is currently a member of Moody's Academic and Advisory Research Committee. He is on the editorial board of three international finance journals. Before joining the Copenhagen Business School, he was a professor at the Department of Applied Mathematics and Statistics at the University of Copenhagen. Among his recent publications is the book *Credit Risk Modeling – Theory and Applications* from Princeton University Press.

Astrid Van Landschoot works in the Financial Stability Division (Research and Analysis) of the National Bank of Belgium. Before joining the Bank, she completed a PhD entitled "empirical credit risk analysis of corporates, sovereigns, and banks" at Gent University, Belgium. During her PhD, she obtained grants to go to Tilburg University (the Netherlands), the

European Central Bank (Germany), and Scuola Normale Superiore (Italy). Her research interests include credit risk modelling, structured finance, bank risk management, and term structure modelling. She has had papers published in *Review of World Economics* (2004), *CentER Discussion Paper series* (2003), *Capital Markets and Economic Perspectives* (2003), and *ECB Working Paper series*.

Matthias Neugebauer is a director in Fitch Ratings' European Structured Finance team. As a member of the CDO team, he is responsible for conducting rating analysis for cashflow, balance sheet and credit derivative CDOs. Matthias is also a member of the CDO criteria development team, and played a key role in the development of the new VECTOR methodology. Matthias joined Fitch in November 2000 as a member of the RMBS team. In that role he was responsible for rating German, Dutch and UK RMBS transactions and was involved in criteria development, especially for cashflow modelling and structural analysis. Matthias completed his MSc in finance and economics, with distinction, at Durham University in 2000. At the same time, he was also awarded the degree of Diplomwirtschaftsingenieur from Cottbus University.

Vladislav Peretyatkin is a PhD student in financial economics at Birkbeck College, University of London. His research interests include credit risk modelling and numerical methods, in particular, the pricing and risk analysis of structured products. He holds a BSc form Kazakh State University and an MSc in finance from Birkbeck. He has acted as a consultant in the credit risk field to a range of financial institutions. In the past, he has worked as a lecturer in economics at the Kazakhstan Institute of Economics, Management and Strategic Research.

William Perraudin is a professor of finance at Imperial College, London, and is a special advisor to the Bank of England. As part of his work for the Bank, he has worked extensively on the Basel II proposals, particularly in the area of capital charges for structured products. He holds degrees from Oxford and LSE and a PhD from Harvard University. His research focuses on continuous time pricing, credit risk modelling, strategic contingent claims models and risk management. Before joining Imperial, he worked in the city, and for the International Monetary Fund, and taught at the University of Cambridge and at Birkbeck College, London. He has acted as a consultant for numerous investment banks, central banks, and multilateral organisations. He is a director of Risk Control Limited, a financial risk management software consultancy.

Domenico Picone is a senior analyst in the Asset Securitisation Department of the Royal Bank of Scotland (RBS) in London. He joined RBS seven years ago as part of its ALM Department. He moved to Asset Securitisation three years later, and specialised in modelling RMBS, CMBS, credit card, consumer finance, NPL and CDOs. Before moving to RBS, he was in the risk industry where he worked on IT solutions to manage interest rate risk and to price interest rate options. He holds an MPhil in finance, an MSc in mathematical trading and finance from the Cass Business School (London), an MA in Finance from Exeter University (UK), and he is a qualified Italian chartered accountant "Dottore Commercialista". Domenico is also a PhD student at the Cass Business School. His research interest is in pricing CDOs and nth to default with Copula functions.

Michael Pykhtin is a vice president in the Risk Management Group at KeyCorp in Cleveland, Ohio. His main responsibility is developing portfolio models of credit risk for capital allocation purposes. Michael has been a regular contributor to *Risk* magazine's Cutting Edge section. He has published articles on capital allocation for securitisations, granularity adjustment for loan portfolios, modelling correlations between default and recovery rates, modelling residual risk in auto leases, and analytical methods for multi-factor credit risk models. Prior to joining KeyCorp in 2000, Michael was a researcher in theoretical physics, studying vibrational dynamics at surfaces and interfaces of materials. He holds a PhD in physics from the University of Pennsylvania.

Olivier Renault is an associate director in the Quantitative Analytics Team of Standard & Poor's Risk Solutions, where he focuses primarily on credit risk portfolio modelling projects. Prior to joining Standard & Poor's in 2002, Olivier was a lecturer at the London School of Economics, where he taught derivatives and risk management. He was also a consultant for several asset management companies. Olivier holds an MSc in economics and finance from Warwick University (UK) and a PhD in finance from the University of Louvain (Belgium). He has published articles in many journals and is the joint author of the book *Measuring and Managing Credit Risk*, published in 2004.

Rafael Schmidt is a research fellow at the London School of Economics. His main research area includes dependence modelling, extreme value theory, statistics and their applications in finance. Prior to this, Rafael worked for three years at DaimlerChrysler on credit risk projects within the Financial Services Division. He holds a PhD and two masters degrees from Syracuse University, New York, and the University of Ulm, Germany, in mathematics and economics.

Jeroen de Smet is head of portfolio modelling at ING Group Corporate Credit Risk Management in Amsterdam, The Netherlands. Previously, he was a short- and long-term market and credit risk analyst at F&C Investment Management Limited in Amsterdam. Prior to this, Jeroen worked as a process modeller at the CFT of Philips Electronics in Eindhoven, The Netherlands. Jeroen obtained an MSc in theoretical geophysics and seismology from University of Utrecht. He also holds a PhD in geodynamics and theoretical geophysics from the University of Utrecht, specialising in (high performance) computing to solve systems of coupled non-linear time-dependent PDEs applied to the Earth's interior. During this research period he was an invited researcher at the Minnesota Supercomputer Institute at the University of Minnesota, Minneapolis, USA.

Viktor Tchistiakov is a senior credit risk analyst within portfolio modelling at ING Group Corporate Credit Risk Management in Amsterdam, The Netherlands. Previously he was a risk management analyst at Transtrend BV, Rotterdam. Viktor's educational qualifications include a PhD in mathematics from the University of Twente, The Netherlands, participation in the post graduate program in economics at the Center for Economic Research and Graduate Education (CERGE) in Prague, Czech Republic, and a diploma in mathematics from St. Petersburg State University, Russia.

Structured Credit Products: An Introduction

William Perraudin

Imperial College and Bank of England

Balance sheet structured products have transformed the way in which banks manage the credit risk in their portfolios. In a typical transaction, a bank will sell a pool of loans it has originated to a bankruptcy-remote special purpose vehicle (SPV). The SPV will pay for the assets by issuing a set of tranches of liabilities with different seniorities. Investors buying part of a tranche assume some of the credit risk of the underlying pool of collateral to the extent that losses on the loans may exceed the par value of more junior tranches.

Initially, much of the growth in structured credit markets was driven by banks' attempts to reduce the regulatory capital they must hold under the 1988 Basel Accord rules. Suppose that a bank securitises a pool of loans but retains most of the SPV's more junior liabilities and therefore retains almost all of the credit risk. Even if regulators required banks to deduct the "toxic waste" junior tranches from their capital, the total increase in capital that this implies will often be substantially less than the capital that the bank would have to hold if the loan pool remains on balance sheet, ie, 8% of the total pool par.

As the market has matured and the motive of economising regulatory capital has become less important, banks have increasingly employed structured products for genuine transfers of their risk to other financial institutions. Put another way, structured products increasingly permit banks to economise their economic capital, not just their regulatory capital.

These developments must surely be regarded as positive. Banks that can manage their risks by adjusting their exposure to different types of credit risk are much better equipped to weather downturns in markets. In the past, debt origination generally amounted to a buy and hold strategy by the originating bank. Now, instead of being locked into a particular credit market sector by its past decisions, a bank may adjust its exposures dynamically.

There may be some concerns that the traditional monitoring role that banks perform in debt markets will be diminished if they do not face the full consequences of their decisions. But where this consideration is significant, one would expect to see SPV designs that leave the bank with a relatively large fraction of the credit risk.

Just as the broad category of balance sheet structured products has revolutionised banking, so-called arbitrage structured products and, in particular, arbitrage collateralised debt obligations (CDOs) have transformed investment in previously illiquid bond markets. In a typical transaction, a collateral manager issues liabilities through an SPV and purchases a pool of illiquid bonds that he then manages, following a more or less active investment strategy. The effect of this has been to create valuable liquidity in corporate bond markets, allowing investors to take positions with differing levels of risk in diversified pools of hitherto illiquid credit sensitive instruments.

The complex nature of structured products means that ratings agencies play a key role as gatekeepers in this market. Issuers setting up an SPV generally consult ratings agencies early on about the ratings that the tranches of the SPV's liabilities will receive if the structure is designed in different ways. The agencies may specify particular levels of over-collateralisation or tranche thickness for senior tranches to attract given high credit ratings. After a structure has been established, ratings agencies play a significant role in monitoring the secondary market performance of structured products, assisting investors' decision-making through changes they make in the ratings they accord to structured exposures.

New markets in financial products often require new techniques of analysis. For example, the growth in interest rate derivatives in the 1980s was accompanied by a big expansion in research activity in firms and universities on term structure modelling. A similar development is under way in the modelling of structured products. The new problem faced by those wishing to model these instruments is that of modelling portfolios of correlated credit-sensitive exposures.

This volume is aimed at readers who wish to understand the latest developments in the pricing, rating and risk management of structured products. Domenico Picone describes the nature of typical structured products in detail, lucidly explaining the different categories of transactions and features of the market. Alexander Batchvarov sets out the many considerations (some hard to model formally) that influence the valuation of structured products. The chapters by David Lando and by Rüdiger Kiesel and Rafael Schmidt exposit new techniques for modelling statistically the losses on pools of correlated credit exposures, focusing on how correlation between defaults may be described. The contributions by Jeroen de Smet and Viktor Tchistiakov and by Olivier Renault, Tom Dewyspelaere and João Garcia examine how different models applied to structured product exposures compare in their implications for expected losses and capital.

The chapters by Kai Gilkes and Norbert Jobst, and by Richard Hrvatin consider methodological aspects of structured exposure ratings. Jian Hu, and John Ammer and Nathanael Clinton contribute significantly to the (at present) limited state of knowledge of the empirical behaviour of structured product ratings. William Perraudin and Astrid Van Landschoot examine the risks in structured product investments by analysing the volatilities and other statistics of secondary market spreads on US asset-backed securities (ABS).

Michael Pykhtin surveys an important new class of asymptotic models that are useful for analysing capital for structured products. The chapters by Michael Gordy and by Vladislav Peretyatkin and William Perraudin examine the underpinnings of the new Basel II framework for structured exposures. Alexander Batchvarov, Domenico Picone, Peter-Paul Hoogbruin, Jeroen de Smet, and Viktor Tchistiakov give a critical industry perspective on some of the Basel II proposals for structured products.

Taken together, these chapters constitute a formidable contribution to our understanding of the risk management, pricing, rating and regulation of structured products. Readers new to the field of structured products, as well as those who already have expertise in the field, should find much to interest them.

Section 1

Pricing

1

A Survey of Dependency Modelling: Copulas, Tail Dependence and Estimation

Rüdiger Kiesel; Rafael Schmidt

University of Ulm; London School of Economics

Modern credit risk management has identified the adequate modelling of dependency in credit portfolios as one of the most important and pressing issues to be addressed. In particular, the new concepts for credit-risk regulation, proposed by the Basel Committee on Banking Supervision (2003) in the New Basel Capital Accord, regard the correlation between asset returns as one of the driving factors for an adequate determination of risk-capital charges. In this context, the application of copulas has been recognised as a promising tool to analyse and model the dependence structure of credit risky portfolios (Bouyé *et al*, 2000; Frey and McNeil, 2001; Embrechts *et al*, 2003). In order to manage and control portfolio credit risk, a new generation of financial instruments, eg, basket credit derivatives and collateralised debt obligations (CDOs) among others, have been introduced to financial markets. The pricing and hedging of these instruments also require a careful analysis of the dependence structure between the respective underlying. For the active management of portfolio credit risk, copulas have recently been applied to model the dependence structure between default times involved in the pricing and hedging of basket credit derivatives and CDOs. For example, Li (2000) utilised the so-called Gaussian copula to price first-to-default credit derivates.

Rafael Schmidt gratefully acknowledges support by a fellowship within the Postdoctoral Programme of the German Academic Exchange Service (DAAD).

Laurent and Gregory (2003) and Schönbucher (2003) extended the copula-based pricing to other basket credit derivatives and CDOs by applying other types of copulas.

This chapter provides a survey of the most important techniques of modelling and measuring dependence with a view towards pricing and hedging these financial instruments. After a short review of the relevant literature, we introduce in the first section the concept of copulas and outline their importance for analysing dependence structures. We then discuss various dependence measures related to copulas and provide examples of copulas together with their current financial applications. The fourth section is devoted to selected aspects of statistical inference for copula functions such as efficient parameter estimations and tests of goodness-of-fit. The following section shows copula modelling in action: we outline a few recent applications of copulas in various fields of finance and insurance. Finally, we focus on the dependence modelling of extreme events such as large credit losses or credit default events.

Let us mention in passing that the interest and need for adequate identification and modelling of dependence in asset portfolios has likewise significantly increased during the last decade. In particular, the precise analysis of the (extreme) return of an asset portfolio, which depends heavily on the dependence structure of the individual (extreme) asset returns, has been studied extensively and provides important insights into asset return behaviour. For example, it is a well-known fact that dependencies between negative financial asset returns increase strongly during bear markets, which leads to the failure of conventional diversification strategies in times when they are most needed. Among the large body of finance literature on various aspects of dependency modelling we mention the empirical studies by Karolyi and Stulz (1996), Longin and Solnik (2001), and Campbell *et al* (2002), who focus on the so-called "correlation break-down", which refers to the significant increases of dependencies between financial asset returns during bear markets. For applications of copula-based techniques in this context, see Patton (2001) for a time series approach with copulas and Goorbergh *et al* (2004), who apply copulas in the framework of multidimensional option pricing.

COPULAS

The common practice of measuring dependency between random variables is via the well-known correlation coefficient. However, if it is used outside the family of multivariate Gaussian distributions, the concept of correlation comprises major insufficiencies. For example, a well-known but often overlooked fact is that uncorrelated random variables, ie, with correlation coefficient zero, may show a very strong dependency (a concrete example of this stylised fact is given below). The latter fact implies that although the dependency between the assets in a credit risky portfolio could be very strong, the correlation coefficient may lead to a completely wrong impression about the real dependency if it is close to zero. To circumvent this shortcoming, we propose alternative dependence measures such as Kendall's tau. Further, the dependence structure of extreme events, such as extreme market movements, is also usually poorly or incorrectly described by the correlation coefficient. However, we need adequate measures for dependencies of extreme events in order to support appropriate asset-allocation strategies, since particularly in credit risk management dependencies between large credit losses are of principal interest. In this context, we show that even the bivariate t-distribution with zero correlation constitutes a strong dependency between extreme events. Embrechts *et al* (2002) provided further reasoning of why traditional dependence measures such as the covariance and linear correlation are not always suited to a proper understanding of dependencies in financial markets.

In order to fully understand the dependence structure between arbitrary random variables and to point out the desirable properties of dependence measures (see the next section), we need to familiarise ourselves with the concept of copulas.

Copulas link multivariate distributions and their corresponding univariate marginal distributions. In other words, copulas allow the dependence structure of random vectors to be studied, irrespective of their marginal distributions. Further, copulas can be utilised to build flexible multivariate distribution functions in two steps: first model the dependence structure via some copula and then plug in appropriate marginals. Recently, the theory of copulas has been introduced to mathematical finance (see Bouyé *et al* (2000), Embrechts *et al* (2001) and Bingham *et al* (2003)), eg, in order to study the dependence structure of asset returns irrespective of the marginal asset-return distributions, and as a starting point to construct multivariate distributions for asset-return vectors or to develop powerful simulation algorithms.

In the following we will assume that all univariate distribution functions are continuous. This will keep the exposition simpler (all important results are still valid under more technical condition for the general case).

Definition (copula). Let $X = (X_1, \ldots, X_n)'$ *be an n-dimensional random vector with distribution function* $F(x_1, \ldots, x_n) = P(X_1 \leq x_1, \ldots, X_n \leq x_n)$ *and marginal distribution functions* $F_i(x_i) = P(X_i \leq x_i)$ *for all* $i = 1, \ldots, n$. *Then the distribution function C of the n-dimensional random vector* $(F_1(X_1), \ldots, F_n(X_n))'$ *is called the copula (or copula function) of X or F.*

It can be shown that the copula function is uniquely determined by the multivariate distribution function F and that

$$F(x_1, \ldots, x_n) = C(F_1(x_1), \ldots, F_n(x_n))$$

Copula functions represent standardised distributions in the sense that their one-dimensional marginals are uniformly distributed on the interval $[0,1]$. An important property is that the copula of a random vector X stays the same irrespectively of any strictly increasing transformation of the marginals X_j, $j = 1, \ldots, n$. This invariance property (also called "scale invariance") is a desired feature of dependence functions and dependence measures as we understand dependency itself to represent the association between "large" and "small" realisations of random vectors irrespective of their scale. A detailed treatment of copulas and other dependence concepts can be found in Joe (1997) and Nelsen (1999).

Survival copula

In credit risk and insurance modelling we study the relation of the joint survival functions

$$\bar{F}(x_1, \ldots, x_n) = P(X_1 > x_1, \ldots, X_n > x_n)$$

and the corresponding univariate survival functions $\bar{F}_j(x_j) = P(X_j > x_j)$, $j = 1, \ldots, n$. Here, the survival copula, $\hat{C}(u_1, \ldots u_n)$, $0 \leq u_i \leq 1$, $i = 1, \ldots, n$, links the marginal and the multivariate survival functions via

$$\bar{F}(x_1, \ldots, x_n) = \hat{C}(\bar{F}_1(x_1), \ldots, \bar{F}_n(x_n))$$

In the bivariate framework it is straightforward to show that

$$\hat{C}(u_1, u_2) = u_1 + u_2 - 1 + C(1 - u_1, 1 - u_2)$$

The multidimensional analogue of the survival copula is of a similar form although notationally rather complex.

Copula density

Existence provided, the n-dimensional copula-density c can be written as

$$f(x_1, \ldots, x_n) = c(F_1(x_1), \ldots, F_n(x_n)) \times \prod_{i=1}^{n} f_i(x_i) \qquad \textbf{(CD)}$$

where f and f_i denote the density functions of F and F_i, respectively.

DEPENDENCE MEASURES

We require proper dependence measures for multivariate distributions to be invariant with respect to the univariate marginal distributions. Now, all dependence measures that can be derived from the copula are scale invariant and so are in line with our basic requirement. The correlation coefficient $\rho(X_i, X_j)$ measures linear dependency and, therefore, is not scale invariant. Intuitively, we might substitute the standardised random variables $F_i(X_i)$ and $F_j(X_j)$ for the random variables X_i and X_j in order to obtain the scale-invariant correlation coefficient $\rho(F_i(X_i), F_j(X_j))$. Indeed, this dependence measure is well known and is called Spearman's rho, $\rho_S(X_i, X_j)$. Its relationship to the copula function C of X is as follows:

$$\begin{aligned}\rho_S(X_i, X_j) &= 12 \iint_{[0,1]^2} C_{ij}(u_i, u_j)\mathrm{d}u_i\mathrm{d}u_j - 3 \\ &= \rho(F_i(X_i), F_j(X_j)) = \frac{E[F_i(X_i)F_j(X_j)] - E[F_i(X_i)]E[F_j(X_j)]}{\sqrt{\mathrm{VAR}(F_i(X_i))}\sqrt{\mathrm{VAR}(F_j(X_j))}}\end{aligned}$$

with $C_{ij}(u_i,u_j) = C(1, \ldots, 1, u_i, 1, \ldots, 1, u_j, 1, \ldots, 1)$.

Another frequently used scale-invariant dependence measure is Kendall's tau. The finite-sample version of Kendall's tau is defined as the ratio of the number of concordant minus the number of discordant pairs of sample points with respect to the number of concordant and discordant pairs of sample points. Recall that a pair of sample points (x_i, x_j) and $(\bar{x}_i, \bar{x}_j)$ is called concordant if $x_i < (>) \bar{x}_i$ and $x_j < (>) \bar{x}_j$ and discordant otherwise. Formally, Kendall's tau is

$$\tau = \frac{\text{concordant pairs} - \text{discordant pairs}}{\text{concordant pairs} + \text{discordant pairs}} \qquad \textbf{(KT)}$$

The latter dependence measure is obviously scale invariant and it represents one of the most intuitive dependence measures. Note that Kendall's tau and Spearman's rho of a random vector refer to its bivariate marginal distributions; this is in line with the correlation coefficient. However, in contrast to the correlation coefficient, the latter two dependence measures are always 1 or -1, respectively, if one random variable is an increasing function (completely positively correlated) or decreasing function (completely negatively correlated) of the other random variable. Recall that the correlation coefficient might be zero in both cases. An illustrative example where the correlation coefficient is zero, despite strong dependency between two random variables, is given by taking a standard normal distributed random variable X and the transformed random variable $Y = X^2$. These two random variables have zero correlation since the first and the third moment of the standard normal distribution are zero.

Another important dependence measure, namely the tail-dependence coefficient, describes the dependency in the tail region of multivariate distributions. In contrast to the dependence measures discussed so far, tail dependence focuses solely on the dependence structure of extreme events. Loosely speaking, tail dependence describes the limiting proportion of a bivariate random vector that one margin exceeds a certain threshold given that the other margin has already exceeded that threshold. We use the following definition of tail dependence.

The n-dimensional random vector X is said to have upper tail dependent marginals X_i and X_j if

$$\lambda_{ij}^{U} = \lim_{q \to 1-} P(X_i > \mathrm{VAR}_q(X_i) \mid X_j > \mathrm{VAR}_q(X_j)) > 0 \qquad \textbf{(TDC)}$$

in the case when the limit exists, where $\mathrm{VAR}_q(X_i)$ denotes the value-at-risk of X_i at a confidence level q. Consequently, we say X_i and X_j are upper tail independent if $\lambda_{ij}^U = 0$. Further, we call λ_{ij}^U the upper tail-dependence coefficient. Similarly, we may define the lower tail-dependence coefficient λ_{ij}^L, if it exists. If C denotes the copula of X then

$$\lambda_{ij}^U = \lim_{q \to 1^-} \frac{1 - 2q + C_{ij}(q, q)}{1 - q}$$

and

$$\lambda_{ij}^L = \lim_{q \to 0^+} C_{ij}(q, q)/q \tag{TDC2}$$

This shows that tail dependence is again a copula property. In particular, the tail-dependence coefficients are invariant under strictly increasing transformations of the marginals.

EXAMPLES OF COPULAS

The list of analytically tractable copulas is large within the two-dimensional and three-dimensional framework. However, for arbitrary dimensions n there are only few copulas, which compromise a satisfactory trade-off between a limited number of parameters and a flexible enough dependence structure. A suitable class of copula functions can be constructed from the family of elliptically contoured distributions. The family of elliptical contoured distributions includes many well-known distributions such as the multivariate normal distribution, the multivariate Student's t-distribution, the multivariate logistic distribution, the multivariate symmetric stable distribution, and the multivariate symmetric generalised-hyperbolic distribution, all of which have been frequently used for financial applications (see, for example, Bingham and Kiesel (2001, 2002), Eberlein (2001), Eberlein and Prause (2002) and Rachev and Mittnik (2000)).

Elliptical copula

We start with the definition of the family of elliptically contoured distributions: let X be an n-dimensional random vector and Σ be a symmetric positive semi-definite $n \times n$ matrix. If $X - \mu$, for some n-dimensional location vector μ, possesses a characteristic function of the form $\Psi(t) = \Psi(t' \Sigma t)$ for some real-valued function Ψ, then X is said to be an elliptically contoured distributed with parameters μ (location), Σ (dispersion) and Ψ. We use $E_n(\mu, \Sigma, \Psi)$ to denote the class of elliptically contoured distributions and call Ψ the characteristic generator. The density function, if it exists, of an elliptically contoured distribution is of the form

$$f(x) = \det(\Sigma)^{-1/2} g\left((x-\mu)'\Sigma^{-1}(x-\mu)\right), \quad x \in R^n \qquad \textbf{(ELD)}$$

for some positive function g, which we call the density generator of an elliptically contoured distribution. Note that the term "elliptically contoured" distribution is related to the elliptical contours of the latter density. For a more detailed treatment of this family of distributions we refer the reader to Fang *et al* (1990).

Definition (elliptical copula). We say that C is an elliptical copula if it is the copula of an elliptically contoured distribution (constructed as in the definition of a general copula).

The copula of an n-dimensional normal distribution, the so-called normal or Gaussian copula, is given by

$$C(u_1, \ldots, u_n; R) = \Phi_R(\Phi^{-1}(u_1), \ldots, \Phi^{-1}(u_n))$$

where Φ_R denotes the n-dimensional standardised normal distribution with correlation matrix R and Φ^{-1} stands for the inverse distribution function of the univariate standardised normal-distribution. Thus, the n-dimensional normal copula comprises $n(n-1)/2$ different parameters that are contained in the correlation matrix. The n-dimensional normal copula density is obtained by

$$c(u_1, \ldots, u_n; R) = \frac{\exp\left(-\frac{1}{2} \varsigma'(R^{-1} - I)\varsigma\right)}{\sqrt{\det(R)}}$$

where $\varsigma = (\Phi^{-1}(u_1), \ldots, \Phi^{-1}(u_n))'$ and I denotes the unity matrix. Financial applications utilising the normal copula (implicitly or explicitly) are numerous (note that each multivariate normal distribution has a normal copula). For example, Li (2000) used the normal copula to explicitly model the dependency between credit default times.

The copula of the n-dimensional Student's t-distribution, the so-called t-copula, also constitutes an important representative of copulas with useful dependency properties (as we will see later). In practice, the t-copula represents the immediate alternative to the above normal copula because it inherits many useful properties of the latter; see Bingham *et al* (2003) and Bluhm *et al* (2003) for applications to credit portfolio modelling and basket derivatives pricing, respectively. The t-copula is defined by

$$C(u_1, \ldots, u_n; R, \upsilon) = T_{R,\nu}(t_\nu^{-1}(u_1), \ldots, t_\nu^{-1}(u_n))$$

where $T_{R,\nu}$ denotes the n-dimensional Student's t-distribution function and t_ν^{-1} stands for the inverse distribution function of the standardised Student's t-distribution with $\nu > 0$ degrees of freedom. The description of the matrix R requires some care as it only coincides with the (Pearson's) correlation matrix for $\nu > 2$. Otherwise, the correlation matrix does not exist and in this case we refer to R as some dependence matrix. The n-dimensional t-copula density function (see Figure 1) is given by

$$c(u_1, \ldots, u_n; R, \nu) = \frac{1}{\sqrt{\det(R)}} \frac{\Gamma((\nu+n)/2)}{\Gamma(\nu/2)} \left[\frac{\Gamma(\nu/2)}{\Gamma((\nu+1)/2)}\right]^n \times \frac{(1+\varsigma' R^{-1}\varsigma/\nu)^{-(\nu+n)/2}}{\prod_{i=1}^{n}(1+\varsigma_i^2/\nu)^{-(\nu+1)/2}} \qquad \textbf{(TCDF)}$$

where $\varsigma = (t_\nu^{-1}(u_1), \ldots, t_\nu^{-1}(u_n))'$.

Figure 1 illustrates the huge difference between the uncorrelated bivariate Student's t-copula (with correlation coefficient 0) and the independence copula, which is the dependence structure between stochastically independent random variables. In fact, according to Theorem 4.11 of Fang *et al* (1990) and Theorem 2.10.14 of Nelsen (1999), there exist no parameter constellations such that the Student's t-copula coincides with the independence copula. However, the Student's t-copula with uncorrelated marginals still incorporates a large amount of dependency, especially in the tail regions of the copula. This phenomenon has to be kept in mind for applications that are sensitive to the dependence structure of extreme events (eg, credit default models). The last section of this chapter investigates this observation in more detail.

Figure 1 Copula-densities $C(u_1,u_2)$ of the bivariate Student's t-copula and the bivariate independence copula. Left upper plot: Student's t-copula with parameters $\nu=3$ and $\rho=0$ (ρ refers to the single parameter of freedom in R). Right upper plot: Student's t-copula with parameters $\nu=3$ and $\rho=0.5$. Left lower plot: Student's t-copula with parameters $\nu=1$ and $\rho=0$. Right lower plot: density of the independence copula $C(u_1,u_2)=u_1 \cdot u_2$

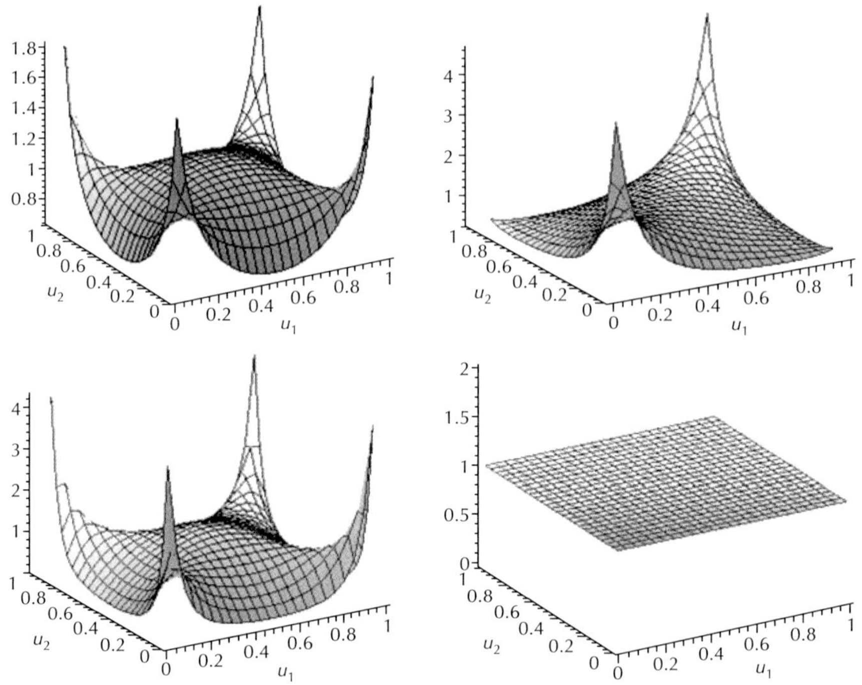

The striking properties of elliptical copulas are their straightforward construction for arbitrary dimensions n and their flexibility due to a reasonable number of parameters. However, the obvious drawback of most copulas of this family lies in the non-explicit representation of the copula function. Although this drawback does not affect a fast simulation, multidimensional copula quantiles require arduous numerical calculations.

Archimedean copula

Archimedean copulas form another important class of copulas that are easy to construct and comprise appealing analytical properties. Financial applications of Archimedean copulas to model loss distributions of credit portfolios and price basket credit derivatives can be found in Schönbucher (2003).

Definition (Archimedean copula). An n-dimensional Archimedean copula has the form

$$C(u_1, \ldots, u_n) = \varphi^{[-1]}(\varphi(u_1) + \cdots + \varphi(u_n))$$

for some continuous, strictly decreasing, and convex generator function $\varphi: [0, 1] \to [0, \infty]$ *such that* $\varphi(1) = 0$ *and the pseudo-inverse function* $\varphi^{[-1]}$ *is defined by*

$$\varphi^{[-1]}(t) = \begin{cases} \varphi^{-1}(t), & 0 \le t \le \varphi(0) \\ 0, & \varphi(0) < t \le \infty \end{cases}$$

We call φ strict if $\varphi(0) = \infty$. In this case $\varphi^{[-1]} = \varphi^{-1}$. Three important representatives of Archimedean copulas are the Clayton copula, the Gumbel copula and the Frank copula, which have the following generator functions:

$$\begin{aligned} &\text{Clayton copula:} && \varphi(t) = t^{-\theta} - 1, \ \theta \ge -1, \quad \theta \ne 0 \\ &\text{Gumbel copula:} && \varphi(t) = (-\ln t)^{\theta}, \quad \theta \ge 1 \qquad \textbf{(ARC)} \\ &\text{Frank copula:} && \varphi(t) = -\ln\left[(\exp(-\theta t) - 1)/(\exp(-\theta) - 1)\right], \\ &&& \theta \ne 0 \end{aligned}$$

Further examples of Archimedian copulas are listed in Nelsen (1999, p. 94). The family of Archimedean copulas is useful since it gives many n-dimensional copula functions in a closed analytical form. For financial applications, the latter property is essential because it forms the fundament for fast simulation and evaluation algorithms. However, Archimedean copulas suffer from two drawbacks; first, they impose too much structure on the dependency between random variables and, second, the number of parameters for higher dimensions is too low in order to represent realistic dependence structures. The first drawback results in the fact that the random vector $U = (U_1, \ldots, U_n)'$, which is distributed according to an Archimedean copula, possesses exchangeable components U_i, $i = 1, \ldots, n$. This means that the multivariate distribution of any permutation of the marginals stays the same.

Another drawback arises in the circumstance that Archimedean copulas only comprise positive correlations. To tackle this disadvantage one could simply consider linear-affine transformations of the resulting random vector: this kind of transformation describes, for example, the relationship between standard normal distributions and general normal distributions.

Empirical copula

Finally, we present the family of empirical copulas and empirical copula functions that are an immediate counterpart to the well-known family of empirical distributions and distribution functions. In statistical analysis, the empirical copula serves as the starting point for the construction of non-parametric statistics and goodness-of-fit tests, which focus on the dependence structure and dependence measures between random variables. In the following we provide some of these applications.

Definition (Empirical copula and empirical copula function). The empirical copula of an n-dimensional statistical sample $\{(X^j_{1m}, \ldots, X^j_{nm})' : j = 1, \ldots, m\}$ *of sample size m is defined as*

$$\hat{C}_m(u_1, \ldots, u_n) = \hat{F}_m(\hat{F}^{-1}_{1m}(u_1), \ldots, \hat{F}^{-1}_{nm}(u_n))$$

Here $\hat{F}_m$ *denotes the multivariate empirical distribution,*

$$\hat{F}_m(x_1, \ldots, x_n) = \frac{1}{m}\sum\nolimits_{j=1}^{m} I(X^j_{1m} \le x_1, \ldots, X^j_{nm} \le x_n)$$

with $I(\cdot)$ *being the usual indicator function, and* $\hat{F}_{im}$, $i = 1, \ldots, n$, *are the corresponding marginal empirical distributions. Let* $\{(x^j_{1m}, \ldots, x^j_{nm})' : j = 1, \ldots, m\}$ *be a realisation of the latter statistical sample. Then the empirical copula function has the form*

$$C_m(u_1, \ldots, u_n) = F_m(F^{-1}_{1m}(u_1), \ldots, F^{-1}_{nm}(u_n)) \qquad \textbf{(ECF)}$$

where F_m *is the well-known empirical distribution function and* F_{im}, $i = 1, \ldots, n$, *are the corresponding empirical marginal distribution functions of the above sample realisation.*

Figure 2 (a) Empirical copula function $C_m(u_1,u_2)$ (left) and the corresponding contour plot (right) of daily DAX and FTSE log-returns for September 2003. (b) Empirical copula function $C_m(u_1,u_2)$ (left) and the corresponding contour plot (right) of completely negatively correlated random variables

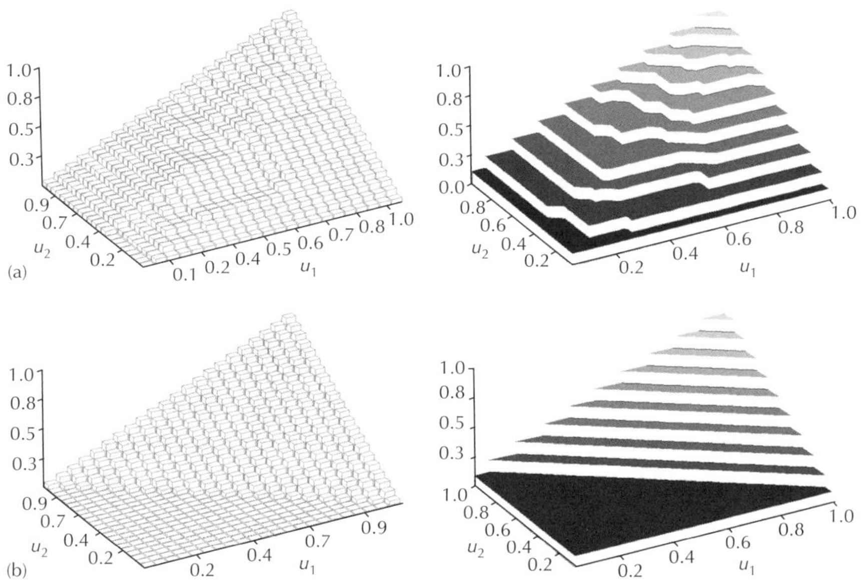

Figures 2(a) and 2(b) illustrate the general structure of a bivariate empirical copula function. Note the similarity to the univariate empirical distribution function is quite obvious in the left plot of both figures. The complementing right plots show the contours of the respective empirical copula function. The data in Figure 2(a) implicate a strong positive correlation since the contours nearly form rectangles. In the case of a strong negative correlation, the contours are straight lines as shown in Figure 2(b).

STATISTICAL INFERENCE

The right choice of the copula in higher dimensions immediately imposes some difficulties in the context of most financial applications. However, once the copula is decided, questions still remain regarding an efficient parameter estimation. In this context we distinguish between three different methods: the usual maximum-likelihood estimation (MLE); the MLE based on parametric inference functions for margins (parametric IFM); and the MLE based on non-parametric inference functions for margins (non-parametric IFM). For the latter two methods, the sample data have to be standardised in order to provide copula-distributed realisations. This standardisation uses the inverse marginal distribution functions (that are referred to as inference functions), which might be either of parametric or non-parametric form.

MLE

Consider an n-dimensional statistical sample of sample size m, ie, $\{(X^j_{1m}, \ldots, X^j_{nm})' : j = 1, \ldots, m\}$, distributed according to the distribution function

$$F(x_1, \ldots, x_n; \theta, \nu_1, \ldots, \nu_n) = C(F_1(x_1; \nu_1), \ldots, F_n(x_n; \nu_n); \theta)$$

where $\nu_1, \ldots, \nu_n$ represent the unknown parameters of the marginals and θ stands for the unknown copula parameter (all parameters might be vectors). In this setting, according to formula (CD), the log-likelihood function l for the MLE of all parameters takes the following form

$$l(\theta, \nu_1, \ldots, \nu_n) = \sum_{j=1}^{m} \log c(F_1(x^j_{1m}; \nu_1), \ldots, F_n(x^j_{nm}; \nu_n); \theta) + \sum_{j=1}^{m} \sum_{i=1}^{n} \log f_i(x^j_{im}; \nu_i)$$

where $\{(x^j_{1m}, \ldots, x^j_{nm})' : j = 1, \ldots, m\}$ denote a realisation of the considered statistical sample. The estimation of the copula parameter θ is therefore obtained from the simultaneous MLE of the parameter vector $(\theta, \nu_1, \ldots, \nu_n)'$. In other words, the estimator for θ is extracted from the MLE

$$l(\hat{\theta}_m, \hat{\nu}_{1m}, \ldots \hat{\nu}_{nm}) = \arg\max l(\theta, \nu_1, \ldots, \nu_n)$$

The popularity of the MLE is justified both by its many attractive properties, such as consistency or asymptotic normality, and its straightforward statistical interpretation. However, for higher dimensions, the previous log-likelihood function turns out to be rather complex and its surface might be too flat for an efficient numerical optimisation.

It is important to note that for the multivariate Student's t-distribution with d degrees of freedom, the one-dimensional marginal distributions are also Student's t-distributed with d degrees of freedom and the copula also contains the parameter d. In other words, the parameter d governs the marginals as well as the copula. However, the concept of copulas strictly splits the set of parameters of a multivariate distribution function into the set of parameters belonging solely to the dependence structure and the set of parameters referring to the marginal distribution functions. Along this line we may therefore construct a multivariate distribution possessing marginal Student's t-distribution functions $F_i(x_i; d_i)$, $i = 1, \ldots, n$ and possessing a t-copula $C(u_1, u_2; R, d)$ (as defined in formula (TCDF)), which only coincides with the multivariate Student's t-distribution if all parameters d_i and d are equal.

IFM

At this point we remind ourselves that the copula function is invariant with respect to the marginal distributions. This suggests a separate estimation of the unknown parameters. This approach is known as the MLE based on inference functions for margins, the so-called IFM method. We distinguish between the parametric and non-parametric inference function and the estimation methods are consequently named parametric and non-parametric IFM. According to the definition of copulas, the transformation of the sample data with the respective marginal distribution functions generates a new data set with distribution according to the copula. This can also be seen from the representation

$$C(u_1, \ldots, u_n) = F(F_1^{-1}(u_1), \ldots, F_n^{-1}(u_n)).$$

Thus, the aim is to transform the sample data via the respective fitted distribution-functions of the marginals in order to obtain new sample data, which are approximately distributed in a similar manner to the copula of the original data. The estimation of the unknown copula parameter θ via the IFM method now takes place in two consecutive steps.

Step one: parametric or non-parametric estimation of the marginal distribution functions

In the first case, we estimate the unknown parameters $(\nu_1, \ldots, \nu_n)'$ of $F_i(x_i; \nu_i)$, $i = 1, \ldots, n$, and denote the resulting estimator of the marginal distribution functions by

$$F_i(x_i; \hat{\nu}_{im}), \qquad i = 1, \ldots, n$$

From the point of view of implementation, many robust and efficient estimation algorithms exist for a large number of flexible univariate parametric distributions. Therefore, the issue is not the estimation of the parameters but the adequate choice of the marginal distribution functions. The proposed transformation of the sample data via inference functions depends heavily on the fit of the marginal distribution functions as illustrated in Figure 3. Hence, a careful testing of the goodness-of-fit is absolutely mandatory.

Figure 3 illustrates that the empirical dependence structure is quite sensitive towards marginal transformations. Although the copula function is theoretically invariant under any marginal transformation, the statistical behaviour of a copula sample with finite sample size is not invariant at all. In particular, the dependence structure of large or extreme events is strongly affected by

Figure 3 Scatter-plots of one and the same copula under different marginal transformations. The original data set are 3,000 realisations of a Gumbel copula with Student's t-marginals. The left plot illustrates the approximate copula realisations after the data have been transformed with the corresponding empirical marginal distributions, whereas the right plot shows copula-realisations obtained via fitted normal-distributed marginals

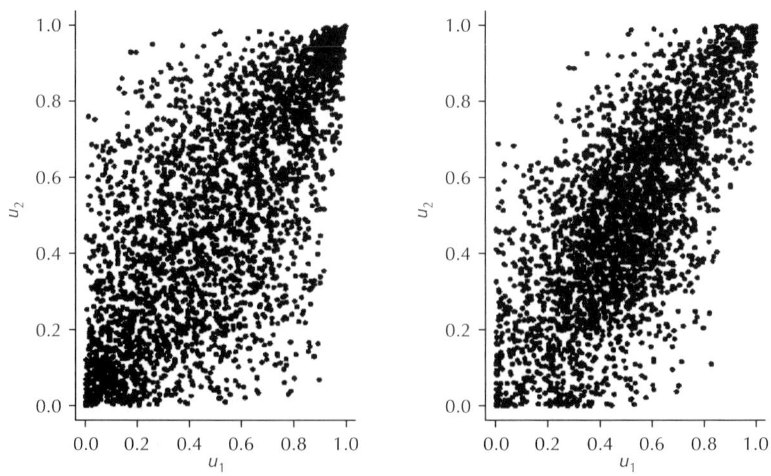

the wrong transformation as shown in the right-hand plot of Figure 3.

The non-parametric estimation, in contrast, utilises the respective empirical distribution as an estimator for the inference functions and therefore circumvents the latter pitfall, which is caused by an incorrect fit. On the other hand, empirical distributions are quite volatile and imprecise if the sample size is too small. However, if the marginal distribution functions are asymmetric or multi-modal, we definitely recommend the non-parametric IFM estimation method. Recall that empirical distributions are referred to as

$$\hat{F}_{im}(x_i), \quad i = 1, \ldots, n$$

Step two: transformation of the marginals by means of parametric or non-parametric IFM

The transformed sample data, after utilising parametric IFM, are

$$\left\{(F_1(X_{1m}^j; \hat{\nu}_{1m}), \ldots, F_n(X_{nm}^j; \hat{\nu}_{nm}))' : j = 1, \ldots, m\right\}$$

Similarly, with the non-parametric IFM transformation, we obtain

$$(\hat{F}_1(X_{1m}^j), \ldots, \hat{F}_n(X_{nm}^j))': \quad j = 1, \ldots, m$$

Note that the latter statistic only takes values on the grid $\{(l_1/m, \ldots, l_n/m)', 1 \leq l_i \leq m, i = 1, \ldots, n\}$ and its distribution function coincides on the grid with the empirical copula function stated in (ECF). Let us denote a set of realisations originated by either of the above statistics by $\{(\widehat{u}_{1m}^j), \ldots, \widehat{u}_{nm}^j))' : j = 1, \ldots, m\}$. This set of sample realisations can be now used for the estimation of the unknown copula parameter θ. Suppose, for example, that θ is estimated via MLE. Then the log-likelihood function is given by

$$l(\hat{\theta}) = \arg\max \sum_{j=1}^{m} \log c(\widehat{u}_{1m}^j, \ldots, \widehat{u}_{nm}^j; \theta). \qquad \textbf{(NP-IFM)}$$

Various asymptotical properties of the parametric IFM estimation, where all parameters are consecutively estimated via MLE, are provided by Joe and Xu (1996). Empirical simulations reveal that the performances, measured by the mean-squared error, between the simultaneous MLE and the MLE based on IFM methods do not deviate significantly for reasonable sample sizes (see, for example, Frahm *et al* (2003)). These facts emphasise the importance of the concept of copulas for both distribution modelling and parameter estimation.

Example: non-parametric IFM estimation for the Student's *t*-copula

Recall that the density function of the Student's t-copula as stated in formula (TCDF) contains the unknown parameters R and ν. The matrix R can be easily estimated via the following well-known relationship:

$$R_{ij} = \sin(\pi\tau_{ij}/2) \text{ and } R_{ii} = 1 \quad \text{with} \quad i \neq j,\, i, j = 1,\ldots,n \qquad \text{(ST)}$$

where Kendall's tau is substituted by its finite-sample version as stated in formula (KT). This relationship even holds, in general, for the class of elliptically contoured distributions (see Fang *et al* (2002)). Recall that Kendall's tau is a scale-invariant dependence measure and therefore the marginal transformations via IFM make no difference for the estimation. In contrast, the estimation of the parameter ν utilises formula (NP-IFM).

Estimation via dependence measures

It happens quite often that some parameters of the copula have a one-to-one relationship to a particular dependence measure. For example, in formula (ST) we illustrated that the parameter (matrix) R of the Student's t-copula has a bijective relationship to Kendall's tau. Therefore, the parameter R (which may not correspond to the correlation coefficient (matrix)) could be estimated via the finite sample version of Kendall's tau. Also, the Clayton copula and the Gumbel copula, which have been introduced as Archimedean copulas, possess parameters having a functional relationship to Kendall's tau. In particular, it is straightforward to show that

Clayton copula: $\theta = 2\tau/(1 - \tau)$
Gumbel copula: $\theta = 1/(1 - \tau)$

Note that Kendall's tau coincides for each bivariate marginal of an Archimedean copula due to symmetry.

Goodness of fit

Goodness-of-fit tests are mainly developed for one-dimensional distributions: among them we mention the well-known chi-square test, the Kolmogorov test and the Cramér–Smirnov–Von Mises test (cf, Casella and Berger (2002)). We have already illustrated that the quality of the IFM method depends primarily on the goodness of fit of the marginal distribution functions. In order to test the latter fit, we may utilise one of the above named tests.

Unfortunately there are only few goodness-of-fit tests available for multidimensional distributions. The following approach is tailored to general multivariate distribution functions and uses a particular probability integral transformation as described by Rosenblatt (1952) and Diebold *et al* (1997). However, we will state the following result in the framework of copulas.

Theorem (goodness-of-fit). Let X be an n-dimensional random vector with distribution function F and marginal distribution functions F_i, $i = 1, \ldots, n$. *If* $(F_1(X_1), \ldots, F_n(X_n))'$ *is distributed according to the copula C, then the random vector*

$$\big(F_1(X_1), C_2(F_2(X_2) \mid F_1(X_1)), \ldots, \\ C_n(F_n(X_n) \mid F_1(X_1), \ldots, F_{n-1}(X_{n-1}))\big)' \qquad \textbf{(GOF)}$$

has a mutually independent component. If the functions

$$C_k(u_1 \ldots, u_k) = C(u_1 \ldots, u_k, 1, \ldots, 1),\ k = 1, \ldots, n$$

denote the k-dimensional marginal functions of C, the conditional distribution of $F_k(X_k)$ *given the random variables* $F_1(X_1), \ldots, F_{k-1}(X_{k-1})$, $k = 2, \ldots, n$, *takes the following form:*

$$\begin{aligned} &C_k(F_k(X_k) \mid F_1(X_1), \ldots, F_{k-1}(X_{k-1})) \\ &= P(U_k \le F_k(X_k) \mid U_1 = F_1(X_1), \ldots, U_{k-1} = F_{k-1}(X_{k-1})) \\ &= \frac{\partial^{k-1} C_k(u_1, \ldots, u_k)}{\partial u_1 \ldots \partial u_{k-1}} \Big/ \frac{\partial^{k-1} C_{k-1}(u_1, \ldots, u_{k-1})}{\partial u_1 \ldots \partial u_{k-1}} \end{aligned}$$

where we substitute $u_1 = F_1(X_1), \ldots, u_k = F_k(X_k)$.

Since the random vector in formula (GOF) has mutually independent marginal distributions that are uniformly distributed on the interval [0, 1], we may now easily utilise one of the previous mentioned goodness-of-fit tests to each one-dimensional marginal.

APPLICATION OF COPULAS

Copulas are currently being applied to a wide field of problems from pricing and risk management. In particular, the modern aspects of credit risk are being modelled with the help of copulas. Out of the vast amount of literature, we present four areas where copulas have recently been applied and where we see the need for further detailed investigations into how to adequately model relevant dependence structures.

Portfolio credit risk models

A popular approach to modelling portfolios of credit-risky assets that has been employed in the CreditMetrics framework and the New Basel Agreement is a Gaussian one- (or multi-) factor model. Here the random vector $(X_1, \ldots, X_n)$ is related to the financial well being of the credit-risky assets and modelled as a Gaussian vector with

$$X_i = \rho Y + \sqrt{1-\rho^2} Z_i$$

where Y, Z_i; $i = 1, \ldots, n$ are independent standard Gaussian random variables. This approach can also be associated with the classical Merton (asset-based) model for the evaluation of a corporate bond. The parameter ρ can be readily identified as a correlation parameter and, because of the Gaussian setting, completely specifies the dependence structure. From our copula-based viewpoint, we find that the model uses a Gaussian copula structure and, therefore, does not possess any tail dependence. We can address this issue without leaving the factor-modelling approach by using alternative factor distributions, such as a multivariate t-distribution. A very flexible general approach is to use a mean–variance mixture. Then

$$X_i = \mu_i(Y) + \sigma_i(Y) Z_i$$

where Y is an one-dimensional mixing variable and Z_i; $i = 1, \ldots, m$ are independent standard Gaussian variables (also independent from Y). Now we naturally work in the framework of elliptical copula functions and can utilise their well-understood dependence structure (see Bingham *et al* (2003) and the section on dependence measures).

CDOs and multi-name credit derivatives

CDOs and multi-name credit derivatives, such as credit default swaps, have become very popular in recent years and now constitute an important asset class (see Bluhm *et al* (2003) for further discussion). Both types of asset are associated with a pool of credit-risky instruments and therefore require an appropriate modelling of the dependence structure of the underlying assets. In standard mathematical models of these assets we consider a portfolio of m obligors and let τ_i represent the default time of the ith obligor. Let $F_i(t) = P(\tau_i \leq t)$ be the marginal distribution function of the default time of obligor i and $f_i(t)$ the corresponding density (which we assume to exist). We can now use a copula function C to obtain the multivariate default-time distribution $F(t_1, \ldots, t_m) = C(F_1(t_1), \ldots, F_m(t_m))$, which allows straightforward simulation of the dependent default. We can furthermore choose the copula function to consider several features of the default times with respect to their dependence structure when performing stress tests and a scenario analysis in our evaluation procedure.

It is possible to calibrate a default-time model that is compatible in distribution with a one-period asset value model (as above). The basic example is a geometric Brownian motion

$$\mathrm{d}A_t^{(i)} = A_t^{(i)} \left(\mu_i \mathrm{d}t + \sigma_i \mathrm{d}W_t^{(i)}\right)$$

with constant coefficients and standard Brownian motions $W_t^{(i)}$ which are correlated and admit a correlation matrix Σ. Thus

$$A_t^{(i)} = A_0^{(i)} \exp\left\{\left(\mu_i - \sigma_i^2/2\right)t + \sigma_i \mathrm{d}W_t^{(i)}\right\}$$

Now, fix a time horizon T and default threshold $\tilde{c}_T^{(i)}$ for obligor i. Then the Bernoulli variable indicating whether a default has occurred or not is $D_T^{(i)} = I(A_T^{(i)} \le \tilde{c}_T^{(i)})$. So, given credit curves $p_t^{(i)}$, we can use the identity $\mathrm{P}\left(D_T^{(i)} = 1\right) = \mathrm{P}\left(A_T^{(i)} \le \tilde{c}_T^{(i)}\right) = p_T^{(i)}$ to specify the threshold. For the example of a geometric Brownian motion, we find

$$\mathrm{P}\left(D_T^{(i)} = 1\right) = \mathrm{P}\left(W_1^{(i)} \le c_T^{(i)}\right)$$

with

$$c_T^{(i)} = \frac{\log(\tilde{c}_T^{(i)}/A_0^{(i)}) - (\mu_i - \sigma_i^2/2)T}{\sigma_i\sqrt{T}}$$

Furthermore, if we define (under regularity conditions) the intensity $\gamma_i(t) = f_i(t)/(1 - F_i(t))$, then the survival probability is

$$1 - F_i(t) = \exp\left(-\int_0^t \gamma_i(u)\mathrm{d}u\right)$$

We can now model the default dependency of the obligors via dependent intensities by means of a joint survival function with intensity obtained by linking the marginal intensities using a copula function (see, for example, Li (2001) and Schönbucher (2003)).

To generate a multivariate default-time distribution, we thus have a choice of modelling the dependence structure using marginal default-time distributions linked by a copula (as in the asset-based factor models) or marginal default intensities, which may be linked via a copula.

Multivariate option pricing

It is quite natural to utilise copula functions to analyse the dependence structure of financial asset returns and quite a few authors have used the technique to investigate the so-called correlation break-down effect (see the introduction). It is also obvious that changing dependence structures must also affect any options written on two or more underlying securities. Examples of these multivariate (or rainbow) options are calls (or puts) on the best (worst) performer of a number of underlying assets. Standard approaches within the Black–Scholes framework rely on the multivariate Gaussian distribution for the underlying assets. Thus a Gaussian copula is used to model the dependence structure and any possible tail dependence is neglected. An empirical study by Goorbergh *et al* (2004) tries to overcome this problem by modelling the joint (risk-neutral) distribution of the underlying by choosing a copula from one of the one-parametric Clayton, Gumbel or Frank families, where the one-to-one relation to Kendall's tau can be used for estimation (see the section on examples of copulas). They find that non-normal copulas produce prices that are significantly different from the normal copula approach.

Dependency modelling in insurance

A topical issue in the current discussion of life insurance and pension contracts is the valuation of embedded guarantees and options. Only recently have insurance companies realised that these contract features have to be reflected in premium calculations. As an example consider a standard unit-linked life insurance with payoff at expiry T,

$$G(T)+\max\{S(T)-G(T),0\}$$

where $S(T)$ is the value of the underlying investment portfolio and $G(T)$ the value of the guarantee at time T. Assuming a simple guarantee structure, such as $G(T) = G\exp(r_G T)$ with r_G some fixed rate and G some fixed face value, the valuation of such a contract can be done within a standard option-pricing framework (see Aase and Nielsen (1994)). However, more involved guarantee structures are used in practice. For instance, in Masala and Micocci (2003) a defined contribution pension plan is considered that guarantees a minimum rate of return that depends on two risky assets, namely a financial portfolio and a consumer price index. They show that the value of the guarantee is highly sensitive to variations of Kendall's tau, and thus also to the copula function used to model the dependence structure.

EXCURSUS: DEPENDENCY OF EXTREME EVENTS

We now continue to investigate and explore the issue of useful dependence structures and dependence measures, and we put the main emphasis on the dependency modelling of extreme events. The preceding applications pointed out that dependencies among extreme events (in short, extremal dependencies) such as extreme asset-returns play an important role in market and credit risk management. According to Ong (1999), the primary issue that risk managers have always been interested in is assessing the size, rather than the frequency, of losses. Presumably, the most well-known risk measure is VAR (which describes the amount of extreme portfolio loss that is exceeded only with a certain small probability) and depends strongly on the dependence structure of extreme events (for a background on VAR measures we refer the reader to Dowd (1998), Brockhaus *et al* (2000) and Jorion (2000)).

Two issues are addressed in this section. We first derive the (lower and upper) tail-dependence coefficient, which we introduced as a measure of extremal dependency in formulas (TDC) and (TDC2) for the copula functions discussed so far. Further, we provide a straightforward generalisation of the latter measure leading to the family of so-called tail copulas. The second issue addresses the statistical estimation of the tail-dependence coefficient and the tail copula. In particular, we provide useful properties such as strong consistency and asymptotic normality for fully non-parametric statistics.

Example

Similarly to formula (ST), there exists a simple relationship between the lower and upper tail-dependence coefficient of an elliptically contoured distribution (such as the multivariate normal or Student's *t*-distribution) and the parameters of the corresponding copula. Recall that the family of n-dimensional elliptically contoured distributions (in short, elliptical distributions) is denoted by $E_n(\mu, \Sigma, \Psi)$ or $E_n(\mu, \Sigma, g)$ if the density generator g exists (see formula (ELD) for the definition of the density generator). However, the existence of the density generator is equivalent to the existence of the density function, which we assume to be given in the following. By the symmetry of the elliptical distributions, the lower and upper tail-dependence coefficients coincide. If X has an n-dimensional elliptical distribution with distribution function F and the corresponding density generator g or any randomly chosen marginal density-function

f_i decreases asymptotically like a power function (called a regularly varying function), ie,

$$g(t) \sim \text{const} \cdot t^{-(\alpha+n)/2} \quad \text{or}$$
$$f_i(t) \sim \text{const} \cdot t^{-\alpha-1}, \quad \alpha > 0, \text{ as } t \to \infty \qquad \textbf{(RV)}$$

(Student's t-distribution and the symmetric stable distribution are well-known examples), then

$$\lambda_{ij}^{u} = \lambda_{ij}^{L} = \frac{\int_0^{h(R_{ij})} \frac{u^\alpha}{\sqrt{1-u^2}}\,du}{\int_0^1 \frac{u^\alpha}{\sqrt{1-u^2}}\,du}$$

where $R_{ij} = \Sigma_{ij}/\sqrt{\Sigma_{ii}\Sigma_{jj}}$ and $h(R_{ij}) = \left(1+(1-R_{ij})^2/(1-R_{ij}^{\;2})\right)^{-1/2}$. The parameter α is called the tail index. A thorough proof of the above result as well as necessary and sufficient conditions for tail dependence can be found in Schmidt (2002). Note that tail dependence is a property of the (elliptical) copula. Therefore, the parameter α and the matrix R are deducible from the copula function. For example, for the Student's t-copula the matrix R can be retrieved directly from its density function as stated in (TCDF) and the parameter α coincides with the parameter ν.

The Archimedean copulas, which have been discussed so far in formula (ARC), possess a quite different behaviour of tail dependence. Due to the strong symmetry of Archimedean copulas, the lower and the upper tail-dependence coefficients coincide for all bivariate marginals. The following tail-dependence coefficients are derived:

Clayton copula: $\lambda^L = 2^{-1/\theta}$ and $\lambda^u = 0$ for $\theta > 0$ (lower tail dependent and upper tail independent),

Gumbel copula: $\lambda^L = 0$ and $\lambda^u = 2 - 2^{1/\theta}$ for $\theta \geq 1$ (lower tail independent and upper tail dependent),

Frank copula: $\lambda^L = 0$ and $\lambda^U = 0$ (lower and upper tail independent).

The empirical copula, of course, does not exhibit tail dependence since the empirical copula function is eventually constant for small or large arguments. However, we may construct the following non-parametric estimator for the tail-dependence coefficient of an unknown copula by utilising the empirical copula. Consider an n-dimensional statistical sample of sample size m, ie, $\{(X^l_{1m}, \ldots, X^l_{nm})': l = 1, \ldots, m\}$, having distribution function F and copula C. Let C_m be the empirical copula function as defined in (ECF) and let $(R^l_{1m}, \ldots, R^l_{nm})'$ denote the ranks of $(X^l_{1m}, \ldots, X^l_{nm})'$, $l = 1, \ldots, m$. We define the following estimators which are motivated by formula (TDC2):

$$\hat{\lambda}^L_{ij} = \frac{m}{k} C^{ij}_m\left(\frac{k}{m}, \frac{k}{m}\right) = \frac{1}{k}\sum_{l=1}^{m} I(R^l_{im} \le k, R^l_{jm} \le k) \qquad \textbf{(LTDCE)}$$

and

$$\begin{aligned}\hat{\lambda}^U_{ij} &= \frac{m}{k} C^{ij}_m\left(\left(1-\frac{k}{m}, 1\right] \times \left(1-\frac{k}{m}, 1\right]\right) \\ &= \frac{1}{k}\sum_{l=1}^{m} I(R^l_{im} > m-k, R^l_{jm} > m-k) \qquad \textbf{(UTDCE)}\end{aligned}$$

where $k = k(m) \to \infty$ and $k/m \to 0$ as $m \to \infty$, $I(\cdot)$ is the indicator function, and the first expression in formula (UTDCE) has to be understood as the empirical copula "measure" of the interval $(1 - k/m, 1] \times (1 - k/m, 1]$ with $C^{ij}_m(u_i, u_j) = C_m(1, \ldots, 1, u_i, 1, \ldots, 1, u_j, 1, \ldots, 1)$. The parameter k governs the amount of extreme sample data that are taken into account for the estimation. Note that k increases with increasing sample size m; however, it increases much slower than m. The optimal choice of the parameter k is known as the variance-bias problem and is illustrated in Figure 4 for the estimation of the lower tail-dependence coefficient of BMW versus Dt. Bank daily stock log-returns. Thereby, too small a k is accompanied by a high variance of the latter estimator whereas too large a k ends up with a strong bias. The parameter k is usually chosen such that the estimation lies on a plateau between the decreasing variance and increasing bias. For example, in Figure 4 we take k between 80 and 110.

Figure 4 Scatter plot of BMW versus Dt. Bank daily stock log-returns with 2,325 data points (left) and the corresponding tail-dependence coefficient (TDC) estimates for various thresholds k (right)

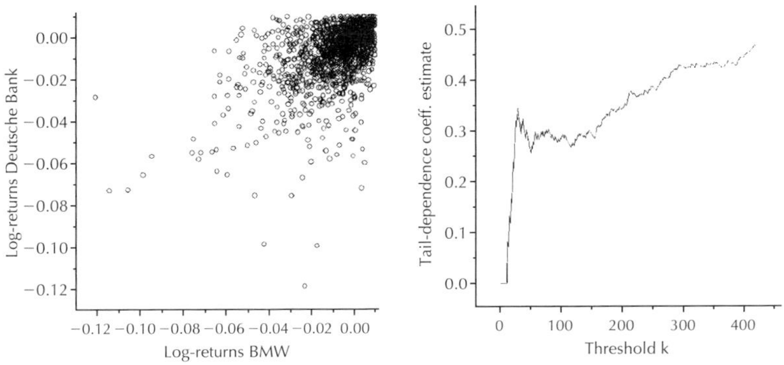

We remark that tests for tail dependence or tail independence are not yet well established in the literature. Among the few papers, we mention Ledford and Tawn (1996) and Draisma *et al* (2001).

The statistical properties of the estimators (LTDCE) and (UTDCE) were established in Schmidt and Stadtmüller (2003). In particular, they showed that the estimators are strongly consistent and asymptotically normal under certain conditions. However, the proof of these results needs the concept of tail copulas, which is interesting in itself since it describes the dependence structure of extreme events in a comprehensive manner. The latter concept constitutes a generalisation of the definition of tail dependence. For reasons of simplicity we provide all further results in the bivariate setting. The corresponding multivariate extensions can be found in Schmidt and Stadtmüller (2003).

Definition (tail copula). Consider the two-dimensional random vector X with distribution function F. The real-valued functions Λ^L and Λ^U, respectively, with domain $[0, \infty]^2 \setminus \{(\infty, \infty)\}$ are called lower and upper tail copula associated with X if the following limiting functions exist:

$$\Lambda^L(x_1, x_2) = \lim_{t \to \infty} P(X_1 \leq F_1^{-1}(x_1/t) \mid X_2 \leq F_2^{-1}(x_2/t))$$

and

$$\Lambda^U(x_1, x_2) = \lim_{t\to\infty} P(X_1 > F_1^{-1}(1-x_1/t) \mid X_2 > F_2^{-1}(1-x_2/t))$$

where F_i, $i = 1, 2$, denote the marginal distribution functions of F.

Note that the lower and upper tail dependence is equivalent with the existence of $\Lambda^L(1, 1) = \lambda_{12}^L > 0$ and $\Lambda^U(1, 1) = \lambda_{12}^U > 0$ (in the following, we drop the subscripts for convenience). Without loss of generality we may substitute the distribution function F in the latter definition by the corresponding copula C.

Theorem (asymptotic normality and strong consistency). *Let F be a bivariate distribution function (for example, a copula C) with continuous marginal distribution functions. Assume that the tail copulas $\Lambda^L \neq 0$ and $\Lambda^U \neq 0$ exist, possess continuous partial derivatives, and the so-called second-order condition holds (this condition refers to the speed of convergence to the limit of tail copula and is usually fulfilled; see Schmidt and Stadtmüller (2003) for a precise definition). Then as the sample size m tends to infinity,*

$$\sqrt{k}(\hat{\lambda}^L - \lambda^L) \xrightarrow{d} N_{0,\sigma_L} \quad \text{and} \quad \sqrt{k}(\hat{\lambda}^U - \lambda^U) \xrightarrow{d} N_{0,\sigma_U}$$

where $k = k(m) \to \infty$, $k/m \to 0$, and N_{0,σ_L} and N_{0,σ_U} are centered normal-distributed random variables with variances

$$\sigma_L^2 = \lambda^L + \left(\frac{\partial}{\partial x_1}\Lambda^L(1,1)\right)^2 + \left(\frac{\partial}{\partial x_2}\Lambda^L(1,1)\right)^2$$
$$+ 2\lambda^L\left(\left(\frac{\partial}{\partial x_1}\Lambda^L(1,1) - 1\right)\left(\frac{\partial}{\partial x_2}\Lambda^L(1,1) - 1\right) - 1\right)$$

and σ_U^2 is defined analogously by substituting L with U in the latter formula. Additionally,

$$\hat{\lambda}^L \to \lambda^L \quad \text{and} \quad \hat{\lambda}^U \to \lambda^U \quad \text{almost surely}$$

if $k / \log\log m \to \infty$ and $k/m \to 0$ as $m \to \infty$.

For further parametric and non-parametric estimators of the lower and upper tail-dependence coefficient we refer to Frahm *et al* (2003) and Schmidt (2004).

Example

To illustrate the latter results, we calculate the lower tail copula Λ^L and the asymptotic variance $\sigma^2{}_L$ of the corresponding non-parametric estimator of the tail-dependence coefficient for the Clayton copula (which we introduced as an Archimedean copula). According to formula (ARC) and the definition of Archimedean copulas, the Clayton copula is given by

$$C(u_1, u_2) = \max\left([u_1^{-\theta} + u_2^{-\theta} - 1]^{-1/\theta}, 0\right), \quad \theta \geq -1, \quad \theta \neq 0$$

Recall that the Clayton copula comprises the lower tail dependence with lower tail-dependence coefficient $\lambda^L = 2^{-1/\theta}$ for $\theta > 0$. Further, the lower tail copula exists for $\theta > 0$ and can be expressed by

$$\Lambda^L(x_1, x_2) = \left(x_1^{-\theta} + x_2^{-\theta}\right)^{-1/\theta}$$

Thus, the partial derivatives are

$$\frac{\partial}{\partial x_1} \Lambda^L(x_1, x_2) = \left(x_1^{-\theta} + x_2^{-\theta}\right)^{-(1/\theta+1)} x_1^{-(\theta+1)}$$

and

$$\frac{\partial}{\partial x_2} \Lambda^L(x_1, x_2) = \left(x_1^{-\theta} + x_2^{-\theta}\right)^{-(1/\theta+1)} x_2^{-(\theta+1)}$$

Figure 5 Lower tail-dependence coefficient λ^L (left) and asymptotic variance σ_L^2 of the corresponding estimator $\hat{\lambda}^L$ (right), as given in the theorem on previous page, for the bivariate Clayton copula

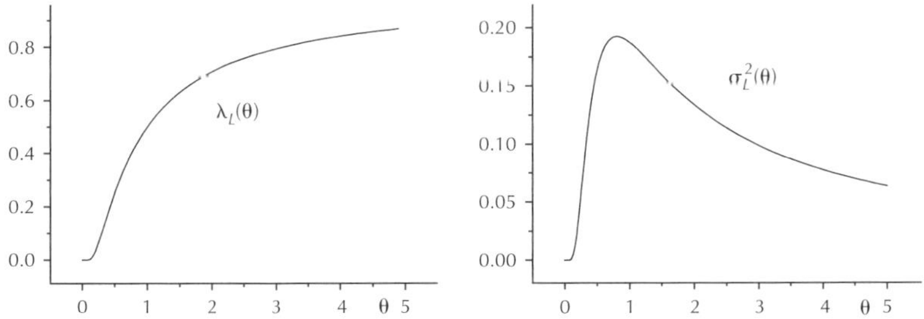

Consequently, the asymptotic variance σ_L^2 in the latter theorem is of the following form (see also Figure 5)

$$\sigma_L^2 = 2^{-1/\theta} - \frac{3}{2}\cdot 4^{-1/\theta} + \frac{1}{2}\cdot 8^{-1/\theta}$$

REFERENCES

Aase, K., and J. Nielsen, 1994, "Pricing of Unit-linked Life Insurance Policies", *Scandinavian Actuarial Journal,* **1**, pp. 26–52.

Basel Committee on Banking Supervision, 2003, "The New Basel Capital Accord", BIS Basel, Switzerland, URL: http://www.bis.org/bcbs, April.

Bingham, N. H., and R. Kiesel, 2001, "Modelling Asset Returns with Hyperbolic Distributions", in J. Knight and S. Satchell (eds), *Asset Return Distributions,* pp. 1–20 (Butterworth-Heinemann).

Bingham, N. H., and R. Kiesel, 2002, "Semi-parametric Modelling in Finance: Theoretical Foundation", *Quantitative Finance,* **2**, pp. 241–50.

Bingham, N. H., R. Kiesel, and R. Schmidt, 2003, "A Semi-parametric Approach to Risk Management", *Quantitative Finance,* **3**, pp. 426–41.

Bluhm, C., L. Overbeck, and C. Wagner, 2003, *An Introduction to Credit Risk Modelling* (London: Chapman and Hall).

Bouyé, E., V. Durrleman, A. Nikeghbali, G. Riboulet, and T. Roncalli, 2000, "Copulas for Finance: A Reading Guide and Some Applications", Groupe de Recherche Opérationnelle, Crédit Lyonnais, Technical Report.

Brockhaus, O., M. Farkas, A. Ferraris, D. Long, and M. Overhaus, 2000, *Equity Derivatives and Market Risk Models* (London: Risk Books).

Campbell, R., K. Koedijk, and P. Kofman, 2002, "Increased Correlation in Bear Markets", *Financial Analysts Journal,* pp. 87–94, January–February.

Casella, G., and R. L. Berger, 2002, *Statistical Inference,* 2nd edn (Pacific Grove, CA: Duxbury Press).

Diebold, F. X., T. A. Gunther, and A. S. Tay, 1997, "Evaluating Density Forecasts", Federal Reserve Bank of Philadelphia, Technical Report.

Dowd, K., 1998, *Beyond Value at Risk: The New Science of Risk Management* (Chichester: John Wiley and Sons).

Draisma, G., H. Drees, A. Ferreira, and L. de Haan, 2004, "Bivariate Tail Estimation: Dependence in Asymptotic Independence", *Bernoulli,* **10**, pp. 251–80.

Eberlein, E., 2001, "Application of Generalized Hyperbolic Lévy Motions to Finance", in O. E. Barndorff-Nielsen, T. Mikosch, and S. Resnick (eds), *Lévy Processes: Theory and Applications.*

Eberlein, E., and K. Prause, 1999, "The Generalized Hyperbolic Model: Financial Derivatives and Risk Measures", Freiburg Center for Data Analysis and Modelling, University of Freiburg, Technical Report 56.

Embrechts, P., F. Lindskog, and A. McNeil, 2003, "Modelling Dependence with Copulas and Applications to Risk Management", in S. Rachev (ed), *Handbook of Heavy Tailed Distributions in Finance*, Chapter 8, pp. 329–84 (Amsterdam: Elsevier).

Embrechts, P., A. McNeil, and D. Straumann, 2002, "Correlation and Dependency in Risk Management: Properties and Pitfalls", in M. A. H. Dempster (ed), *Risk Management: Value at Risk and Beyond*, pp. 176–223 (Cambridge: Cambridge University Press).

Fang, H.-B., K.-T. Fang, and S. Kotz, 2002, "The Meta-elliptical Distributions with Given Marginals", *Journal of Multivariate Analysis*, **82**, pp. 1–16.

Fang, K.-T., S. Kotz, and K.-W. Ng, 1990, *Symmetric Multivariate and Related Distributions* (London: Chapman and Hall).

Frahm, G., M. Junker, and R. Schmidt, 2003, "Estimating the Tail Dependence Coefficient", Caesar Center Bonn, Technical Report 38, URL: http://stats.lse.ac.uk/schmidt.

Frey, R., and A. McNeil, 2001, "Modelling Dependent Defaults", Working Paper, ETH Zuerich.

Goorgergh, R. W. J., C. Genest, and B. Werker, 2004, "Multivariate Option Pricing Using Dynamic Copula Models", Working Paper.

Joe, H., 1997, *Multivariate Models and Dependence Concepts* (London: Chapman and Hall).

Joe, H., and J. J. Xu, 1996, "The Estimation Method of Inference Function or Marginals for Multivariate Models", Department of Statistics, University of British Columbia, Technical Report 166.

Jorion, P., 2000, *Value at Risk*, 2nd edn (New York: McGraw-Hill).

Junker, M., and A. May, 2002, "Measurement of Aggregate Risk with Copulas", Caesar Center Bonn, Germany, Technical Report.

Karolyi, G. A., and R. M. Stulz, 1996, "Why Do Markets Move Together? An Investigation of US–Japan Stock Return Comovements", *Journal of Finance*, **51**, pp. 951–89.

Laurent, J.-P., and J. Gregory, 2003, "Basket Default Swaps, CDO's and Factor Copulas", Working Paper.

Ledford, A. W., and J. A. Tawn, 1996, "Statistics for Near Independence in Multivariate Extreme Values", *Biometrika*, **83**, pp. 169–87.

Li, D. X., 2000, "On Default Correlation: A Copula Function Approach", *Journal of Fixed Income*, **9**, pp. 43–54.

Longin, F., and B. Solnik, 2001, "Extreme Correlation of International Equity Markets", *The Journal of Finance*, **LVI**, pp. 649–76.

Masala, G., and M. Micocci, 2003, "Pricing Pension Funds Guarantees Using A Copula Approach", Working Paper.

Nelsen, R. B., 1999, An *Introduction to Copulas* (New York: Springer).

Ong, M. K., 1999, *Internal Credit Risk Models* (Haymarket: Risk Books).

Patton, A., 2001, "Modelling Time-Varying Exchange Rate Dependence Using the Conditional Copula", UCSD, Working Paper, September.

Rachev, S., and S. Mittnik, 2000, *Stable Paretian Models in Finance* (New York: John Wiley and Sons).

Rosenblatt, M., 1952, "Remarks on a Multivariate Transformation", *Annals Mathematical Statistics*, **23**, pp. 470–72.

Schmidt, R., 2002, "Tail Dependence for Elliptically Contoured Distributions", *Mathematical Methods of Operations Research*, **55**, pp. 301–27.

Schmidt, R., 2004, "Tail Dependence", in P. Cizek, W. Härdle and R. Weron (eds), *Statistical Case Studies* (Berlin: Springer).

Schmidt, R., and U. Stadtmüller, 2002, "Nonparametric Estimation of Tail Dependence", LSE Department of Statistics, Technical Report 101, URL: http://stats.lse.ac.uk/schmidt.

Schönbucher, P., 2003, *Credit Derivatives Pricing Models* (New York: John Wiley and Sons).

2

Pricing European Structured Product Securities

Alexander Batchvarov

Merrill Lynch

Structured (also referred to as securitisation) products have developed over the last ten or so years to become a major sector of the overall European fixed income market. From a small sector of mostly privately placed securities with a specialised investor base in the early 1990s, it has grown today into a clearly identified, independent sector within the broad European fixed income portfolio with a constantly expanding investor following. Most market observers now regard the European structured product market as a fully mature part of the mainstream fixed income sector. These developments have affected the pricing of the struc tured product securities both on the primary and secondary markets. While we focus here on the European structured products' pricing, many of the observations and conclusions are applicable to the respective US, Australian, Asian and Japanese markets.

KEY PRICING FACTORS FOR STRUCTURED PRODUCTS

We examine first the main characteristics of structured products; these characteristics themselves represent the key factors which are taken into consideration in pricing and trading such products.

Factor 1: the inherent diversity of the structured product universe

Several years ago we developed a diagram, as presented in Figure 1, to explain the diversity in credit profiles of structured products.

Figure 1 Credit dependence of structured product credits from originator (horizontal axis) and from third party (vertical axis)

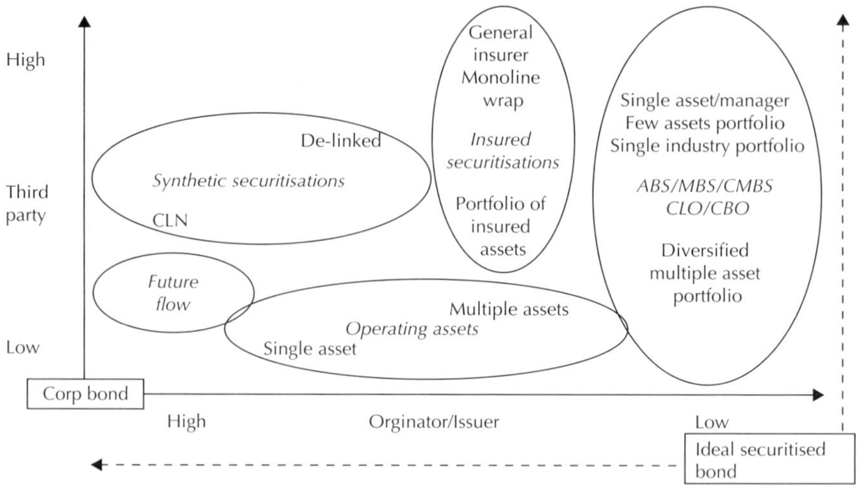

Source: Merrill Lynch

They comprise the following main types:

- *Securities backed by large granular consumer related portfolios*, such as residential mortgage-backed securities (RMBS), credit and retail cards receivables, and consumer and auto-loan asset-backed securities (ABS). These securities represent very granular consumer pools, whose behaviour is driven primarily by the state of the general economy and by the specific pool composition reflecting the underwriting policy of the loan originator and specific servicing policies and the capabilities of the pool servicer. These sectors are by far the largest in terms of volume of new issuance (see figure) and securities outstanding, and by far the best understood by the market.
- *Securities backed by large granular corporate-related portfolios*, such as commercial mortgage-backed securities (CMBS), equipment and vehicle leases ABS, pub and care home receivables ABS, large static pools of corporate loans or funded or unfunded lines of credit (collateralised loan obligations, also known as CLOs), and small and medium-size enterprise loans (SME CLOs), etc. In this category, one may include mixed pools of corporate and

consumer-related portfolios, such as commercial and residential mortgage pools, auto-loan and auto-lease pools, etc. (The reason for including them in this category is that the corporate-related exposures are often the dominant sources of credit risk in these pools.) The behaviour of the corporate pools depends on both macro-economic and industry specific factors, and is again affected by origination and servicing considerations. These securities come a distant second in terms of volume of new issuance and volume outstanding, and are well understood by pockets of investors and are subsequently less broadly incorporated in structured product portfolios.

- *Securities backed by individual corporate exposures* often with a strong real estate component, such as trophy property sale-and-lease-back securitisations (CMBS) and whole business securitisations (WBS). While small in volume they are subject to intense interest and scrutiny by specialised investors, and their performance is closely linked to the idiosyncratic single corporate and industry sector exposure they represent.
- *Arbitrage bond securitisations of corporate bonds or loans*, referred to as CDOs, CBOs and CLOs, *and of other securitisations or CDOs*, often referred to as re-securitisations or master CDOs. While the underlying exposures may vary and should be taken into account in the pricing of the securities, the predominant features that attract attention are the arbitrage and managed nature of the transaction, the relatively smaller number of exposures and securities included (ranging from several dozen to a hundred), its derivative nature with regards to the corporate bond/loan market and its structure. The derivative and managed nature of most CDO securities closely links their performance to the cycles in the underlying corporate or ABS markets, modified to a degree by the capabilities and mandate of the manager.
- *Supported securitisations or structured products*, whose performance depends on the performance of two independent parts. The first is related to a specific securitisation or structured product (any of the above) and the second is related to a bond guarantee provided by a highly rated insurance company or another guarantor. These structured products are viewed as dual in nature, whose current and future performance is influenced by the degree of the exposure to each of the two parts and their own behaviour.

- *Form of execution – cash or synthetic.* This is related either to the way the exposures pool backing the structured product is created or to the way the particular investors undertake a given exposure. The pool may be constructed with cash assets (bonds, loans, etc) – the assets are sold or pledged to the issuer of the structured product, known as the special purpose vehicle (SPV), or with credit default swaps (CDSs) on single corporate names or ABS – the SPV sells protection by writing CDSs to other market participants, interested in buying protection. Investors in the structured product who face the SPV may undertake to buy the bonds issued by the SPV (cash bonds) or to enter into a CDS (selling protection) with the SPV. While the form of execution may have some, but not major, impact on the credit risk and performance of the given structured product, it affects the type and availability of investors willing to invest in it, and, hence, its pricing.

This diversity in terms of credit product and pool, type of execution, structure, investor base and factors affecting performance has a substantial impact on the pricing of structured products. It is the driver for the establishment and existence of spread tiering by product type, which we call *a pricing hierarchy in the structured product market*, that we discuss below. The fact that structured products are backed by given assets suggests that the expectation regarding the performance of such assets and the similarities and deviation of the actual from expected performance should have an on-going impact on the pricing of such products, both on the primary and the secondary markets.

Factor 2: the parties to a specific structured product

As mentioned above, the performance of a given pool of assets depends on the underwriting criteria of the originator of such assets and the strength of the servicer of the asset pool.

The former affects the expectation about future asset performance. In the case of transactions where modifications of the pool are allowed (such as revolving securitisations or replenishments), the expectations about future pool composition and performance are affected, as well as the expectations about the probability to continue revolving or replenishment of the pool. The servicer's capabilities and availability also influence actual pool performance and investors' views and forecasts about it. A pending change of a servicer due to its bankruptcy, take over and exit from the business introduces uncertainty about the future servicing of a transaction pool and its performance in terms of cashflow generation, leading to uncertainty about the repayment of the structured product. The degree of uncertainty will also depend on whether there is a supporting second servicer and its degree of readiness to assume the responsibilities of the primary servicer. In most European transactions the originator also acts as a servicer of the asset pool and is, more often than not, highly rated. The risk of a lower rated servicer and the potential replacement of the primary servicer exists in the UK and US sub-prime mortgage sectors and in the US and Japanese sub-prime consumer loan sectors.

Hence, developments (such as change in underwriting and servicing policy, credit strength, change in corporate status and related changes in underwriting business strategy and so on) related to the originator and/or servicer of a given pool, supporting a structured product, will inevitably have an impact on the actual pool performance and on the view investors have regarding such performance. This suggests the presence of event risk associated with the originator/servicer of a structured product transaction, whether actual or perceived, may affect the related pricing of such transactions on the primary and secondary markets. An interesting illustration of this, in a European context, was the movement in auto-loan ABS secondary spread levels. In late 2001 and throughout 2002 Fiat was experiencing credit problems, which resulted in Fiat CDS widening from 200 bps in late 2001 to 900 bps by the end of 2002 (see Figure 2). During that period Fiat auto-loan ABS spreads widened from 28 bps to nearly 70 bps, before returning to their initial levels. Ironically, Fiat itself was not the servicer of the ABS transaction and its performance had little, if any, bearing on its performance. In this case, we can talk about event risk contagion by association.

In many cases, though, the market appears to discount, or disregard outright, such event risk associated with the originator/servicer of a securitisation transaction. We demonstrate this by comparing CDS spreads of originators/servicers as an expression of the market view regarding their pure credit risk and the spreads on ABS they sponsor/service. The originator/servicer pure credit

Figure 2 FIAT CDS spreads (mid, bps)

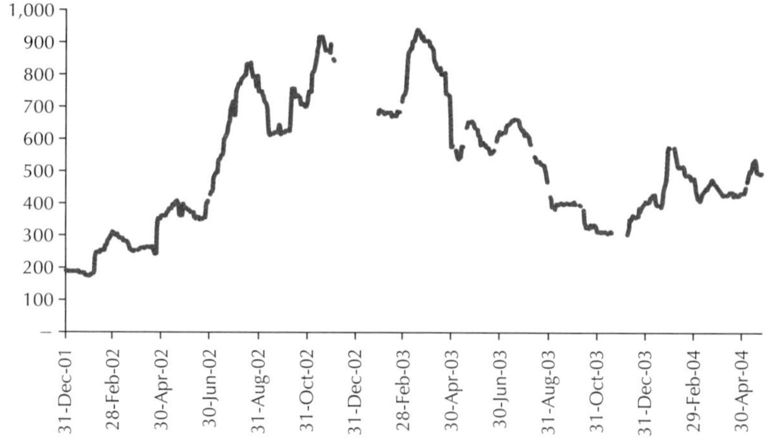

Source: Merrill Lynch

Figure 3 Monoline five-year CDS holding company bid spreads and monoline wrapped five-year triple-A RMBS launch spreads over LIBOR (bp)

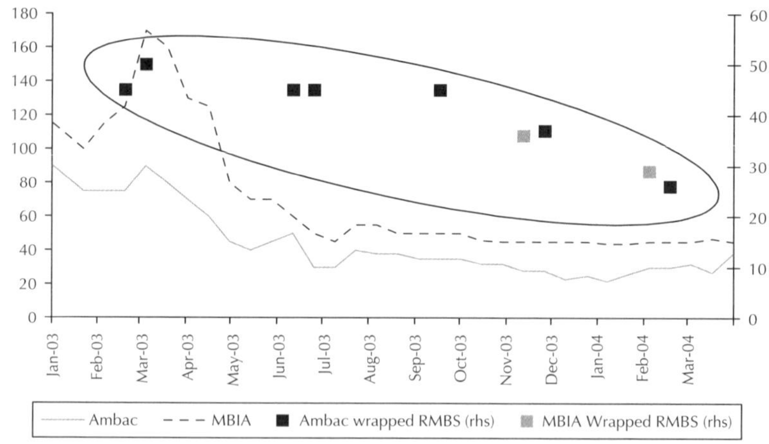

Source: Merrill Lynch

Figure 4 German bank CDS and RMBS spreads

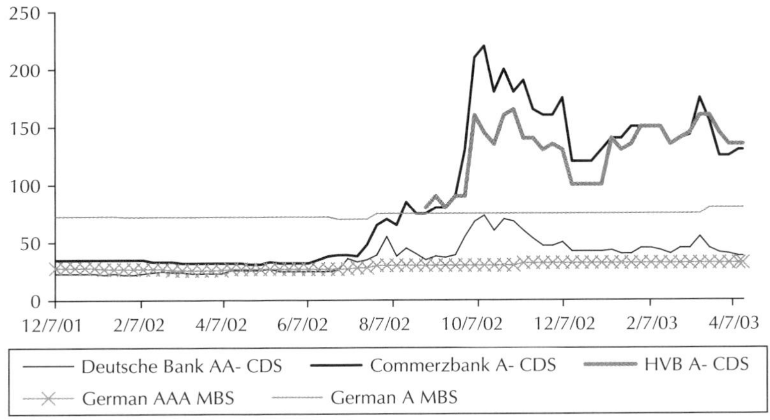

Source: Merrill Lynch

risk as expressed in the CDS should be viewed as the risks of: (a) bankruptcy of originator and subsequent termination of replenishment/revolving period of a transaction and related commencement of its amortisation; and (b) bankruptcy of servicer and its subsequent replacement with potential temporary or permanent deterioration in servicing standards and pool performance.

The data included in Figures 4–9 serves as a basis for the following preliminary conclusions:

- corporate CDS spreads are more volatile than the securitisation bonds' spreads of related transactions (although CDS spread volatility cannot be attributed only to credit factors);
- ABS spreads do not react at all to CDS spread movements at triple-A level, but have some, albeit often negligible reaction, at single-A level;
- the relationship between CDS spreads and single-A spread appears stronger in some countries, eg, Italy, and negligible in others, eg, Holland, UK.

Factor 3: the tranching of structured products

With very few exceptions, structured products are tranched with the seniormost tranche rated triple-A, several mezzanine tranches

Figure 5 UK bank CDS and credit card ABS spreads

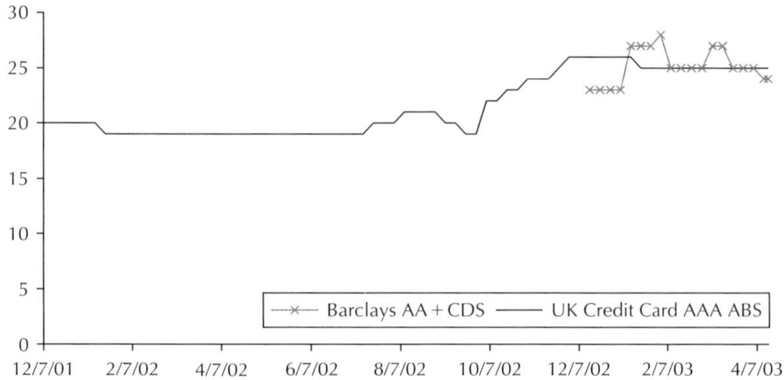

Source: Merrill Lynch

Figure 6 Italian bank CDS and RMBS spreads

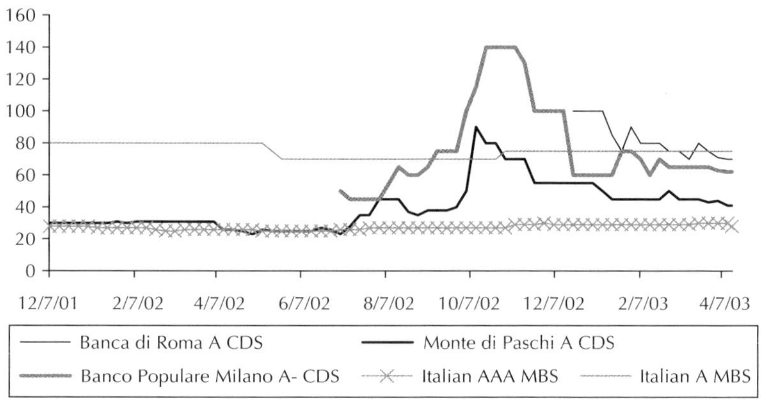

Source: Merrill Lynch

rated anywhere from double-A to double-B, and a non-rated juniormost tranche often referred to as equity. Different asset classes tend to lead to different tranching in terms of the number of tranches and their rating, and in terms of the thickness of those tranches. For example, double-B tranches are very rare in European MBS, but are often seen in CDOs and CMBS. Triple-A tranches tend to be thickest (roughly between 85 and 90% of the security) in prime RMBS, credit cards and other consumer assets, but much less

Figure 7 Dutch bank CDS and RMBS spreads

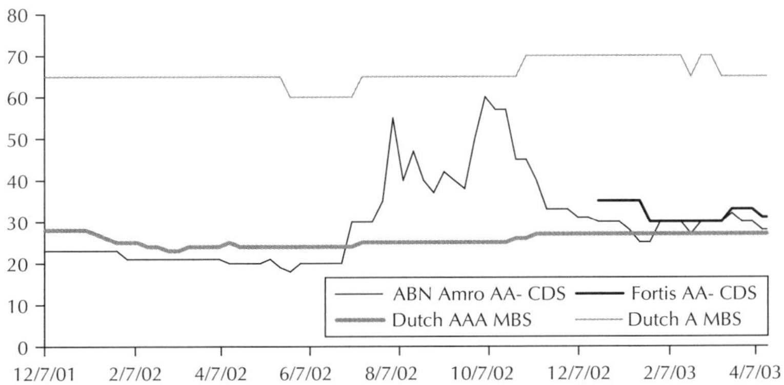

Source: Merrill Lynch

Figure 8 Auto manufacturers CDS and auto-loan ABS spreads

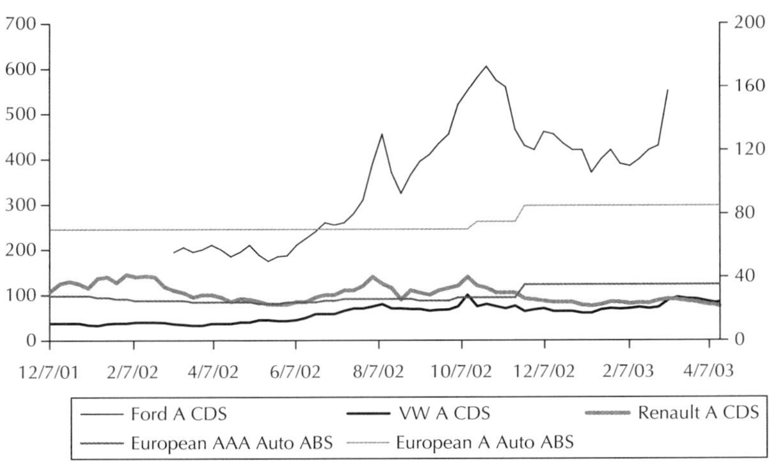

Source: Merrill Lynch

thick in CDOs (say between 70 and 85%). Tranche size, in turn, affects the number of investors that take on that tranche.

The tranching reflects the seniority in distribution of cashflows to payment of interest and repayment of principal, as well as the priority in loss allocation – both cashflows and losses emanate from the underlying pool of assets or the single asset backing the

Figure 9 UK bank CDS and RMBS spreads

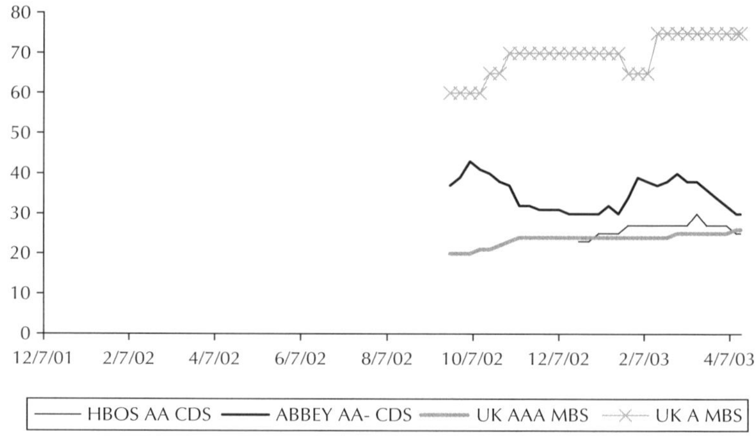

Source: Merrill Lynch

structured product. The allocation of generated cashflows to the different tranches and the probabilistic nature of such allocation underlies the tranches' credit risk, reflected in its rating. The different mechanisms for allocation and re-allocation of the cashflows, even when they give the same probability of repayment of a given tranche, may actually suggest a different timing of such repayment. For example, sequential and pro rata repayment of the senior and upper mezzanine tranches of a securitisation in two transactions backed by the same asset pool may result in the same probability of repayment (the same rating of the respective tranches in each transaction), but different timings of repayment (the senior tranche in the sequential pay transaction will be repaid faster than the same tranche in the pro rata pay transaction).

Alternatively, the timing and extent to which losses occur in the asset pool backing a given structured product affects the timing and extent of cashflows received by the juniormost tranches, that is, their return. This is most evident in the CDO sector, where the juniormost tranche, also known as equity, is placed with investors more often than not. Early accumulation of losses would mean a lower return for the equity tranches, and even downgrade and losses for the junior mezzanine tranches. The opposite will be true if losses are concentrated towards the end of the life of the asset pool and the transaction it is supporting – in this case, equity investors have received large amounts of cashflow (investment return) and may be indifferent to the final payment.

Factor 4: the available investor base for different asset types, tranches, structures and executions of structured products

As the structured product sector is not static, neither is the investor base. Different investors tend to choose different parts of the capital structure of the structured product (tranches) or different asset types of the structured products altogether. The majority of them, however, are predominantly buy-and-hold investors.

Composition of investor base

As Figures 10 and 11 below indicate, the leading investors in European structured products are banks and bank-related entities

Figure 10 Structured product investors, by country, 2003

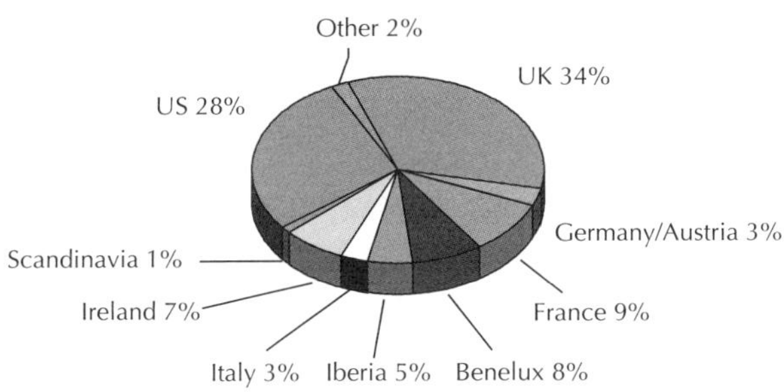

Source: Merrill Lynch

Figure 11 Structured product investors, by type, 2003

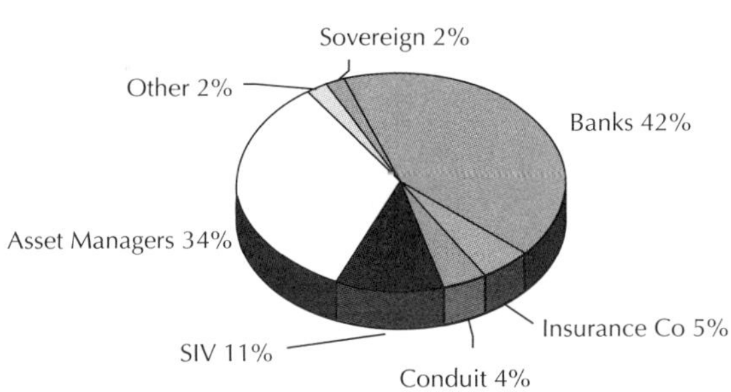

Source: Merrill Lynch

Figure 12 Corporate investors, by country, 2003

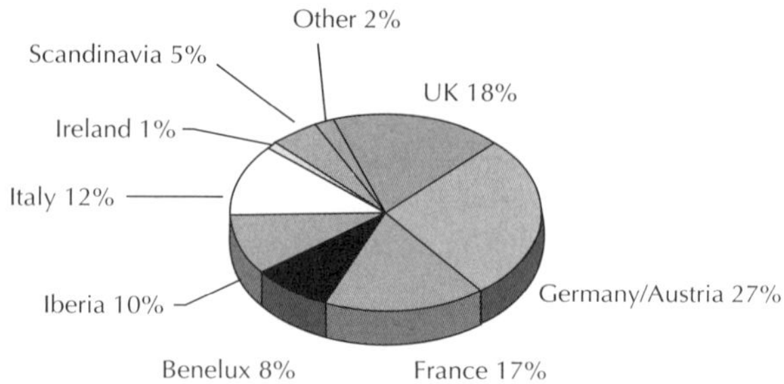

Source: Merrill Lynch

Figure 13 Corporate investors, by type, 2003

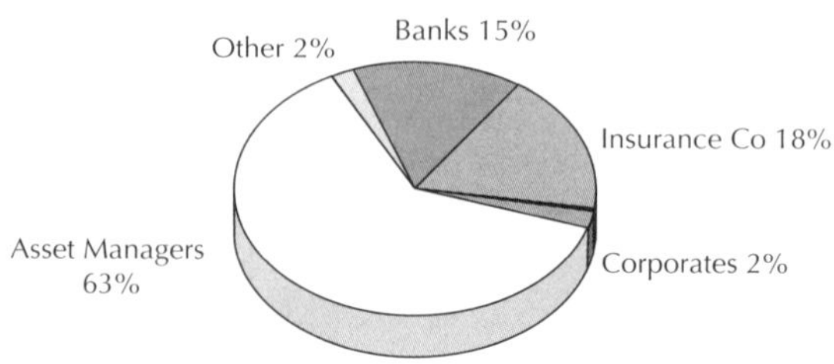

Source: Merrill Lynch

(asset-backed commercial paper (ABCP) conduits). This is in contrast to the investor base for corporate bonds highlighted in Figures 12 and 13. Structured investment vehicles (SIVs) are another strong buyer; in fact their portfolios consist predominantly of structured products. In other words, the entities holding the majority share of the investor base are not active traders as far as their structured product holdings are concerned. The share of asset managers in the overall investor base for structured products in Europe is relatively small – this is in contrast to the investor base for corporate bonds. The role of pension funds is rising, primarily due to the secular increase in their fixed income holdings in comparison to their equity holdings. Insurance companies are also increasing their structured product holdings and viewing them as a mainstream product rather than alternative investment.

Preferences along the capital structure

Different investor types concentrate on different parts of the capital structure. Banks tend to focus on the senior tranches, while pension funds and insurance companies do buy along the entire capital structure with a bias on the lower mezzanine tranches. SIVs are primarily triple-A and occasionally upper mezzanine buyers; so are the ABCP conduits. Such buying preferences are not only related to credit ratings, but are also driven by size. Senior tranches, being the largest part of the capital structure (70–90%), naturally support large lot buying. Large and diversified investor base, and large size holdings are the prerequisit for active secondary trading. This in turn, depends on the investment strategy adopted by the respective investors. The more junior the tranche, the smaller its size and the more private in nature the investor market becomes. Smaller sizes and limited numbers of buyers suggest a buy-and-hold investment strategy by design.

Other preferences

The investor base for structured products differs also depending on the structure (pass-through or bullet), maturity (usually in the 5–7 year range, but much longer maturities up to 30 years and much shorter maturities of about 1–2 years also exist) and coupon type (floating or fixed) of the respective security. Asset managers, for example, tend to like bullet maturities. Pension funds and insurers would prefer longer maturities, while banks would favour pass-through three-to-five year bonds. There is a very small European investor base for fixed rate pass-through securities (contrary to the US market), due to the difficulties in determining prepayment speed in the amortising pool of mortgages, for example.

Country composition

The investor base for structured products in Europe differs by country. While the above statements remain valid within most countries in Europe, investors from the different European countries have different degrees of participation in the market due to national regulatory guidelines, sophistication of investor base, precedents, etc.

For example, the access of the retail investor base to structured products varies among countries. While in some countries certain products are widely purchased by retail investors (say, Italian

Government securitisations in Italy), other products are just beginning to make inroads into the retail sector and only at the very top levels (say, CDOs for high net worth individuals).

Regulatory considerations

There may also be regulations affecting the access of institutional investors to the product. For example, Italian regulations require specific approval for each foreign structured product transaction before it is made available to Italian institutional investors. Against the background of rising demand for structured products across Europe and declining deal marketing time as a result, this ruling from 2003 effectively decimated the Italian investor base for European (non-Italian) structured products. Tax considerations have in the past occasionally prevented investors from certain countries (say, Germany) investing in structured products originating from other countries (say, Italy). In Spain, currently, there is a lack of clarity regarding the regulatory treatment of synthetic securitisations, which excludes Spain's investors from the overall investor pool for such products. In addition, many investors across Europe are still hesitant about the structured synthetic product, which by itself severely limits the demand for such product and impacts on its pricing.

Another important regulatory consideration is the risk weighting of the respected structured product. While the general risk weightings are fairly simple (50% of triple-A RMBS and 100% for all other structured products), variations exist from one country to the next and special risk weightings may be adopted for given structured products, which in turn can also significantly vary among countries.

The repo eligibility of structured products is not standardized either. While many RMBS are included in the repo collateral lists, many other structured products and asset classes are not. This affects investor interest particularly at a triple-A level for the purposes of leveraged triple-A trades, which gain prominence during tight spread market conditions.

Factor 5: liquidity, as it is difficult to characterise the sector as liquid or illiquid without qualifications

Reviewing the characteristics of the structured product sector, it is obvious that its different sub-sectors will have different liquidity profiles. Senior tranches will be theoretically more liquid than junior tranches, based on size and investor penetration. Conversely, junior tranches will be much less liquid and restricted to a smaller investor base. In the last two or so years, the development of ABS CDOs has created a demand for mezzanine tranches, so that a primary investor could sell them to a CDO manager – cashing in on the capital gain as a result of spread tightening along the way – who in turn holds them to maturity. The RMBS sector should be more liquid than the CMBS sector based on supply and homogeneity. However, in reality this only partially holds true, given that UK sterling CMBS deals based on large trophy properties have been traded fairly actively on occasions. The same can be said about some of the WBS bonds. Figure 14 provides a subjective ranking of different classes of European structured products in terms of liquidity; this ranking may also be viewed as 'perceived liquidity'.

Furthermore, structured products with repeat issuers and regular issuance, such as RMBS and credit cards, tend to be more liquid, as investors may roll over from one issue to the next with a negligible amount of new credit work. Selling investments, when their maturity

Figure 14 Liquidity continuum in European structured products

Most Liquid ↑

Italian Treasury Sponsored
UK–Prime RMBS
Dutch RMBS
UK Credit Cards
Top-Tier Auto Loans
Spanish RMBS
Italian RMBS
Spanish SME
Portuguese RMBS
Irish and Swedish RMBS
Spanish/Portuguese Consumer Loans
Portuguese Auto Leases
UK Sub–Prime RMBS
Utilities
Pubs
UK CMBS
German RMBS
German SME
Non-UK CMBS
Italian/French Credit Crads
Italian Leases
CDOs
Italian NPLs

Least Liquid ↓

Source: Merrill Lynch

falls to one year or less, is not that common in Europe due to the lack of a specialised investor base for such short maturities – unlike the existence of the large money market sector in the US.

When discussing liquidity for structured products, we must point out that it is common on the market to have many bids, but no offer under normal conditions and expected performance of the respective structured product securities. The opposite is true once a given security experiences a performance problem – there are more sellers than willing buyers, a situation clearly experienced in the CBO sector in 2000–2003. Tables 1 and 2 compare the bid–offer spreads for select structured products and corporate bonds – the bid–offer spread is the quantifiable expression of liquidity and appears to favour structured products at triple-A level and corporate bonds at single-A and triple-B level.

Table 1 Indicative bid–offer spreads by European asset class* (bp)

	AAA	% of bid	A	% of bid	BBB	% of bid
Italian Treasury ABS	1–2	6	NA	NA	NA	NA
UK Prime RMBS Master Trust	1	5	3	5	5	3
Dutch RMBS	1–2	≤8	5	8	10	9
UK Prime RMBS Other	2	9	5	8	10	7
Spanish/Portuguese Consumer	3	11	10	15	NA	NA
German SME	5	11	15	10	25	9
Autos	2	12	7	10	NA	NA
Spanish SME	3	12	10	14	NA	NA
Italian, Spanish, Portuguese RMBS	1–3	≤13	5	8	10–15	≤13
Credit Cards	3	14	10	14	15	10
UK Sub-Prime RMBS	5	14	10	7	20	8
German RMBS	5	14	10	11	25	12
CMBS	7	16	15	14	25	12
Utilities	5	18	10	18	15	13
Pubs	5	18	10	15	15	12
Italian Lease	10	26	25	25	NA	NA
Arbitrage CBO/Bank Balance Sheet CLO/A BS CDO	10–20	≤31	50	25	25–100	≤27

Source: Merrill Lynch
*Most are 5-year, CDO typically 7–9 years.

Table 2 Indicative corporate 5-year bid–offer spreads – select names

Rating category	Ticker	Bid–offer spread (bp)	Bid–offer as % of bid
AA	Lloyds	5	5
AA	HBOS	4	3
AA	Gaz De France	4	15
AA	EDF	5	18
AA	EON	3	6
A	Deutsche	2	2
A	RWE	4	8
A	Carrefour	3	8
A	Peugeot	4	9
A	VW	5	8
A	BMW	4	12
BBB	Ford	5	2
BBB	GM	5	3
BBB	Daimler-Chrysler	5	4
BBB	Sainsbury's	5	8
BBB	Renault	4	5
BBB	Deutsche Telekom	5	5
BBB	France Telecom	5	6
BB	Xerox	22	6

Source: Merrill Lynch

The liquidity of the structured finance market is heavily influenced by the asset type as discussed above, the inclusion or not in an index and by the interest rate type (fixed or floating of the bonds). The fixed rate sterling and Euro-denominated bonds are included as part of the Sterling and Euro corporate indices and can be viewed as sub-sectors (rather small ones) of those indices. The performance of such a "sub-index" can then be used for comparison with the overall corporate index. As far as stand-alone structured product indices are concerned, to our knowledge there is only one dedicated ABS index currently in use in Europe – the Lehman Brothers ABS index, which is effectively a sum of four indices: fixed and floating rate indices denominated in Sterling and in Euros. While both the dedicated indices and the small "sub-indices" of the general corporate Euro and Sterling indices can be useful tool for investors, they all suffer from the same shortcoming – the structured product securities included in them are priced by the broker, who is running the indices, and there is no market-wide derived pricing for them. This situation is in sharp contrast to the US, where several large brokers run their own indices and, in addition to the general ABS index, there exist indices for some asset classes as well, such as mortgages, credit cards, etc.

Liquidity in the structured product sector has been affected in recent years by several developments:

- The introduction of currency- and maturity-tranched transactions, particularly for UK master trust RMBS deals, conducive to very large size issuance. This allows issuers to issue tranches denominated in Euros, Sterling and US dollars, thus reaching wide investor base and sizing the currency tranches according to existing investor demand, and hence achieving the best price execution possible under given market conditions. It further helps create short- and longer-term tranches addressed to investors focusing on different parts of the curve and creating the optimal blended pricing.
- The development of the CDO of ABS, which created demand from CDO managers for structured products of all ratings, and particularly for the mid and lower mezzanine tranches. This in turn created a thin secondary market for mezzanine tranches.
- The increase in the number of repeat issuers and the size of repeat issuance, which has resulted in some degree of standardisation and transparency in the market, therefore boosting liquidity.
- The introduction of UK mortgage master trusts by a number of UK large mortgage lenders, which has introduced to the market a certain level of commoditisation and transparency, besides the other benefits discussed earlier. Certain structural innovations, such as the introduction of the de-linked issuance in credit card master trusts, should boost liquidity for the mezzanine credit card ABS in the future.
- The emergence of CDSs for structured products will also have an impact on liquidity, but at this stage the outcome is uncertain.

Factor 6: transparency, in a sense of availability of information regarding the structured product transaction and the performance of its underlying asset over time

Transparency was not a strong point of the European structured credit market for a long time, but significant improvements have been made since the beginning of the 1990s. This was supported by the increase in the number of repeat issuers and debacles in some market sectors (for example, high yield CBOs), which prompted investors to demand more information and the disclosure of rating agencies' models and modelling assumptions. However, in many sectors the data supporting the initial and ongoing rating analysis remains undisclosed (be it for competitive or other reasons). A number of problems exist with regards to the comparability of publicly available data across countries or asset classes.

Some improvements have been registered in the area of performance reporting, but significant differences remain among asset classes – for example, the availability of information in the residential mortgage sector and in the credit card sector is very high in comparison with the commercial real estate sector. Sell-side research coverage of structured products has expanded in recent times, although, from the perspective of performance analytics, it is as good as the data provided by the issuers of structured products directly to the market or through the rating agencies.

The more transparent the specific structured product sector, the easier it is to understand and adequately price the risks of the respective structured product, and the easier it is to trade, therefore making the security itself more liquid.

Factor 7: one more factor influencing the pricing of structured products is the developments in other fixed income sectors

The growth of the structured product market and its comparability with the corporate bond market in terms of size of new issuance has attracted the attention of traditional corporate bond investors and hedge funds. The hedge funds have entered primarily the area of CDOs and distressed CDOs. Traditional corporate bond investors have directed their interest to the mezzanine and lower mezzanine tranches of structured products, primarily because of the significant tightening of spreads in their main markets and the resultant attractive relative value of the structured universe.

Their motivation being relative value and positioning, they may prove to be the swing factors in the demand for structured products in the future. However, this is difficult to predict with a high degree of certainty. On the one hand, one can argue that spread widening for corporate bonds should restore their attractiveness; on the other hand, traditional corporate bond investors are now much more familiar with the structured product sector than they were a few years back and are now aware of some of its advantages in comparison with corporate bonds (say, relative rating and spread stability), so they may decide to keep some allocation to structured products for the long term. Furthermore, hedge funds are likely to retain high commitment to the rapidly growing synthetic structured product sector with its promise for high relative value trades.

Figures 15–17 illustrate the issuance volume in the corporate Euro and Sterling markets in Europe and compare them to the ABS

Figure 15 Euro corporate bond issuance, 2000–2004 (EURmn)

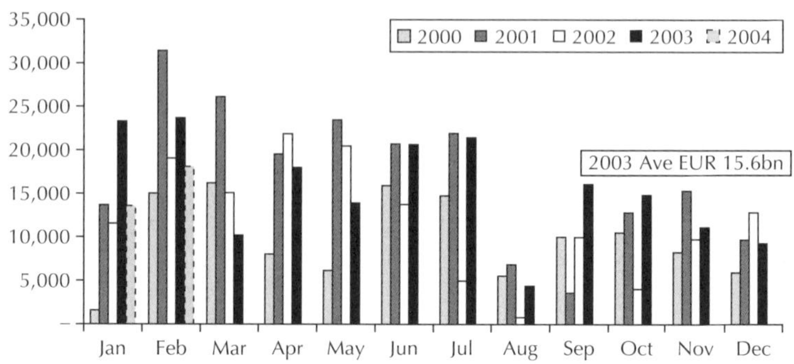

Source: Merrill Lynch

Figure 16 Sterling corporate bond issuance, 2000–2004 (EURmn)

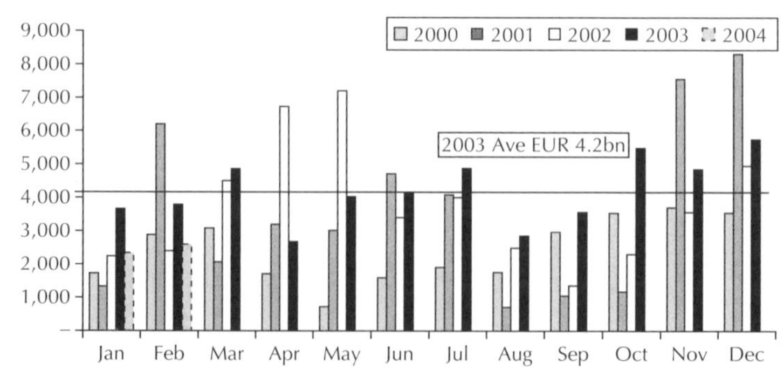

Source: Merrill Lynch

Figure 17 Structured product issuance, 2000–2004 (EURmn)

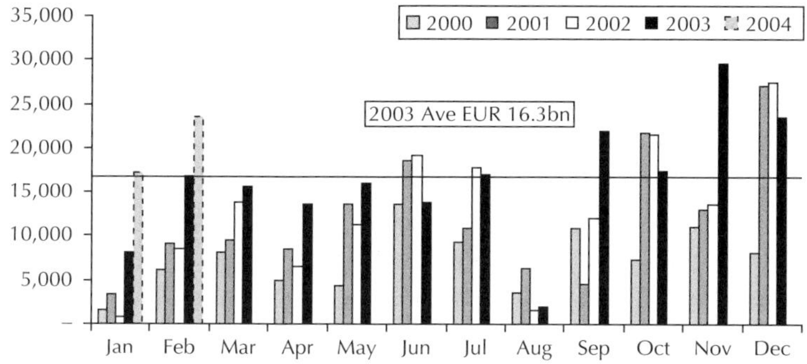

Source: Merrill Lynch

issuance volume in Euro and Sterling together. The data illustrates the declining availability of corporate bonds and the rising availability of structured products in recent years.

Weighing the factors

We have highlighted several different factors, which we believe affect the pricing of structured products in Europe and elsewhere. We must note that such factors are not assigned equal weights in the pricing process.

We emphasise that the general state of the fixed income market provides the background for pricing decisions. The next section examines this aspect in more detail. In a "buyer's market", the differences among asset classes and different issues within an asset class are carefully scrutinised and priced accordingly – the market is "tiered". In general, the tiering in the European market is not sufficient given the overall chronic state of the market with "demand exceeding supply". In a "seller's market", even the embryonic tiering disappears.

In the past, given infrequent issuance of new structured product securities, secondary pricing in Europe re-aligned to the levels set up by new issuance. As secondary trading increased in 2003–2004, the relationship between the primary and the secondary markets has become more balanced. With a larger amount of the European issuance going into the US market, US spread levels have also had an impact on European pricing.

All the factors above need to be taken into account, in their complexity, when determining the pricing of any one structured product, be it in the primary or secondary markets. In many cases, however, one factor may become dominant; such as the level of issuance of a particular asset class up to the moment when a new structured product of the same asset class comes to market. For example, a high supply of UK RMBS will have an impact on the pricing of the next RMBS transaction, and a low general supply of Swedish RMBS over the years will support the tight pricing of a new transaction regardless of the overall pan-European RMBS issuance.

'Black box' issuance will always price wider than other comparable structured products with more transparency or it may not price at all given a lack of takers on the market. Occasionally, the market in Europe may have no takers for a given product regardless of the price.

With the advent of CDOs of ABS, a driving factor in the pricing of mezzanine tranches has become the demand for them, as expressed by the number of CDOs currently ramping up. The diversification requirements imposed on CDOs has also affected the pricing of new product offerings, especially those which are not widely available (asset classes, countries of issuance, etc).

LAUNCH SPREADS FOR STRUCTURED PRODUCTS

So far we have identified a series of characteristics of the structured product market, which have input with regard to the pricing of its securities. Overall, the structured product market presents a wide diversity by asset class and exposure, type of execution, deal structure, tranching, investor base, transparency, liquidity, related parties' involvement and creditworthiness, etc. We can define these to be the sector-specific factors, which determine the pricing of its securities.

Spread tiering within the structured product market

The existence of sector-specific pricing factors suggests the existence of a hierarchy of prices. In such a hierarchy the most liquid, transparent, widely held and traded bonds act as a benchmark for the pricing of the rest of the structured product universe. Such bonds in a European context are the RMBS, particularly those from the UK mortgage master trusts. In Table 3 we highlight the pricing of structured products backed by different asset types in order to demonstrate the existing hierarchy in their pricing.

A vertical read of the information by asset class demonstrates the following.

- Prime RMBS tend to price tightest over time at all rating levels, followed by credit card and unsecured consumer loan ABS, auto ABS and then immediately non-prime RMBS. In short, the consumer-related structured products demonstrate the tightest pricing. This could be expected given the preceding discussion on credit characteristics, granularity, transparency, size, availability and investor base.
- The corporate-related securitisations in the form of CMBS tend to price wider than the consumer deals, followed farther out by CDOs. This is also logical on the basis of lower granularity, higher event risk, less transparency historically (although recent changes may make transparency comparable) and fluctuation of available investor base (consistently expanding for CMBS, widely variable over time for CDOs).

A vertical read of the same information by rating suggests the following.

- There is no constant differential in pricing of the tranches even in the same asset classes, let alone across asset classes. This is consistent with the different types of investor base for the different tranches, and the more private nature of the placement of the junior tranches.
- Pricing of double-B tranches is not included, given the paucity of double-B supply and the private nature of the market.

We note that the data presented is of a more generic nature, for example, we do not elaborate on sector spreads by geography – say auto-loan ABS in Portugal versus Germany. From that angle, pricing dispersion should be interpreted carefully, as it may be geographically driven within the generic class.

Overall, while the spread differentials in the hierarchy of spread (tiering) among asset classes fluctuate over time, they remain preserved due to the many reasons (pricing factors) discussed earlier.

However, the tiering within each asset sector occasionally disappears when overall spread levels decline. This can be verified in Table 4, where the pricing for the same type of product – prime RMBS, in different European countries – is presented.

Table 3 Monthly average launch spreads by asset class and rating, 1998–2004 ytd

Asset class	Sub-type	Rating	1998			1999			2000		
			Ave	Max	Min	Ave	Max	Min	Ave	Max	Min
MBS	NCF	AAA	27	58	14	41	65	31	35	55	28
MBS	PRM	AAA	18	24	11	23	28	18	25	28	14
CMBS	CMBS	AAA	47	47	47	44	55	27	34	51	25
CDO	CDO	AAA	15	39	7	15	30	11	37	43	26
ABS	CAR	AAA	45	45	45	32	50	19	31	35	26
ABS	CCD	AAA	22	30	14	18	20	15	20	30	16
ABS	UCC	AAA	23	36	17	24	36	16	28	33	25
MBS	NCF	A	70	83	40	125	160	85	124	150	85
MBS	PRM	A	57	80	35	63	77	50	69	86	48
CMBS	CMBS	A				112	138	73	89	115	65
CDO	CDO	A	66	120	36	59	93	45	100	120	48
ABS	CAR	A	75	75	75	65	90	51	76	85	65
ABS	CCD	A				45	48	40	54	75	37
ABS	UCC	A	55	72	47	62	75	40	69	79	50
MBS	NCF	BBB	139	175	92	244	275	200	256	300	200
MBS	PRM	BBB	88	93	82	153	160	150	145	188	130
CMBS	CMBS	BBB	140	140	140	248	375	165	199	275	140
CDO	CDO	BBB	131	183	77	124	188	59	159	200	85
ABS	CAR	BBB	175	175	175	75	75	75	178	180	175
ABS	CCD	BBB				90	90	90	112	150	88
ABS	UCC	BBB	130	130	130	160	160	160	175	175	175

Asset class: MBS = mortgage backed securitisations; CMBS = commercial mortgage backed securitisations; CDO = collateral debt obligations; ABS = asset backed securitisations;
Sub-types: NCF = non-conforming; PRM = prime; CMBS = commercial mortgage backed securitisations; CDO = collateral debt obligations; CAR = automobiles; CCD = credit cards; UCC = unsecured consumer loans.
Source: Merrill Lynch

Historically the market has priced a 4–5 bps differential between UK RMBS, on the one hand, and Italian and Portuguese RMBS, on the other, due to the market's perception of the differences in the credit quality of the respective mortgage pools, data availability, legal framework for mortgage lending and foreclosure, etc. This differential has virtually disappeared during the first half of 2004 even though none of the above considerations have evolved.

The data in Table 4 reflects triple-A spreads only. Tiering remains to some degree at a triple-B level, although we believe that it is difficult to say how much of that is determined by

2001			2002			2003			2004 ytd		
Ave	**Max**	**Min**	**Ave**	**Max**	**Min**	**Ave**	**Max**	**Min**	**Ave**	**Max**	**Min**
35	55	19	27	50	22	35	54	26	19	19	19
24	30	22	24	28	18	24	40	20	17	22	12
37	44	24	43	63	28	45	50	40	38	38	38
45	57	35	55	68	25	71	81	61	57	64	48
24	28	14	24	38	13	30	42	11	15	15	15
25	28	23	20	22	16	20	27	5	13	22	3
32	35	28	31	36	28	25	31	20			
139	203	100	109	125	98	164	188	135	95	95	95
68	77	63	64	83	45	71	85	65	52	62	39
99	108	83	97	110	83	109	118	93	103	103	103
118	146	97	182	223	125	216	279	174	202	203	200
65	68	47	58	80	43	74	100	35	40	40	40
74	77	70	57	62	50	59	78	30	37	55	19
82	120	47	75	88	43	72	75	69			
256	300	218	240	270	207	326	350	300	212	212	212
144	165	135	141	179	120	140	163	127	103	121	81
194	220	183	201	280	138	214	232	200			
238	311	168	322	467	215	348	490	285	375	500	300
225	225	225	150	150	150	160	170	155			
151	165	138	149	168	120	159	187	110	83	120	45
217	275	188	150	170	125	153	170	140			

Table 4 European 5-year weighted average life (WAL) prime RMBS triple-A secondary spreads (bp)

	25-Jun-04	**19-Jan-04**	**12-Dec-03**
UK	17	17	19
Belgium	16	17	19
Switzerland	16	18	19
Sweden	16	20	21
Italy	16	22	25
Portugal	17	23	24
Ireland	17	21	23
France	20	23	22
Greece	18	23	24
Holland	17	23	24
Spain	18	24	25

Source: Merrill Lynch

Figure 18 European residential housing market position at the end of 2003

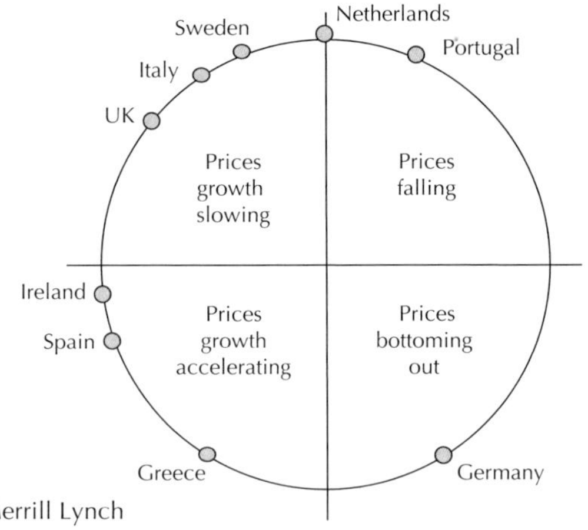

Source: Merrill Lynch

fundamental credit factors associated with the state of each market and how much is due to demand factors.

If we compare the pricing on the triple-A tranches of the respective RMBS (Table 4) and compare the state of the housing market (Figure 18), which directly affects the performance of RMBS geographically, we can see that there is barely any direct connection. The most telling discrepancy, on a pure housing market credit basis, will be the pricing between the Dutch and German RMBS, for example. However, the spread levels are distorted and should be interpreted on the basis of cash execution for Holland and synthetic execution for Germany, which attracts different investors by type and investment appetite–the former pan-European, large size portfolios and large lot size; the latter primarily German, restricted to several types of institutions.

Structured product spreads trends within the fixed income universe

So far we have highlighted the relative spread levels within the structured product sector. The developments in this sector, however, cannot be fully isolated from the spread developments in the overall fixed income market, and particularly in the corporate sector. All spreads are quoted over London Interbank Offer Rate (LIBOR).

Figure 19 Average AAA launch spreads of prime and sub-prime MBS *versus* AAA corporate index

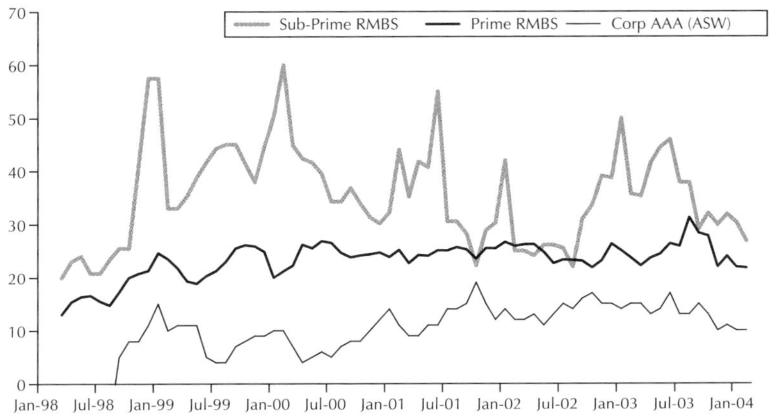

Source: Merrill Lynch

Figure 20 Average AAA launch spreads of CMBS and non-SME CDOs *versus* AAA corporate index

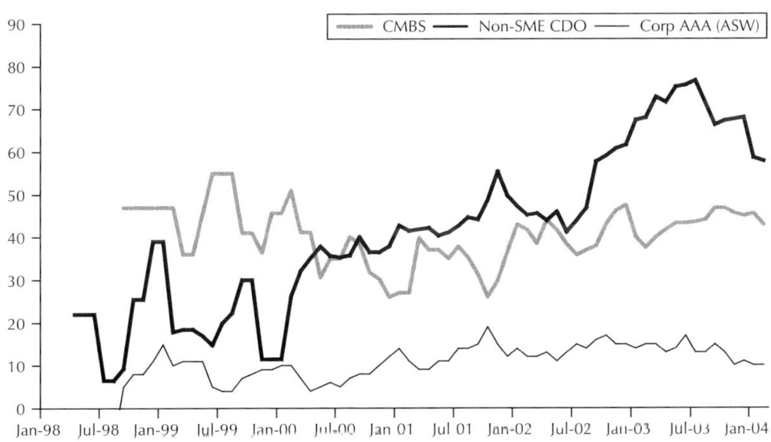

Source: Merrill Lynch

Figure 19–26 demonstrate the relationships that exist between the two. We emphasise again that such relationships are on a level of general trends rather than specific bond pricing. Examination of the figures brings the following preliminary conclusions.

Figure 21 Average AAA launch spreads of consumer ABS *versus* AAA corporate index

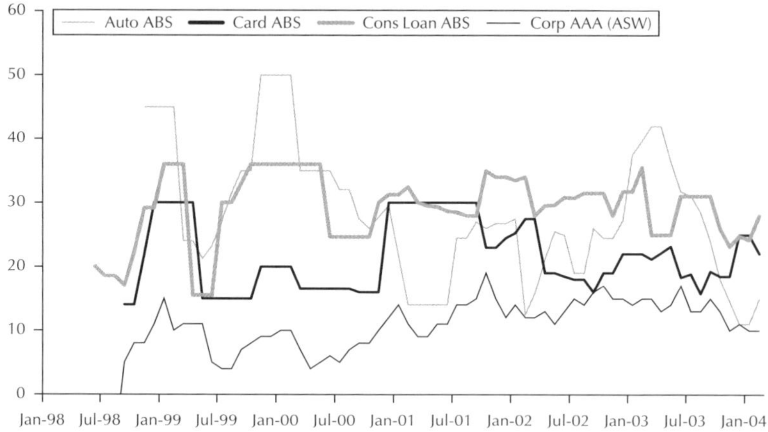

Source: Merrill Lynch

Figure 22 Average A launch spreads of prime and sub-prime MBS *versus* A corporate index

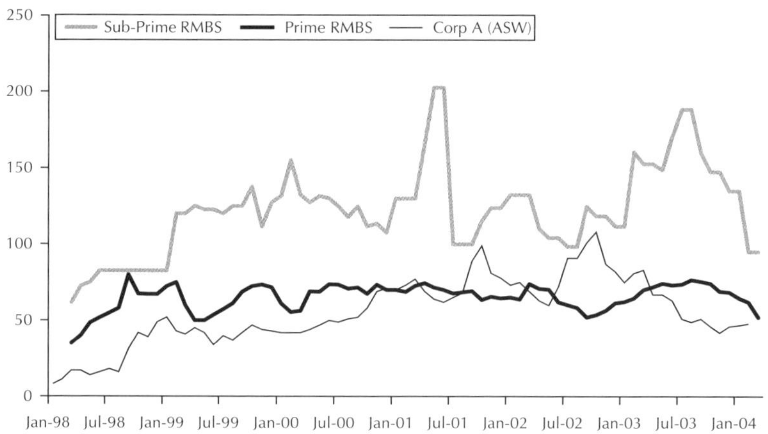

Source: Merrill Lynch

- Structured product spreads appear to show a broadly similar trend to corporates, although lagged. The timing and magnitude of the lag differs by asset class, and is especially evident in the single-A and triple-B tranches.

Figure 23 Average A launch spreads of CMBS and non-SME CDOs *versus* A corporate index

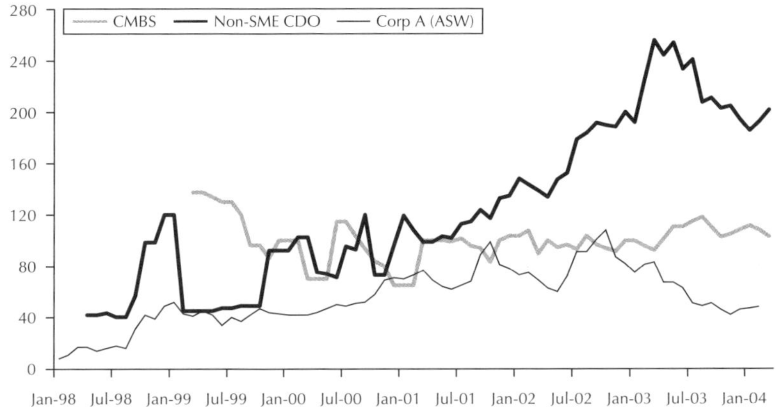

Source: Merrill Lynch

Figure 24 Average A launch spreads of consumer ABS *versus* A corporate index

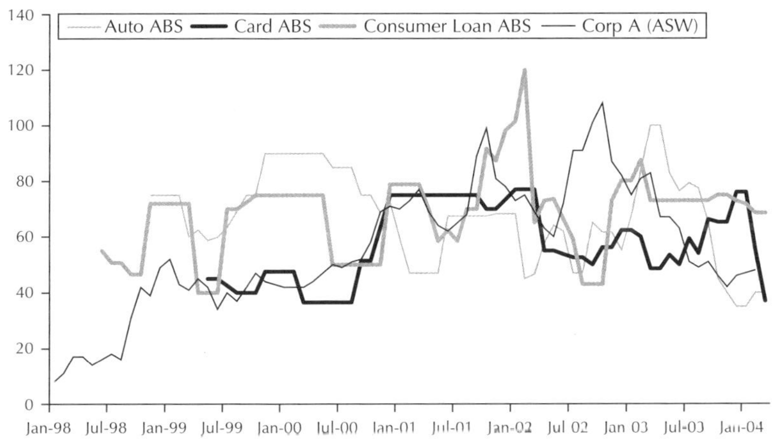

Source: Merrill Lynch

- ❑ Structured product spreads have rarely experienced the same degree of tightening as that of the corporate sector in 2003.
- ❑ Triple-A structured products have consistently priced wide of similarly rated corporates (Figures 19–21).

Figure 25 Average BBB launch spreads of prime and sub-prime MBS *versus* BBB corporate index

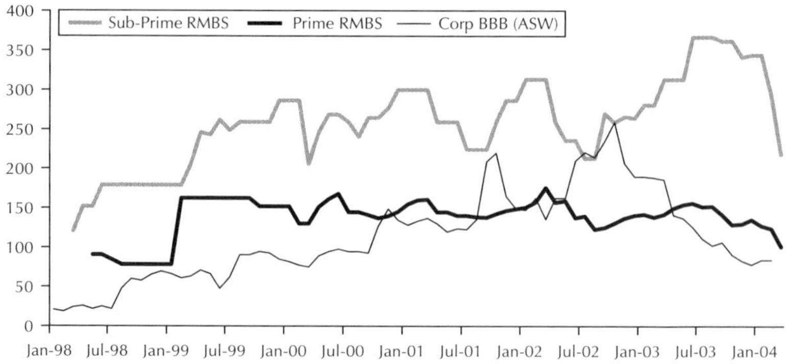

Source: Merrill Lynch

Figure 26 Average BBB launch spreads of CMBS and non-SME CDOs *versus* BBB corporate index

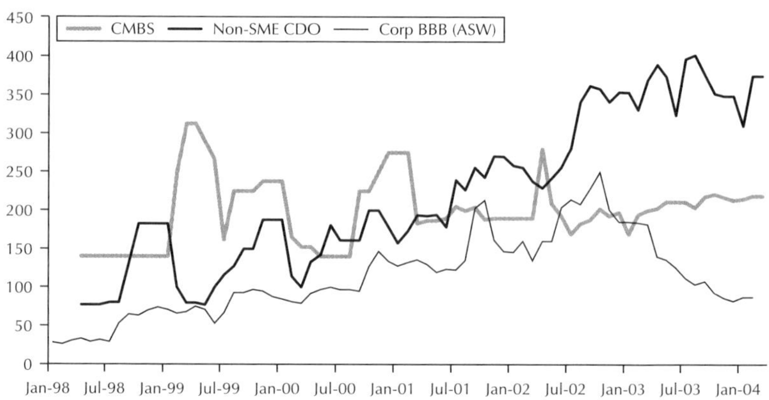

Source: Merrill Lynch

- ❑ Single-A ABS price at similar levels to corporates, with the exception of sub-prime RMBS, CMBS and non-SME CDOs (Figures 22–24).
- ❑ Only prime RMBS price close to triple-B corporates, with most other asset classes pricing at wider levels (Figures 25 and 26).
- ❑ Although differences in underlying asset mix may result in launch spreads that appear volatile over time, spread volatility

for like ABS deals is much lower than for similarly rated corporate debt. This has been the traditional wisdom for a long time now. Nonetheless, ABS spread volatility has increased slightly from these low levels, commensurate with increased secondary trading volumes.

Pricing dual exposure structured products

We have highlighted the existence of dual exposure structured products, such as the combination of a bond and a guarantee provided by highly rated specialised bond insurers (known as monoline due it its single, "mono", line of business of insuring bonds).

In Figure 3, we compare secondary CDS spreads of the US monoline insurers MBIA and AMBAC with the launch spreads on RMBS wrapped by this monoline from a single issuer. We feel compelled to make two observations:

- despite the monoline CDS widening significantly in spring 2003, spreads on wrapped UK RMBS widened by only about 5 bp, in line with the overall ABS market jitters linked to fears about UK house price inflation;
- conversely, in late 2003 and in 2004, the spreads on the monoline wrapped RMBS paper tightened significantly, from 50 bp to 26 bp, again commensurate with the movements in the overall market; in contrast, the CDS spreads on the monolines have remained relatively stable.

This raises a number of interesting questions regarding the relationship between the market view on the credit quality of the monoline, the monoline wrapped paper and that of the underlying exposure subject to the wrap.

- Significant changes in the credit views on the monolines expressed in the massive CDS spread widening did not appear to affect the spreads on the wrapped paper in the case of UK RMBS. Given the understanding that the swap spreads represent a "pure credit view", one would expect that such a widening was reflective of credit deterioration of monolines. However, while there were concerns related to monolines' exposures (particularly to the CDO sector) and their capital adequacy, these concerns were neither substantiated by rating agencies' actions nor detailed factual information.

- ❑ When a pool's originator/servicer experienced credit stress, another counter party to an ABS transaction, the market reacts in a very different way – the spread on the ABS widens sympathetically, even if not to the same degree.

In the case of UK RMBS, investors appear to have focused primarily on the underlying asset or pool of assets subject to the wrap, that is the specific RMBS transaction and the dynamics in the UK RMBS market, rather than the credit developments and concerns regarding the monoline area.

CONCLUDING REMARKS

The analysis and pricing of structured products is a complex undertaking. We have identified a set of factors, which should be taken into consideration in pricing such products. The weight of these factors in pricing decisions at launch and during the life of any given transaction may vary.

One particularly important factor, however, is the state of the fixed income market in general and relative value across fixed income sectors and within structured product sectors. Given the chronically short supply and constantly expanding demand, the structured product market has not maintained the sufficient spread tiering that the fundamentals will otherwise suggest. The credit fundamentals and the other key pricing factors highlighted in the body of this chapter seem to play an important role in determining the prices of structured products, particularly during difficult markets.

In reviewing the pricing of corporate and structured product bonds, we have naturally concentrated on generic products and corporate indices. The observed relationships, however, could be considerably different for individual securities and more custom-tailored structured products.

REFERENCES

Batchvarov, A., J. Collins, and W. Davies, 2004, *Launching Your ABS Portfolio.*

Batchvarov, A., J. Collins, and W. Davies, 2004, *Are ABS Spreads AT Their Tightest.*

Batchvarov, A., and W. Davies, 2004, *European MBS – Can They Go Tighter?.*

Collins, J., A. Batchvarov, and W. Davies, 2003, *Assessing Liquidity in European ABS.*

Batchvarov, A., J. Collins, and W. Davies, 2004, *Monoline Wraps in European ABS.*

Batchvarov, A., J. Collins, and W. Davies, 2004, *International Structured Product Monthly (June) –ABS, RMBS, CMBS, CDO.*

Batchvarov, A., J. Collins, and W. Davies, 2003, *ABS/MBS/CMBS/CDO 101.*

Batchvarov, A., J. Collins, and W. Davies, 2003, *European Structured Credit 2003–2004 (Annual Review).*

3

*On Correlation in Intensity Models**

David Lando

Copenhagen Business School

The big challenge of portfolio credit risk modelling and the modelling of CDO structures is the modelling of default correlation in a way which is mathematically tractable and in which the parameters of the model can readily be interpreted. Intensity models have a lot to offer in this respect. This chapter reviews approaches to modelling correlation within the intensity setting, points to some recent advances and discusses some of the problems that remain in specifying models for groups of issuers within the intensity setting.

THE MIXED BINOMIAL DISTRIBUTION

To appreciate the flexibility that is offered by focusing on intensities, it is useful to start by reviewing the static approach which relies on the binomial distribution. The simplest world of portfolio modelling would consider a group of N issuers all with probability p of defaulting before a given time horizon T. The probability that the number of defaults D equals k in this setting is equal to

$$P(D - k) = \binom{N}{k} p^k (1-p)^{N\ \ k} \tag{1}$$

We consider two ways of introducing correlation into this setting: one is by randomising the default probability, ie, using a

*This chapter is based in part on a survey lecture given at the Moody's/NYU inaugural credit risk conference at NYU, May 19–20, 2004.

mixed binomial distribution, and the other is by introducing direct contagion as in Davis and Lo (2001). The mixed binomial approach starts with the assumption that the default probability p is really a random variable, reflecting, for example, different states of the economy, but that given an outcome of this random variable, defaults are independent. From the homogeneity assumption that all have the same default probability, the conditional probability of there being k defaults given $\tilde{p} = p$ is then just Equation 1. The unconditional probability of k defaults is obtained by taking the expectation of the binomial probability over the distribution of $\tilde{p}$. If we assume that $\tilde{p}$ has a density function ϕ defined on [0, 1], then

$$P(D = k) = \int_0^1 \binom{N}{k} p^k (1-p)^{N-k} \phi(p)\, dp \qquad \textbf{(2)}$$

The unconditional default probability of an individual issuer is just the mean $\bar{p}$ of $\tilde{p}$. The randomisation introduces correlation between defaults through the common dependence on $\tilde{p}$. It is straightforward to check that the variability of $\tilde{p}$ increases the correlation between default events. Let X_i be the indicator function which is 1 if firm i defaults; then one can show that the correlation ρ_{ij} between the default indicators X_i, X_j is

$$\rho_{ij} = \frac{\mathrm{VAR}\,\tilde{p}}{\bar{p}(1-\bar{p})}$$

and hence holding the unconditional default probability $\bar{p}$ constant while increasing its variance will increase the default event correlation. A recurrent discussion in this simple setting and in the general intensity framework below is precisely whether empirically plausible variation in the mixture probability can induce enough correlation in the models.

The choice of mixing distribution is usually either the beta distribution, because it is a flexible family of distributions on the unit interval, or a more economically motivated distribution derived from the Merton model. In the latter case we think of firms whose asset values evolve as Brownian motions

$$dV_t^i = rV_t^i\, dt + \sigma V_t^i\, d\tilde{B}_t^i$$

and assume that the geometric Brownian motion driving V^i can be decomposed into a common factor B^0 and a firm specific factor B^i such that

$$\tilde{B}_t^i = \rho B_t^0 + \sqrt{1-\rho^2} B_t^i$$

This means that the asset value processes (or to be precise the increments in log-asset value) have correlation ρ. We stipulate that a firm defaults if the terminal asset value falls below the default threshold D at maturity. Assume now that all firms start at V_0. Then the unconditional default probability of a firm is

$$\bar{p} = \Phi(-c)$$

where Φ is the distribution function of a standard normal and

$$c = \frac{\log V_0/D + (r - \sigma^2/2)T}{\sigma\sqrt{T}}.$$

Given the outcome of the common factor B_T^0, defaults of firms are independent, and we are therefore, as shown in Vasicek (1991), in a mixed binomial setting with the mixture distribution having the distribution function

$$F(x) = \Phi\left(\frac{1}{\rho}\left(\sqrt{1-\rho^2}\Phi^{-1}(x) + c\right)\right)$$

This is a nice expression in that it uses only the default probability and the correlation ρ in asset returns as inputs. The homogeneity assumption is of course strong, but the distribution is also useful as an approximation device; see, for example, Glasserman (2003), who approximate probabilities of large fractional losses in inhomogeneous loan portfolios by working with a distribution of this form, concentrating on finding a value of ρ which makes the tail decay the same in the approximating and the true distribution.

We have considered a fixed time horizon above, but we can of course make the dependence of the time horizon on the default probability explicit. The problem then is to specify a consistent family of default probabilities as we vary T. An easy way of doing this is to assume that default occurs when asset value hits a lower boundary defined for every time point, but in this case we lose the simplicity of the conditioning argument which works for one fixed time horizon. We are therefore forced to do a full simulation of sample paths in this case. We could also just specify a distribution of the default time exogenously, but we want to be able to update this probability in response to varying conditions. This is what the intensity framework of the next section achieves.

An alternative to using the mixed binomial setting is the contagion model of Davis and Lo (2001). Here, default of a firm i can happen either as a direct default, symbolized by $X_i = 1$, or because of the default of another firm j, ie, of $X_j = 1$, combined with a contagion effect from firm j to i represented by another Bernoulli variable Y_{ji} being equal to 1. Assume that all X_i, Y_{ij} are independent Bernoulli variables whose probabilities of being 1 are $P(X_i = 1) = p$ and a $P(Y_{ij} = 1) = q$. Then the default indicator of firm i is

$$Z_i = X_i + (1 - X_i)\left(1 - \prod_{j \neq i}(1 - X_j Y_{ji})\right)$$

One can check that this expression is 1 either if there is a direct default of firm i or there is no direct default and at least one of the factors $X_j Y_{ji}$ is 1, which happens when firm j defaults and infects firm i. Although further from the binomial, the homogeneity of the firms with respect to both the probability of direct default and the contagion probability is vital to the closed-form solution given in Davis and Lo (2001) and it is therefore still fair to think of this model as an extension of the binomial setting.

The homogeneity assumption has been maintained above. Of course, there are several methods which extend the scope of the binomial distribution. For example, we can use "multiple binomials" when there is heterogeneity in the population, but a subdivision into homogeneous groups of issuers is still possible. Such "bucketing" approaches are universal and can be applied in the intensity approach as well in the following section. There are also diversity score methods for approximating the loss on a pool of inhomogeneous loans (having different default probabilities and different face values, say) with a binomial distribution matching the first two moments of the loss distribution. Finally, there are methods for treating inhomogeneous populations through moment generating function methods. These methods will not be covered here. Many of these methods also apply to the intensity setting to which we will turn next. However, as we will see, the intensity setting adds a lot of flexibility to how we model dependence dynamically while to a large extent preserving computational simplicity.

THE INTENSITY SETTING

There are multiple ways of formulating correlation on intensity settings – and much of the flexibility derives simply from the fact that the model is dynamic. We will now see how the intensity setting can be used to model dependence in several different ways.

The analogue of the mixed binomial setting with fixed time horizon is the Cox process or doubly stochastic setting, in which we have a state variable process X and an issuer i has an intensity of default $\lambda^i(X_s)$ at time s which depends on the state variable process. The fundamental assumption is that, given the outcome of the state variable process (up to the relevant time horizon), the probability of the default τ happening later than time T is

$$P\left(\tau > T \mid (X_s)_{0\leq s\leq T}\right) = \exp\left(-\int_0^T \lambda^i(X_s)\,\mathrm{d}s\right)$$

so that unconditionally

$$P(\tau > T) = E\exp\left(-\int_0^T \lambda^i(X_s)\,\mathrm{d}s\right).$$

The direct analogue with the mixed binomial is as follows. If we fix the time horizon T and we assume that a group of issuers have the same default intensity function λ, then the common random default probability is

$$\tilde{p}(T) = 1 - \exp\left(-\int_0^T \lambda(X_s)\,\mathrm{d}s\right).$$

If we make the additional assumption of conditional independence of default times of the issuers given the history of the state variable, then we have exactly the setting of the mixed binomial distribution for a given time horizon. How does one think of the conditional independence assumption? An analogue from medicine would perhaps be that the level of air pollution affects the onset of respiratory problems – the higher the pollution, the more individuals are struck. However, since the respiratory problems are not contagious, the only source of correlation is through the common dependence of the level of pollution. Given that we know the level of pollution, the fact that one individual has been hit with respiratory problems does not lead us to revise the probability of another individual being affected.

The great advantage of the Cox setting is that we have a dynamic model in which we can update our knowledge of the state variable (which can of course be a vector of state variables, including information on the term structure, the business cycle, etc) as time passes, and we observe the evolution of the state variables: under standard assumptions we get

$$P\left(\tau > T \mid (X_a)_{0 \le a \le t}\right) = \mathbf{1}_{\{\tau > t\}} E \exp\left(-\int_t^T \lambda(X_s)\,\mathrm{d}s\right)$$

where the indicator checks that the firm is still alive at time t. The setting is extremely convenient to work with because of the machinery of affine models being right at our disposal. Even with non-homogeneous issuers with different intensity functions (and perhaps different relevant state variables) it offers computational advantages in the simulation in that we can compute default times.

The problem here is the level of correlation that we can achieve. Duffie and Gârleanu (2001) use the Cox setting for pricing CDOs and obtain sizable correlation effects by having large jumps in state variables that drive intensities, but it is hard to say if these are unreasonably high. Note that it is possible to tie the jumps in intensities to defaults of large firms outside the collateral pool, but it is not defaults inside the pool that actually trigger the higher intensities. This is because of the conditional independence assumption.

There is a remarkably simple way of obtaining jumps in hazard rates even in a setting of conditional independence, namely by thinking of the state variables as being latent variables. This is not feasible in the mixed binomial model, even if we are in a way thinking of the default probability as a latent variable. The problem is that there is no updating in the light of defaults in that model. At the end of a fixed time horizon, we cannot experimentally distinguish between the outcome of a mixed binomial and a binomial, so we would need repeated experiments to say anything about the mixture distribution. The dynamic intensity model automatically allows for updating. The most simple example of this is specified in Arjas (1989). Here, the outcome of a single latent stochastic variable determines the level (according to a known function) of the intensities of independent issuers. Since the intensities are not observable but assuming that the distribution of the intensities are known (since the distribution of the latent variable is known), the actual default of one firm allows us to update through Bayes' rule what the outcome of the latent variable is. When a default of firm 2 occurs, say, this causes us to revise upwards our assessment of the latent variable, and thus the intensity of the surviving firm jumps upwards. For a graphical illustration, see Lando (2004). For more on the much harder case of updating default intensities when they are modulated by latent stochastic processes, see Collin-Dufresne *et al* (2003).

A huge advantage of the Cox setting is the automatic consistency that we achieve when specifying background state variables and intensities and we have conditional independence. We do not need to include issuers outside a given pool of issuers to model the defaults of issuers in the pool. This is lost with latent state variables. If defaults of firms cause us to update our beliefs of the values of state variables, then modelling of a pool of issuers will have to consider a larger universe consisting of all firms whose defaults would cause us to update our distribution of state variables on which the intensities depend.

If we insist on modelling contagion effects and do not use the latent variable method, the intensity setting still offers much flexibility as well, at least in terms of formulating models with concrete interpretation of parameters and ease of calculation. We demonstrate this now through a series of examples.

These examples all rely on a very nice tool for setting up the model assumptions, namely the generator matrix of a continuous-time, finite-state Markov chain. The generator matrix describes the evolution of a Markov chain through transition intensities. More precisely, the transition probability matrix $P(t)$ over a time horizon $t \geq 0$ of a time-homogeneous Markov chain on a finite-state space with K states can be described by an associated generator matrix, ie, a $K \times K$ matrix Λ for which

$$P(t) = \exp(\Lambda t)$$

where the exponential of the matrix Λt (obtained by multiplying all entries of Λ by t) is defined as

$$\exp(\Lambda t) = I + \sum_{k=1}^{\infty} \frac{\Lambda^k t^k}{k!}$$

Hence all the transition probabilities can be obtained from the generator.

The elements of a generator matrix satisfy

$$\lambda_{ij} \geq 0 \quad \text{for } i \neq j$$
$$\lambda_i = \sum_{j \neq i} \lambda_{ij}$$

ie, all elements off the diagonal are non-negative and the diagonal element makes the sum of the rows equal to zero. A row of zeros corresponds to an absorbing state.

It is useful for our interpretation of the parameters of the generator to recall the way in which a Markov chain can be simulated from its generator. Consider an example with three states and a generator given by

$$\Lambda = \begin{pmatrix} -\lambda_1 & \lambda_{12} & \lambda_{13} \\ \lambda_{21} & -\lambda_2 & \lambda_{23} \\ \lambda_{31} & \lambda_{32} & -\lambda_3 \end{pmatrix}$$

Let $Ex(\lambda)$ denote the exponential distribution with mean $1/\lambda$. To simulate the chain proceed as follows:

1. given an initial state, say state 1;
2. simulate the outcome of an $Ex(\lambda_1)$-distributed random variable, let the chain stay this amount of time in state 1;

probability $\lambda_{12}/(\lambda_{12} + \lambda_{12}) = \lambda_{12}/\lambda_1$ or
$_3/\lambda_1$;
nulate an $Ex(\lambda_2)$-distributed random
hat amount of time;
probability λ_{23}/λ_2, and to state 1 with

ros, the chain is absorbed in that state
imulation then stops.

of how the generator matrix can be
ependencies in default models. In all
. To compute the transition probabil-
ach case one needs to multiply each
and then compute the matrix expo-
v of how to actually compute the
a method which works for very large
lo (2004).

...on of the binomial model is what is known as a "pure death" process in Markov chain theory. Think of a population of N issuers, each of whom has a constant default intensity of λ, ie, the probability of surviving past time t is $\exp(-\lambda t)$. If the state space is the number of issuers which have not defaulted, we can let the first row of the generator correspond to the state where all issuers are alive, the next row correspond to the state with $N-1$ firms not in default, etc. The generator would then be a matrix with non-zero elements only in the diagonal and one place to the right of the diagonal:

$$\begin{pmatrix} -N\lambda & N\lambda & 0 & \cdots & \\ 0 & -(N-1)\lambda & (N-1)\lambda & 0 & \cdots \\ \vdots & & \ddots & \ddots & \end{pmatrix}$$

Example 2. We can do a number of things to introduce different kinds of contagion or different kinds of influence from background variables in this setting. In this example, we assume that the default of one issuer causes an increased intensity of defaults for a random amount of time. We therefore add an extra state to all the states to allow for the default intensity of issuers to be "excited". To save space, we will write down just those transition intensities which are non-zero. As always, one constructs the generator by numbering the different states, listing the intensities of transitions between states and making sure that the diagonal element is minus the sum of the remaining elements of the same row. The model is from Davis and Lo (2001). Instead of having a constant intensity of default equal to λ as in the example above, we assume that the intensity of default increases to $\lambda + \mu$ right after a firm has defaulted. This higher default intensity remains valid for an exponentially distributed amount of time but then drops (unless there is a new default) to the "normal level" λ. Assume that the parameter of the exponential distribution is ν. The description (see also Lando, 2004) is then as follows. Let the state space be $0, 1, \ldots, 2N$ and let state $2n$ for each n denote a state in which n firms are alive and the default level is normal, and let $2n + 1$ denote the state where there are n non-defaulted firms but the default intensity is high. Hence

$$\begin{aligned}\lambda_{2n+1,2n} &= \gamma \\ \lambda_{2n+1,2n-1} &= n(\lambda + \mu) \\ \lambda_{2n,2n-1} &= n\lambda\end{aligned}$$

All other transition intensities are zero. The matrix exponential can be readily calculated. As the model stands here, it has the consequence that firms change their marginal default rates through time, since fewer issuers will mean that the time spent in the excited state decreases relative to the time spent in the non-excited state. This is a problem when focussing in a contagion model only on the issuers in a given pool of loans. One can mitigate the problem by choosing state-dependent values of the parameters μ and ν to keep the marginal default rates constant.

Example 3. We can also introduce a more direct contagion similar to that introduced in the extended binomial setting of Davis and Lo (2001). Then we would modify the pure death process above and make it possible to go from a state with n firms to any state below. Given that a default occurs, one could let a binomial distribution determine the number of firms that ate pulled down together. If one wants to keep the marginal default rate constant in this model for individual firms, this requires a condition on the contagion parameter as the number of firms decreases. For more on this, see Lando (2004).

Example 4. Another simple extension is to have the Cox process setting, where the driving state variable is itself a continuous-time Markov chain. Assume that the "state variable" X is such a process with M states and the generator matrix A. We let α_{ij} for $i \neq j$ denote an off-diagonal element of this matrix. Assume that the state of X determines the default intensity of a firm in our homogeneous pool. Hence, the default intensity of a firm is λ_x when the environment X is in state x. Let (N, X) denote the state of the Markov chain where N records the number of surviving firms. Then we have the following specification of the transition intensities:

$$(n, x) \to (n-1, x) \text{ has intensity } n\lambda_x \quad (3)$$

$$(n, i) \to (n, j) \text{ has intensity } \alpha_{ij} \quad (4)$$

All other transition intensities are zero. As noted above, this is simply a representation of the Cox setting where the driving state variable is a continuous-time Markov chain. Since continuous-time Markov chains can be used to approximate jump-diffusion processes, this example also provides a way of approximating models with more complicated state-variable dynamics. In addition, one can easily add new possibilities of transitions assuming, for example, that a default triggers a change in the environment. This is an example of a case where the "usual" computations that apply for Cox processes break down. However, in the generator specification, one can still just compute the matrix exponential and obtain transition probabilities.

Example 5. The above examples have all been restricted by the assumption of homogeneous issuers. For some applications, we may wish to focus on a few issuers. For example, we could be interested in understanding the role of correlation in default risk between three issuers: the protection buyer and protection seller in a default swap, and the reference entity of the default swap. Of course the main concern here is with correlation between the protection seller and the reference entity, but even a protection seller could be hit with default risk if a protection buyer stops paying premia in a scenario where the credit quality of the reference entity has improved. Representing complicated dependence patterns for such a small group of issuers is simple. We give an example here to illustrate the idea. Consider three issuers which can each be in the non-default state N or the default state D. The state NNN is the state where all three are alive, the state DNN is where the first issuer has defaulted and the others have not, etc. In the example we think of the first issuer as "large" in the sense that the default of this issuer can trigger the simultaneous default of the two others. If the first issuer defaults, this simultaneous default happens with probability α/λ_1. Note that we have specified intensities in the generator so that the initial marginal default intensity of firm i is λ_i. When the default of firm 1 does not trigger the default of the two others, the default intensity of the remaining two will change (and one should think of this as an increase). For example, in the state DNN the default intensities of the remaining small firms have changed from λ_i to μ_i for $i = 2, 3$. This notion of a primary firm and secondary firms was introduced in Jarrow and Yu (2001). Here we add the possibility of simultaneous defaults. Note that when firm 1 has not defaulted, but one of the small firms has, there is still a chance that the large firm 1 will pull the remaining small firm with it in default. The generator for this example is shown in Table 1.

For this example to work, we must assume that $\alpha < \lambda_i$ for all i. With this in place, one can fill in numbers for the intensities and, to compute transition probabilities for a time horizon t, simply multiply each entry by t and compute the matrix exponential. Of course, the theme can be varied. For methods to introduce a random driving state variable, see Lando (2004). Models with this kind of contagion are studied in, for example, Collin-Dufresne *et al* (2003), Jarrow and Yu (2001) and Kusuoka (1999). The generator formulation of this problem was used in Lando (1998).

CONCLUDING REMARKS

It is clear that the intensity models offer a very flexible and highly interpretable framework for thinking about correlated defaults. We have indicated cases where computation can be made simpler, but it is clear that for complicated waterfall structures in CDOs and

Table 1 The generator matrix

	NNN	DNN	NDN	NND	DDN	DND	NDD	DDD
NNN	$-\left(\sum_{i=1}^{3}\lambda_i - 2\alpha\right)$	$\lambda_1 - \alpha$	$\lambda_2 - \alpha$	$\lambda_3 - \alpha$	0	0	0	α
DNN	0	$-(\mu_2 + \mu_3)$	0	0	μ_2	μ_3	0	0
NDN	0	0	$-(\lambda_1 + \lambda_3 - \alpha)$	0	$\lambda_1 - \alpha$	0	$\lambda_3 - \alpha$	α
NND	0	0	0	$-(\lambda_1 + \lambda_3 - \alpha)$	0	$\lambda_1 - \alpha$	$\lambda_2 - \alpha$	α
DDN	0	0	0	0	$-\mu_3$	0	0	μ_3
DND	0	0	0	0	0	$-\mu_2$	0	μ_2
NDD	0	0	0	0	0	0	$-\lambda_1$	λ_1
DDD	0	0	0	0	0	0	0	0

with large inhomogeneity among issuers the intensity framework must also rely on simulation. There are well-known techniques for simulating default times in intensity settings, see, for example, Duffie and Singleton (1999) and Yu (2004).

However, even if in principle it is possible to include very intricate dependence patterns in intensity models, it is also clear that the modelling easily becomes very "partial" and this raises consistency problems. If we are certain that there are contagion effects present among (say) corporate bonds, then we cannot restrict the modelling universe to the loans underlying a portfolio, but must instead look at the entire universe of bonds relevant for determining the dynamics of our portfolio. Similarly, if we think updating of latent variables is important, defaults outside the portfolio we are modelling matter, and to be consistent we must model the entire universe of defaultable claims that depend on the same state variables. A possible way around this is to designate, as in Jarrow and Yu (2001), a small collection of primary firms whose defaults are state variables and then let the rest of the universe remain conditionally independent given observed state variables. This would bring us back to the Cox setting – at least for the secondary firms – and computation can also be handled for a small group of primary defaulters.

Although markets seem to believe in strong correlation patterns, it is not clear that the Cox (or doubly-stochastic) assumption, by which correlation of defaults is only a consequence of correlation between intensities, is strongly at odds with empirical evidence of default clustering, see Das *et al* (2004). This is an exciting empirical question.

REFERENCES

Arjas, E., 1989, "Survival Models and Martingale Dynamics", *Scandinavian Journal of Statistics*, **16**, pp. 177–225.

Collin-Dufresne, P., R. Goldstein, and J. Helwege, 2003, "Is Credit Event Risk Priced? Modelling Contagion Via the Updating of Beliefs", Working Paper, Carnegie Mellon University.

Collin-Dufresne, P., R. Goldstein, and J. Hugonnier, 2003, "A General Formula for Valuing Defaultable Securities", Working Paper, Carnegie Mellon University.

Das, S., D. Duffie, and N. Kapadia, 2004, "Common Failings: How Corporate Defaults are Correlated", Working Paper, Santa Clara University and Stanford University.

Davis, M., and V. Lo, 2001, "Infectious Defaults", *Quantitative Finance,* **1**, pp. 382–7.

Duffie, D., and N. Gârleanu, 2001, "Risk and Valuation of Collateralized Debt Obligations", *Financial Analysts Journal,* **57(1)**, pp. 41–59.

Duffie, D., and K. Singleton, 1999, "Simulating Correlated Defaults", Working Paper, Stanford University.

Glasserman, P., 2003, "Tail Approximations For Portfolio Credit Risk", Working Paper, Columbia Business School.

Jarrow, R., and F. Yu, 2001, "Counterparty Risk and the Pricing of Defaultable Securities", *Journal of Finance,* **56(5)**, pp. 1765–99.

Kusuoka, S., 1999, "A Remark on Default Risk Models", in *Advances in Mathematical Economics,* pp. 69–82, (Springer Verlag).

Lando, D., 1998, "On Rating Transition Analysis and Correlation", in R. Jameson (ed), *Credit Derivatives – Applications for Risk Management, Investment and Portfolio Optimization,* pp. 147–55 (London: Risk Books).

Lando, D., 2004, *Credit Risk Modeling – Theory and Applications* (Princeton, New Jersey: Princeton University Press).

Vasicek, O., 1991, "Limiting Loan Loss Probability Distribution", Working Paper, KMV Corporation.

Yu, F., 2004, "Default Correlation in Reduced-form Models", Working Paper, University of California at Irvine.

Section 2

Rating

4

Rating Transitions in Global Structured Finance

Jian Hu

Moody's Investors Service

Credit ratings are opinions of the relative credit quality of individual obligations. Ratings play an important role in structured finance markets by increasing transparency and thereby permitting greater liquidity. The credit quality of securities and hence their ratings evolve over time. Changes or "transitions" in the structured finance ratings published by Moody's signal changes in the rating agency's assessments of expected loss, ie, the product of the default frequency and losses in the event of default.

In this chapter, we present a comprehensive review of rating transition statistics for structured finance securities rated by Moody's. We compare transitions in structured exposures with those of corporate issuer ratings and across sectors and regions. We focus on rating transitions in 2003 relative to 2002, but also include comparisons with historical rating transition rates.[1] In addition to the one-year horizon, rating transition statistics over multiple-year horizons are also discussed.

We note, however, that rating transition statistics are based on a relatively short historical sample period and may not necessarily represent the future. This is especially true at the sector specific level because some structured finance sectors are young and have yet to experience a full credit cycle, while others have experienced only one cycle. In addition, with the evolvement of structured finance markets, new assets and new structures are introduced continuously. As a result, ratings may sustain changes because the nature of the securities rated has changed.

MEASURES OF RATING TRANSITION FREQUENCIES

Throughout this chapter, we have adopted the following measures of rating transition frequencies.[2]

Downgrade (or upgrade) rate

A security is downgraded (upgraded) if its rating at the end of a year is lower (higher) than at the beginning of the year on the basis of ratings with numeric modifiers (Moody's ratings use both alphabetical and numeric symbols). The downgrade rate is the number of securities downgraded (or upgraded) divided by the total number of outstanding securities at the beginning of the year that excludes ratings withdrawn during the year. In measuring downgrade rates and upgrade rates, only ratings at the beginning and the end of the year are considered.

Weighted-downgrade (or upgrade) rate

This term refers to the number of securities downgraded (or upgraded), weighted by the total number of notches changed per downgrade (upgrade) from the beginning to the end of a year, divided by the total number of outstanding securities at the beginning of the year, after excluding ratings withdrawn during the year. For example, a security downgraded from Baa1 at the beginning of the year to Ba1 at the end of the year is counted as three downgrades to get a weighted downgrade rate, but counted as only one downgrade to get the unweighted downgrade rate.

Rating stability rate

This is the number of securities that did not change ratings, on the basis of ratings with numeric modifiers, from the beginning to the end of the year, divided by the total number of outstanding securities at the beginning of the year, after excluding ratings withdrawn during the year. Only ratings at the beginning and the end of the year are used.

Number of notches downgraded (upgraded) per year

This refers to the number of total notches downgraded (upgraded) over an entire year, averaged across all securities downgraded (upgraded) during the year. A security can experience multiple rating actions during the year. Therefore, this is different from the number of notches changed per rating action.

Rating drift

This is the weighted upgrade rate minus the weighted downgrade rate.

Rating volatility

This is the weighted upgrade rate plus the weighted downgrade rate.

Downgrade-to-upgrade ratio

This refers to the total number of unweighted downgrades divided by the total number of unweighted upgrades.

Downgrade (upgrade) rate by broad rating

A downgrade (upgrade) occurs only if a security changes its rating across two broad rating categories (alphabetical ratings without numeric modifiers). For example, a rating change from Baa1 to Ba2 is considered a downgrade by broad rating (from Baa to Ba). A rating change from Baa1 to Baa3 is not counted as a downgrade by broad rating (since it moves from Baa to Baa), but is considered to be a downgrade by alphanumeric rating (this is the standard case).

Cohort

A cohort contains all rated securities outstanding at the beginning of a year regardless of when a security was issued. The length of a cohort is the number of years during which a security's rating will be examined. For example, a one-year cohort is formed for the purpose of examining rating changes over a one-year period. A three-year cohort is formed for the purpose of examining rating changes over a three-year period. Only the ratings outstanding at the beginning and end of the three-year period are used.

Rating transition matrix

A one-year rating transition matrix specifies the frequencies of ratings changed from a starting rating category at the beginning of a year to an end rating category at the end of a year (typically by broad rating). A multi-year rating transition matrix reports the frequencies of ratings changed from a starting rating category at the beginning of a multi-year cohort to an end rating category at the end of the multi-year cohort (typically by broad rating).

Treatment of withdrawn ratings (WRs)

In calculating rating transition rates, ratings that were withdrawn during a given cohort period (one-year or multiple-year) were excluded from the total number of outstanding securities at the beginning of the cohort period. Alternatives include deducting only half of the WRs from the denominator or including all WRs in the denominator.

DATA SAMPLE

Our data sample contains a total of 30,278 structured securities from 10,720 deals in asset-backed securities (ABS, home equity loan (HEL)-backed securities included), collateralised debt obligations (CDOs), commercial mortgage-backed securities (CMBS) and residential mortgage-backed securities (RMBS) over the entire sample period from 1983 to 2003. Only structured securities with a Moody's long-term bond rating were included. Tranches wrapped by financial guarantors, government agencies or government sponsored enterprises (GSEs) were excluded.

Tranches carrying the same rating from the same deal were collapsed into a single rating tranche. To better reflect rating transition performance in the structured finance universe and to reduce direct corporate influence on structured rating transition statistics we made two adjustments. First, we excluded deals that were entirely dependent on a single corporate rating, such as the single borrower credit tenant lease (CTL) deals. Second, we excluded the derivatives sector from this study. The derivatives sector contains mainly re-packaged securities, structured notes and credit derivatives. Most of them are heavily dependent or based on one corporate rating, such as the rating of a swap counterparty or a single reference credit.

The four major sectors – ABS, CDO, CMBS and RMBS – combined, with the exclusion of derivatives, are the subject of this chapter. We refer to these sectors as "all structured finance" (or "structured finance as a whole").

Figure 1 Distributions of number of rated securities on January 1, 2004

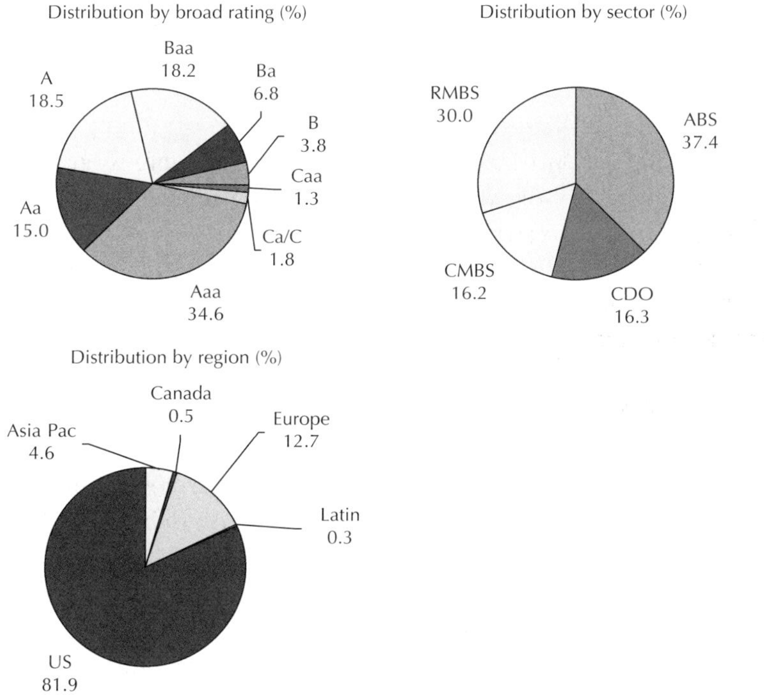

Figure 1 reports the number of rated securities outstanding on 1 January, 2004 by broad rating group, sector and region. As indicated, global structured securities were predominantly rated as investment grade with the Aaa-rated securities making up more than one third of the entire sample.

By sector, the number of outstanding ABS securities included in the data sample grew by 33.3% from the beginning of 2003 to the beginning of 2004, driven by an impressive growth rate of 64.3% in HEL asset class. At the beginning of 2004, the share of HELs in the ABS sector reached 45.7%. As a result, the share of ABS in all structured finance was 37.4%, the largest among the four sectors.

In RMBS, the growth was equally remarkable in 2003, with a rating growth rate of 27.5%, making RMBS the second largest sector with a 30% share of the total at the beginning of 2004, and the largest if HELs are not included in the ABS sector.

Rated securities in the CDO and CMBS sectors also recorded significant growth in 2003, with a growth rate of 36.5% for CDOs and 20.8% for CMBS. The shares of CDOs and CMBS as a percentage of all outstanding structured securities remained about the same at the beginning of 2004 as it was in 2003.

By the number of deals, the share of ABS at the beginning of 2004 stood at 42.3%, while the shares of RMBS, CDO and CMBS were 29.9%, 20.2% and 7.6%, respectively.

By region, rated structured securities in Europe and the Asia Pacific also saw extraordinary growth. European structured securities grew at a rate of 43.3% in 2003, while Asia Pacific structured securities grew by 36.5% from the beginning to the end of 2003.

RATING TRANSITIONS IN THE ALL STRUCTURED FINANCE CATEGORY

Out of a total universe of 18,947 ratings at the beginning of 2003, the global structured finance sector downgraded 1,279 ratings from 570 deals and upgraded 569 ratings from 216 deals, resulting in a 2-to-1 downgrade-to-upgrade ratio. In comparison, out of 14,345 ratings in 2002, 958 ratings from 420 deals were downgraded and 194 ratings from 102 deals were upgraded, resulting in a 5-to-1 downgrade-to-upgrade ratio.

The frequency of rating downgrades was about the same at 7.2% in 2003 as in 2002, while the frequency of rating upgrades climbed to 3.2% in 2003 from 1.5% in 2002, signalling an overall improvement of credit quality among global structured finance securities in 2003.

Of all the securities downgraded in 2003, 48.2% were ABS, 39.4% were CDOs, 10.4% were CMBS and 2% were RMBS.

Of all the securities upgraded in 2003, 17.2% were ABS, 6.5% were CDOs, 27.8% were CMBS and 48.5% were RMBS.

Historically, 2002 and 2003 experienced substantially higher downgrade rates and lower upgrade rates than any recent period prior to 2002. Figure 2 presents the downgrade and upgrade rates from 1983 to 2003.

The average number of notches changed per downgrade action increased to 3.5 in 2003, from 3.1 in 2002. However, the number of rating actions per downgraded security in 2003 declined. Because fewer securities sustained downgrades, the average number of total notches downgraded decreased to 4.2 in 2003 from 4.7 in 2002.

Figure 2 Historical downgrade and upgrade rates in the all structured finance category

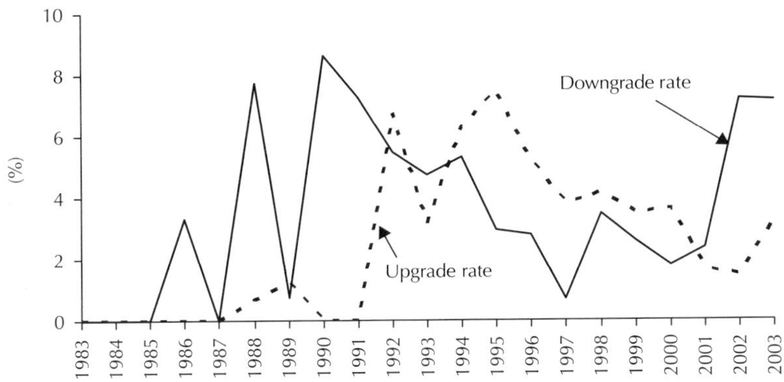

Figure 3 Weighted downgrade and upgrade rates in the all structured finance category

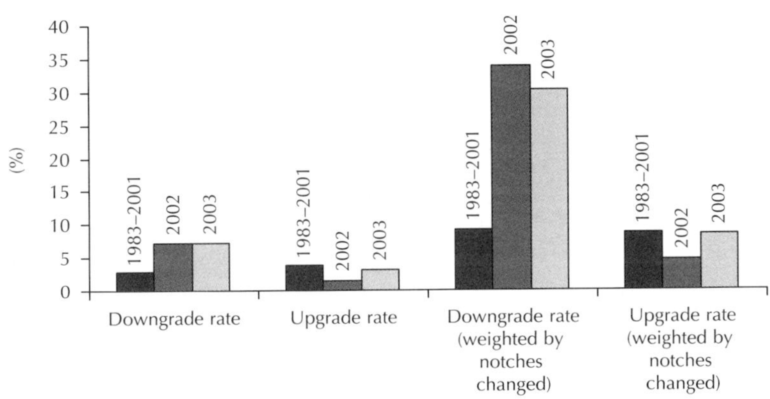

In the meantime, the average number of notches changed per upgrade action fell from 3.1 to 2.6 and the average number of total notches upgraded per year also fell from 3.2 to 2.6.

Weighted by the magnitude of downgrades, the downgrade rate declined to 30.2% in 2003, from 33.9% in 2002. However, the downgrade rates in 2003 and 2002 were both substantially higher than the historical average of 9.0% during 1983–2001 (Figure 3).

The rating drift in 2003 was negative at −21.9%, significantly higher than the historical average of −0.5% during 1983–2001,

Figure 4 Rating drift and downgrade-to-upgrade ratio in the all structured finance category

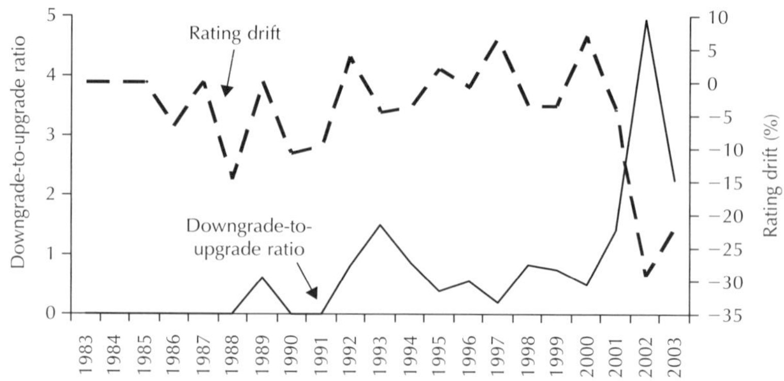

despite a seven-percentage-point improvement over 2002. Meanwhile, the downgrade-to-upgrade ratio dropped to 2-to-1 from 5-to-1 in 2002 (Figure 4).

Ratings were volatile in 2003 in the all structured finance category. Overall rating volatility stood at 38.5% in 2003, the same as in 2002, which was the highest level historically. In comparison, the historical average rating volatility during 1983–2001 was 17.5%.

Meanwhile, the frequency of ratings that remained unchanged in 2003 stood at about 89.6%, slightly lower than 91.3% in 2002, and an average of 93.4% during 1983–2001.

Of all the 2003 downgrades, 32% sustained a downgrade in 2002, while of all the 2003 upgrades, only 2% had experienced an upgrade in 2002. This suggests that in 2003 the downgrade momentum persisted and was stronger than the upgrade momentum.[3]

The one-year rating transition matrix (Table 1) provides downgrade and upgrade rates by rating category by reviewing rating changes at the beginning and the end of a year. Table 1 compares the 2003 one-year rating transition matrix with an average matrix during 1983–2003.

On the basis of broad rating categories, Table 1 reveals that rating stability rates were about the same as the long-term average since 1983. Rating stability rates stayed above 80%, and above 88% for the investment-grade rating categories, with the Aaa rating remaining the most stable.

Table 1 One-year rating transition matrices in the all structured finance category

2003 Ratings from:	Ratings to: Aaa	Aa	A	Baa	Ba	B	Caa or below
Aaa	98.21%	1.06%	0.50%	0.20%	0.03%		
Aa	5.02%	89.13%	3.43%	1.58%	0.60%	0.19%	0.04%
A	0.65%	3.22%	89.62%	3.75%	1.57%	0.95%	0.24%
Baa	0.31%	0.28%	2.83%	88.20%	3.68%	2.49%	2.20%
Ba	0.07%	0.07%	0.22%	3.26%	83.20%	4.74%	8.44%
B	0.28%			0.98%	3.66%	81.01%	14.06%
Caa or below						0.21%	99.79%
1983–2003 average							
Ratings from:	Ratings to: Aaa	Aa	A	Baa	Ba	B	Caa or below
Aaa	98.86%	0.82%	0.20%	0.07%	0.01%	0.01%	0.04%
Aa	5.48%	91.15%	2.25%	0.77%	0.19%	0.09%	0.08%
A	1.03%	2.42%	93.14%	2.20%	0.72%	0.29%	0.20%
Baa	0.44%	0.50%	2.20%	90.34%	3.65%	1.57%	1.31%
Ba	0.12%	0.06%	0.64%	3.56%	85.92%	3.62%	6.09%
B	0.07%		0.07%	0.67%	1.52%	87.16%	10.51%
Caa or below					0.09%	0.26%	99.65%

Significantly, Table 1 also shows that the annual rate of downgrades into the Caa or below category was generally higher in 2003 than for the weighted average period from 1983–2003. However, while 2003 evidenced a higher than normal downgrade rate into the Caa category or below, it was nonetheless an improvement when compared to 2002 (Table 2). Specifically, the rate of downgrades into the Caa category or below from a Baa rating was about the same in 2003 relative to 2002, but was significantly lower for securities rated Aaa, Aa and A (Table 2).

COMPARING STRUCTURED RATING TRANSITIONS WITH CORPORATE RATING TRANSITIONS

Out of a total universe of 4,692 corporate ratings in 2003, 717 ratings were downgraded and 319 ratings were upgraded, as compared to 986 downgrades and 250 upgrades out of a total universe of 4,591 ratings in 2002.[4] The one-year downgrade rate (unweighted by the magnitude of downgrades and including defaults as downgrades)

Table 2 Rates of downgrades into the Caa category or below in the all structured finance sector

Rating at the beginning of a year	2003 (%)	2002 (%)	1983–2001 (%)
Aaa		0.15	0.02
Aa	0.04	0.55	0.02
A	0.24	0.43	0.12
Baa	2.20	2.25	0.61
Ba	8.44	12.39	2.72
B	14.06	15.10	7.32

Figure 5 Rating stability rates in the structured and corporate sectors

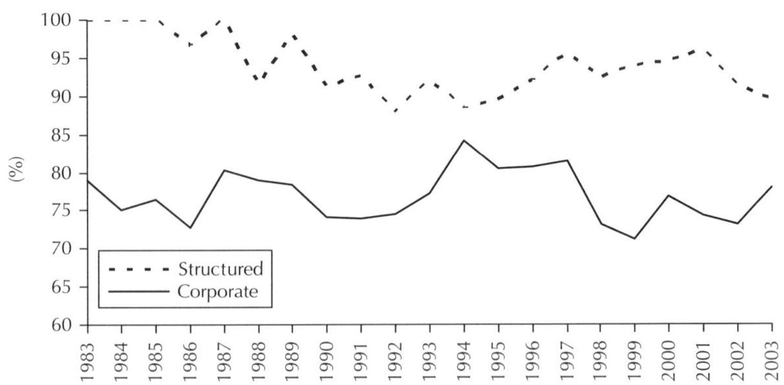

fell to 15.3% in 2003, from 21.5% in 2002, while the upgrade rate went to 6.8%, from 5.5%.

Additionally, corporate ratings were more stable in 2003 than in 2002, as the one-year stability rate rose to 77.9% from 73.1% in 2002. Despite the improvement, corporate ratings were less stable than those in the all structured finance category. Overall, rating stability in structured finance was more than ten percentage points higher than in corporate finance in 2003, as it has been since 1983.

Figures 5 and 6 detail rating stability trends and transition rates since 1983 in the structured and corporate sectors.

In Table 3 we present a more detailed comparison between the two sectors through one-year rating transition matrices.

Figure 6 Downgrade and upgrade rates in the structured and corporate sectors

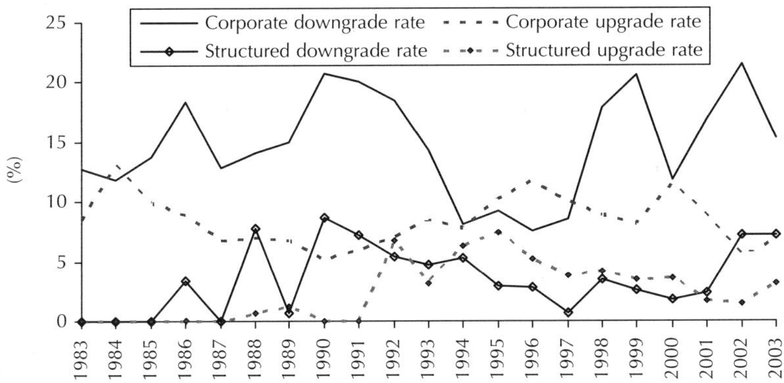

Table 3 One-year rating transition matrices in the structured and corporate sectors for 2003

Global corporate in 2003

Ratings from:	Ratings to: Aaa	Aa	A	Baa	Ba	B	Caa or below
Aaa	99.44%				0.56%		
Aa	1.44%	91.79%	6.77%				
A	0.08%	1.28%	90.91%	7.58%	0.08%	0.08%	
Baa			1.79%	90.89%	5.45%	1.79%	0.09%
Ba			0.38%	4.19%	82.29%	10.67%	2.48%
B				0.29%	4.03%	83.88%	11.80%
Caa or below						6.67%	93.33%

Global structured in 2003

Ratings from:	Ratings to: Aaa	Aa	A	Baa	Ba	B	Caa or below
Aaa	98.21%	1.06%	0.50%	0.20%	0.03%		
Aa	5.02%	89.13%	3.43%	1.58%	0.60%	0.19%	0.04%
A	0.65%	3.22%	89.62%	3.75%	1.57%	0.95%	0.24%
Baa	0.31%	0.28%	2.83%	88.20%	3.68%	2.49%	2.20%
Ba	0.07%	0.07%	0.22%	3.26%	83.20%	4.74%	8.44%
B	0.28%			0.98%	3.66%	81.01%	14.06%
Caa or below						0.21%	99.79%

By broad rating category, we can see that corporate and structured rating stability rates in 2003 were similar, but the overall downgrade rates for the Aaa and Baa rating categories were higher in the structured than in the corporate sector, but lower for the Aa and A rating categories. Furthermore, in 2003, there were more upgrades in the Aa, A and Baa rating categories in the structured than in the corporate sectors, but more upgrades in the Ba and B categories in the corporate than in the structured sectors.

Additionally, the rates of downgrades into the Caa category or below by rating were higher in the structured than in the corporate sectors, and were particularly so among securities rated as investment grade at the beginning of 2003. The findings are reported in Figure 7.

Similar to the structured sector, corporate issuers also demonstrated slower negative rating drift in 2003. Negative rating drift fell to –17.4%, from –37.2% in 2002. Per our discussion above, negative drift in the structured sector fell to –21.9% from –29.2%.

As indicated in Figure 8, the structured and corporate sectors displayed strong similarity with respect to their rating drifts in the last five years, suggesting a positive correlation between the two sectors during this period.

Despite the similarity and correlation, the average rating drift from 1983 to 2001 was significantly different across the two sectors,

Figure 7 Rates of downgrades into the Caa category or below in the corporate and structured sectors for 2003

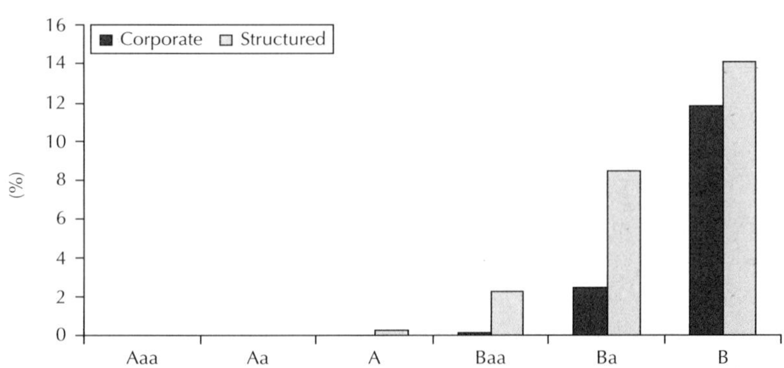

Figure 8 Rating drift in the structured and corporate sectors

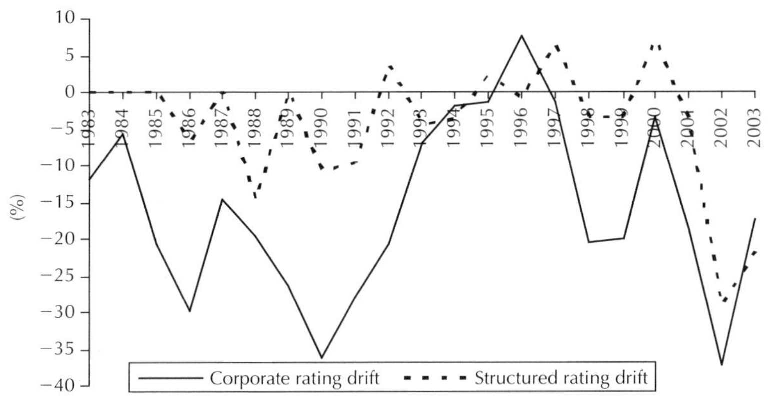

Figure 9 Rating volatility in the structured and corporate sectors

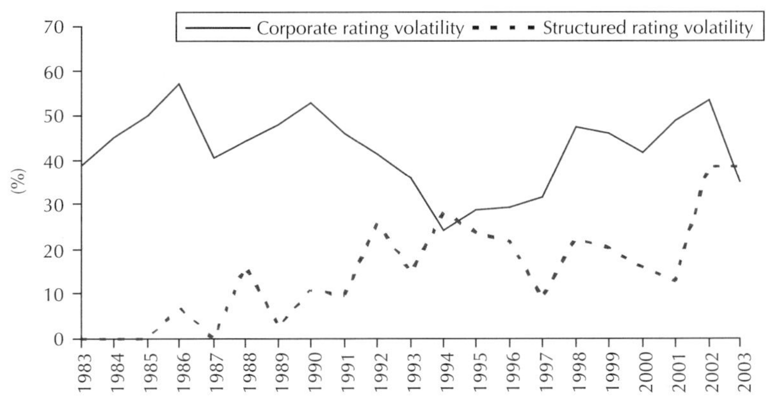

with the average rating drift among structured securities only at 0.5%, and the drift among corporate issuers at –13.7%.

In contrast, the corporate rating volatility declined to 35.3% in 2003 from 53.5% in 2002, while the structured rating volatility stayed at the same level at 38.5% (Figure 9).

The average number of total notches downgraded per year in the corporate sector fell to 1.7 in 2003 from 2.1 in 2002. Total notches upgraded fell to 1.3 from 1.5. The number of total notches downgraded and upgraded in the corporate sector were both

Figure 10 Average number of notches downgraded and upgraded per year in the structured and corporate sectors

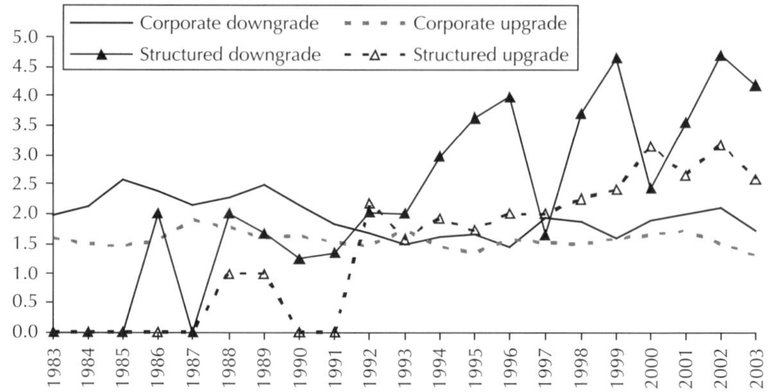

significantly lower than those in the structured sector, which were 4.2 for downgrades and 2.6 for upgrades in 2003. Figure 10 illustrates the differences.

SECTOR SPECIFIC ANALYSIS OF RATING TRANSITIONS

ABS

Out of a total universe of 6,905 ABS ratings at the beginning of 2003, 616 ratings from 243 deals were downgraded and 98 ratings from 52 deals were upgraded in 2003.

As in 2002, the downgrade rate in 2003 greatly exceeded the upgrade rate, with a downgrade rate of 9.5% and an upgrade rate of 1.5%. Figure 11 depicts the patterns of downgrade and upgrade rates in ABS from 1995 to 2003.

Within the ABS sector, transactions backed by franchise loans, manufactured housing loans, leases and tobacco settlement bonds were most affected by downgrades. ABS securities backed by traditional consumer credit, such as auto loans, credit card receivables and home equity loans, continued to perform well. Table 4 takes a closer look at the downgrade rate and the upgrade rate for a few selected asset classes within the ABS sector.

As indicated, securities backed by manufactured housing (MH) or franchise loans continued to deteriorate in 2003. In 2003, Moody's

Figure 11 Downgrade and upgrade rates in ABS

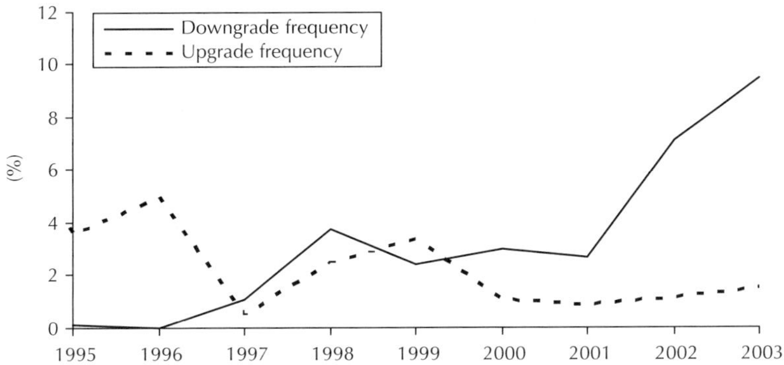

Table 4 Rates of downgrades and upgrades in 2003 and 2002 for selected ABS

	Number of outstanding ratings		Downgrade rate		Upgrade rate	
ABS asset classes	**1 January 2003**	**1 January 2002**	**2003 (%)**	**2002 (%)**	**2003 (%)**	**2002 (%)**
Autos	499	395	1.85		3.70	4.55
Credit cards	1073	939	1.77	3.48	0.73	0.12
Franchise loans	157	150	40.76	44.00		
HEL	2558	1615	3.09	0.70	2.06	1.33
Leases	468	424	22.00	11.02	1.00	0.28
MH	656	594	39.72	23.49	0.77	0.17
Small business loans	117	108	9.48			
Tobacco settlement bonds	52	31	100			

downgraded more than 250 tranches from 81 MH deals, most of which were associated with a large number of Green Tree/Conseco transactions, although deals issued by Oakwood Mortgage Investors (OMI) and UCFC Funding also contributed to the total.

Eighty eight securities backed by 11 equipment lease deals, represented by DVI Receivables transactions, and 14 aircraft lease deals were also downgraded in 2003, doubling the downgrade rate in the lease class of ABS to 22% in 2003 from 11% in 2002. Additional downgrades in tobacco settlement bonds, securities backed by small business loans and the HEL asset class further exacerbated the ABS downgrade rate.

The auto and credit card asset classes in ABS, however, continued to outperform. Both sustained a downgrade rate lower than 2% in 2003. In addition, auto ABS sustained a 3.7% upgrade rate in 2003, again showing the strength in this segment.

More than 20% of the 2003 ABS downgrades came from the 2000 vintage, while the 1999, 2000 and 2001 vintages together added up to more than 50% of the total ABS downgrades in 2003.

Table 5 compares the ABS rating transition matrix in 2003 with the average from 1983 to 2003. It shows that the rating stability rates by rating in 2003 were all lower than their long-term averages. Nonetheless, the stability rates of investment-grade ratings remained above 85%, with the Aaa rating being the most stable.

In Table 6, we provide two-year and five-year rating transition matrices for the ABS sector. The matrices reveal that multi-year rating stability rates have generally been much lower over longer horizons.

Table 5 One-year rating transition matrices in ABS

2003

Ratings from:	Ratings to: Aaa	Aa	A	Baa	Ba	B	Caa or below
Aaa	97.30%	1.21%	0.94%	0.45%	0.09%		
Aa	3.35%	87.66%	4.08%	2.93%	1.57%	0.42%	
A	0.79%	1.22%	89.10%	4.81%	2.01%	1.71%	0.37%
Baa	0.71%	0.09%	1.15%	86.74%	2.83%	3.80%	4.69%
Ba	0.34%			0.69%	70.69%	5.17%	23.10%
B					3.13%	51.04%	45.83%
Caa or below							100.00%

1983–2003 average

Ratings from:	Ratings to: Aaa	Aa	A	Baa	Ba	B	Caa or below
Aaa	98.71%	0.85%	0.24%	0.10%	0.02%	0.01%	0.08%
Aa	2.59%	93.22%	2.22%	1.17%	0.42%	0.10%	0.27%
A	0.71%	1.01%	94.93%	1.89%	0.87%	0.42%	0.16%
Baa	0.55%	0.31%	0.87%	89.78%	4.81%	1.92%	1.76%
Ba	0.26%	0.17%	0.34%	4.74%	76.21%	5.09%	13.19%
B			0.30%	0.60%	0.90%	73.19%	25.00%
Caa or below							100.00%

Table 6 Two-year and five-year rating transition matrices in ABS (1983–2003)

Two-year

Ratings from: \ Ratings to:	Aaa	Aa	A	Baa	Ba	B	Caa or below
Aaa	97.65%	1.52%	0.34%	0.19%	0.08%	0.06%	0.15%
Aa	5.17%	87.43%	3.33%	1.73%	0.99%	0.64%	0.71%
A	1.69%	1.96%	91.48%	2.37%	1.07%	0.63%	0.80%
Baa	1.32%	0.66%	1.56%	82.22%	7.21%	2.84%	4.19%
Ba	0.60%	0.48%	0.84%	0.84%	65.90%	5.78%	25.54%
B	0.45%		0.90%	1.35%	1.35%	67.57%	28.38%
Caa or below							100.00%

Five-year

Ratings from: \ Ratings to:	Aaa	Aa	A	Baa	Ba	B	Caa or below
Aaa	96.67%	2.11%	0.67%	0.39%	0.06%		0.11%
Aa	16.41%	73.48%	4.28%	1.66%	1.19%	2.62%	0.36%
A	5.13%	3.71%	86.39%	1.50%	1.35%	0.43%	1.50%
Baa	2.69%	1.95%	2.08%	63.00%	12.21%	4.88%	13.19%
Ba	2.86%	1.90%	1.90%	3.81%	49.05%	3.33%	37.14%
B	4.44%		4.44%	6.67%	4.44%	60.00%	20.00%
Caa or below							100.00%

Furthermore, over longer horizons, there have been more upgrades than downgrades in the Aa and A rating categories, but more downgrades than upgrades in the Baa rating categories and below.

CDOs

The CDO sector showed significant improvements in 2003, although the sector still remained under stress after an extremely volatile 2002. The downgrade rate dropped to 17.9% in 2003 from 25.1% in 2002, and the upgrade rate rose from 0.6% to 1.3%. Despite improvement, the CDO downgrade rate was still the highest in the structured finance universe.

The one-year downgrade rate, weighted by the number of total notches changed per year, dropped from a record high of 123.4% in 2002 to 58.9% in 2003, cutting the 2002 level by more than a half. However, the weighted downgrade rate in 2003 was still substantially higher than the historical average level of 21.0% during

Figure 12 Downgrade and upgrade rates in CDOs and corporate downgrade rates

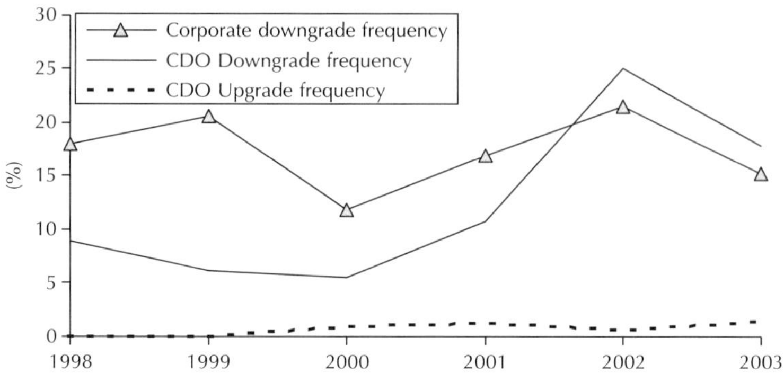

1991–2001, marking 2002 and 2003 as two extremely stressful years since the inception of the CDO sector.

Relative to the downgrade rate, the upgrade rate in CDOs has been particularly low and was 1.3% in 2003 (Figure 12). Figure 12 illustrates the trends in the CDO migration rates from 1998 to 2003.

For comparison, Figure 12 also includes the downgrade rates in the corporate sector. It points out a strong and positive correlation between the corporate and CDO downgrade rates.

Within the CDO sector, declines in the downgrade rate were evident in both synthetic and cashflow transactions (Table 7).

The downgrade rate for balance sheet synthetic securities fell to 16.2% in 2003, from 30.5% in 2002. Among synthetic arbitrage securities, the downgrade rate fell to 33.7% from 61.1%, although the main cause of such a huge decline in downgrade rate for this asset class could also be attributed to the large increase in the number of rated securities. For ACF CBO securities, the downgrade rate in 2003 was 15.4 percentage points lower than in 2002.

Although few CDOs were upgraded, balance sheet cashflow CDOs posted an upgrade rate of 8.57% in 2003. This is attributable to nine upgrades in two European balance sheet cashflow deals.

About 40% of the downgraded CDO securities in 2003 had experienced a downgrade in 2002, exhibiting strong downgrade momentum in the CDO sector.

Table 7 Downgrade and upgrade rates in 2002 and 2003 for selected CDOs

	Number of outstanding ratings		Downgrade rate		Upgrade rate	
CDO types	**1 January 2003**	**1 January 2002**	**2003 (%)**	**2002 (%)**	**2003 (%)**	**2002 (%)**
ACF CBO	543	538	33.46	48.86	0.56	0.19
ACF CLO	494	331	5.47	7.27		
BalSh CF	123	135	3.81	1.89	8.57	0.94
BalSh Syn	284	209	16.21	30.53	1.98	1.05
IG CBO	141	109	29.93	20.18	0.73	
Resecuritisations	372	200	8.92	4.52	0.54	
Syn Arb	472	126	33.71	61.06	0.89	

Notes: ACF CBO – arbitrage cashflow collateralised bond obligations; ACF CLO – arbitrage cashflow collateralised loan obligations; BalSh CF – balance sheet cashflow deals; BalSh Syn – balance sheet synthetic deals; IG CBO – investment-grade collateralised bond obligations; Resecuritisations – including cashflow resecuritisations and synthetic resecuritisations; Syn Arb – synthetic arbitrage deals including both managed and static.

In addition, the majority of the 2003 CDO downgrades were from the most recent vintages. In fact, 74% of them were from three vintages: 2000, 2001 and 2002. The 2000 vintage experienced 136 downgrades – the highest among all vintages.

Table 8 compares two one-year rating transition matrices in the CDO sector: one for 2003 only and one for an average from 1991 to 2003.

As indicated, rating stability rates for CDOs in 2003 were above 80% for all investment-grade rating categories, with 93.3% for the Aaa rating category, 86.5% for the Aa rating category, 84.5% for the A rating category and 82.5% for the Baa rating category in 2003. Long-term averages of CDO rating stability rates since 1991 were even higher, as CDO rating transitions were much less frequent before 2002.

The large number of CDO downgrades in the last two years has resulted in higher CDO downgrade rates over multi-year horizons. Longer horizon rating stability rates were markedly lower in the CDO sector than in other sectors (Table 9).

A particularly interesting observation from Table 9 is the fact that the CDO rating transition rates were much higher over a five-year horizon than over a two-year horizon. This is primarily because most of the growth within the relatively young CDO

Table 8 One-year rating transition matrices in CDOs

2003 Ratings from:	Ratings to: Aaa	Aa	A	Baa	Ba	B	Caa or below
Aaa	93.27%	5.20%	1.22%	0.31%			
Aa	0.65%	86.52%	9.35%	3.04%	0.22%	0.22%	
A		1.77%	84.48%	8.65%	3.77%	0.89%	0.44%
Baa		0.16%	0.97%	82.47%	9.42%	4.71%	2.27%
Ba				0.85%	77.46%	10.70%	10.99%
B				1.92%	1.92%	66.35%	29.81%
Caa or below							100.00%
1991–2003 average							
Ratings from:	Ratings to: Aaa	Aa	A	Baa	Ba	B	Caa or below
Aaa	94.14%	4.06%	1.10%	0.58%	0.06%	0.06%	
Aa	0.56%	87.89%	6.93%	3.29%	0.91%	0.35%	0.07%
A	0.09%	1.24%	87.01%	7.33%	2.65%	0.88%	0.80%
Baa		0.11%	0.64%	84.77%	7.29%	4.15%	3.04%
Ba				1.09%	80.71%	7.42%	10.78%
B				0.56%	0.56%	70.14%	28.73%
Caa or below							100.00%

sector has occurred in the recent five years, resulting in only a small number of five-year cohorts. When the sector was severely impacted by the troubles in the corporate sector in 2001 and 2002, this limited number of five-year cohorts recorded extremely high downgrade rates.

CMBS

Out of a total universe of 3,301 CMBS ratings at the beginning of 2003, 133 ratings from 50 deals were downgraded, while 158 ratings from 53 deals were upgraded in 2003.

The downgrade rate declined to 4.3% in 2003, from 5.3% in 2002, while the upgrade rate rose to 5.1% in 2003, from 2.4% in 2002 (Figure 13).

Of all 2003 CMBS downgrades, less than 20% sustained a downgrade in 2002, suggesting some CMBS rating downgrade momentum, but the momentum was weaker than those in the ABS and CDO sectors.

Table 9 Two-year and five-year rating transition matrices in CDOs (1991–2003)

Two-year

Ratings from: \ Ratings to:	Aaa	Aa	A	Baa	Ba	B	Caa or below
Aaa	86.99%	7.32%	2.95%	1.93%	0.41%	0.30%	0.10%
Aa	1.10%	77.12%	9.13%	7.48%	3.08%	1.32%	0.77%
A	0.16%	2.80%	76.81%	8.22%	5.92%	2.47%	3.62%
Baa		0.17%	1.01%	70.32%	9.11%	7.25%	12.14%
Ba				2.24%	64.10%	8.81%	24.84%
B						54.62%	45.38%
Caa or below							100.00%

Five-year

Ratings from: \ Ratings to:	Aaa	Aa	A	Baa	Ba	B	Caa or below
Aaa	88.68%	3.77%		3.77%		1.89%	1.89%
Aa	1.05%	60.21%	16.75%	11.52%	5.24%	1.57%	3.66%
A		14.63%	63.41%	2.44%	4.88%	9.76%	4.88%
Baa			0.54%	43.24%	11.35%	10.81%	34.05%
Ba				4.08%	48.98%	6.12%	40.82%
B						28.21%	71.79%
Caa or below							100.00%

Figure 13 Downgrade and upgrade rates in CMBS

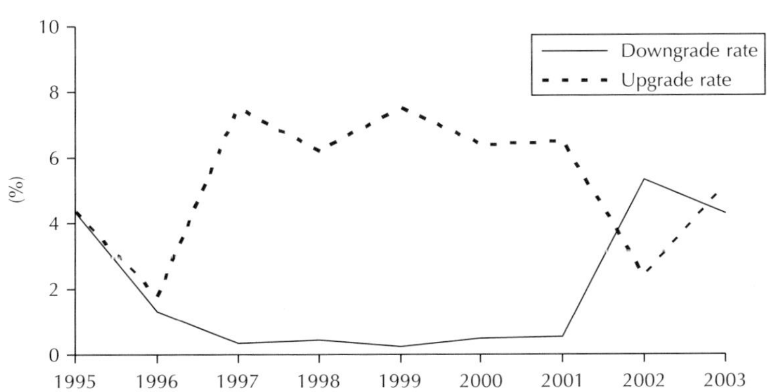

Moreover, of the 133 CMBS downgrades in 2003, 47 were from the 2000 vintage, 22 were from the 2001 vintage and 25 were from the 2002 vintage. In total, more than 70% of the 2003 CMBS downgrades came from the latest three vintages, with the 2000 vintage alone contributing more than 35%.

In contrast, CMBS upgrades were less concentrated in recent vintages. In addition to 2000, 2001 and 2002 vintages, 1997, 1998 and 1999 vintages also made substantial contributions to the rise in CMBS upgrades in 2003.

Table 10 presents two one-year CMBS rating transition matrices, one for 2003 alone and one for an average from 1988 to 2003.

As indicated in Table 10, from 1988 to 2003 (the first CMBS rating transition experience appeared in our data sample in 1988), CMBS rating stability rates across all rating categories were well above 90%. The same was also true in 2003, with the exception of the Aa rating category that had a rating stability rate of 88%.

By rating category, upgrade rates were significantly higher than downgrade rates for the Aa and A rating categories in 2003, while

Table 10 One-year rating transition matrices in CMBS

2003

Ratings from:	Ratings to: Aaa	Aa	A	Baa	Ba	B	Caa or below
Aaa	99.34%	0.50%	0.17%				
Aa	10.20%	88.03%	1.77%				
A	0.96%	4.24%	92.87%	1.35%	0.58%		
Baa		0.42%	1.82%	93.57%	3.64%	0.56%	
Ba			0.25%	1.47%	95.10%	2.70%	0.49%
B	0.59%			0.29%	0.29%	92.65%	6.18%
Caa or below						2.27%	97.73%

1988–2003 average

Ratings from:	Ratings to: Aaa	Aa	A	Baa	Ba	B	Caa or below
Aaa	98.73%	1.23%	0.04%				
Aa	6.55%	92.05%	1.01%	0.22%		0.11%	0.06%
A	1.21%	3.42%	93.61%	1.49%	0.28%		
Baa	0.38%	0.88%	2.52%	93.25%	2.43%	0.42%	0.13%
Ba			0.59%	2.20%	94.58%	2.12%	0.51%
B	0.19%		0.10%	0.58%	1.17%	94.36%	3.60%
Caa or below						2.50%	97.50%

Table 11 Two-year and five-year rating transition matrices in CMBS (1988–2003).

Two-year

Ratings from:	Ratings to: Aaa	Aa	A	Baa	Ba	B	Caa or below
Aaa	97.88%	1.86%	0.26%				
Aa	10.47%	86.78%	1.50%	0.58%	0.42%	0.08%	0.17%
A	2.17%	6.10%	88.13%	2.34%	1.09%	0.08%	0.08%
Baa	1.13%	1.93%	5.18%	86.91%	3.52%	0.93%	0.40%
Ba		0.41%	1.23%	3.68%	89.50%	3.68%	1.50%
B			0.15%	1.36%	2.26%	89.61%	6.63%
Caa or below						5.41%	94.59%

Five-year

Ratings from:	Ratings to: Aaa	Aa	A	Baa	Ba	B	Caa or below
Aaa	94.96%	2.80%	1.96%	0.28%			
Aa	31.33%	61.45%	1.20%	1.20%	3.61%		1.20%
A	8.11%	16.99%	67.18%	3.47%	3.86%		0.39%
Baa	6.54%	6.21%	17.32%	66.67%	1.63%	0.65%	0.98%
Ba		7.34%		9.17%	69.72%	8.26%	5.50%
B			0.88%	5.26%	7.89%	71.05%	14.91%
Caa or below						23.08%	76.92%

downgrade rates were higher than upgrade rates for the Baa, Ba and especially the B rating categories.

In Table 11 we show two rating transition matrices, one for the two-year horizon and the other for the five-year horizon.

Table 11 demonstrates that CMBS ratings have been stable over longer horizons. Moreover, from the two-year horizon to the five-year horizon, upgrade rates of all rating categories increased significantly, with the upgrade rates at the five-year horizon about three times as high as those at the two-year horizon. In other words, there is a strong tendency for ratings to be upgraded over long horizons such as five years.

RMBS

Out of a total universe of 5,795 RMBS ratings, only 26 ratings from 19 deals were downgraded, while 276 ratings from 90 deals were upgraded in 2003.

Figure 14 Downgrade and upgrade rates in RMBS

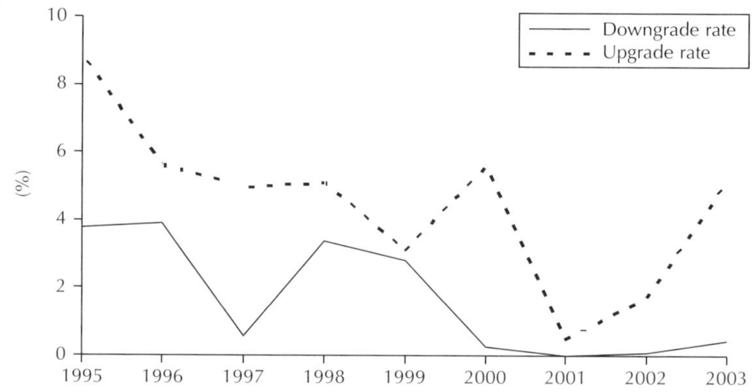

The downgrade rate remained low at 0.45% in 2003, and the upgrade rate increased significantly to 5.1% in 2003, from 1.7% in 2002 (Figure 14).

Of all RMBS upgrades in 2003, 141, or 51%, came from the 2002 vintage. The 2001 and 2000 vintages contributed 88 and 20 upgrades, respectively. In total, the 2002, 2001 and 2000 vintages combined made up 90% of all 2003 RMBS upgrades. The upgrades are attributable to strong housing economics and record-setting prepayment incentives.

A comparison of downgrade and upgrade rates across all four sectors shows that RMBS clearly outperformed ABS, CDO and even CMBS (Figure 15).

Table 12 provides two one-year rating transition matrices for RMBS, one for 2003 only and one for an average during 1983–2003.

As indicated, RMBS ratings have been highly stable and upgrades greatly exceeded downgrades in all rating categories in 2003. The upgrade rates of speculative-grade RMBS securities were particularly noteworthy, as 11.1% of the Ba-rated securities were upgraded into the Baa rating category and 11.7% of the B-rated securities were upgraded into the Ba rating category. The trend is largely attributable to deal deleveraging, which resulted in higher upgrade rates in lowly rated securities.

Rating transition matrices in RMBS over multi-year horizons further demonstrate that RMBS ratings have been stable across the

Figure 15 Downgrade and upgrade rates in RMBS and other structured sectors

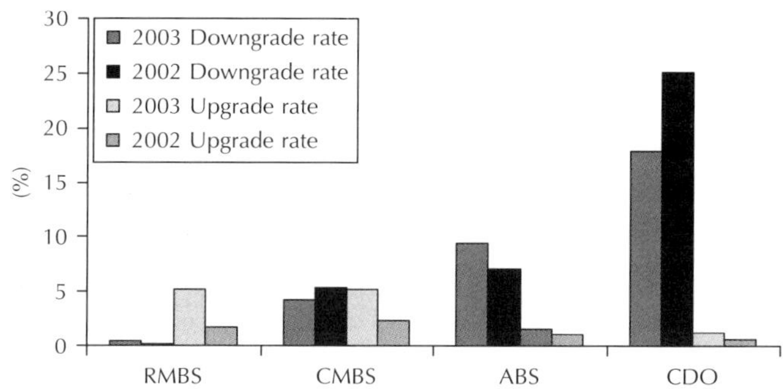

Table 12 One-year rating transition matrices in RMBS

2003

Ratings from: \ Ratings to:	Aaa	Aa	A	Baa	Ba	B	Caa or below
Aaa	100.00%						
Aa	6.64%	93.10%	0.13%				0.13%
A	0.52%	7.65%	91.57%	0.26%			
Baa	0.28%	0.56%	8.10%	90.08%	0.14%	0.42%	0.42%
Ba		0.34%	0.67%	11.07%	85.91%		2.01%
B				2.34%	11.70%	83.63%	2.34%
Caa or below							100.00%

1983–2003 average

Ratings from: \ Ratings to:	Aaa	Aa	A	Baa	Ba	B	Caa or below
Aaa	99.44%	0.43%	0.10%	0.02%			0.02%
Aa	7.15%	90.63%	1.81%	0.34%	0.02%	0.04%	0.01%
A	1.73%	4.68%	91.49%	1.73%	0.16%	0.02%	0.20%
Baa	0.55%	0.65%	3.97%	91.69%	1.62%	0.74%	0.78%
Ba	0.16%	0.05%	1.20%	5.06%	89.34%	1.58%	2.61%
B				0.81%	2.43%	90.48%	6.28%
Caa or below					0.18%		99.82%

longer term as well. Additionally, the rating stability rate of the Aaa rating category in RMBS has been the highest among all sectors. In Table 13, we present two-year and five-year rating transition matrices for RMBS.

Table 13 Two-year and five-year rating transition matrices in RMBS (1983–2003)

Two-year

Ratings from:	Ratings to: Aaa	Aa	A	Baa	Ba	B	Caa or below
Aaa	98.72%	0.87%	0.23%	0.06%			0.11%
Aa	14.61%	80.81%	3.35%	0.98%	0.12%	0.05%	0.09%
A	4.75%	8.46%	82.74%	2.49%	0.91%	0.23%	0.42%
Baa	1.29%	1.64%	7.10%	83.87%	2.01%	1.58%	2.50%
Ba	0.41%	0.07%	2.91%	8.60%	81.10%	1.90%	5.01%
B				1.72%	1.72%	86.49%	10.07%
Caa or below					0.47%		99.53%

Five-year

Ratings from:	Ratings to: Aaa	Aa	A	Baa	Ba	B	Caa or below
Aaa	96.72%	1.93%	0.57%	0.19%	0.02%	0.06%	0.52%
Aa	36.63%	53.98%	5.04%	2.28%	0.50%	0.45%	1.12%
A	16.91%	17.82%	57.36%	3.55%	1.15%	0.86%	2.35%
Baa	4.61%	4.40%	15.45%	62.81%	1.47%	2.15%	9.11%
Ba	1.46%	0.97%	9.47%	18.33%	58.98%	1.94%	8.86%
B				5.32%	2.13%	72.61%	19.95%
Caa or below					3.08%		96.92%

REGIONAL COMPARISONS OF RATING TRANSITIONS

At the end of 2003, there were more than 3,000 European structured securities in our data sample. This represents a share of 12.7% in global structured finance. By comparison, at the end of 2002, European securities totalled about 2,200, roughly 11.5% of the global total.

In the Asia Pacific region (Japan included), the number of outstanding securities increased to 1,123 at the beginning of 2004 from 823 at the beginning of 2003. Its share as a percentage of the global total reached 4.6% in 2003.

In addition, at the end of 2003, there were about 200 structured finance ratings in Canada and Latin America. The combined share from these two regions comprised less than 1% of the global sample in 2003.

The share of US structured securities in the global data sample declined slightly in 2003 to 81.9%, from 83.6% in 2002. Despite the

Figure 16 Downgrade and upgrade rates in Europe and the US

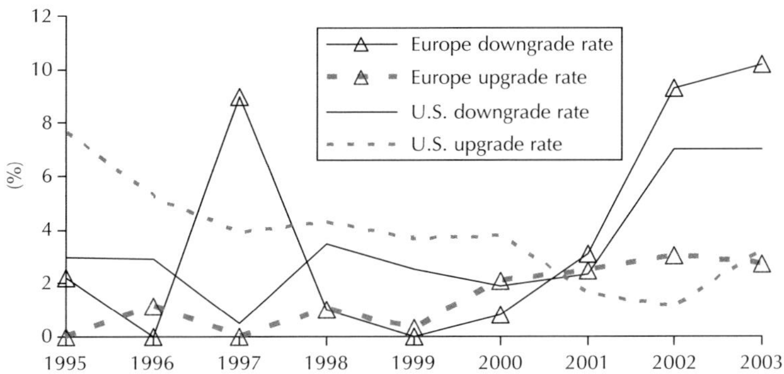

decline in its share, rating transitions of US structured securities continued to dominate the rating transitions of global structured finance as a whole.

European and US rating transition rates

Out of a total universe of 2,180 European ratings at the beginning of 2003, 209 were downgraded and 56 were upgraded in 2003, while in the US, out of a total of 15,834 ratings, 1,041 were downgraded and 483 were upgraded. Of the 209 European securities downgraded, 177, or about 84%, were CDOs.

In both Europe and the US, the downgrade rate continued to exceed the upgrade rate in 2003. In Europe, the downgrade rate was 10.2% and the upgrade rate was 2.7%. In the US the downgrade rate was 7.0% and the upgrade rate was 3.2%. Figure 16 compares the rating transition trends across Europe and the US.

Figure 16 shows that in recent years both downgrade and upgrade rates among European structured securities have been higher than those in the US.

In Europe, the downgrade-to-upgrade ratio rose to 3.7:1 in 2003 from 3:1 in 2002, and the rating stability rate was 87%, as in 2002. In comparison, the 2003 US downgrade-to-upgrade ratio was 2:1, and the rating stability rate was about 90%. The high downgrade-to-upgrade ratio in Europe was the result of a large percentage of CDOs among European structured finance securities.

Table 14 European and US one-year rating transition matrices in 2003

Europe Ratings from:	Ratings to: Aaa	Aa	A	Baa	Ba	B	Caa or below
Aaa	97.06%	2.63%	0.31%				
Aa	0.86%	90.54%	5.44%	3.15%			
A	0.20%	2.81%	90.18%	5.01%	1.80%		
Baa			2.70%	91.11%	4.58%	0.81%	0.81%
Ba				0.73%	81.75%	13.14%	4.38%
B				6.90%	6.90%	62.07%	24.14%
Caa or below							100.00%

US Ratings from:	Ratings to: Aaa	Aa	A	Baa	Ba	B	Caa or below
Aaa	98.27%	0.91%	0.54%	0.24%	0.04%		
Aa	5.48%	88.89%	3.18%	1.43%	0.74%	0.23%	0.05%
A	0.73%	3.24%	89.38%	3.67%	1.53%	1.16%	0.29%
Baa	0.38%	0.26%	2.86%	87.56%	3.65%	2.78%	2.52%
Ba	0.09%	0.09%	0.17%	3.61%	83.23%	3.87%	8.94%
B	0.30%			0.75%	3.44%	81.74%	13.77%
Caa or below							100.00%

Table 14 compares 2003 rating transition matrices in Europe and in the US.

As indicated, rating stability rates were generally similar across European and the US structured securities except for the B rating category in Europe. This category sustained both higher downgrade and upgrade rates in 2003.

Asia Pacific and US rating transition rates

At the beginning of 2003, our data sample contained 823 ratings in the Asia Pacific region. Of these, 17 ratings downgraded and 22 upgraded. The downgrade rate in the Asia Pacific region fell to 2.3% in 2003, from 3.4% in 2002, while its upgrade rate also declined to 3% from 4.5%. The rating stability rate increased to 94.7% from 92.1%. Figure 17 compares downgrade and upgrade rates in the Asia Pacific and the US.

Figure 17 reveals that the downgrade rate has been lower in the Asia Pacific region since 2000, while the upgrade rate has been higher than in the US, although the total number of securities was still small in the Asia Pacific region.

Figure 17 Downgrade and upgrade rates in the Asia Pacific region and the US

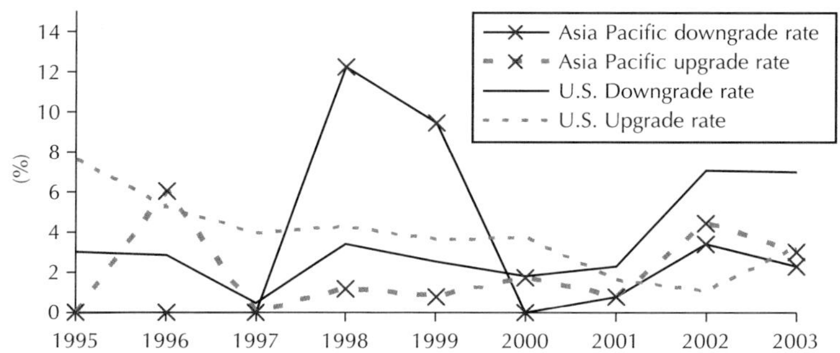

CONCLUDING REMARKS

This chapter has found that structured finance ratings have been less volatile than corporate ratings overall, even though the average number of notches changed per rating action has historically been higher in structured finance than in corporate finance.

Relative to historical averages, rating volatility in 2003 and 2002 was particularly high. Downgrades mostly concentrated in the ABS and CDO sectors, while upgrades concentrated in the RMBS and CMBS sectors.

Driving the increase of downgrade rates in the ABS sector were the troubles in the manufactured housing loan, franchise loan and equipment lease sectors, while in the CDO sector high yield arbitrage cashflow deals and synthetic arbitrage deals contributed the majority of downgrades.

Driving the increase of the upgrade rates in the RMBS and CMBS sectors were the strong real estate markets and record-setting prepayment incentives, a result of historically low interest rates.

More than 80% of all Europe's downgrades in 2003 and 2002 occurred in the CDO sector. Average downgrade rates in Europe were slightly higher than in the US but signs of improvement were evident in Europe in 2003.

Average downgrade rates in Asia Pacific were lower than in the US while average upgrade rates were higher, signalling the strength of this segment of the global structured finance market.

1 For a detailed analysis of historical rating transitions in structured finance during 1983–2002, compared with corporate rating transitions, please see Hu and Cantor (2003).
2 Moody's rating addresses expected loss rate, which is the product of default frequency and loss severity. For a comprehensive study of default and loss given default in structured finance, please see Hu and Cantor (2004).
3 Structured finance rating transition momentum was first studied in Hu and Cantor (2003).
4 Detailed statistics on Moody's corporate rating transition experiences prior to 2003 can be found in Hamilton, Varma, Ou and Cantor (2003).

REFERENCES

Hamilton, D. T., P. Varma, S. Ou, and R. Cantor, 2003, "Default & Recovery Rates of Corporate Bond Issuers (1920–2002)", Moody's Investors Service *Special Comment*, February.

Hu, J., and R. Cantor, 2003, "Structured Finance Rating Transitions: 1983–2002", *Journal of Fixed Income*, June.

Hu, J., and R. Cantor, 2004, "Defaults and Losses Given Default of Structured Finance Securities", *Journal of Fixed Income*, March.

5

Credit Risk Analysis and Structured Finance Ratings: Qualitative and Quantitative Methods

Kai Gilkes, Norbert Jobst

Standard & Poor's

The core of the risk analysis in assigning ratings to structured finance transactions is the assessment of the potential for default and subsequent loss arising within a portfolio of financial contracts – the portfolio credit risk. This chapter describes and compares some of the qualitative and quantitative methods used by Standard & Poor's to address this risk, highlighting the relative merits of each type of approach. We emphasise the need for the combination of qualitative and quantitative methods in the development of robust analytical models. In particular, we address an important issue, which is the *coherence* of qualitative methods based on stress-testing, and quantitative methods involving Monte Carlo simulation.

The rise and rise of the structured finance market

The growth of residential mortgage securitisation was fuelled by the crisis within the US savings and loans institutions in the late 1970s. The rating of these mortgage-backed securities (MBS) involved the risk analysis of large diversified pools of mortgage loans. Other large homogeneous portfolios of consumer debt soon followed, such as credit cards, home equity loans and auto loans New asset classes then emerged, such as commercial real estate loans and collateralised debt obligations (CDOs), backed by portfolios of corporate bonds and loans.

Over the past decade, the boundaries of the structured finance market have widened considerably, away from traditional funding considerations and balance sheet management towards risk management and risk transfer in the broadest sense. There has also been significant convergence between different markets. For example, the synthetic CDO market now routinely makes use of both the financial contracts (credit default swaps) and the quantitative models developed for the burgeoning credit derivatives market.

Portfolio credit risk analysis

Whether financial contracts involve consumers, SMEs or large corporate institutions, the analysis of portfolio credit risk attempts to answer one fundamental question: What level of default and loss could a portfolio of such contracts generate? We distinguish here between *default*, the breach of contract arising – for example – from a missed payment, and *loss*, the financial loss resulting from the default event. Clearly, the loss resulting from a default will depend on the level of recovery achieved by the creditor.

This question can be addressed in a number of ways, of which the following is an illustrative, but not exhaustive, set of examples:

1. analysis of historical default and loss data on similar portfolios;
2. analysis of historical "market-wide" default and loss data, with extrapolation of the results to the portfolio of interest;
3. development of quantitative models for portfolio default and loss.

There are some clear – and some subtle – differences between these alternative approaches. The first is clearly the most direct method, but relies on the availability of data specific to portfolios with similar characteristics to the portfolio of interest. In the case of the second method there is likely to be more data available, but this method involves the need to infer portfolio behaviour from market behaviour. Qualitative solutions to this problem are discussed in the section "Subordination level – lessons from history". The third method has the promise of increasing the overall accuracy of portfolio analysis, and extending the analysis to portfolios where it is difficult or impossible to apply the first two methods. Of course, this does not escape the need for historical portfolio and/or market data, as good models always require good data! These challenges are discussed in the section on "Model risk".

Stress-testing rated tranches

Given that a structured finance rating is generally an opinion of the creditworthiness of a security, the analysis of portfolio credit risk must be accompanied by an analysis of the impact of portfolio losses on the security itself. Structured finance transactions contain specific rules governing the allocation of payments and losses to investors. These rules are generally replicated within a transaction cashflow model, and can be quite complex, especially when the transaction is structured to allow the issuance of several "tranches" of rated securities with different levels of seniority. In some cases, where the portfolio risk is transferred "synthetically", ie, without relying on the actual payments made under each contract (eg, synthetic CDOs), the rules are simple enough to remove the need for a cashflow model.

The advantage of the transaction cashflow model is that it can be used both to determine a price for each tranche of debt *and* to examine whether each tranche can survive certain levels of portfolio loss. The second of these is crucial in the determination of the likely performance of the tranche over a period of economic stress, and hence the adequate rating for the tranche. The value of stress testing is discussed further in the sections "Assessing ratings performance – constructing economic scenarios" and "The value of stress tests".

QUALITATIVE ANALYSIS – SURVIVING RECESSIONARY ENVIRONMENTS

In the analysis of credit risk within a given asset class, we start with the assumption that a rated security must be able to withstand some level of economic stress to the asset portfolio. The resilience of the security will depend on the rating. For example, "AAA" securities must be capable of surviving much higher levels of economic stress than "BBB" securities. Note that these are qualitative statements, in that we are so far only interested in *relative* ability to withstand stress. No absolute measure of resilience has yet been defined. A direct result of this requirement is the observation that ratings are "through-the-cycle" measures of credit quality, as opposed to "point-in-time" measures. (If ratings only reflected creditworthiness at a point in time, it would be possible to imagine very high ratings being assigned to all healthy companies in a booming industry sector, regardless of their leverage and management structure, which is clearly nonsensical.)

To illustrate the above ideas, consider the following hypothetical example. A large homogeneous mortgage portfolio is securitised, and "AAA" securities are issued backed by the mortgage payments. What protection should investors be given against losses within the mortgage pool? Ignoring interest payments for the moment, there are two main ways in which this protection can be provided.

i. By obtaining an insurance contract from an insurer rated "AAA" for all payments to "AAA" bondholders. In this way, the risk of the investor not being paid in full can be equated to the AAA likelihood of the insurer becoming insolvent.
ii. By issuing "AAA" securities with a face value lower than the principal balance of the mortgage pool by some amount (known as the "overcollateralisation" amount). Investors will therefore only lose money if losses on the portfolio exceed this level of overcollateralisation.

These two sources of protection are very different. In (i) above, the insurer faces the risk of mortgage defaults and losses, and the investor effectively becomes an unsecured creditor of the insurance company. In (ii), the investor faces the risk of mortgage defaults and losses exceeding some predetermined threshold, ie, the overcollateralisation amount. This can also be thought of as a level of "subordination" to the "AAA" securities, which could itself take the form of securities, either unrated or with a lower rating.

Subordination levels – lessons from history

The example above leads to a crucial question – what level of subordination is required in order to provide "AAA" protection to investors? The qualitative approach would be to identify a recessionary period in history that can be considered to represent "AAA" stress to the assets in the portfolio. For example, in the case of the US mortgage market, the Great Depression of the early 1930s is an appropriate period. The cumulative losses experienced over this period could then be used as an estimate of the required subordination. For ratings lower than "AAA", some reduction in this level would be possible, down to some lower limit at (say)

"B", where the level would be much closer to "normal" market conditions.

The above estimates can be thought of as "benchmark" levels of stress to a very large, diversified portfolio. For smaller, less diversified portfolios, some adjustments would need to be made to account for the potential deviation of the behaviour of the portfolio from that of the market as a whole. These adjustments would need to be made on an asset-by-asset basis, and could be based on qualitative "scoring" of each asset to establish relative riskiness across the portfolio. In this way, portfolios containing higher proportions of "high-risk" assets would attract levels of subordination higher than the benchmark level, while those dominated by "low-risk" assets would attract levels of subordination lower than the benchmark level.

The qualitative methods described above formed the basis for the analysis of early residential mortgage portfolios. This analysis combined historical market data with loan level "semi-quantitative" analysis, and provided a straightforward, transparent and consistent method for assessing the relative riskiness of a wide range of different mortgage portfolios. For other portfolios of consumer debt, such as credit cards and auto loans, historical data from such a severe recessionary environment was not readily available. In these cases, multiples of historical losses were often used as proxies for recessionary losses, using the empirically observed relationships between "normal" and "stressed" loss levels in other markets.

Assessing ratings performance – constructing economic scenarios

Once the portfolio credit risk is assessed, its impact on rated securities needs to be determined. As mentioned previously, if the contractual payments from the portfolio are used to service the rated securities, a cashflow model would be used to replicate the transaction rules for allocating portfolio payments and losses to investors. Additional features would be needed within the model to allow the separation of portfolio losses into defaults and (lagged) recoveries, interest rate paths (for floating rate assets), prepayments, etc. In this way, different *scenarios* can be constructed and analysed to assess whether investors would receive full and timely payment of interest and principal. For example, the impact of defaults in a rising interest rate environment can be thoroughly examined for a particular portfolio and transaction structure.

The criteria for rating a certain tranche of debt can then be summarised by a matrix of economic scenarios appropriate to the given rating. For the tranche to be assigned that rating, it must be capable of surviving these scenarios. In general, the higher the rating required for the tranche, the more stressful the economic scenarios, and the more stringent the requirements regarding the ability of the tranche to withstand them. For example, "AAA" tranches might be required to survive a number of very stressful scenarios without exception, whereas "BBB" tranches would need to survive a similar number of less stressful scenarios, with some tolerance over the percentage of scenarios in which the tranche survives.

The advantage of this qualitative framework is the ability to create rules that are intuitive, transparent and consistently applied across different transactions. Market participants can replicate the scenarios independently as part of their own risk analysis, and form their own views of the relative riskiness of different tranches. One disadvantage of this approach is that it does not readily allow for an analysis of the likely default and loss characteristics of the rated securities themselves. In order to achieve this, quantitative methods are required.

QUANTITATIVE METHODS – UNIFIED APPROACHES TO PORTFOLIO CREDIT RISK

As the structured finance market has developed, there has been significant convergence and cross-fertilisation of structures and analytics across different asset classes, such as the CDO and credit derivatives markets. In addition, considerable effort has recently been devoted to quantitative portfolio credit risk modelling, both by market participants and academics. This has given rise to a rich variety of theoretical approaches, many of which are beyond the scope of this chapter. Here, we do not attempt to provide a detailed overview of the quantitative methods used in the marketplace, only to outline themes that occur across different asset classes. For such an overview, the recent book by de Servigny and Renault (2004) serves as an excellent reference.

Whereas qualitative methods have largely been "top-down" approaches, making use of both intuition and historical portfolio/market data to infer the behaviour of portfolios of assets, quantitative approaches tend to be "bottom-up" in nature, focusing first on individual assets, and then determining the joint portfolio behaviour within a given dependency framework.

There are several advantages to a quantitative approach, some of which are listed below:

- the potential for increased accuracy in determining the probability of default and loss associated with a given asset;
- the ability to accurately capture portfolio dependency, such as the correlation between pairs of assets;
- the reduction or removal of the subjective bias inherent in qualitative approaches;
- the ability to explore outcomes that are not covered (or not covered to a sufficient level of statistical significance) by the available historical data.

In this section, we outline the quantitative methods currently used in the rating analysis of structured finance transactions. We start by discussing the essential ingredients of portfolio credit risk models – namely transition matrices, default probabilities and recoveries – and then show how these can be linked together *via* a dependency model of the joint behaviour of portfolios of assets. At the end of the section, we provide detailed examples of the development and use of these methods by focusing on a specific asset class – synthetic CDOs. We also discuss ways of mitigating model risk, such as undertaking sensitivity analysis, and investigate and compare the results of different models.

Transition and default

The starting point for many credit risk models is the estimation of the transition and default behaviour of each asset in the portfolio, referred to as the *marginal* (or univariate) behaviour.

Consumer assets

Modelling of consumer transition and default behaviour is made possible by the large amounts of consumer delinquency and default data available to both credit bureaux and consumer lending institutions. Credit scoring models based on various types of regression analysis have been widely and successfully employed in the prediction of consumer default. For example the LEVELS product used by Standard & Poor's in the analysis of US residential mortgage portfolios makes use of the predictive power of the Fair Issac & Company (FICO) credit score in ranking the default risk of US consumers.

Corporate assets

Large corporates are not amenable to credit scoring methods, mainly due to their size and complexity. In the case of publicly traded corporate debt, knowledge of the structure of the balance sheet prompted the use of models that determine default risk directly from the difference between the value of a company's assets and its liabilities. This "firm-value" approach was pioneered by Merton (1974), and formed the basis for the development of a class of so-called "structural" models. A key assumption in many of these models is that the asset values of a company are *normally distributed* at the end of a given horizon.

In the case of rated companies, a simpler and more efficient approach is to assume that the rating is a proxy for the likelihood that the company defaults. Since ratings are "through-the-cycle" opinions of creditworthiness, their main appeal for quantitative analysis is in the estimation of long-term average default probabilities for companies in a given rating class, *when these companies are part of a portfolio*. This last point is crucially important. Given that ratings are ordinal, not cardinal, measures of creditworthiness, a single rating cannot be explicitly linked to a probability of default.

In order to determine estimates of default probabilities associated with ratings, Standard & Poor's uses its extensive global database of rating migration and default history to construct "idealised" transition matrices. These matrices are then used to create estimates of cumulative default probabilities associated with each rating – or *credit curves* – which serve as key inputs to a portfolio model. The determination of these credit curves is discussed further in the section on "Estimating credit curves".

Asset-backed securities

Given that structured finance securities themselves are often included in CDO portfolios, their likely transition and default behaviour also needs to be estimated. On average, these securities have exhibited considerable ratings stability over the past two decades, and, as a result, there have been very few cases of default. Given the relative paucity of default data, Standard & Poor's has so far adopted a conservative treatment of these securities by using corporate default rates as proxies for their long-term default behaviour.

Recoveries

Unlike transition and default probabilities, the study of recoveries is still plagued by the paucity of historical data. Empirical studies have nonetheless shown that recovery clearly depends on such factors as seniority, security and overall market conditions. In cases where recovery depends on a physical asset, recoveries can be quantitatively derived from models of the underlying asset price, which themselves need to be developed using historical price data.

Consumer assets

Unsecured consumer loans generally exhibit very low recoveries. In cases where the loans are secured, such as residential mortgages and auto loans, models can be developed for the analysis of future asset values, which in turn allow quantitative estimates of likely recoveries. For example, Standard & Poor's makes use of historical house price data within each country to determine stressed levels of asset value decline. These are the key inputs into its mortgage recovery models.

Corporate assets

The simplest quantitative model is a statistical distribution fitted to the historical data, aggregated for instance by industry, region and level of security provided. For example, the simple *beta* distribution is widely used. Some approaches go one step further, attempting to model recovery through the use of enhanced regression models based on explanatory variables, including economic factors. See Friedman and Sandow (2003).

Asset-backed securities

Given the high historical stability of these securities, recovery data is very limited. However, the security provided by the underlying assets is likely to lead to relatively high levels of recovery in the event of default, especially for senior asset-backed securities (ABS). Current efforts to provide additional recovery information involve the dynamic modelling of recoveries for structured finance transactions, utilising a "drill down" approach. An example of the application of this approach to CDOs can be found in Gilkes and Drexler (2003).

Dependence

Once the appropriate default probability and recovery have been estimated for each asset in the portfolio, the joint default and loss behaviour of all assets in the portfolio must be determined through some kind of dependency model. A simple model might assume that all assets behave independently, reducing the calculation to a simple combinatorial problem. Another simplification – albeit a very extreme one – would be to assume perfect positive correlation, where all assets either default or survive together. Both of these models are unrealistic, as most portfolios contain neither zero nor perfect dependency, but some intermediate level.

Dependence in large homogeneous portfolios

In the case of large homogeneous portfolios (LHPs), analytical approximations can be employed, in which portfolio defaults and losses are driven by a single systematic risk factor (eg, the state of the economy). These approximations are based largely on the original work of Vasicek (1987), who extended the Merton's firm-value approach to consider the probability distribution of the default rate L of an infinitely fine-grained portfolio. This is given by

$$P(L \leq x) = \Phi\left[\frac{1}{\sqrt{\rho}}(\Phi^{-1}[x]\sqrt{1-\rho} - \Phi^{-1}[p])\right], \quad \text{where } 0 \leq x \leq 1$$

In the above expression, Φ and Φ^{-1} are the standard and inverse normal cumulative distribution functions, respectively, p is the average default probability of the portfolio and ρ is the correlation of the portfolio to the systematic risk factor.

As mentioned earlier, the portfolio default probability can be obtained from consumer credit scoring models applied to each loan in the portfolio. Accurate estimation of correlation requires a detailed analysis of the historical correlation between consumer asset performance and macroeconomic variables, such as GDP or unemployment rates. Note that this correlation will, in general, not

Figure 1 Default distribution for an LHP assuming an average portfolio default probability of 5%, and a one-factor correlation of 30% (broken line) and 50% (solid line)

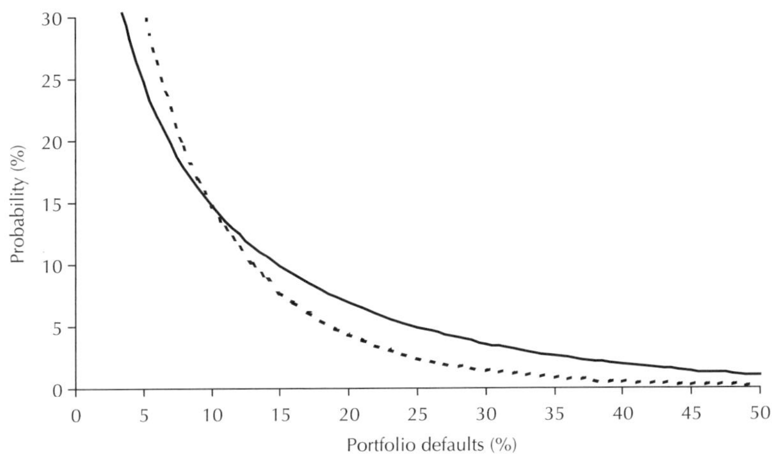

be static, but will vary depending on the choice of dataset and time period.

An example of the default distribution obtained using this approach is shown in Figure 1, assuming a portfolio default probability of 5%, and different correlation parameters. This distribution expresses the potential levels of default within an LHP as the systematic risk factor (the economy) varies from very low (booming economy) to very high (recessionary economy), and allows for the stress-testing of rated tranches under many different economic scenarios.

Copula dependency models

For the valuation and risk management of credit portfolio products, the Gaussian copula model has become the industry standard for modelling dependence (clustering) between default times or default events. Initiated by Li (2000), this model is currently used by many trading desks to price synthetic CDO tranches and basket credit derivatives. Standard & Poor's CDO Evaluator – a Monte Carlo simulation tool for the credit analysis of CDOs – is also based on the Gaussian copula. For details, see Gilkes and Watson (2004). Among the reasons for the success of this model are its ease of simulation and the fact that the dependence structure can be linked to the asset (or equity) correlations *via* the re-interpretation of the model as a variant of Merton's structural model. Furthermore, with certain modifications the model can be used for fast pricing and hedging calculations (see, eg, Gregory and Laurent (2003); Anderson *et al* (2003)).

In the Gaussian (survival) copula approach we consider marginal survival functions $S^i(t) = P(\tau_i > t)$ for the ith company, $i = 1, \ldots, N$. These functions describe the survival probabilities for each company over time, with τ_i denoting the default time of the ith company. The need to estimate this survival function directly for each company is avoided by using a rating-based credit curve. This is given by $p_t^k = 1 - S^k(t) = P(\tau \leq t)$, where p_t^k is the cumulative probability of a default before time t for rating k, and τ denotes the default time of the company in rating k. In a pricing or valuation context, these survival functions are frequently calibrated from default swap prices.

In both cases, we are interested in the joint survival function

$$S(t_1, \ldots, t_N) = P\left(\tau_1 > t_1, \ldots, \tau_N > t_N\right)$$

Given the marginal survival functions, we need only to specify the copula (or dependence) function in order to fully specify the joint distribution. The Gaussian copula is given by

$$C(u_1, \ldots, u_N) = \Phi_\Sigma\left(\Phi^{-1}(u_1), \ldots, \Phi^{-1}(u_N)\right).$$

In the above expression, Φ is the univariate standard normal cumulative distribution function with uniform random variates u_i, and Φ_Σ is the multivariate normal distribution function with correlation matrix Σ. Default times are then given by $\tau_i = S^{-1}\left(\Phi(y_i)\right)$, where S^{-1} denotes the quasi-inverse of the survival function and $(y_1, \ldots, y_N)$ denotes a vector drawn from Φ_Σ.

The flexibility of modelling the marginals and the dependence structure separately leads to several extensions where alternative copulae can be considered. In particular, Schönbucher and Schubert (2001) and Rogge and Schönbucher (2003) consider Archimedian copulas. By investigating the dynamics of credit spreads (or default intensities) before and after credit events, they conclude that the Gaussian copula has certain undesirable properties (eg, front-loaded defaults), whereas a Clayton copula results in somewhat more favourable dynamics.

Marshal *et al* (2002) show that joint equity price dynamics are more adequately described by a *t*-copula, and propose the use of this copula (which contains the Gaussian copula as a special case) for risk management and pricing of credit products. However, Greenberg *et al* (2004) show that the *t*-copula does not lead to an improvement in replicating the market prices of Trac-X II tranches, and hence does not better capture the price dynamics such as the correlation smile. Furthermore, for long-term risk management, de Servigny and Renault (2003) show that equity and/or asset correlations are at best noisy estimates of the "true" dependence parameters, when comparing model-induced and historic default correlation.

Alternative approaches to credit portfolio modelling

The success of copula techniques stems to a large extent from the separation of marginal and dependency models, which greatly enhances model estimation and calibration. On the other hand, the choice of copula function is also driven by analytic tractability or ease of calibration. In recent years, several alternatives have been proposed in the literature. For example, Duffie and Garleanu (2001) and Yu (2002) propose that dependency can be captured by modelling correlated default intensities. Although it is frequently stated that these models are incapable of "imposing" enough dependency, Yu (2002) shows that the problem lies in adequately conditioning the intensity processes, and not in the model set-up *per se*.

Default infection or *contagion* models provide another approach to modelling realistic dependency between assets. Here, given the default of an obligor, the intensity of default of dependent obligors increases (or jumps), which is intuitively appealing. For example, Davis and Lo (2001) propose a simple model that exhibits similar dynamics to the Clayton copula model. An overview and extensions can be found in Giesecke (2002), Yu (2002) and Frey and Backhaus (2003). Very recently, Schönbucher (2003) discussed the application of *frailty* models, where additional stress is added to individual default intensities by introducing an "unobservable" random factor – the frailty. This concept has been successfully applied in survival analysis studies, for example, in biomedicine, and allows more detailed modelling of individual default risk by adding extra (unobservable) dependency in an intuitive way.

Synthetic CDO analysis – a case study

In the following examples, we use the Gaussian copula model to analyse the risk posed to investors by a number of different hypothetical CDO tranches (0–6%, 6–12%, 12–18% and 36–42%). Each tranche is characterised by its attachment point A and its detachment point D. The tranche thickness is equal to $D - A$, ie, all of the tranches discussed here have a thickness of 6%. Each tranche is assumed to reference a portfolio of 100 "BBB" companies. We assume a maturity of 5 years, a "BBB" default probability of 2.72%, a constant recovery of 33% and a constant pairwise (asset) correlation of 20%.

In order to model the loss on a given CDO tranche, the loss following default of the ith company is $(1 - \delta_i)E_i$, where δ_i denotes the recovery rate and E_i the notional exposure. The cumulative portfolio loss up to time t is given by $L(t) = \Sigma_i(1 - \delta_i)E_iN_i(t)$, where $N_i(t) := 1_{\{\tau_i \leq t\}}$ is the default indicator of the ith company.

Our quantitative model allows the calculation of several useful measures of risk to investors in the above CDO tranches, which are listed below.

Tranche default probability. We analyse the probability that a tranche is hit by a loss, or equivalently that portfolio losses at maturity T exceed A. This is given by

$$\mathrm{PD}^{\mathrm{Tranche}} = P(L(T) \geq A) = E\left[1_{\{L(T) \geq A\}}\right]$$

Expected tranche loss. The cumulative loss on the tranche at time t, $M(t)$, is given by

$$M(t) = (L(t) - A)\,1_{\{A \leq L(t) \leq D\}} + (D - A)\,1_{\{L(t) \geq D\}}$$

The expected tranche loss

$$E[M(t)] = E\left[(L(t) - A)\,1_{\{A \leq L(t) \leq D\}} + (D - A)\,1_{\{L(t) \geq D\}}\right]$$

can be easily derived using Monte Carlo simulation.

Table 1 Default probabilities (PD), expected losses (EL), loss-given-default (LGD) and leverage calculated for four CDO tranches referencing a portfolio of 100 "BBB" companies

Tranche	0–6%	6–12%	12–18%	36–42%
PD, %	70.00	6.98	0.95	0.00
EL, %	27.13	2.68	0.40	0.00
LGD, %	38.76	38.40	42.59	–
Leverage, %	14.92	1.48	0.22	–

Expected tranche loss-given-default. The tranche loss-given-default is given by

$$\mathrm{LGD}^{\mathrm{Tranche}} = \frac{E(M(t))}{\mathrm{PD}^{\mathrm{Tranche}}}$$

Tranche leverage. The tranche leverage is equal to the expected tranche loss divided by the expected portfolio loss,

$$\mathrm{Leverage}^{\mathrm{Tranche}} = \frac{E(M(t))}{E(L(t))}$$

Table 1 shows the results obtained from our model for each of the four CDO tranches mentioned above.

As expected, more senior tranches exhibit both lower tranche default probabilities and expected losses, and would therefore attract higher ratings. However, it is important to bear in mind that there are several other risk measures that investors should consider in order to form an opinion on the credit risk of different CDO tranches. For example, the sensitivity of tranches to changes in default probabilities (or spreads), recovery assumptions and correlations, or the contribution of individual assets to the risk of a given tranche, also provide valuable information.

COMBINING QUALITATIVE AND QUANTITATIVE APPROACHES

Despite the frequently reported drawbacks of the basic Gaussian copula model, none of the alternatives have yet been shown to outperform this approach consistently in either a pricing or risk management context. There is, however, no doubt that the Gaussian copula approach is only a first attempt at modelling the true dynamics and dependency of credit portfolios. Given the uncertainty in the choices of correct models and model parameters, what value do these portfolio credit models add in the risk analysis of credit derivatives and structured finance transactions?

In our view, the main advantage of using quantitative models is the ability to assess credit risk in an objective and consistent fashion. This is particularly important when there is limited historical data on the underlying assets, or when novel structures are proposed with new portfolio characteristics. An additional benefit lies in the possibility of conducting detailed sensitivity analysis of tranche performance to the underlying risk factors, such as marginal default probabilities, recovery rates and correlations. Such an analysis is required for two main reasons. The first is the need to analyse in detail the new risks posed by each transaction and the second is the need to understand the behaviour of the model, in order to quantify the inherent model risk.

In this section, we start by addressing model risk, and then discuss the coherence between qualitative methods based on stress testing and quantitative methods that utilise Monte Carlo simulation. Throughout this section, we emphasise the need for the combination of qualitative and quantitative approaches in order to develop robust and realistic models.

Model risk

Models can be no better than the information used to develop them, both in terms of the specification of the model (eg, a Gaussian copula) and the calibration of the parameters of the model (such as correlation assumptions). Some judgement is required to determine the relevance and usefulness of both the model and the assumptions used within it. The lower the quantity and/or quality of the available information, the more important qualitative factors become in choosing the appropriate model. Once a model is chosen, its behaviour needs to be properly understood through careful sensitivity analysis. In this section, we discuss the sensitivity of ratings-based marginal default probabilities to different estimation techniques and then examine the sensitivity of the Gaussian copula model to these inputs.

Estimating credit curves

In order to examine the sensitivity of the estimation of credit curves to different estimation techniques, we analysed Standard & Poor's extensive global ratings and default database, containing ratings information on over 10,000 obligors between 1981 and 2003. We used two different methods to construct transition matrices from the underlying data – the *cohort* and *duration* methods. The first of these is a well-known method for estimating a discrete transition matrix from empirical data, and involves observing the transition of cohorts of firms with the same initial rating. Indeed, Standard & Poor's annual transition study ("Ratings Performance 2003", Standard & Poor's, March 2004) is based on such a cohort analysis.

An alternative to the simple cohort method – which simply compares the initial and final ratings over a certain period – is the duration method, which takes into consideration the exact points in time at which rating transitions take place, using the instantaneous probability of transition, the *transition intensity*. We then directly estimate the generator matrix of a time-homogenous Markov chain, from which a transition matrix can be easily derived (see Lando and Skødeberg, 2002; Jobst and Gilkes, 2003).

Although based on exactly the same data, the two techniques result in quite different transition matrices (Tables 2 and 3).

Generally, the resulting investment grade default probabilities are lower in the duration exercise, whereas, for example, CCC default rates appear to be significantly higher. These differences stem mainly from the more efficient use of historical data in the duration method, ie, both the timing of default and the duration of

Table 2 Transition matrix obtained using cohort analysis (all numbers are in per cent)

	AAA	AA	A	BBB	BB	B	CCC	D
AAA	92.08	7.09	0.63	0.15	0.06	0.00	0.00	0.000
AA	0.62	90.83	7.77	0.60	0.06	0.10	0.02	0.010
A	0.05	2.09	91.38	5.79	0.44	0.16	0.04	0.053
BBB	0.03	0.21	4.10	89.39	4.82	0.86	0.24	0.359
BB	0.03	0.08	0.40	5.53	83.25	8.15	1.11	1.447
B	0.00	0.08	0.27	0.34	5.39	82.41	4.92	6.585
CCC	0.10	0.00	0.29	0.58	1.55	10.54	52.80	34.14

Table 3 Transition matrix obtained using duration analysis (all numbers are in per cent)

	AAA	AA	A	BBB	BB	B	CCC	D
AAA	92.17	6.88	0.76	0.14	0.06	0.01	0.00	0.0003
AA	0.61	91.20	7.49	0.56	0.08	0.05	0.01	0.004
A	0.06	1.87	91.86	5.60	0.45	0.14	0.02	0.009
BBB	0.03	0.22	3.81	89.81	5.13	0.81	0.08	0.103
BB	0.03	0.09	0.50	4.68	84.17	9.10	0.79	0.645
B	0.00	0.07	0.24	0.45	4.50	83.35	6.31	5.076
CCC	0.05	0.01	0.29	0.42	1.11	8.31	44.05	45.75

a company in a given rating class are taken into consideration. Another interesting property of the duration method is that non-zero, 1-year default probabilities are obtained, even though no "AAA" defaults have occurred over such a short horizon. Companies in high investment grade ratings stay, on average, longer in their rating class than firms in a CCC state, which is frequently only passed through on the way to default. Further details on these two estimators and on the construction of confidence intervals around these estimates can be found in the papers cited above.

Credit curves are frequently estimated from transition matrices by assuming the first-order time-homogeneous Markov property. For the cohort case, a T-year transition matrix is then simply given by the Tth power of the 1-year matrix. Similarly, in the duration method, the T-year matrix is obtained first by multiplying the estimated generator matrix by T and then taking the exponential of this product. Credit curves can then be directly extracted from these matrices. However, time homogeneity of rating transitions is an assumption that may be questionable, given ratings momentum and business cycle effects. Although Lando and Skødeberg (2002) show that introducing time inhomogeneity does not change results dramatically, some qualitative adjustment of these credit curves is clearly required in order to bring the results into line with "real-world" behaviour. Extensions of the duration approach to incorporate macro-economic and ratings momentum effects are discussed in Kavvathas (2000) and Christensen *et al* (2004).

However, even if we assume that rating transitions follow a Markov chain, significant differences in the multi-year default

Table 4 Comparison of the 5-year default probabilities obtained using cohort and duration analyses (all numbers are in per cent)

5-yr PD	AAA	AA	A	BBB	BB	B	CCC
Cohort	0.03	0.23	0.66	2.72	10.74	43.43	76.62
Duration	0.02	0.13	0.29	1.42	7.93	47.87	87.11

Table 5 Default probabilities, expected losses, loss-given-default and leverage calculated for four CDO tranches referencing a portfolio of 100 "BBB" companies

Tranche	0–6%	6–12%	12–18%	36–42%
PD, %	52.11	2.06	0.17	0.00
EL, %	15.06	0.64	0.06	0.00
LGD, %	28.91	30.96	37.06	–
Leverage	15.92	0.67	0.06	–

probabilities can be observed between the cohort and duration approach, even though the underlying transition and default data are identical in both cases. Table 4 shows the 5-year default probabilities obtained from the two transition matrices (Tables 2 and 3). Again, low speculative grade names appear to be more risky in the duration analysis, whereas investment grade firms appear to be less risky.

The impact on portfolio performance – and, in particular, tranche performance – is significant. Table 5 shows how various tranche risk measures change when the duration results are used to analyse CDO tranches referencing a portfolio of "BBB" companies (see the section on "Synthetic CDO analysis – a case study" and Table 1) within our Gaussian copula model. Apart from the leverage of the subordinated tranche, all risk measures decrease relative to the cohort results. This further highlights the need for risk managers to carefully analyse all model inputs before applying the model to a given portfolio or transaction.

Coherence between quantitative and qualitative methods

The LHP default distribution shown in Figure 1 is an example of the application of a quantitative method to determine potential levels of default within a consumer asset portfolio. As discussed in the section on "Subordination levels – lessons from history", qualitative methods are often used to determine portfolio default levels in different rating scenarios for consumer asset-backed transactions. It is interesting to ask whether these different methods would produce similar results for the same portfolio, that is, whether the qualitative and quantitative methods are *coherent*.

Before answering this question, it is important to remember that the information provided by each type of method is fundamentally different. While qualitative methods provide estimates of portfolio defaults and losses in certain recessionary scenarios, quantitative methods create probability distributions of potential defaults and losses. A framework is therefore required that allows reliable comparison of the two sets of results.

One possible framework involves specifying a tolerance for default (or loss) at certain rating levels. Why is this necessary? For example, if the tolerance for default were zero at all rating levels, one would have to apply the maximum default level produced by the model at all rating levels, which is clearly inconsistent with the qualitative analysis, which effectively "tiers" the level of default according to the required rating. This implicitly assumes higher tolerance for default at lower rating levels, without specifying its exact value. Only by specifying these tolerances explicitly can we usefully compare the output of the model with the results of qualitative analysis.

For example, if we assumed a tolerance of 1% for "AA" ratings, we would compare the "AA" default assumption from the qualitative method with the 99th percentile of the model-derived default distribution. By suitable choice of these tolerances at each rating level, we can determine whether the quantitative approach is indeed consistent with the results of qualitative analysis. If the two are inconsistent, then one (or both) will need some adjustment in order to achieve coherence. These tolerances can naturally be interpreted as measures of the long-term average default probabilities of the rated securities.

Table 6 illustrates this approach for the "BBB" portfolio mentioned previously, using our Gaussian copula model to determine the portfolio default distribution. The tolerance levels correspond to the 5-year corporate default probabilities – obtained using the

Table 6 Levels of default over a 5-year maturity for a portfolio of 100 "BBB" companies in different rating scenarios (all numbers are in per cent)

Scenario	Tolerance	Portfolio defaults
AAA	0.03	23.98
AA	0.23	16.75
A	0.66	13.40
BBB	2.72	8.71
BB	10.74	4.69
B	43.43	1.34

cohort method – of companies with the rating shown on the "Scenario" column of the table. The levels of portfolio default in each scenario correspond to these quantiles of the portfolio default distribution.

It is clear from the table that higher rating scenarios are associated with lower tolerances and correspondingly higher levels of portfolio default. Another way of expressing this is that a highly rated tranche should experience losses less often than a tranche with a lower rating, and therefore more loss protection should be provided to the highly rated tranche. This quantitative requirement is analogous to the qualitative requirements discussed in the section "Assessing ratings performance – constructing economic scenarios".

The value of stress tests

The usefulness of qualitative methods goes beyond simple "reality checks" on our models. They are also crucial in the process of ensuring that models perform well under stress, and produce extreme – but not nonsensical – results. As discussed in the section "Assessing ratings performance – constructing economic scenarios", economic stress testing within a qualitative framework is an integral part of the rating analysis for many structured finance asset classes. A disadvantage of this is the inability to accurately analyse the default and recovery behaviour of the rated securities, as they are required to "survive" the stresses applied. In the section "Synthetic CDO analysis – a case study", we discussed how a quantitative framework takes the analysis one step further, by no longer requiring a rated tranche to survive all levels of default or loss experienced in a relevant period of history. Instead, a tranche is required to survive a level of default or loss produced by a model.

Using a quantitative model does not remove the need for stress tests; it only changes the way these stresses are applied. For example, stressed default patterns are replaced by stresses to default probabilities and correlation, or the use of different copula functions. Both methods will produce extreme scenarios (such as front-loaded defaults), but the advantage of the quantitative method is that it weights both "normal" and "extreme" economic/market events according to the frequency with which they occur. The correct frequencies can, of course, be debated. As discussed earlier, this will require qualitative judgement.

Once a good model has been developed, the results may need to be communicated to a wider audience than the modelling community. This is always a challenge for regulators, rating agencies and other market participants who need to maintain a transparent framework for risk analysis. While the provision of a "black box" with good documentation may suffice in some cases, it is often necessary to distil the output of a model (or set of models) into a discrete set of criteria for use in determining approximate levels of economic or regulatory capital. This is the spirit of the advanced internal ratings-based (IRB) approach under the revised Basel II accord.

Standard & Poor's adopts both practices, providing its models to market participants with full transparency, while providing qualitative criteria to allow economic stresses to be consistently applied across different asset classes. As the quantitative methods employed by Standard & Poor's develop further, these criteria are likely to change over time. However, the combination of quantitative and qualitative analysis utilised by Standard & Poor's is likely to ensure that these criteria will always remain consistent with the lessons from history.

REFERENCES

Andersen, L., J. Sidenius, and S. Basu, 2003, "All Your Hedges in One Basket", *Risk,* Vol. 16, pp. 67–72, November.

Christensen, J., E. Hansen, and D. Lando, 2004, "Confidence Sets for Continuous-time Rating Transition Probabilities", Working Paper, Copenhagen Business School.

Davis, M. H. A., and V. Lo, 2001, "Infectious Defaults", *Quantitative Finance,* **1**, pp. 382–6.

de Servigny, A., and O. Renault, 2003, "Correlation Evidence", *Risk,* Vol. 16, pp. 90–94, July.

de Servigny, A., and O. Renault, 2004, *Measuring and Managing Credit Risk* (McGraw-Hill).

Duffie, D., and N. Garleanu, 2001, "Risk and the Valuation of Collateralised Debt Obligations", *Financial Analysts Journal,* **57**, pp. 41–59.

Friedman, C., and S. Sandow, 2003, "Ultimate Recoveries", *Risk,* Vol. 16, pp. 69–73, August.

Frey, R., and J. Backhaus, 2003, "Interacting Defaults and Counterparty Risk: A Markovian Approach", Working Paper, Department of Mathematics, University of Leipzig.

Giesecke, K., 2002, "An Exponential Model for Dependent Defaults", Technical Report, Humboldt-Universität zu Berlin.

Gilkes, K., and M. Drexler, 2003, "Drill-Down Approach for Synthetic CDO Squared Transactions", Standard & Poor's Special Report.

Gilkes, K., and R. Watson, 2004, "CDO Evaluator Technical Document", Working Paper, Standard & Poor's.

Greenberg, A., R. Marshal, M. Naldi, and L. Schloegl, 2004, "Tuning Correlation and Tail Risk to the Market Prices of Liquid Tranches", *Quantitative Credit Research Quarterly,* Q1, Lehman Brothers.

Gregory, J., and J. P. Laurent, 2003, "Basket Default Swaps, CDOs and Factor Copulas", Working Paper, BNP Paribas and ISFA Actuarial School, University of Lyon.

Jobst, N., and K. Gilkes, 2003, "Investigating Transition Matrices: Empirical Insights and Methodologies", Working Paper, Standard & Poor's.

Kavvathas, D., 2000, "Estimating Credit Rating Transition Probabilities for Corporate Bonds", Working Paper, Department of Economics, University of Chicago.

Lando, D., and T. M. Skødeberg, 2002, "Analyzing Rating Transitions and Rating Drift With Continuous Observations", *Journal of Banking and Finance,* **26**, pp. 423–44.

Li, D., 2000, "On Default Correlation: A Copula Function Approach", *Journal of Fixed Income,* **9**, pp. 43–54.

Marshal, R., M. Naldi, and A. Zeevi, 2002, "The Dependence Structure of Asset Returns", *Quantitative Credit Research Quarterly,* Q4, Lehman Brothers.

Merton, R., 1974, "On the Pricing of Corporate Debt: The Risk Structure of Interest Rates", *Journal of Finance,* **29**, pp. 449–70.

Rogge, E., and P. Schönbucher, 2003, "Modelling Dynamic Portfolio Credit Risk", Working Paper, ABN AAMRO Bank and ETH Zürich.

Schönbucher, P., and D. Schubert, 2001, "Copula Dependent Default Risk in Intensity Models", Working Paper, Bonn University.

Schönbucher, P., 2003, "Information-Driven Default Contagion", Working Paper, Department of Mathematics, ETH Zürich.

Vasicek, O., 1987, "Probability of Loss on a Loan Portfolio", Working Paper, KMV Corporation.

Yu, F., 2002, "Correlated Defaults in Reduced-Form Models", Working Paper, University of California.

6

CDOs and Correlation Analysis

Richard V. Hrvatin, Matthias Neugebauer

Fitch Ratings

The repackaging of corporate debt in the form of collateralised debt obligations (CDOs) has been around since the inception of the high yield or junk bond market in the late 1980s. The credit risk of defaults in the portfolio underlying the CDO is absorbed *via* multiple tranches of debt of varying levels of seniority, the equity holder being the most junior and the first loss provider. CDOs allow the equity holders to leverage their investment through the issuance of rated debt funded in the credit markets.

The majority of these transactions have been cash funded, but newer, more innovative structures, rely on synthetic structures to transfer the credit risk through the use of credit default swaps. However, the economics of the credit risk is virtually the same when compared with cash funded transactions. Synthetic structures offer the advantage of allowing more flexibility for custom-crafted transactions to suit a particular investor's needs or risk tolerance. Hence, over the past few years single-tranche CDOs, custom crafted for a particular investor, have gained in popularity.

A logical extension of the single-tranche concept is the repackaging of many single-tranche CDOs into a master CDO, colloquially known as a CDO of CDOs, or a CDO-squared transaction. However, leveraging an already leveraged transaction can magnify the risks that might be more transparent and easier to comprehend in a single stand-alone transaction. To understand the interplay of how the credit performance of each single-tranche CDO behaves relative to the other single-tranche CDOs, it is necessary to look through to the portfolios underlying each CDO and to analyse the correlation amongst the corporate credits. Transactions that may appear to be diverse, and thus shielded from the risk of multiple credit events, may experience more defaults than anticipated due to correlation and overlap of the underlying corporate credits. Due to the leveraged nature of these transactions, even modest amounts of overlap and correlation can lead to severe losses that at first may not be obvious.

Although CDO-squared transactions appear to provide additional diversification, the limited universe of liquid corporate single-name credit default swaps ("CDSs") has resulted in substantial overlap among the reference portfolios in the underlying CDOs.

The assumed asset correlation between the corporate entities ("asset correlation") being referenced by the underlying CDOs is a key driver of the default correlation among the underlying CDOs themselves. Asset correlation assumptions are therefore an important determinant of required credit enhancement (CE) levels at the master CDO level itself.

Importantly, correlation studies have shown that significant correlation exists between companies in different industries as well as those in the same industries.[1]

The highlights of this chapter may be listed as follows.

- A standard CDO model can be extended to allow a look-through analysis of the universe of assets underlying CDOs of CDOs. The look-through model, which is used to determine the CE required for synthetic CDOs that include a substantial proportion of CDO collateral, eliminates the need to make specific recovery and correlation assumptions for CDO tranches. The correlation between the underlying CDO tranches is determined by the following:
  - the assumed correlation between the different corporate reference entities that populate each underlying CDO portfolio;
  - the extent to which each underlying CDO references the same corporate obligations (the "level of overlap").
- The results reported below show that the correlation between CDO tranches in a CDO-squared transaction is generally significantly higher than the correlation between stand-alone corporates in a typical corporate CDO.

- The assumed asset correlation between the corporate reference entities is found to be a key driver of the default correlation between CDO tranches in a CDO-squared transaction. It is therefore an important determinant of required CE levels.
- For a relatively well-diversified portfolio of corporates, correlations across industries (inter-industry correlation) generally have a greater impact on the portfolio average level of correlation than correlations within the same industry (intra-industry correlation).
- Using the look-through model, the effect of asset correlation between the underlying corporates on tranche default correlation and the CE necessary to achieve a particular rating on a given tranche is shown.

THE LOOK-THROUGH APPROACH

The look-through model is an extension of a standard Monte Carlo structural form model (see Panel 1) which is used by many market participants to approximate the default behaviour of credit portfolios. Default events on the underlying CDOs in a CDO squared are modelled by "looking through" to the simulation results for the universe of underlying names that make up the individual CDO portfolios. This allows one to model the correlation between CDO tranches based on the correlation assumption for the underlying assets and requires no additional assumptions.

Table 1 sets out results from an application of the look-through approach to a master CDO comprising exposures to five underlying CDOs. The pools for the underlying CDOs contain exposures to 20 distinct reference entities (obligors). The steps involved in this application are as follows.

Step 1. The asset notional shows the reference notional of each of the obligors for each of the five CDO portfolios. For example, CDO 1 comprises seven corporate entities with a total portfolio notional of 800. CDO 3 also includes seven corporates, three of which are included in both CDO 1 and 3.

Step 2. For each scenario, the model simulates the performance of the universe of corporate names and identifies how many and which names defaulted. In the example above, the simulation is

PANEL 1 STRUCTURAL FORM MODELS/MONTE CARLO SIMULATION

Structural form models are widely used in evaluating the credit risk of individual firms or credit portfolios, including CDOs. They are based on option pricing theory and were first developed by Black–Scholes and Merton. The approach is built on the assumption that companies default if the value of their assets falls below the value of their liabilities (also referred to as the default threshold). Graphically, this is shown in Figure 1a below. The probability of default (p_i) for the issuer (i) can therefore be expressed as the probability that the value of the assets (V_i) falls below the default threshold (D_i).

$$p_i = \Pr(V_i \leq D_i)$$

Structural form models can be used in conjunction with Monte Carlo simulation to approximate the default distribution of credit portfolios. In the Monte Carlo framework, the change in asset values is typically assumed to follow a particular distribution. For ease of computation, most models use the normal distribution due to its well-defined characteristics. In each simulation run, a standard normal random number is drawn for each name in the portfolio, representing the change in the obligor's asset values over the holding period or the time to default. The default threshold can be inferred from the default probability, which may be derived from an obligor's rating. For example, if the default rate for a "BBB"-rated entity over five years is assumed to be 1.89%, the default threshold can be computed by using the inverse of the standard normal cumulative distribution,

$$\Phi^{-1}(1.89\%) = -2.08$$

Figure 1a Structural default modelling

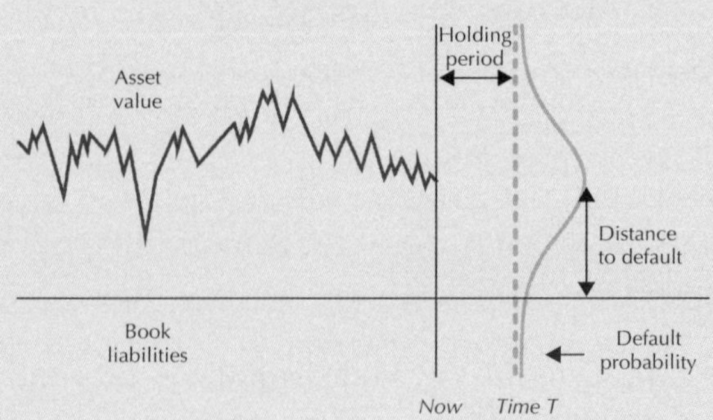

Most models today define the holding period as the time to asset maturity and draw a single random number representing the change in asset value until maturity of the asset. Such single-period models, although fast, do not allow for changes to the inputs such as correlation and default probabilities over time. Fitch has adopted a multi-period approach in its VECTOR model, with a holding period of one year. For each year of a transaction's life, the VECTOR model repeatedly applies the single-period model. For example, for assets that survive in the first year, the model assigns a second standard normal random variable representing the change in asset value over the second year, and so on until maturity. This allows for the incorporation of time varying parameters such as correlation and default probabilities. The default threshold for each period is based on the conditional probability of default, which is derived as follows:

$$p_{\text{conditional};k|k+1} = \frac{p_{\text{marginal};k|k+1}}{1 - p_{\text{cumulative};k}}$$

where $p_{\text{marginal};k|k+1} = p_{\text{cumulative};k+1} - p_{\text{cumulative};k}$.

Structural form Monte Carlo simulations are appealing, as they can easily be extended to take into account the correlation between the asset values of individual obligors in a portfolio. This is typically achieved through the use of copula functions, of which the standard Normal Copula is the most widely used (also used in the VECTOR model). A copula function is, essentially, an approximation of the joint asset value distribution for the obligors in a portfolio. The marginal distributions are linked through asset correlation. Mathematically, this is achieved through the use of Cholesky decomposition. The resulting correlated, normally distributed asset values are again compared to the respective default threshold. For the bivariate normal distribution, the probability that both assets default (joint probability of default) is represented by

$$P(V_A < D_A \cap V_B < D_B) = \Phi(D_A; D_B; \rho_{AB})$$

run five times. Scenario 1 yields six defaulted entities out of the total universe of 20.

Step 3. The model computes the cumulative portfolio loss for each of the CDOs by summing the loss given default (the notional multiplied by one minus the recovery rate) for each of the

Table 1 Look-through model example

		Step 1					Step 2				
		Asset notional					Simulation results (1 = default/0 = survival)				
Obligor	**Recovery rate (%)**	**CDO 1**	**CDO 2**	**CDO 3**	**CDO 4**	**CDO 5**	**Scen 1**	**Scen 2**	**Scen 3**	**Scen 4**	**Scen 5**
Corp 1	25	100	0	0	100	0	0	0	1	0	1
Corp 2	30	0	0	0	0	100	0	0	0	0	0
Corp 3	35	100	0	100	0	0	0	0	0	0	0
Corp 4	25	100	0	0	50	0	0	0	0	0	1
Corp 5	25	0	150	0	0	100	0	0	0	1	0
Corp 6	25	0	150	0	100	0	0	0	0	1	0
Corp 7	25	0	0	100	0	100	1	0	0	1	0
Corp 8	25	100	0	0	0	100	0	1	0	0	0
Corp 9	30	0	0	100	50	0	1	0	0	0	1
Corp 10	15	0	0	0	100	0	0	0	1	0	0
Corp 11	15	0	0	100	0	100	1	0	0	0	0
Corp 12	15	0	0	0	100	0	1	0	0	0	1
Corp 13	15	0	0	200	100	0	0	0	0	0	0
Corp 14	20	100	0	0	0	100	1	0	0	1	1
Corp 15	20	0	100	0	100	0	0	0	1	0	0
Corp 16	20	200	0	100	0	0	0	1	1	0	0
Corp 17	20	0	100	0	0	100	0	1	0	0	0
Corp 18	20	100	0	100	0	0	1	0	1	0	1
Corp 19	25	0	100	0	100	0	0	0	0	0	0
Corp 20	25	0	100	0	0	100	0	0	0	0	0
Portfolio notional		**800**	**700**	**800**	**800**	**800**	**6**	**3**	**5**	**4**	**6**

Step 3

Total CDO portfolio loss for each scenario					
	CDO 1	**CDO 2**	**CDO 3**	**CDO 4**	**CDO 5**
Scen 1	160	0	310	120	240
Scen 2	235	80	80	0	155
Scen 3	315	80	160	240	0
Scen 4	80	225	75	75	230
Scen 5	310	0	150	232.5	80

	CDO 1	**CDO 2**	**CDO 3**	**CDO 4**	**CDO 5**
AP	200	300	200	200	200
TS	100	100	100	100	100
DP	300	400	300	300	300

Step 4

CDO tranche loss: Min(*TS*; Max(Portfolio Loss – *AP*, 0))					
	CDO 1	**CDO 2**	**CDO 3**	**CDO 4**	**CDO 5**
Scen 1	0	0	100	0	40
Scen 2	35	0	0	0	0
Scen 3	100	0	0	40	0
Scen 4	0	0	0	0	30
Scen 5	100	0	0	32.5	0

TS = tranche size; *AP* = attachment point; *DP* = detachment point.
Source: Fitch Ratings

defaulted assets included in the particular CDO portfolio. In scenario 1, the cumulative portfolio loss is 160 for CDO 1 and 310 for CDO 3.

Step 4. For synthetic structures that do not include structural enhancement features, such as overcollateralisation (OC) triggers and excess spread, the CE is provided by a loss threshold or attachment point. A cash settlement payment would be made once the cumulative portfolio loss exceeds the attachment point. Most synthetic CDO-squared transactions allow for multiple cash settlement payments in respect of the underlying CDOs. In the example, scenario 1 would lead to a breach of the attachment point for CDOs 3 and 5. Losses exceeding the attachment point are passed on to the master CDO. For CDO 3 in scenario 1, the excess loss is 110. However, the maximum loss that is passed on to the master CDO cannot exceed the size of the individual CDO tranche, which for CDO 3 in our example is 100. The total loss incurred by the master CDO in scenario 1 is 140.

The results of each individual scenario are used to produce the loss distribution for the master CDO. This shows the likelihood of observing a particular loss within the master CDO portfolio over the life of the transaction. In synthetic CDOs, which typically do not include structural protections such as excess spread and diversion of cashflow, the CE is provided only by subordination. The required CE would be sized to ensure that, based on the portfolio loss distribution, the probability of observing a loss that exceeds available subordination on the master is in line with the expected default rate associated with the rating of that tranche.

CORRELATION AND DIVERSIFICATION

Correlation is a measure of co-movement between two variables, based on their historically observed values – for example, the correlation between two companies' equity prices or asset values.

Correlation may be thought of as reflecting exposure to common economic factors that affect individual variables such as equity returns, causing them to move in the same direction. This is captured in so-called factor models, which relate the change in returns to changes in the underlying factors, in addition to idiosyncratic or asset-specific risk factors.

PANEL 2 DEFAULT CORRELATION

For binary variables such as default/survival, the correlation coefficient is calculated as follows:

$$\rho_{12} = \frac{p_{12} - p_1 p_2}{\sqrt{p_1 p_2 (1-p_1)(1-p_2)}}$$

where p_1 and p_2 are the individual default probabilities and p_{12} is the joint probability of default for the two entities. The maximum default correlation between two entities is given by

$$\max(\rho_{12}) = \frac{\min(p_1, p_2) - p_1 p_2}{\sqrt{p_1 p_2 (1-p_1)(1-p_2)}}$$

ie, since joint probability of default between two entities cannot be lower than the lower of the two individual default probabilities, the maximum possible default correlation is reached if the joint probability of default is equal to the lower of the two individual default rates. This is relevant when we consider two CDO tranches from the same underlying portfolio.

It is difficult to measure default correlation directly since there has not been deep enough historical default experience, relatively speaking, to adequately observe and measure default correlation. Therefore, a significant amount of research has been dedicated to the development of

Figure 2a Credit correlations

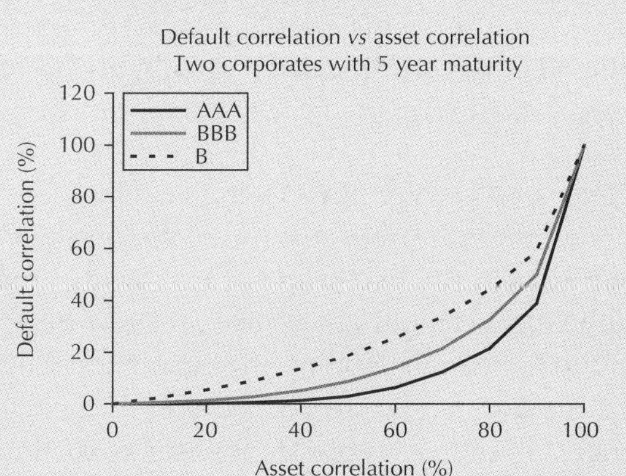

Source: Fitch Ratings

models that can derive the default correlation between two or more entities from available data. One of the most widely used models is based on the structural form methodology, which was initially developed by Merton (1974). The model is based on the assumption that a company defaults once the value of the asset falls below the value of the liabilities. This can be used in conjunction with the Monte Carlo simulation to derive the default correlation from asset or equity correlation. (For more details on this methodology please see *"Default Correlation and its Effect on Portfolios of Credit Risk"*, Fitch Ratings, February 17, 2004).

Figure 2a shows the relationship between default and asset correlation for two identically rated corporates (same default probability). The default correlation is generally lower than asset correlation (except at 0% and 100% asset correlation) and increases as asset correlation increases.

Interestingly, the higher the rating of the individual entities, the more non-linear the relationship between asset and default correlation. For higher ratings the asset correlation needs to be significantly higher for the default correlation to increase.

The degree of correlation between the returns of two assets depends on the proportion of the total volatility of each asset's returns that is due to systematic risk factors (such as region and industry) and idiosyncratic (asset-specific) factors.

$$\text{Total risk} = \text{Systematic risk} + \text{Idiosyncratic risk}$$

As idiosyncratic (ie, asset-specific) risk is by definition independent, it follows that the higher the proportion of idiosyncratic risk within the total risk, the less correlated the returns of the two assets.

This notion is at the centre of modern portfolio theory. Investors can increase their risk–return profile by creating portfolios of assets with low correlation (high level of idiosyncratic risk), thereby diversifying the total amount of idiosyncratic risk inherent in individual portfolio assets. Therefore, systematic and idiosyncratic risks are equivalent to non-diversifiable and diversifiable risk, respectively. Portfolio theory shows that the higher the proportion of idiosyncratic risks inherent in an asset, the greater the benefit of diversification. However, by diversifying the idiosyncratic risk inherent in the underlying assets, the investor is left with a high level of systematic risk inherent in the portfolio return. Therefore, one would expect the level of correlation between the returns of two diverse portfolios to be significantly higher than between two individual assets.

Example

To show this empirically, two equally weighted stock portfolios were constructed, each including 10 names. Portfolio 1 includes 10 randomly chosen bank stocks and portfolio 2 includes 10 randomly chosen telecommunication stocks. Table 2 shows the individual pairwise return correlations between the constituents in the two portfolios, based on weekly returns for the period between 1999 and 2002.

The average pairwise correlation between each of the individual entities is approximately 19%. For comparison, we computed the correlation between the two portfolios over the same time period using the weekly portfolio returns. The correlation coefficient was 50%.

This is what one would expect, given that the level of idiosyncratic risk inherent in the portfolio returns is significantly reduced as a result of diversification. Hence, the proportion of portfolio risk attributable to systematic factors is much larger, leading to a higher correlation between the portfolio returns.

Therefore, we would expect the correlation between CDO tranches to be significantly higher than the correlation between individual corporates. Moreover, the correlation between CDOs should be higher for highly diversified CDOs.

CORRELATION BETWEEN CDO TRANCHES

For credit portfolios such as CDOs, investors are primarily interested in the default correlation between two entities, since this provides a measure for the joint default behaviour between the two entities (see Panel 2).

To illustrate this point, Figure 1 shows the distribution of losses on a portfolio of 50 "B"-rated assets under different assumptions about the correlation of the underlying exposures. As may be seen from the figure, higher asset correlation for the underlying claims translates into substantially greater risks of substantial losses on the portfolio as a whole.

Table 2 Pairwise correlation between equity returns (%)

	Telco 1	Telco 2	Telco 3	Telco 4	Telco 5	Telco 6	Telco 7	Telco 8	Telco 9	Telco 10
Bank 1	17.04	15.59	21.09	−4.54	25.06	25.06	27.50	22.62	4.38	12.23
Bank 2	16.51	16.66	15.91	6.00	16.36	16.36	20.19	21.43	10.51	13.91
Bank 3	17.11	5.62	21.62	1.94	21.30	21.30	18.62	19.07	17.63	9.41
Bank 4	18.42	16.67	20.81	−6.43	29.65	29.65	33.79	22.41	15.59	17.42
Bank 5	26.62	30.12	35.30	12.05	24.38	24.38	31.84	34.05	21.82	21.39
Bank 6	26.83	24.43	31.55	5.73	30.91	30.91	26.69	38.43	28.63	23.13
Bank 7	18.89	25.33	23.33	−1.64	29.51	29.51	29.46	35.16	14.12	19.11
Bank 8	18.25	10.80	37.37	6.71	27.71	27.71	28.64	39.94	12.96	25.83
Bank 9	−3.77	7.03	−3.36	1.65	−5.54	−5.54	0.77	−6.97	−11.56	4.04
Bank 10	23.52	25.18	33.50	−0.54	36.26	36.26	34.16	39.83	24.94	28.37

Source: Fitch Ratings

Based on general principles of portfolio theory (as outlined above), we would expect the pairwise correlation between any two CDOs to depend on the following:

- the assumed asset correlation between the different corporate reference entities that populate each underlying CDO portfolio;
- the extent to which each underlying CDO references the same corporate obligations (the "level of overlap");
- the level of diversity of each of the underlying CDO portfolios, which is driven by the number as well as the regional and industry distribution of the assets included in each of the portfolios.

To assess the impact of each of these factors on correlation, we used the look-through model to calculate the pairwise default correlation between CDO tranches.

The model was run 100,000 times for homogeneous hypothetical portfolios of "BBB" assets with a five-year maturity. The reference notional of each asset was assumed to be 100,000, with a fixed recovery rate assumption of 25%.

The joint probability of default between any two tranches needed to compute the default correlation was approximated by dividing the number of scenarios in which both tranches defaulted by the total number of scenarios run. Based on the joint probability of default and the individual default probabilities of each tranche, we then derived the default correlation using the formula shown in Panel 2.

Figure 1 Losses on portfolios with different exposure asset correlations

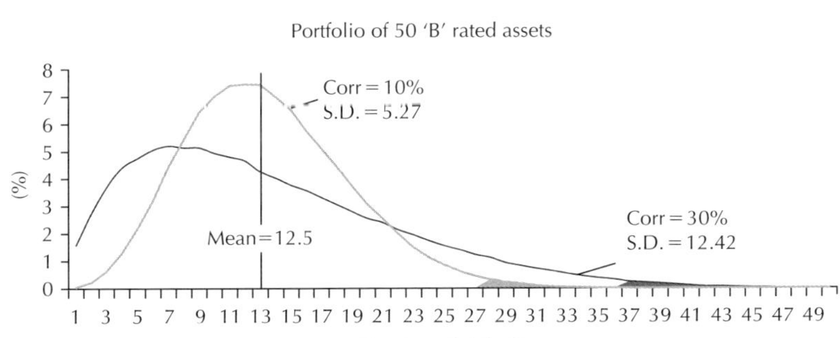

Four sets of tests were run. In each test, we changed one factor, keeping everything else constant.

Test 1: Asset correlation between the reference obligations

The first test shows the impact of asset correlation between the corporate reference entities on the pairwise default correlation between "BBB"-rated CDO tranches. The attachment point required for a "BBB" rating was sized individually (see *"CDO Squared: A Closer Look at Correlation"*, Fitch Ratings, February 2, 2004) every time the asset correlation was changed.

We realise that default correlation is a relatively abstract concept. Therefore, we also presented the "AAA", "AA" and "A" loss rate and associated required CE for the master CDO produced by the look-through model for a portfolio of 25 "BBB"-rated CDO tranches, each derived from a hypothetical portfolio of 100 "BBB" assets (as outlined above) with an overlap of 10%. The CDO tranche size was assumed to be 2% of the underlying portfolio, which represents a typical CDO-squared structure. The results are summarised in Table 3 and Figure 2.

The default correlation between the CDOs in a CDO squared is significantly higher than the default correlation between corporates in a standard corporate CDO. This is true even where there is low overlap of corporate names in the underlying CDOs.

For example, with a 15% asset correlation (and an overlap of 10%) among the universe of the underlying corporate names, the default correlation between the CDO tranches is 32%. By contrast, the pairwise default correlation between "BBB"-rated corporates is less than 10% for asset correlation levels up to 50%.

Furthermore, the level of default correlation across underlying CDOs in a CDO-squared transaction is very sensitive to the level of asset correlation of the underlying corporates within the CDOs. An increase in asset correlation from 5% to 15% (among the underlying corporate entities) increases the CDO default correlation from 5.8% to 32%; simultaneously, the required CE at the "AAA" level in our example CDO squared rises from 25.2% (corresponding to 10 defaulted CDO tranches) to 59.6% (corresponding to 18 defaulted CDO tranches). By comparison, the default correlation between corporates and the CE required for CDOs of individual corporates are much less sensitive, especially where levels of asset correlation are low.

Table 3 Pairwise default correlation *versus* asset correlation (%)

Corporate asset correlation (intra and inter industry)	**0.0**	**5.0**	**10.0**	**15.0**	**20.0**	**25.0**	**30.0**
Corporate default correlation	0.0	0.3	0.5	1.0	1.6	2.2	3.1
CDO tranche default correlation	0.0	5.8	17.6	32.0	40.8	50.0	60.0
Required CE							
AAA	8.3	25.2	40.8	59.6	77.0	89.8	96.1
AA	6.9	18.3	25.5	36.0	50.5	63.1	74.8
A	5.6	13.7	16.2	20.9	26.5	33.2	40.3

Assumptions: 25 "BBB"-rated CDO tranches; 10% overlap; 100 "BBB"-rated corporates each; 2% tranche size; five-year maturity
Source: Fitch Ratings

Figure 2 Pairwise default correlation *versus* asset correlation

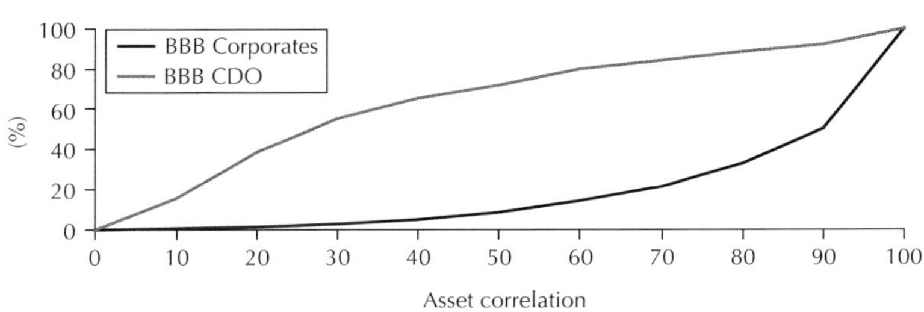

Source: Fitch Ratings

Test 2: Overlap between CDO portfolios

The level of default correlation also depends crucially on the level of overlap between two CDO portfolios, which is shown in Table 5.

For this test we modelled pairs of "BBB"-rated CDO tranches with a maturity of five years, which were linked to portfolios of 100 equally weighted "BBB" reference entities each. The test was run at different levels of overlap between the two portfolios. For example, 10% overlap means that 10 of the underlying reference names are common to both portfolios.

As expected, the level of overlap has a significant impact on the pairwise default correlation between the "BBB"-rated CDO

Table 4 Underlying corporate correlation assumptions (%)

Companies in same industry	30	30	30	30	30	30	30
Companies in different industries	0	5	10	15	20	25	30
CDO tranche default correlation	11.0	19.0	27.0	36.0	45.0	53.0	60.0

Assumptions: 25 "BBB"-rated CDO tranches; 10% overlap; 100 "BBB"-rated corporates each; 2% tranche size; five-year maturity
Source: Fitch Ratings

tranches, which is approximately 28% at zero overlap but increases to 40% with an overlap of 30%.

Test 3: Number of reference entities

Next we analysed the effect of the number of reference obligors included in each CDO portfolio on the level of default correlation (assuming zero overlap). A higher number of obligors increases the level of diversity, which should increase correlation. This is indeed the case as shown in Table 5. Raising the number of reference entities from 20 to 100 causes the default correlation to increase from 4.6% to 28%.

Test 4: Industry and regional diversity

The previous tests have confirmed that the increased diversity in the underlying CDOs increases the correlation between these CDO tranches. In the final test, we examined the effect of regional and industry diversity between the two portfolios. Generally, the correlation across industries and/or regions is lower than the correlation within industries and/or geographic regions. Therefore, CDO tranches derived from portfolios that are highly concentrated across industries or regions should be less correlated than diverse portfolios.

To test this, we increased the level of pairwise asset correlation between assets from the same regional portfolios relative to the correlation between assets from different portfolios (to simulate the effect of regional and/or industry concentration). The results are shown in Table 6.

As expected, the default correlation between the two CDO tranches declines as the asset correlation within each of the underlying portfolios increases relative to the correlation between assets

Table 5 Number of reference entities *versus* CDO default correlation

No of reference entities	20	30	40	50	60	70	80	90	100	110	120
CDO default correlation (%)	4.6	7.8	13.0	14.5	15.3	20.8	22.3	24.8	28.0	29.5	31.2
Impact of overlap											
Overlap (%)	0	10	20	30	40	50	60	70	80	90	100
CDO default correlation (%)	28.0	32.0	36.0	40.0	44.0	49.0	54.0	59.0	67.0	77.0	100.0

Five years; 15% asset correlation; 100 reference names; "BBB" tranches
Source: Fitch Ratings

Table 6 Industry and regional concentration (%)

Asset correlation within portfolios	15	20	25	30
Asset correlation across portfolios	15	15	15	15
CDO default correlation	28	15.5	10.2	6.6

Five year; no overlap; 100 reference names; "BBB" tranche
Source: Fitch Ratings

from different CDO portfolios. The default correlation between two tranches from different CDO portfolios is very sensitive to the relative level of asset correlation between assets from the same portfolio and assets from different portfolios. For example, a relative increase in asset correlation within portfolios from 15% to 20% reduces the default correlation of the two CDOs from 28% to 15.5%.

CONCLUDING REMARKS

The correlation between CDOs within CDO-squared transactions is higher than the correlation between stand-alone corporates in a corporate CDO. Correlation between CDOs depends on the diversity of underlying portfolios – in particular, the size, industry and regional concentration, and overlap. Typically, correlation increases for larger portfolios, more diverse industry and regional distributions, and higher levels of overlap. In particular, asset correlation between the underlying reference entities appears to have a significant impact on CDO correlation. The relatively high correlation in CDOs is even higher in synthetic CDOs of investment-grade corporate entities, which exhibit significant overlap because of the limited universe of liquid single-name CDSs.

Correlation has no effect on the mean or expected loss on a portfolio, but does affect the volatility of portfolio defaults and losses. Generally, higher correlation leads to increased volatility and more frequent extreme events (ie, very high and no losses), as shown in Figure 1. Therefore, correlation increases the expected loss on senior tranches while reducing the expected loss for equity holders and junior tranches.

1 "Default Correlation and its Effect on Portfolios of Credit Risk", Fitch Ratings, February 17, 2004.

REFERENCES

Black, F., and M. Scholes, 1973, "The Pricing of Options and Corporate Liabilities," *Journal of Political Economy,* **81**, pp. 637–654.

Merton, R. C., 1974, "On the Pricing of Corporate Debt: The Risk Structure of Interest Rates", *Journal of Finance,* **29(2)**, pp. 449–470.

7

The Impact of Credit Rating Changes on the Pricing of Asset-Backed Securities*

John Ammer, Nathanael Clinton

Federal Reserve Board

INTRODUCTION: CREDIT RATINGS AS A SOURCE OF MARKET INFORMATION

Although conventional notions of efficient markets imply that the pricing of debt securities will reflect any available information about the creditworthiness of the obligor, financial theory alone offers little information about how market participants acquire it. For about a century in US corporate bond markets, ratings assigned by private independent agencies such as Moody's and Standard and Poor's (S&P) have been one of the possible channels through which investors might obtain credit information. Despite the long history, the available evidence about the importance of credit ratings to debt markets is somewhat conflicting and inconclusive.

There are a number of pieces of circumstantial and anecdotal evidence that imply that credit ratings may be quite important to the functioning of bond markets. As documented in Estrella *et al* (2000), most public debt securities have at least one agency rating, and a majority of the issuers voluntarily pay fees to be rated. A United States Securities and Exchange Commission (2003) report argues that ratings have become more important over time, and notes their increasing use in private contracts (such as ratings-based "triggers" in debt covenants) and in financial regulation worldwide. Ferri *et al* (1999) and Reisen and von Maltzan (1999)

*The views expressed here are those of the authors and not necessarily those of the Board of Governors of the Federal Reserve System or its staff.

conjecture that by the time of the 1998 Asian financial crisis, investors' reliance on emerging market sovereign bond ratings had reached the point where the ratings became a potentially destabilising factor, and perhaps a focal point for herd behaviour, as too many investors accepted them uncritically.

However, there is also a body of empirical research that points to a fairly limited marginal contribution by credit ratings to market information about corporate and sovereign borrowers. Cantor and Packer (1996) showed that most of the credit information in a cross-section of sovereign ratings is also present in a set of readily observable macroeconomic variables, so that the ratings serve largely as a convenient summary measure of the relevant public information. For US corporate bonds, Campbell and Taksler (2003) concluded that yield spreads are more closely associated with the recent historical volatility of the bond issuer's stock price than with the bond rating, and this is broadly consistent with the asset pricing models that emphasise second moments.

Event studies of bond ratings changes have typically discovered average pricing reactions that were in the expected direction but were small in magnitude. For example, in a study of the changes in US corporate bond ratings between 1977 and 1982, Hand *et al* (1992) reported an average impact from a downgrade of −1.27% on the bond return and −1.52% on the associated stock return, with the effect going in the opposite of the expected (negative) direction in roughly 40% of the cases. For upgrades, the results are even weaker: a mean of 0.35% for the bond return and 0.24% for the stock return. Analyses of rating changes in other bond markets have generally documented similarly modest effects.[1]

We are unaware of any previous event studies on the impact of changes in the credit ratings of asset-backed securities (ABS), which, for a number of reasons, may have somewhat different properties and implications than corporate bond ratings. In particular, ABS issuers are limited-purpose trusts of finite duration with relatively inflexible restrictions on managerial discretion. Accordingly, the underlying risks, as well as the incentives and scope for action in the face of financial distress, may be rather different than for an operating firm, which in turn may affect the dynamics of fluctuations in credit quality. Hu and Cantor (2003) characterised Moody's structured finance ratings as more stable than the corporate ratings, in the sense that changes in ratings are rarer events, which is particularly true for Aaa-rated securities. However, Moody's structured finance rating migrations are more likely to entail moves of several notches at a time, compared with an average change of about 1.5 notches for corporate bonds.[2] As a consequence, precipitous declines in credit standing to Caa or lower within a year of an investment-grade rating are much more common in structured finance than for bonds, and Hu *et al* (2004) document this effect for ABS in particular. However, Hu *et al* (2003) pointed out that the higher probability of near-term impairment on investment-grade structured finance securities is offset by a significantly lower historical average loss given default than on corporate bonds. The combination of more frequent but less severe defaults is a natural consequence of diversification in the underlying portfolios.

Another fundamental difference is that most ABS tranches are claims against a portfolio of payment obligations from borrowers with much smaller balance sheets than the typical bond issuer. Thus, some of the means by which credit information about large borrowers is disseminated simply do not exist for the individual credits in the portfolios underlying ABS. Relative to the credit information available to managers of bond portfolios, it is not clear as to what extent that sources specifically geared toward ABS investors (such as the ABSNet service, industry trade journals, and investment bank newsletters) provide comparable intelligence at a similar cost. Clark *et al* (2003) speculated that investors in structured financial products such as ABS have both less capacity and less incentive to monitor the creditworthiness of borrowers themselves, and, as a consequence, will need to rely on third parties, such as rating agencies, to a greater degree. Given that the majority of ABS bear less credit risk and have shorter maturities than the typical corporate bond, the payoff to the ABS holder for additional monitoring effort is likely to be less than that gained by a corporate bond investor.

DATA DESCRIPTION

The data we use for our event study of ABS credit rating changes is based on Merrill Lynch's Asset-Backed Fixed and Floating Rate Index, going back to the end of 1996. Specifically, from Bloomberg we downloaded a sequence of cross-sectional files containing various data fields for each constituent member, including security identifiers, maturity, composite credit rating, amount outstanding, price, yield, duration, option-adjusted spread, total return, and the general category of the underlying collateral assets. Table 1 contains summary statistics for the data as of the end of each year in our sample.

The index covers a variety of types of ABS, with a heavy emphasis on collateral assets based on sundry forms of consumer credit. In all cases, the underlying assets are located in the United States and the securities are denominated in US dollars. The categories that are broken out separately in the dataset are automobile loans, credit card receivables, home equity loans, manufactured housing loans, and utility company receivables. There is also a miscellaneous category within which we were able to identify deals based on streams of receivables such as student loan payments, aircraft leases, payments to state governments under a legal settlement with tobacco companies, recreational vehicle loans, and industrial equipment leases. At the end of 2003, the 3,673 securities in the index had an aggregate market value of about US$650 billion. The proportion of floating-rate instruments in the index had risen to nearly a half. We use data on the floaters in empirical exercises based on returns, but the files do not provide estimates of yields, spread or duration for floaters (and we did not have enough information about the terms of the instruments to compute these figures independently). At the very beginning of the sample, however, credit rating data were missing for all of the floating-rate instruments.

Each security has a three-part description field that consists of a ticker, series code and a class identifier. In general, the ticker corresponds to the sponsor of the deal, the series code identifies the specific special-purpose trust that holds the underlying assets and issued the security (the "deal", in common parlance) and the class identifier specifies the particular tranche of notes. We were able to use the ticker and series to infer relationships among the securities. In many cases, we were able to infer the name that corresponded to a ticker and crosscheck deal information in other sources. In most cases, the CUSIP[3] identifier was also available. Price data are available at a daily frequency, but the rating and amount outstanding (and the index membership) are only updated at the end of the month.

The credit ratings given in the dataset are a composite of Moody's and S&P, using the average based on the standard mapping between their respective rating scales (rounding down, if necessary), when both are available. As calculated by Carron *et al* (2003), Moody's rated a somewhat greater number of ABS than S&P over our sample period, although deals rated either by S&P only or by both are fairly common occurrences. Fitch also rated many of the ABS in the Merrill Lynch index, but their ratings are not incorporated into the composite rating.

Note also that a majority of the index securities are rated AAA. The data set systematically excludes securities that are speculative-grade (rated below BBB3) or have outstanding principal of less than US$25 million, which are mechanically deleted from the index. The median values that are shown in Table 1 reveal a prototypical ABS that is shorter in maturity and duration and has a smaller market value than the average corporate bond that trades in secondary markets in the United States (For comparison, at the end of 2003, the bonds in Merrill Lynch's Corporate Master index had a median market value of US$324 million, a median maturity of 6.8 years, and a median duration of 5.2 years). Mean yield spreads, shown separately in the table for AAA and for lower-rated ABS, have widened over the seven-year sample, and stood substantially higher for these ABS by the end of 2003 than for a comparable portfolio of short-term investment grade corporate bonds.

Because the composite credit ratings are only updated at the end of the month, we conduct the analysis at a monthly frequency. An upgrade or downgrade is inferred when a different rating for a security is shown than that of the previous month.[4] This means that we may miss some single-notch rating changes by either S&P or Moody's that leave the composite rating unchanged, but all of our inferred rating change events should include at least one genuine move in the same direction. Table 2 reports summary statistics for the 819 downgrades and 473 upgrades of index securities that we identify between 1997 and 2003. Because of the cases in which more than one tranche of a deal was included in a rating change, the number of events is reduced from 1,292 to 1,051 when we count them at the issuer level. Furthermore, in many instances ratings were changed simultaneously for related issuers with the same sponsor, as implied by a common ticker. Accordingly, the number of events would be further reduced to just 395 if we were to count them at the sponsor level. ABS rating changes are also clustered over time, with very few

Table 1 Sample statistics for Merrill Lynch ABS index members

	31/12/96	31/12/97	31/12/98	31/12/99	31/12/00	31/12/01	31/12/02	31/12/03
Usable number of securities	607	1,029	1,192	1,335	1,348	1,142	2,094	3,673
Median:								
maturity (years)	5.8	5.0	4.2	3.7	2.8	2.5	2.4	2.2
duration (years)	1.9	1.8	1.9	2.2	2.1	2.4	1.6	1.4
market value (US$ millions)	32.7	39.9	41.6	44.5	47.4	57.9	60.4	76.1
Yield spread (basis points):								
AAA-rated	39	61	110	95	110	132	93	84
below AAA-rated	49	103	205	233	262	297	401	469
Proportion which are:								
fixed rate	100.0%	81.2%	84.1%	87.6%	83.0%	72.3%	57.8%	50.7%
floating rate	0.0%	18.9%	15.9%	12.4%	17.0%	27.7%	42.2%	49.3%
Rated:								
AAA	77.1%	75.4%	73.1%	70.7%	72.0%	68.2%	61.2%	69.3%
AA1	0.0%	0.0%	0.2%	0.3%	0.5%	0.4%	1.6%	0.9%
AA2	8.7%	3.7%	2.7%	4.3%	4.5%	3.8%	7.6%	7.8%
AA3	3.3%	3.1%	4.0%	2.9%	2.8%	3.4%	2.7%	1.0%
A1	0.3%	3.5%	2.4%	1.4%	1.1%	1.1%	1.9%	1.9%
A2	7.9%	3.3%	4.5%	15.9%	16.0%	19.0%	17.0%	12.2%
A3	0.2%	8.6%	10.8%	0.2%	0.2%	0.5%	1.2%	1.0%

BBB1	2.1%	1.9%	0.9%	1.0%	0.8%	1.1%	0.4%	0.7%
BBB2	0.2%	0.3%	0.7%	1.3%	1.6%	2.5%	5.1%	4.2%
BBB3	0.2%	0.2%	0.7%	2.1%	0.5%	0.1%	1.4%	1.1%
With collateral type:								
Auto loans	26.0%	16.1%	14.9%	13.4%	13.2%	11.0%	17.8%	16.7%
Credit card receivables	24.9%	36.2%	33.9%	32.8%	32.1%	40.5%	25.6%	15.4%
Utility company receivables	2.0%	1.0%	0.0%	2.6%	2.8%	3.9%	2.6%	1.6%
Home equity loans	11.2%	20.5%	30.5%	29.7%	31.1%	21.7%	36.4%	49.7%
Manufactured housing loans	35.9%	23.3%	18.2%	19.3%	19.3%	20.8%	13.4%	9.5%
Other	0.0%	2.9%	2.6%	2.2%	1.6%	2.0%	4.2%	7.2%

Notes: Durations and yields are only computed for fixed-rate securities. Proportions are unweighted.

Table 2 Sample totals for ABS composite rating changes

	Downgrades	Upgrades	Total
Security rating changes	819	473	1,292
Issuer rating changes	615	436	1,051
Sponsor rating changes	238	157	395
Number of notches:			
1	429	367	796
2	154	54	208
3	107	31	138
4	50	12	62
5	30	8	38
>5	49	1	50
Rating prior to upgrade or downgrade:			
AAA	167	0	167
AA1	40	13	53
AA2	73	29	102
AA3	121	59	180
A1	91	48	139
A2	171	91	262
A3	29	170	199
BBB1	48	17	65
BBB2	44	21	65
BBB3	35	25	60
Crossed investment grade threshold:	73	–	73
With collateral type:			
auto loans	73	92	165
credit card receivables	270	200	470
utility company receivables	1	3	4
home equity loans	65	85	150
manufactured housing loans	343	80	423
other	67	13	80
Occurring in:			
1997	148	13	161
1998	197	91	288
1999	105	247	352
2000	21	10	31
2001	4	34	38
2002	133	28	161
2003	211	50	261

Notes: Seventy-three "fallen angels" (securities whose ratings changed from investment grade to speculative grade) events are included in the set of downgrades. We identified 13 "rising devils" (rating change from speculative grade to investment grade), but they are not included in either our sample or in the totals above.

occurring in 2000 and 2001 compared with earlier and later years. The manufactured housing sector accounted for a disproportionate share of ABS credit rating downgrades between 1997 and 2003.

A majority of the events involve a change in the composite rating of only one notch. However, it should be noted that for securities that are rated by both Moody's and S&P, these single-notch changes in the composite rating could involve a change of as much as three notches in one agency's rating, if the other agency's rating were unchanged. Because securities are deleted from the index if they drop below investment grade, the impact on pricing of becoming a "fallen angel" cannot be incorporated into the study from the Merrill Lynch file alone, which creates a potential for a "survivorship" bias in our results from the consequent censoring of the sample. To address this problem, we extracted the latest S&P and Moody's ratings given for each ABS that had been deleted from the index during the sample period from Bloomberg, whenever we were able to match it either by the CUSIP identifier, or by ticker, series and class. By this means, we were able to identify 73 securities that were deleted from the index because they had been downgraded to speculative grade, and we include them in our sample for the contemporaneous tests by measuring pricing changes to their last day in the index. In contrast, we only found 13 examples of "rising devils", which had the converse experience of an upgrade to investment grade. No pricing data were available for these ABS until the month after they were raised to investment grade, so these upgrades could not be included in our sample.

ESTIMATION AND RESULTS

The first two columns in Table 3 show our most basic results for the 819 downgrade events and 473 upgrade events – the average returns on the corresponding ABS in the month of the rating change. These figures are expressed as excess returns by subtracting the same month's return on the whole ABS index, thus implicitly controlling for general market movements. An advantage of casting the results in terms of returns, rather than changes in yield spreads, is that we are able to include rating events for floating-rate securities. On average, downgrades are accompanied by a negative return on the affected ABS of nearly three percentage points, a larger impact than found by Hand *et al* (1992) for their earlier

Table 3 Contemporaneous excess return reactions to credit rating changes (%)

	Security downgrades	Security upgrades	Issuer downgrades	Issuer upgrades
Mean excess return	−2.87	−0.00	−1.57	−0.02
	(0.00)	(0.95)	(0.00)	(0.77)
Median	−0.09	0.03	−0.06	0.03
% Positive	39.8%	57.3%	41.5%	57.6%
	(0.00)	(0.00)	(0.00)	(0.00)
Observations	819	473	615	436

Note: Excess return is the security's total return less the full index's total return for each month. *p*-values appear in parentheses in the "Mean excess return" row for *t*-tests of the null hypothesis that the coefficient is zero. In the "% Positive" row, *p*-values appear in parentheses for likelihood ratio tests of the null hypothesis that the coefficient is 50%.

sample of rating announcements for US corporate bonds. The stronger reaction is consistent with a somewhat greater reliance by ABS investors on rating agencies as a source of credit information. Nevertheless, our results are a long way from suggesting that ABS trading decisions depend on ratings alone; almost 40% of our downgraded ABS had positive excess returns during the event month, implying either that market participants are dismissing the rating decision or that the information conveyed by the downgrade had already been incorporated into market prices.

The third column shows results for downgrades at the issuer level. In months in which multiple classes of the same ABS deal have been downgraded, we construct a value-weighted excess return for the affected tranches. Elimination of multiple downgrades among the same ABS series reduces the sample size from 819 to 615, but it avoids double-counting reactions to rating agency judgements about deterioration in a given ABS portfolio, the principal cause of credit rating downgrades. Accordingly, we use this framework to confirm with a *t*-test that the mean excess return associated with ABS downgrades is significantly different from zero. The magnitude of the mean excess downgrade return is smaller for issuer-level downgrades, because the weighting is generally reduced for junior tranches, which tend to have particularly negative price reactions.

Table 4 Contemporaneous yield spread reactions to credit rating changes (basis points)

	All downgrades	Downgrades within investment grade	Fallen angels	All upgrades
Mean yield spread reaction	159 (0.00)	79 (0.00)	733 (0.00)	−5 (0.13)
1st quartile	0	−1	29	−11
Median	19	15	421	−1
3rd quartile	187	134	729	8
Observations	564	495	69	288

Note: *p*-values appear in parentheses for *t*-tests of the null hypothesis that the coefficient is zero.

In contrast, the estimated mean effect of ABS upgrades is virtually zero, although the 57% with pricing reactions in the expected positive direction *is* statistically distinguishable from the 50% probability that would be implicit if ratings had no relevance at all. Accordingly, the median contemporaneous excess return of the ABS upgrades is slightly above zero. Prior event studies with bond ratings have also found weaker results for upgrades. There are at least two possible explanations for this asymmetry. First, the immediate implications for credit risk seem to be somewhat greater for downgrades than for upgrades, because a one-notch difference in bond ratings has greater consequences for both default rates and for market spreads as the rating becomes lower, especially for shorter maturities. The asymmetric effect of this convexity is bolstered in our sample by the fact that multi-notch changes are less common for upgrades and by the relatively short maturity of many of the securities in our sample. Second, in a study of conditional effects in the dynamics of Moody's bond ratings, Hamilton and Cantor (2004) found more serial correlation in downgrades than in upgrades. Hu and Cantor (2003) reported even stronger asymmetry in serial correlation in Moody's structured finance ratings.

To facilitate comparisons with some of the more recent literature on bond ratings, Table 4 reconfigures our event study in terms of changes in the yield spreads over the US Treasury curve. Because spreads on the ABS in our index are only available for the fixed-rate securities, the sample size is somewhat reduced, but the results are nevertheless quite striking. The mean reaction to downgrades is a widening of spreads by 159 basis points in the event month. At first glance, this figure seems at odds with an average excess return of less than 3%, but the apparent conflict is explained by the short duration of most ABS – a median of approximately two years. Two other features of yield-spread reactions to downgrades are worthy of note. First, the median spread change is only 19 basis points, so that the much higher mean change reflects a distinctly skewed distribution, with roughly half of the spread changes near zero, but many others quite large. Second, spreads widen much more (an average of 733 basis points) for fallen angels. Covitz and Harrison (2003), who studied the monthly changes in the composite credit ratings of US corporate bonds over a similar sample period, also report median yield-spread reactions to downgrades that are a lot stronger for fallen angels than for bonds that remained at investment grade. However, they found smaller median reactions than us for both types of downgrade at a one-month event horizon. For corporate bonds upgrades within investment grade, Covitz and Harrison found a median change of −1 basis point, identical to our result for ABS upgrades.

We now explore how various features of ABS affect their sensitivity to credit ratings. Table 5 shows the outcomes of regressions of excess returns in the month of an upgrade or downgrade versus the characteristics of the security, the issuer and the rating event. With an adjusted R^2 of 38%, we are much more successful in explaining the variation in downgrade effects than in accounting for reactions to upgrades, where the adjusted R^2 is only 13%. Downgrade returns are more negative and upgrade returns are more positive for ABS with longer durations, and this probably reflects the combination of two effects. First, an evolutionary development in credit quality is likely to have stronger implications for the risk of loss for securities for which scheduled principal repayment is further into the future. Second, for a given change in the yield spread, the effect on the contemporaneous return will increase directly with the duration of the ABS.

The level of the rating before and after the change also affects the contemporaneous return. Not surprisingly, downgrade returns are more negative and upgrade returns are more positive for sharper changes in agency opinion, as reflected in the number of notches by

Table 5 Determinants of contemporaneous excess returns reactions to credit rating changes

	Security downgrades		Security upgrades	
Intercept	−2.87 (0.00)	−2.86 (0.00)	−0.00 (0.95)	−0.05 (0.67)
Duration		−1.05 (0.00)		0.20 (0.01)
Initial rating		0.35 (0.02)		0.07 (0.21)
Log face value		0.14 (0.77)		−0.34 (0.19)
Number of rating notches changed		−0.70 (0.00)		0.28 (0.01)
Fallen angel		−9.95 (0.00)		
Manufactured housing		0.14 (0.92)		0.73 (0.33)
Home equity		3.64 (0.03)		0.93 (0.20)
Autos		−0.26 (0.86)		1.18 (0.13)
Credit cards		0.27 (0.85)		1.87 (0.02)
Utilities		−1.21 (0.87)		2.52 (0.05)
Time trend (monthly)		−0.07 (0.00)		0.04 (0.00)
Adjusted R^2		0.38		0.13
Observations	819	620	473	308

Note: The variables on the right-hand side are measured as deviations from the sample mean. Excess return is the security's total return less the full index's total return for each month. *p*-values appear in parentheses for *t*-tests of the null hypothesis that the coefficient is zero.

which the composite rating is modified. In addition, downgrade returns are less negative when the initial rating is higher, reflecting the fact that default is still a relatively remote possibility. Third, fallen angels have much larger negative downgrade returns than we see for rating reductions within the investment-grade range. This also arises in event studies of bond ratings, and Steiner and Heinke (2001) suggested that the use of credit ratings in financial regulation has conferred an artificial importance to the investment-grade boundary. However, default rates increase sharply as ratings move below investment grade, and speculative-grade defaults also appear to be more cyclically sensitive, so the strong market reaction to fallen angels might be justifiable on the basis of the pure credit risk implications, particularly if the underlying credit deterioration had gone unnoticed by investors before the rating downgrade.

We also control for broad ABS categories by including dummy variables in the regression specification. To some degree, excess return reactions also appear to depend on the type of underlying collateral, although not all of the estimated effects are statistically significant. All else equal, downgrade reactions are much less negative for home equity ABS, perhaps because the underlying assets are backed by relatively stable real estate collateral. Meanwhile, upgrade returns are substantially higher when the underlying portfolio consists of credit card or utility company receivables, which are not typically backed by collateral. Given that ratings are intended to reflect expected loss, irrespective of the nature of the underlying cash flow, these differences in market reactions may in part reflect investors' independent judgements about relative risk.

We also include a time trend in the equations. To the extent that alternative sources of credit information have developed as the ABS market has matured, one might expect the reliance of investors on credit ratings to have diminished over time, but the signs on our estimated coefficients suggest the opposite. On average, downgrade returns were more negative and upgrade returns were more positive later in the sample period.

In recent years, rating agencies have sometimes been criticised for being too slow to recognise changes in the creditworthiness of rated borrowers. If alternative information sources exist, one might then expect prices to change ahead of ratings. Figures 1 and 2 show the average patterns of a total return index around the event month of an ABS that has been downgraded or upgraded, respectively. The excess return on an ABS with an imminent downgrade tends to be negative in the prior two months, and the tests shown in Table 6 reveal that the effect is statistically significant in the second month before the downgrade. However, the extent of anticipation, as gauged by the proportion of the total pricing reaction that occurs

Figure 1 Average monthly ABS returns around the time of credit rating downgrades

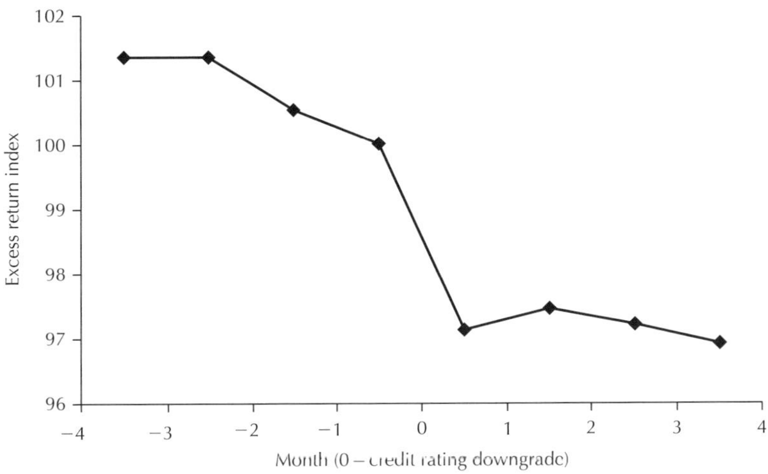

Figure 2 Average monthly ABS returns around the time of credit rating upgrades

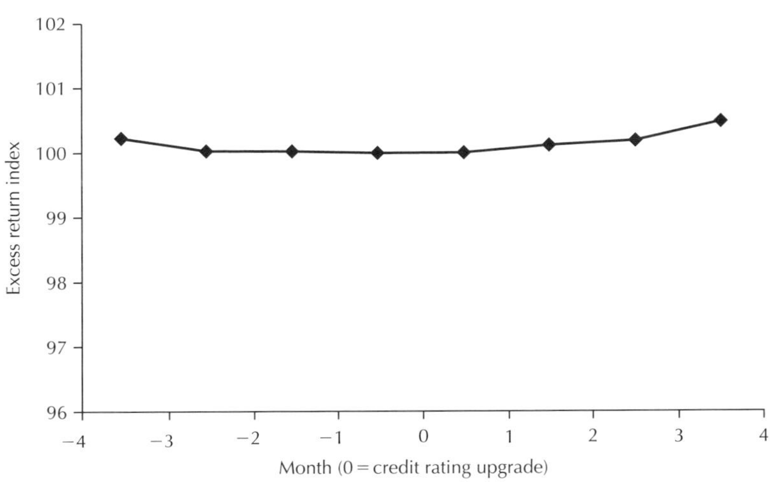

Table 6 Average excess returns in the months near a rating change

	Same month	One month before	Two months before
All downgrades	−2.87	−0.23	−0.83
	(0.00)	(0.16)	(0.00)
Downgrades within investment grade	−1.42	−0.10	−0.65
	(0.00)	(0.33)	(0.00)
Fallen angels	−17.70	−1.53	−2.60
	(0.00)	(0.30)	(0.16)
All upgrades	−0.00	−0.01	0.03
	(0.95)	(0.86)	(0.83)

Note: excess return is the security's total return less the full index's total return for each month. *p*-values appear in parentheses for *t*-tests of the null hypothesis that the coefficient is zero.

before the downgrade, is markedly less than found for corporate bonds by Covitz and Harrison (2003). In contrast, the average total return pattern for upgrades in Figure 2 is puzzlingly flat – before, during and after the upgrade – as if the rating change were completely irrelevant.

The lack of market reaction to rating upgrades raises the question of whether upgraded ABS had already been priced as if they had their future higher ratings, as opposed to these ABS continuing to be priced after the upgrade as if they still had their former lower ratings. To address this issue, we estimate rating-specific yield curves, in which yield to maturity is a locally linear function of duration, using the locally weighted regression method of Cleveland (1979). Figure 3 shows time series of the two-year duration points of several of our estimated yield curves. We estimated separate yield curves for home equity ABS and for manufactured housing ABS, because we noticed that in some periods, yields were significantly higher for these categories than for other types of ABS. Other ABS categories are pooled for the purpose of yield-curve estimation.

For securities about to undergo a ratings change, Table 7 shows the average deviations of their yield at the end of the previous month from each of two yield curves – the curve for their current rating and the curve for the rating they are on the point of obtaining.

Figure 3 Two-year duration yields (December 1996 to December 2003)

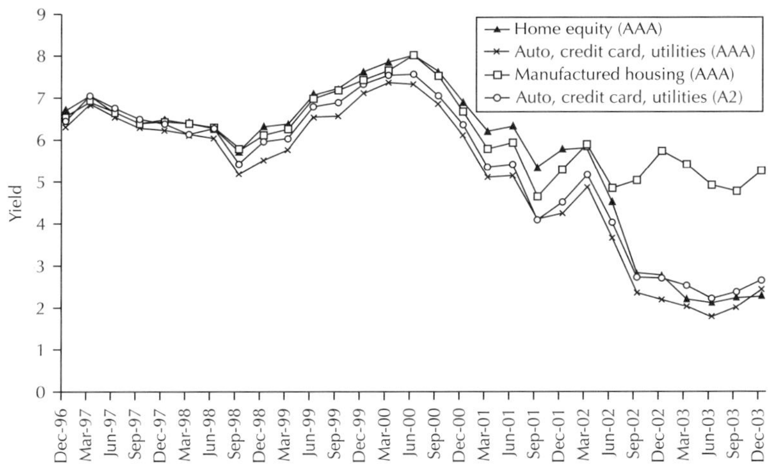

Table 7 Deviations from estimated rating-specific yield curve prior to ratings change (annual percentage points at end of previous month).

	Downgrades		**Upgrades**	
	Prior rating	**Future rating**	**Prior rating**	**Future rating**
Mean deviation (%)	0.18 (0.08)	−1.35 (0.00)	0.22 (0.05)	0.31 (0.01)
Average rating change (number of notches)	−2.18		1.78	
Observations	201		97	

Notes: yield curves fit by locally weighted regression, using a linear local fit (*d*), a tricube weighting function (*W*), two iterations (*t*), and smoothing parameter 0.35 (*f*). See Cleveland (1979) for a discussion of the methodology and parameters. The smoothing parameter was adjusted in cases where there were there were fewer than 15 points with which to estimate the yield curve. Rating categories where there were fewer than five points were excluded. Securities that were upgraded or downgraded were excluded from the yield curve estimates. We estimate separate yield curves for the home equity and manufactured housing collateral types. This is because, especially in later years, these two collateral types tend to systematically differ from the rest of our sample. *p*-values appear in parentheses for *t*-tests of the null hypothesis that the coefficient is zero.

Note that the samples are constrained to ABS for which there were at least five points available to estimate each of the two requisite yield curves, even after securities on the cusp of a ratings change were excluded from the curve fitting. For imminent downgrades, the typical ABS yield stood slightly above their current yield curves and 1.35 percentage points below their future curves, which is consistent with their credit quality being perceived by market participants as in line with their old rating. This result helps to explain the sizable average contemporaneous market reaction to downgrades. In contrast, our estimated deviations for imminent upgrades are somewhat puzzling. On average, the pre-event ABS yield for an imminent upgrade stood 22 basis points above the yield curve applicable to its current rating, which seems to suggest that the market was concerned about a possible downgrade rather than expecting an upgrade.

CONCLUDING REMARKS

In summary, we find that on average, rating downgrades are accompanied by negative returns and widening spreads, with stronger effects than those that have been reported in prior research on corporate and sovereign bond ratings. The sharp increases in yield spreads that we see for downgrades to speculative grade stand out in particular. We also find that a smaller fraction of the negative downgrade return for ABS occurs ahead of the rating action than has been reported for corporate bond downgrades. Taken together, these results suggest that ABS market participants appear to rely somewhat more on rating agencies as a source of *negative* credit news. Nevertheless, because ABS rating downgrades are relatively rare events, their effects account for only a small fraction of the variance of returns. Furthermore, about 40% of the time downgrade returns are not even negative for ABS. In contrast to our results on downgrades, on average, market reactions to ABS rating upgrades are virtually zero. These results imply even greater asymmetry in the value-relevance of ABS rating changes than has been found in the event studies of changes in bond ratings.

It is worth noting that our discussion up to now has been based on an implicit assumption that ABS pricing is informationally efficient. It is at least conceivable that some of the asymmetries we discover in event-month returns arise as the market either over-reacts or under-reacts to certain types of rating changes because of behavioural biases. If so, the pricing error would eventually be corrected in future periods, leading to abnormal excess returns. Our examination of average returns around rating changes does not reveal any systematic pattern in the first three months after the event, but the requisite pricing correction, if any, might occur later – an issue we leave for future research.

1 See Creighton *et al* (2004) for Australian evidence, Steiner and Henke's (2001) work on Eurobonds, and Cantor and Packer (1996) and Brooks *et al* (2004) for the effects of sovereign rating changes. One interesting nuance is reported in a study by Elayan *et al* (2003) of the New Zealand market, where rating changes have a weaker impact on firms that are cross-listed in the United States and thus are covered by a greater number of equity analysts.

2 Although the pattern of rarer but larger rating changes may well arise from differences in the underlying credit risk dynamics, an alternative explanation is the relatively infrequent monitoring by the rating agencies. In our empirical analysis, we encountered a number of examples of simultaneous rating changes for a number of securities of a similar type, also consistent with an only sporadic review of ABS ratings.

3 The CUSIP® Service Bureau, operated by Standard & Poor's for the American Bankers Association, exists for the primary purpose of uniquely identifying issuers of securities and other financial instruments within a standard nine-character framework, and disseminating this information to the financial marketplace.

4 In a few cases, rating changes implied by the rating field in the Merrill Lynch files seemed implausible, so we excluded them from our sample. In a handful of cases, the files included a speculative-grade rating (which, if correct, should have caused the security to be excluded from the index). We checked these ratings against other sources and concluded that these speculative-grade ratings were data recording errors. Second, in a number of cases, there was a multi-notch rating change that was reversed the following month. For these, we assumed that the rating had probably not changed at all.

REFERENCES

Brooks, R., R. Faff, D. Hillier, and J. Hillier, 2004, "The National Market Impact of Sovereign Rating Changes", *Journal of Banking and Finance*, pp. 223–50, January.

Campbell, J., and G. Taksler, 2003, "Equity Volatility and Corporate Bond Yields", *Journal of Finance*, pp. 2321–49, December.

Cantor, R., and F. Packer, 1996, "Determinants and Impact of Sovereign Credit Ratings", *Federal Reserve Bank of New York Economic Policy Review*, pp. 37–53, October.

Carron, A., P. Dhrymes, and T. Beloreshki, 2003, "Credit Ratings for Structured Products", NERA Economic Consulting Report, 6 November.

Clark, A., et al, 2003, "Credit Risk Transfer", report submitted by a Working Group established by the Committee on the Global Financial System, Bank for International Settlements, January.

Cleveland, W., 1979, "Robust Locally Weighted Regression and Smoothing Scatter Plots", *Journal of the American Statistical Association*, pp. 829–36, December.

Covitz, D., and P. Harrison, 2003, "Testing Conflicts of Interest at Bond Rating Agencies with Market Anticipation: Evidence that Reputation Incentives Dominate", *Finance and Economics Discussion Series* paper 2003–68, Federal Reserve Board, December.

Creighton, A., L. Gower, and A. Richards, 2004, "The Impact of Rating Changes in Australian Financial Markets", Research Discussion Paper 2004–02, Reserve Bank of Australia, March.

Elayan, F., W. H. Hsu, and T. Meyer, 2003, "The Informational Content of Credit Rating Announcements for Share Prices in a Small Market", *Journal of Economics and Finance,* pp. 337–56, Fall.

Estrella, A., *et al*, 2000, "Credit Ratings and Complementary Sources of Credit Quality Information", Basel Committee Working Paper No 3, Bank for International Settlements, August.

Ferri, G., L. -G. Liu, and J. Stiglitz, 1999, "The Procyclical Role of Rating Agencies: Evidence from the East Asian Crisis", *Economic Notes*, pp. 335–55, November.

Hamilton, D., and R. Cantor, 2004, "Rating Transitions and Defaults Conditional on Watchlist, Outlook, and Rating History", Moody's Investors Service Special Comment, February.

Hand, J., R. Holthausen, and R. Leftwich, 1992, "The Effect of Bond Rating Agency Announcements on Bond and Stock Prices", *Journal of Finance*, pp. 733–52, June.

Hu, J., and R. Cantor, 2003, "Structured Finance Rating Transitions: 1983–2002 – Comparisons with Corporate Ratings and Across Sectors", Moody's Investors Service Special Comment, January.

Hu, J., *et al*, 2003, "Payment Defaults and Material Impairments of US Structured Finance Securities: 1993–2002", Moody's Investors Service Special Comment, December.

Hu, J., *et al*, 2004, "Structured Finance Rating Transitions: 1983–2003 – Ratings Remain Volatile in 2003 but Downgrade-to-Upgrade Ratio Falls Sharply", Moody's Investors Service Special Comment, February.

Reisen, H., and J. von Maltzan, 1999, "Boom and Bust and Sovereign Ratings", *International Finance*, pp. 273–93, July.

Steiner, M., and V. Heinke, 2001, "Event Study Concerning International Bond Price Effects of Credit Rating Actions", *International Journal of Finance and Economics*, pp. 139–57, April.

United States Securities and Exchange Commission, 2003, "Report on the Role and Function of Credit Rating Agencies in the Operation of the Securities Markets", January.

Section 3

Risk Management

8

A Survey of CDOs and Their Use in Bank Balance Sheet Management

Domenico Picone

Royal Bank of Scotland

This chapter explores the market of collaterised debt obligations (CDOs) and synthetic CDOs and their use in bank balance sheet management. We first review the different types of CDOs that are used in capital markets and their economic rationales and then discuss the growth in synthetic CDOs under structural and balance sheet management perspectives. Following this, we analyse the CDO equity piece and see how it can be used in portfolio management. The last section is dedicated to the table of idealised losses of Moody's.

THE CDO STRUCTURE

A CDO is a special purpose company or vehicle (SPV), complete with assets, liabilities and a manager. Typically, the CDO's assets consist of a diversified portfolio of illiquid and defaultable assets such as high yield bonds (CBOs) or bank leverage loans (CLOs).[1]

We have set up a typical CDO structure in Figure 1. The assets, also called the collateral portfolio, are transferred to the SPV that funds the purchase, from cash proceeds of the notes it has issued.

The CDO structure allocates interest income and principal repayment from a pool of different debt instruments to a prioritised collection of securities notes called tranches. Senior notes are paid before mezzanine and lower rated notes. Any residual cash-flow is paid to the equity investors. This makes the senior notes significantly less risky than the collateral.

On every payment date, the equity investors receive cash-distributions after the scheduled payments and other costs have

Figure 1 CDO diagram

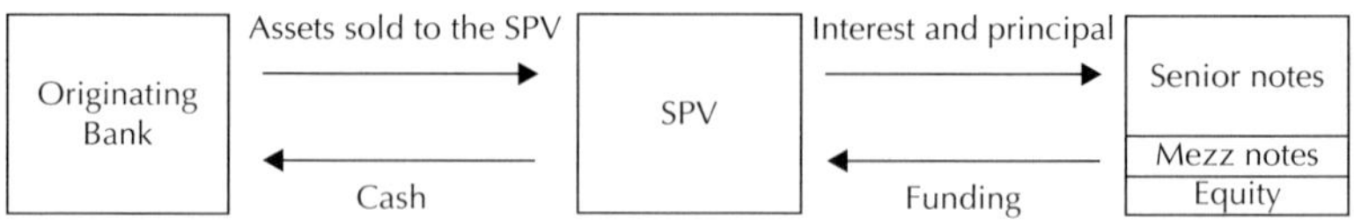

been paid off. The equity is also called the "first-loss" position in the collateral portfolio. This is because it is exposed to the risk of the first pound loss in the portfolio.

The CDO rating is based on its ability to service the notes, with the cashflows generated by the collateral portfolio. The service of the notes depends on the diversification and quality of the collateral, subordination and structural protection.

As we move down the CDO's capital structure, the level of risk increases. The equity investors bear the highest risk, and their gain lies in the residual cash, also called excess spread between the interest income from the assets sold to the SPV, and the interests due to the notes, plus any non-interest costs and losses.

The equity investors also have the option to call the CDO notes after the end of the non-call period, which in most cases lasts three to five years. In this case, the assets are liquidated and the proceeds are used to pay down the notes and interests due.

The typical CDO has a ramp-up period, a reinvestment period and an amortising period. During the ramp-up period the collateral portfolio is formed. In the reinvestment period, all the proceeds received from the matured assets are promptly reinvested in new assets. The amortising period is the terminal phase, when the notes are repaid in order of seniority using the proceeds from the collateral portfolio.

In the ramp-up period, there is the risk of negative carry, which is the condition in which the cost of borrowing money exceeds the return obtained from it. This is because, before the CDO is fully ramped-up, the proceeds received from issuing the notes, are invested in highly rated and secured bonds, such as US Government Bonds and Pfandbriefe, with very little return.[2]

The above problem is rectified in synthetic CDOs, since the notes issued represent only a part of the collateral portfolio.[3]

Figure 2 CDO capital structure

Classes	% of the capital structure
A Moody's/S&P rating: Aaa/AAA Coupon: Libor + 45 bp	69%
B Moody's/S&P rating: A2/A Coupon: Libor+145 bp	15%
C Moody's/S&P rating: Baa2/BBB Coupon: Libor+245 bp	8%
D Moody's/S&P rating: Ba3/NR Coupon: Libor+645 bp	4%
Equity not rated expected return: 15%–25%	4%

Figure 2 displays an example capital structure, where the high yield bonds collateralise CDO liabilities.

ARBITRAGE AND BALANCE SHEET CDOs

Most CDOs can be placed into one of two main groups: arbitrage and balance sheet transactions. Figure 3 shows the conceptual breakdown between the two structures.

A cashflow CDO is one where the collateral portfolio is not actively traded by the CDO manager.[4] The CDO performance depends on whether the notes are fully repaid and there are no interest payment delays. Losses are the main source of risk, not the volatility of the market value of the collateral portfolio.

A market value CDO is one where the performance of the CDO notes is primarily a mark-to-market performance, ie, all securities in the collateral are marked to market with high frequency.

In the case that the collateral market value drops below a certain value, called the market value trigger, the CDO manager is obliged to pay the CDO notes by selling all of the assets of the collateral

Figure 3 CDO structure

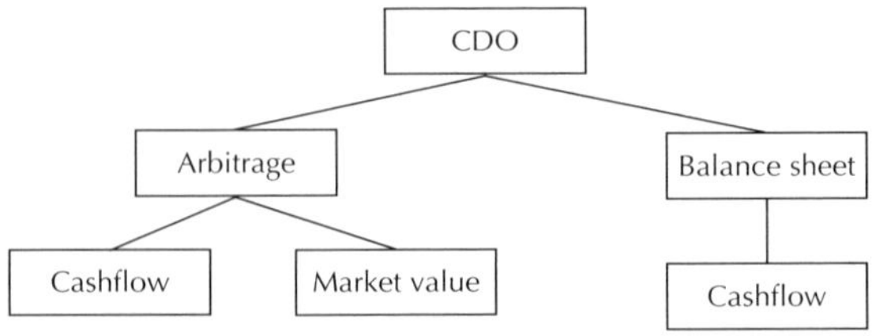

Source: Morgan Stanley (Schorin and Weinreich, 2001)

portfolio. The market value trigger is set to create a reserve between the market value of the collateral portfolio and the par values of the CDO notes. Because the collateral of market value CDOs is constantly traded, the CDO performance depends upon the CDO manager, who will buy and sell the collateral assets. As part of normal due diligence, a potential market value CDO investor needs to evaluate the ability of the manager, the institutional structure around him, and the suitability of the management style to a leveraged investment vehicle.

Balance sheet cashflow CDOs are structures for the purpose of regulatory capital relief, where the assets of the collateral portfolio are lower yield debt instruments. The regulatory capital relief reduces funding costs or increases return on equity, by selling the assets that take too much regulatory capital to the SPV, and thus removing them from the originator's balance sheet.

These transactions rely on the quality of the collateral that is made of guaranteed bank loans with a very high recovery rate.[5] In this case the CDO takes the name of collateralised loan obligations (CLOs).

The relatively low coupon of these assets results in a smaller excess spread than the arbitrage CDOs.[6] Given their relative superior credit quality when compared with assets used in arbitrage CDOs, they require less subordination.[7]

The size of a typical balance sheet CLO is generally larger than an arbitrage CDO, as the transaction must have an impact on the return on regulatory capital (RORC) of the originating bank looking for capital relief. Because the collateral is represented by bank loans with an opaque market value, CLOs are only in the form of balance sheet cashflows.

More recently, active credit portfolio management has been cited as another reason behind CLOs. Through active credit portfolio management, banks are able to measure the risk-adjusted efficiency of their credit portfolio.[8] The CLO is now used as the tool for a bank to redeploy freed-up resources in higher yield and better diversified instruments.

Market value-arbitrage CDOs go through a very extensive trading by the CDO manager, which is necessary to exploit perceived price appreciations. This type of CDO relies on the market value of the collateral portfolio, which is monitored on a daily basis. Every security traded in capital markets with a liquid market price can be included in this type of CDO. The important aspect is the collateral manager's capacity to generate a high total rate of return. In these CDOs, the CDO manager has a great deal of flexibility in terms of the assets included in the deal. They can also increase or decrease the funding amount, which changes the leverage of the structure, during the reinvestment period.

In cashflow arbitrage CDOs, the collateral assets have been purchased at market price and are negotiable instruments, primarily bonds. However, syndicated loans, which are usually tradable, have been included in past transactions. In the majority of the cases, the collateral assets have already been used in a previous CDO, and by merging the collateral with a more diversified pool, or by simply re-tranching the original notes, it is possible to extract an arbitrage benefit. Unlike market value arbitrage CDOs, the collateral assets are not traded very frequently.

The aim of arbitrage CDOs is to capture the arbitrage opportunity that exists in the credit-spread differential, between the high yield collateral and the highly rated notes.[9] Most arbitrage CDOs are private deals, which are small and the number of assets included in the collateral portfolio is very limited compared with the cashflow type.

CREDIT ENHANCEMENT

Credit enhancement is a way to protect senior note and mezzanine note investors from quality deterioration of the collateral portfolio. It is ensured through prioritisation of investor claims, also known as subordination, over-collateralisation and excess spread.

Subordination

The principal repayment and the interest income of the collateral portfolio are generally distributed sequentially to the note investors in the order of their seniority, *via* the principal waterfall and the interest waterfall.

The interest waterfall specifies the order in which interest income is paid in the CDO. The fees, the hedge costs such as interest rate swap payments, are paid before the interest due to the senior notes and the interest due to the mezzanine notes. Any additional income is called extra spread and is paid to the equity investors.

The interest waterfall is subject to changes in cases where certain triggers are breached.[10] For example, a trigger can be defined in such a way that no more than a certain percentage of the par value of the collateral portfolio is rated below BBB. In these instances, the interest proceeds that would normally go to pay the interest due to the mezzanine notes are used to pay down (turbo or accelerate) the senior notes. This form of early amortisation ensures that the investors of the senior notes are insured against further reductions in the value of the collateral portfolio due to rising defaults or downgrades.

The principal waterfall is the distribution of the principal repayment. The senior notes are at the top. The mezzanine notes are repaid as soon as the senior notes are fully redeemed. In this way, the performance of the mezzanine notes is subordinated to the good performance of senior notes.

Over-collateralisation

Over-collateralisation (OC) provides further protection to the senior notes by imposing two quality tests on the collateral portfolio: the par value test and the interest coverage test.

The par value test requires that the collateral portfolio, A, is sufficient to repay the various notes at any future date and until the notes are redeemed. For example, a par value test may be applied on the senior note, L_S, so that they are never greater than a percentage, β, of the collateral portfolio minus defaults. In this case, it is defined as

$$[A_t - \text{defaults}_t] - \beta - L_{S,t} > 0 \quad \text{with } 0 < \beta \leq 1 \tag{1}$$

The par value test is also applicable to the mezzanine note, L_M. In this case, the percentage is selected at a lower rate, and is defined as

$$[A_t - \text{defaults}_t - L_{S,t}]\alpha - L_{M,t} > 0 \quad \text{with } 0 < \alpha < \beta \leq 1 \tag{2}$$

The interest coverage test guarantees that all expenses and interests due on the liability side are fully covered by the interest proceeds from the collateral portfolio.[11] We denote the interests earned on the collateral assets by I_A, the expenses by Ex and the interests on the notes by I_L, and we write the test as

$$I_A - Ex - I_L \geq 0 \tag{3}$$

If either test is breached, the interest waterfall is changed, and the repayment of the senior notes (or mezzanine notes) is accelerated.

Excess spread

The excess spread is what is left in the interest waterfall after paying all expenses and the interests due to the notes. Before the excess spread is distributed to the equity investors, it is used to cover losses in the collateral portfolio. In this way, it represents the first layer of credit protection of the note investors.

In a real life CDO, it is very difficult to estimate the excess spread that can be used to protect the senior notes and be returned to the equity investors. For example, if the CDO suffers a large number of defaults in the last stage of the transaction and the par value test is breached so that the interest waterfall is changed to accelerate the repayment of the senior notes with the extra spread, the equity investors have had plenty of time to collect excess spread and achieve a remarkable return. In contrast, if the CDO suffers a large number of defaults in the early days of the transaction, the equity investors would bear the first loss and would not collect any excess spread, because it would be used to accelerate the senior notes.

CREDIT ENHANCEMENT IN MARKET VALUE CDOs

Market value CDOs have three further forms of credit enhancement: advance rates, the market value over-collateralisation test, and the minimum net worth test.

The advance rate is the maximum percentage of the collateral portfolio market value that can be used to issue senior and mezzanine notes. Rating agencies assign the collateral advance rate according to the historic volatility of the collateral return and on the liquidity of its market price. Assets with a higher return volatility and lower liquidity are given lower advance rates.

Table 1 shows the advance rates that Fitch would apply to different types of assets as collateral. For example, when a portfolio of certificate of deposits (CD) or commercial paper (CP) is used as the collateral of a note rated AA, Fitch allows the use of only 95% of the CD and CP market value. In this instance, 5% of the market value of the CD and CP is the equity that the originating bank retains. The advance rate of CD and CP would rise to 100% where the note is rated BB.

In market value CDOs, the par value OC test is called the market value OC test and is applied on the market value of the collateral portfolio, MVA_t, as follows

$$[MVA_t - defaults_t]\beta - L_{S,t} > 0 \quad \text{with } 0 < \beta \leq 1 \tag{4}$$

To illustrate how the advance rate and the market value OC tests work in practice, we introduce a simple example with the collateral portfolio and the liability structure of Table 2.

In Table 3, we apply the AA advance rates of Table 1 to each asset of the collateral portfolio of Table 2. In column 5, we have calculated the senior advance amounts of each asset, by multiplying the AA advance rates (from Table 1) by the asset market values of column 2 of Table 2. Their sum gives the total advance amount of £402.

To prepare the AA OC test, we take the difference between the total advance amount of £402 (in Table 3) and the senior note face value of £375 (in Table 2). The difference of £27 million is the borrowing amount surplus and is the maximum change in the collateral market value that the CDO can sustain before breaching the AA market value OC test.

A collateral manager must ensure that the market value tests are not violated. A breach of the market value OC test is quite serious and, when it happens, the collateral manager must remedy it within a cure period that is usually between two to 10 business days.

Table 1 Fitch's advance rates

Asset category	AA (%)	A (%)	BBB (%)	BB (%)	B (%)
Cash and Equivalents	100	100	100	100	100
CD and CP	95	95	95	100	100
Senior Secured Bank Loans	85	90	91	93	96
BB-High Yield Debt	71	80	87	90	92
<BB-High Yield Debt	69	75	85	87	89
Convertible Bonds	64	70	81	85	87
Convertible Preferred Stock	59	65	77	83	86
Mezzanine Debt, Distressed, Emerging Market	55	60	73	80	85
Equity, Illiquid Debt	40	50	73	80	85

Source: Fitch

Table 2 Market value CDO

Collateral			Notes			
Assets	**Market value (euro)**	**%**	**Tranche**	**Rating**	**Face value (euro)**	**%**
CD and CP	£230	46	Senior Notes	AA	£375	75
BB-High Yield Debt	£225	45	Mezz. Notes	BBB	£50	10
Convertible Bonds	£10	2	Junior Notes	B	£25	5
Mezz. Debt	£25	5	Equity	NR	£50	10
Equity	£10	2				
Total	£500	100	Total		£500	100

Table 3 Market value OC test

Collateral				
Assets	**Market value (euro)**	**%**	**AA advance Rates**	**Sr. Advance amounts**
CD and CP	£230	46	95	£219
BB-High Yield Debt	£225	45	71	£160
Convertible Bonds	£10	2	64	£6
Mezz. Debt	£25	5	55	£14
Equity	£10	2	40	£4
Total	£500	100	Total advance amount	£402
			Senior notes	£375
			Borrowing amount surplus	£27

There are usually two options:

- to sell one or more assets with lower advance rates and buy one or more assets with higher advance rates; or
- to sell one or more assets with lower advance rates and repay some or a portion of the notes, starting from the most senior notes, until the OC test is in compliance.

The first action is preferred when the OC test is slightly out of compliance. The second is a drastic cure.

The minimum net worth test is designed to offer further credit protection to the senior notes. This is achieved by imposing that the collateral market value, MVA_t, minus the par value of all notes is never lower than the equity face value multiplied by a percentage, δ, indicated by the rating agency (see Yvonne and Gluck (1998, p. 12))

$$[MVA_t - L_{S,t} - L_{M,t} - L_{J,t}]\delta - V \geq 0 \quad \text{with } 0 < \delta \leq 1 \qquad (5)$$

In cases where the test is breached, the manager has a cure period to bring the CDO into compliance, by either:

- redeeming part or all of the senior notes; or
- generating enough capital gains by selling some assets.

The latter is preferable for the equity investors since the manager would not de-leverage the deal.

If the collateral manager cannot comply with the market value OC test or the minimum net worth test, the notes investors have the legal power to take control of the CDO and liquidate the collateral portfolio.[12]

THE CDO MANAGER

The manager of the CDO is responsible for the credit performance of the collateral portfolio and for ensuring that the transaction meets the diversification, quality and structural guidelines specified by the rating agencies. In return for managing the collateral portfolio, the manager receives a fee, typically divided into base and incentive components.

During the reinvestment period, the CDO manager continuously evaluates the state of the collateral portfolio and of the overall market. They trade out positions at risk for credit deterioration and take advantage of appreciation opportunities.

The key to a successful market value CDO is the manager's ability to generate high returns through research, market knowledge and trading ability. Different managers stress different strategies. For example, an insurance company may depend on its portfolio risk management system, a mutual fund group may use its size and market knowledge, and a private equity sponsor may rely on its knowledge of leveraged companies.

The market value CDO is typically only accessible to managers who have established track records and who have demonstrated a high level of organisational commitment to the CDO business.

Today, successful CDO management franchises are found in a variety of asset management organisations, including mutual fund groups, insurance companies, banks, private equity firms and hedge funds.

In recent CDOs, the collateral manager has had the opportunity to use credit default swaps (CDSs) to hedge positions or lock profits, which can then be used to provide a further credit enhancement to the transaction. Where the manager purchases protection without having exposure, these transactions are called *naked short bucket transactions*. This new facility combines elements of a cash-flow arbitrage CDO with elements of a synthetic CDO and further protects the portfolio against credit deterioration.

In more general terms, the collateral manager can enter into short CDSs to buy protection and hedge its credit exposure to the obligors under cash obligations, total return swaps and other CDSs.

The only condition to enter into short CDSs is to have sufficient excess spread available to pay the upfront premium. If, in subsequent periods, there is no longer sufficient excess spread, the manager will close out the trade by entering into offsetting CDSs.

CDSs give extra flexibility to a manager: if a sector is perceived as too risky, rather than simply selling assets, they can close out positions by buying credit protection.

THE MOTIVATIONS FOR CDOs

The main motivations for CDOs are market price inefficiency, funding costs and regulatory capital relief.

Market price inefficiency

CDOs make most economic sense for collateral portfolios in markets where there is limited information (inefficient) with the possibility of high-risk-adjusted returns through active management. Defaultable assets, such as the debt of leveraged corporations, are often difficult to analyse and value, thus limiting their potential investor base and creating a gap in the economy between the demand and supply of risky finance. As a result, corporate debts are relatively illiquid in the secondary market. The CDO structure addresses this market inefficiency by bringing a specialised manager to the transaction and allocating much of the credit risk and liquidity risk to the equity class.

The CDO acts as a cushion and hedges the collateral portfolio from defaults (in a cashflow CDO) and from the direct impact of mark-to-market changes in the value of the collateral (in a market value CDO).

Funding cost

In the case where the main motivation is funding cost, which is the interest paid on the notes, the originating bank would try to reduce the funding costs by minimising the size of the subordinated notes (mezzanine notes and the equity piece).

Funding can be an issue for banks whose rating has declined to a level where funding from other sources is expensive. The advantage of funding through a CDO is that the size of the subordinated notes, and so the funding cost, depends on the quality of the collateral portfolio. To improve it, the originating bank would also fund the cash collateral account (CCA), which is a cash deposit that reinforces the credit protection by creating another layer of protection before the equity piece (usually in the range of 1% of the collateral portfolio).

Regulatory capital

Regulatory capital relief is another important motivation for issuing CDOs. Under the BIS rules, loans require regulatory capital, RC, of the size of 8% of the risk weighted assets, RW_{Loan}, of 100%.[13]

In Figure 4, we have prepared an example to outline the originating bank regulatory capital before and after the CDO: in the left-hand box we have a portfolio of loans before they are transferred to the CDO and in the right-hand box we have a portfolio of loans

Figure 4 Regulatory capital relief and RORC

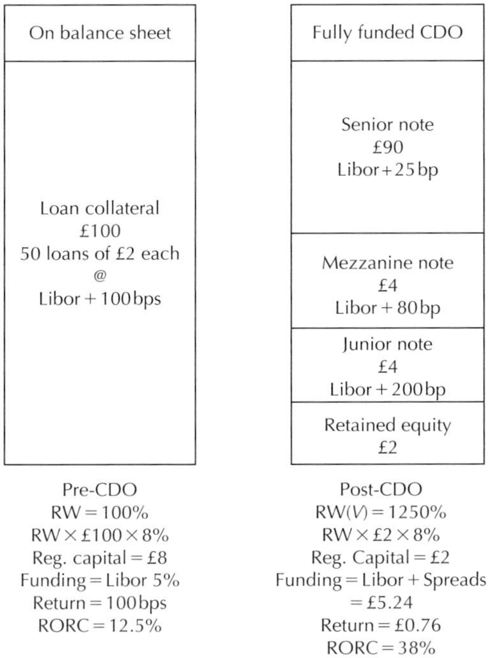

after they have been purchased by the CDO. We assume that the loan collateral, A, is £100, all loans are of the same amount £2 and pay the default free rate $r(t)$, with an assumed libor rate of 5%, plus a spread, s_{Loan}, of 100 bps.

Ignoring any loan eligibility rule for a RW_{Loan} reduction, the regulatory capital charge of the loan portfolio, RCC_{Loan}, before the CDO is

$$\begin{aligned} \text{RCC} &= \text{RW}_{\text{Loan}} \times £100 \times \text{RC} \\ \text{RCC} &= £8 \end{aligned} \tag{6}$$

We also assume that the funding cost of the portfolio is libor (with no spread) and we derive the RORC

$$\begin{aligned} \text{RORC} &= \frac{s_{\text{Loan}}}{\text{RC}_{\text{Loan}}} \\ \text{RORC} &= \frac{100 \text{ bps}}{8\%} = 12.5\% \end{aligned} \tag{7}$$

With the CDO in the right-hand box of Figure 4, the originating bank sells, through senior, mezzanine and junior notes, 98% of the original loan portfolio and only retains 2% on its balance sheet. Under the BIS rules, the only capital charge is on the equity piece, V, which receives full regulatory capital deduction,[14] that is, $RW_V = 1{,}250\%$. With (6) we can calculate the new regulatory capital of the originating bank, which drops from £8 to £2,

$$\begin{aligned} RCC &= RW_V \times £2 \times RC \\ RCC &= £2 \end{aligned} \tag{8}$$

To calculate the RORC, we first compute the funding cost, FC, of the three notes, where L_S, L_M and L_J are, respectively, the notionals of the three notes, and s_S, s_M and s_J, are their spreads over the libor, $r(t)$,

$$\begin{aligned} FC &= L_S(r(t)+s_S)+L_M(r(t)+s_M)+L_J(r(t)+s_J) \\ FC &= £5.24 \end{aligned} \tag{9}$$

After this, we subtract the funding cost in (9) from the interest on the asset, I_{Loan},

$$\begin{aligned} I_{\text{Loan}} - FC &= £6 - £5.24 \\ I_{\text{Loan}} - FC &= £0.76 \end{aligned} \tag{10}$$

(where $I_{\text{Loan}} = (r(t) + s_{\text{Loan}})A$) and divide (10) by (8),

$$RORC = \frac{£0.76}{£2} \Big/ 100\% = 38\% \tag{11}$$

If this transaction had a bigger volume it would have a huge effect on the RORC of the overall bank.[15]

SYNTHETIC CDOs

In the CDOs we have seen so far, assets are actually transferred into the SPV. The process of transferring loans to the SPV requires significant up-front work. A loan-by-loan analysis is necessary to check it complies with the securitisation programme and to verify that there are no special clauses attached to any loan limiting its transfer.

We would like to call these CDOs *conventional*, to distinguish them from a new generation of CDO called *synthetics*.

The term synthetic appeared when the credit risk was transferred into the SPV through a CDS, and the underlying credit ownership of the underlying pool remained in the originating bank's balance sheet.[16] In this instance, the term synthetic was used, since the risk was synthetically transferred out of the originating bank's balance sheet.

With synthetic CDOs, the big advantage is that sensitive client relationship issues arising from loan transfer notification, assignment provisions and other restrictions can be avoided. Client confidentiality is maintained and it also takes less time to complete the transaction.

In the following two sections we review how the CDS can be used to transfer the credit risk from the originating bank to capital markets, with both fully funded and partially funded CDOs.

Fully funded synthetic CDOs

In Figure 5, we illustrate a simplified example of how a fully funded synthetic CDO is structured.

The loan collateral, A, is £100. The SPV issues one note, L_{AAA}, rated as AAA, of £98 that pays the default free rate $r(t)$, assumed to be the libor rate, plus the spread s_{AAA}, and the originator bank, O, retains the equity, V, of £2.

The proceeds of the note are invested in high-quality securities, S, that have risk weight assets of 0%, and return the default free rate, $r(t)$.

In order to transfer the credit risk of the loan collateral, the originating bank enters into a CDS with an OECD bank, referred to the loan collateral A, for a notional amount of £100. With the CDS the originating bank buys credit protection on the loan collateral A, in return for the premium, γ_O. Then, the SPV sells a CDS with reference to the same loan collateral A, to the same OECD bank in return for the premium, γ_{SPV}, where we assume $\gamma_{SPV} = \gamma_O$. At this point, the originating bank has removed the credit risk from its balance sheet and the SPV has acquired the credit risk, both entities via the CDS market. The CDS premium, γ_{SPV}, that the SPV receives, plus the interests on the 0% risk weight assets, $r(t)$, should be large enough to pay the interests on the notes, $r(t)$ plus the spread s_{AAA}. This is the

Figure 5 Fully funded synthetic CDO with CDS with an OECD bank

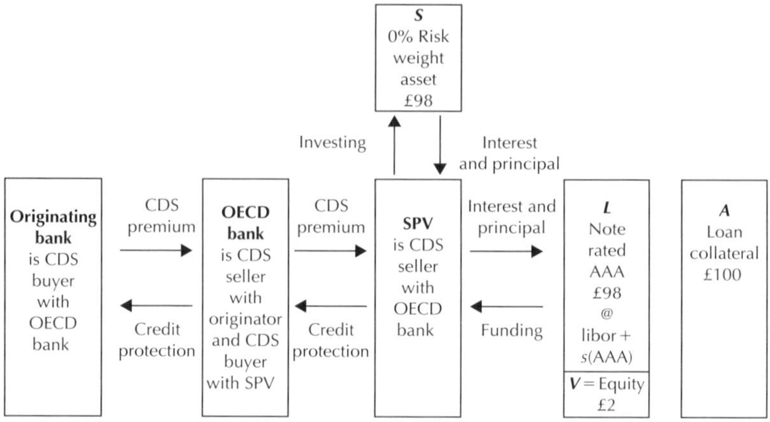

Source: Investing in collateralized debt obligations by Frank J. Fabozzi and Laurie S. Goodman, amended by the author

main condition for the originating bank to go ahead with a fully funded synthetic CDO. We write this condition as

$$\begin{aligned} \gamma_{SPV} A + Sr(t) &> L_{AAA}(r(t) + s_{AAA}) \\ \gamma_{SPV} A + L_{AAA} s_{AAA} &> 0 \qquad \text{with } A > L_{AAA} = S \\ \gamma_{SPV} &> s_{AAA} \frac{L_{AAA}}{A} \end{aligned} \tag{12}$$

Both γ_{SPV} and s_{AAA} are what we like to call market inputs: s_{AAA} is the spread over the default free rate that the AAA investor is willing to earn to hold the AAA note and γ_{SPV} is the credit premium that an OECD bank is willing to earn to take over the credit risk of the loan collateral. As long as the loan collateral A has a greater credit risk than the note L_{AAA}, and $\gamma_{SPV} < s_{AAA}$, the SPV will generate guarantee excess spread that flows back to the originator bank.

We now look at the regulatory capital charge of the originating bank after the fully funded synthetic CDO.

Under the BIS rules, the regulatory capital charge, $RCC_{\%,CDS}$, on the CDS is 1.6%, calculated as the risk weight asset, $RW_{CDS,OECD}$, of 20%, times the regulatory capital, RC, of 8%

$$\begin{aligned} RCC_{\%,CDS} &= RW_{CDS,OECD} \times RC \\ RCC_{\%,CDS} &= 1.6\% \end{aligned} \tag{13}$$

The 1.6% is then multiplied by the notional amount of the CDS of £100, to give the regulatory capital charge, $RCC_{£,CDS}$, of £1.6

$$\begin{aligned} RCC_{£,CDS} &= RCC_{\%,CDS} \times CDS \\ RCC_{\%,CDS} &= £1.6 \end{aligned} \quad (14)$$

The originating bank has retained the equity of £2. The regulatory capital charge of the equity is the risk weight asset, RW_V, of 1,250%, times the regulatory capital, RC, of 8%, times the equity of £2, which is £2,

$$\begin{aligned} RCC_{£,V} &= RW_V \times RC \times V \\ RCC_{£,V} &= £2 \end{aligned} \quad (15)$$

As result, the total capital charge of this transaction is £3.6,

$$RCC_{£,V} + RCC_{£,CDS} = £3.6 \quad (16)$$

With the fully funded synthetic CDO of Figure 5, the originating bank does not achieve a further reduction of regulatory capital when moving from a conventional CDO. Because the CDS is with an OECD bank, there is actually an additional regulatory capital of £1.6.

In Figure 6, we show an alternative structure to that of Figure 5. All the variables are the same, except that the CDS is directly with the SPV. Since the proceeds from the note, L_{AAA}, are invested in high-quality securities that have risk weight assets of 0%, the CDS does not bring any regulatory capital charge and $RW_{CDS,SPV} = 0$. Therefore, the only regulatory capital remains the £2 of the equity.

As in Figure 5, with the structure in Figure 6, the originating bank has synthetically transferred the credit risk to capital markets, and preserved confidentiality: it does not notify to its clients that the loan is transferred to the SPV.

Partially funded structures

In the fully funded synthetic CDO of Figure 5, the SPV has issued a note equal to 98% of the loan collateral. This is a very expensive funding programme and, thus, the originating bank is far from achieving an efficient use of capital.

Figure 6 Fully funded synthetic CDO with CDS with an SPV

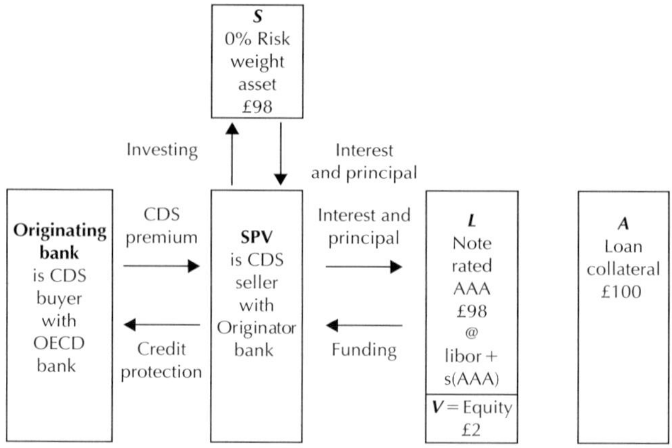

Source: Investing in collateralized debt obligations by Frank J. Fabozzi and Laurie S. Goodman, amended by the author

The alternative is a partially funded synthetic CDO transaction where the originating bank still buys credit protection, either directly from a SPV (Figure 7) or from an OECD bank (Figure 8). The difference is that in this instance, the SPV issues a smaller number of notes.

In Figures 7 and 8, the SPV issues one note, L_A, of £18, rated *A*, that pays the default free rate $r(t)$ plus the spread s_A, whose proceeds are invested in high-quality securities, *S*, that have risk weight assets of 0% and return the default free rate, $r(t)$. The originating bank retains the equity, *V*, of £2.

To transfer the credit risk of the same collateral portfolio, *A*, of £100 to capital markets, the originating bank enters into two CDSs: one called super senior CDS, CDS^S (also called the *un-funded piece*), and a second called junior CDS, CDS^J (also called the *funded piece*).

The notional of the junior CDS, CDS^J, is £20

$$\begin{aligned} \text{CDS}^J &= L_A + V \\ \text{CDS}^J &= £20 \end{aligned} \tag{17}$$

What really characterises this structure is the super senior CDS, CDS^S, whose notional is £80

$$\begin{aligned} \text{CDS}^S &= A - \text{CDS}^J \\ \text{CDS}^s &= £80 \end{aligned} \tag{18}$$

Figure 7 Partially funded synthetic CDO with CDS with a SPV

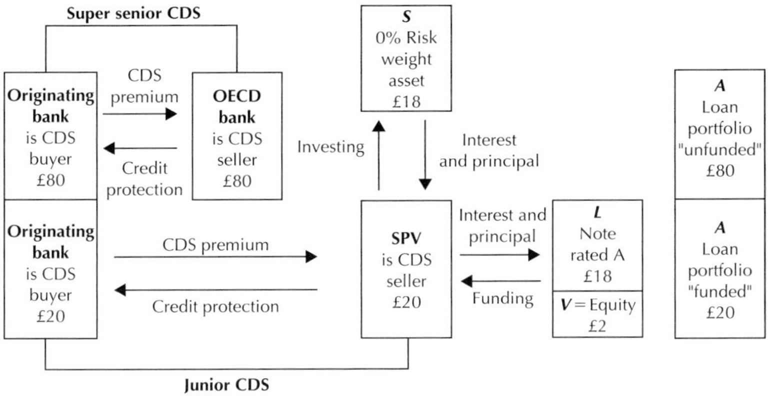

Source: Investing in collateralized debt obligations by Frank J. Fabozzi and Laurie S. Goodman, amended by the author

Figure 8 Partially funded synthetic CDO with CDS with an OECD bank

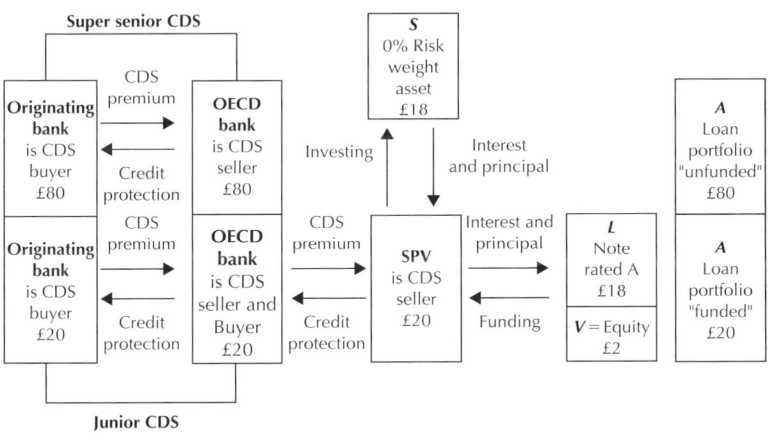

Source: Investing in collateralized debt obligations by Frank J. Fabozzi and Laurie S. Goodman, amended by the author

To see how the super senior CDS affects the funding benefit between a fully funded and a partially funded synthetic CDO, we write the super senior CDS premium and the junior CDS premium as k^S_{SPV} and v^J_{SPV}, respectively, and we assume that market forces preserve the following relationship between the premiums of this example and the premium of the previous example,

$$\nu^J_{\mathrm{SPV}} > \gamma_{\mathrm{SPV}} > k^S_{\mathrm{SPV}} \tag{19}$$

Then, we rewrite the condition of (12) as

$$\begin{aligned} &\nu^J_{\mathrm{SPV}}\mathrm{CDS}^J + Sr(t) > L(r(t) + s_{\mathrm{A}}) \\ &\nu^J_{\mathrm{SPV}}\mathrm{CDS}^J > L_A s_A \quad \text{with } \mathrm{CDS}^J > L_A = S \end{aligned} \tag{20}$$

We can notice two relationships in (20). Firstly, from (17) and (18), larger the notional of CDS^S, smaller the size of the note L_A, and the smaller the funding cost, $L_{\mathrm{A}}(r(t) + s_{\mathrm{A}})$. Secondly, ν^J_{SPV} and k^S_{SPV} are the premiums that two OECD banks are willing to earn to take over the credit risk of the loan collateral. As long as the funded piece CDS^J has a greater credit risk than the note L_A, the SPV generates guarantee excess spread that flows back to the originator bank.

The size, rating and spread of the note L_A are what drive the funding benefit of this structure when compared with the fully funded CDO, which we can write as follows

$$L_{\mathrm{AAA}} s_{\mathrm{AAA}} - L_A s_A > 0 \tag{21}$$

We now look at the regulatory capital charge of the originating bank after the partially funded synthetic CDO.

Under the BIS rules, if the super senior CDS, CDS^S, is with another OECD bank, the risk weight asset, $\mathrm{RW}_{\mathrm{CDS}^S,\mathrm{OECD}}$, is 20% and returns the regulatory capital charge, $\mathrm{RCC}_{£,\mathrm{CDS}^S}$, which is £1.6,

$$\begin{aligned} \mathrm{RCC}_{£,\mathrm{CDS}^S} &= \mathrm{RW}_{\mathrm{CDS}^S/\mathrm{OECD}} \times \mathrm{RC} \times \mathrm{CDS}^S \\ \mathrm{RCC}_{£,\mathrm{CDS}^S} &= £1.6 \end{aligned} \tag{22}$$

The regulatory capital rules on the equity piece and on the junior CDS are the same as those applied on the fully funded synthetic CDOs as seen in Tables 5 and 6, and we have to distinguish between the case where junior CDS is directly with the SPV or with another OECD bank.

Table 4 Regulatory capitals and funding costs of Figures 5–8

	Notional	Figure 5	Figure 6	Figure 7	Figure 8
		Regulatory capital			
CDS	£100.00	£1.60	£0.00	£0.00	£0.00
Senior CDS	£80.00	£0.00	£0.00	£1.60	£1.60
Junior CDS	£20.00	£0.00	£0.00	£0.00	£1.60
Equity	£2.00	£2.00	£2.00	£2.00	£2.00
Total		£3.60	£2.00	£3.60	£5.20
		Funding cost			
Note Notional		£98.00	£98.00	£18.00	£18.00
Note Rating		AAA	AAA	A	A
Libor		5%	5%	5%	5%
spread (bps)		10	10	50	50
		£5.00	£5.00	£0.99	£0.99

Figures 7 and 8 illustrate the mechanics of this type of CDO, whereas Table 4 shows the regulatory capital results of the structures of Figures 5–8, and compares their funding costs, where we have assumed libor rates, $r(t)$, of 5%, and spreads over the libor, s_{AAA} and s_A, of 10 and 50 bps, respectively, of the note rated AAA and A.

BALANCE SHEET MANAGEMENT WITH CDS

Figure 9 contains a new partially funded CDO structure, where the loan collateral is the same as in the previous examples.

This structure is also free of any interest rate risk: it pays libor and receives libor. The spread, s_{Loan}, of 100 bps over libor compensates the bank for taking the credit risk. The spreads on the three notes, ranging from 25 to 200 bps, compensate the notes investors for taking different credit risks.

We can remove the libor, leave the spreads on the note side and write the loan collateral as 50 loans paying the spread, s_{Loan}, of 100 bps over libor, as shown in Table 5.

A CDS is designed to mimic the credit behaviour of a floating rate note, such as the loans in Table 5. The loan spread, which is constant until the loan matures, is equivalent to the fixed leg of a CDS. In fact, the CDS seller, who seeks credit exposure, receives X basis points, ie, a spread per year until the credit reference matures or defaults.

Figure 9 Partially funded synthetic CDO

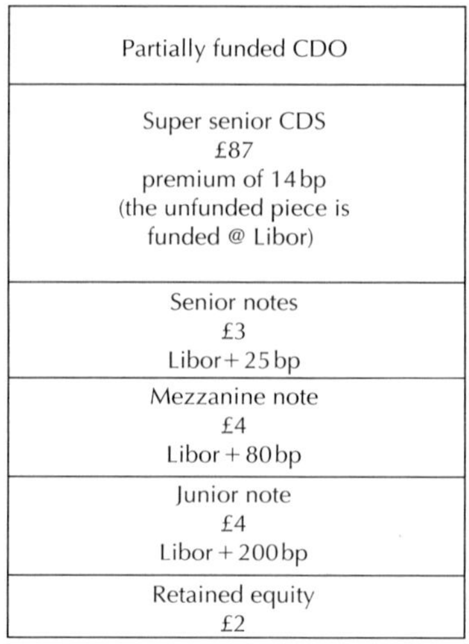

Table 5 CDO structure with hedged interest rate risk

Partially funded synthetic CDO					
Assets	**%**	**Spreads**	**Liabilities**	**%**	**Spreads**
Loan 1	2	100 bps	Super Senior CDS	87	14 bps
Loan 2	2	100 bps	Senior Notes	3	25 bps
Loan 3	2	100 bps	Mezzanine Notes	4	80 bps
...	...	100 bps	Junior Notes	4	200 bps
Loan 50	2	100 bps	Retained Equity	2	Dividend

The constant spread is the fixed leg of the CDS. As a consequence, we can remove the loans and add the CDS on the asset side.

With the CDO in Table 6 the originating bank is now exposed to the credit risk of 50 synthetic assets. To hedge its position, the bank borrows via three different notes and a CDS. Retaining the equity gives it the right to a possible dividend.

Viewed from this angle, a CDO is a hedged portfolio. The assets are a portfolio of CDSs, the liabilities are the notes with different seniorities. By hedging its balance sheet from credit risk, the bank

Table 6 CDO structure with hedged interest rate risk and with CDS in place of loans

Partially funded synthetic CDO					
Assets	**%**	**Spreads**	**Liabilities**	**%**	**Spreads**
CDS1	2	100 bps	Super Senior CDS	87	14 bps
CDS 2	2	100 bps	Senior Notes	3	25 bps
CDS 3	2	100 bps	Mezzanine Notes	4	80 bps
...	...	100 bps	Junior Notes	4	200 bps
CDS 50	2	100 bps	Retained Equity	2	Dividend

is trying to achieve a higher return than could be achieved by investing in risk-less treasury bonds. By partially funding the CDO structure, the bank has also achieved a leverage position, with potentially huge returns. The problem is how to correctly price the portfolio of CDSs.

CDO EQUITY PIECE

The CDO equity piece is a truly hybrid security. It exhibits the features of a coupon bond, a corporate equity, a call option on the collateral and a managed fund.

As a coupon bond, CDO equity is issued at or near par and has a final maturity date.[17] Like convertible bonds, cash payments are not specified, although the range of expected distributions is established at the time of issuance.

In a similar way to a call option, the value of CDO equity increases with the price and volatility of the underlying assets (the collateral portfolio). As with any actively managed investment, the contribution of the manager is a crucial determinant of CDO equity performance.

The CDO equity piece performance

The equity of a CDO represents a leveraged investment in the underlying asset class and in the asset management skills of the CDO manager. The leverage is achieved by issuing investment and sub-investment grade debt as term asset-backed securities.[18]

Credit losses are the obvious drivers of the CDO equity piece performance and can affect investors in two ways. First, as collateral shrinks because of defaults (in cashflow CDO's) or realised price deterioration (in market value CDO's), the amount of the collateral portfolio reduces and with it the size of received interest payments is reduced. Second, if the par size of the collateral drops below the par value test or where the interest coverage test is breached, the excess spread that is normally paid to the equity investors is redirected to pay down the senior liabilities, thereby de-leveraging the CDO. Equity payments only resume after the tests are restored above the trigger levels. Redirection of equity distributions can also be triggered by a drop in the interest income relative to the interest cost of the transaction.

According to Moody's, the average excess spreads in cashflow arbitrage CDOs, in January 2002, was 3.14%.[19] In the same month, the average life, in cashflow arbitrage CDOs, was 5.95 years. This means that, on average, in cashflow arbitrage CDOs the return on the CDO equity was 18.7% (3.14% times 5.95 years).

The CDO embedded call option

Depending on the collateral asset type and the timing of the transaction, the call option embedded in CDO equity may be quite valuable. Figure 10 shows the historical spread over libor on the Goldman Sachs Single B Bond Index and the estimated cost of funding of CDO liabilities (Olberg *et al*, 2001). The wider the gap between the income from the assets and the cost of the liabilities, the greater the investment incentive for CDO equity. There is also a greater capital appreciation for the equity investors as a consequence of calling the CDO.[20]

The upside from calling the transaction hugely depends on the type of collateral, making the distinction between CBOs and CLOs imperative. Those CDOs where the collateral is represented by bonds purchased at low prices (when interest rates were high) and where the structure is financed through cheap term notes (current low interest rates) offer the greatest benefit of a possibility of significant capital appreciation.

Floating-rate collaterals such as leveraged loans can easily be refinanced. The underlying borrowers can prepay outstanding loans and refinance at a lower funding rate. For this reason, a manager of a CLO will be in a very difficult position when trying to generate outsized capital appreciation. In other words, they do not offer as much potential for significant appreciation.

Figure 10 GS Single B Bond Index over Libor and the bond-backed CDO issuance incentive (Olberg *et al*, 2001)

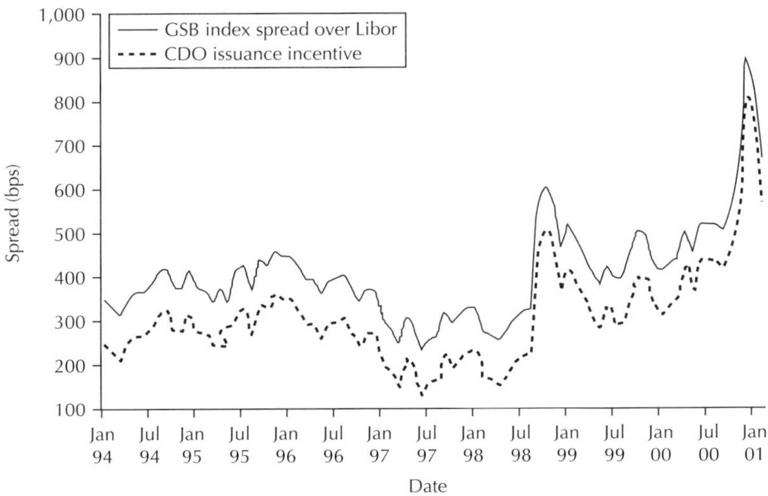

As the remaining expected returns fall, the equity holders are likely to exercise their option during the repayment period, either to take advantage of potential appreciation in CBOs, or to minimise the impact of a difficult credit environment with CLOs.

Investing in CDO equity

For long-horizon investors such as pension plans, endowments and insurance companies, portfolio diversification is an important investment consideration. In principle, diversification across asset classes lowers portfolio volatility without altering expected returns.

Traditionally, investments in real estate and foreign securities have been seen as effective diversification strategies. More recently, as volatilities in financial markets have increased, asset investors have also turned to more illiquid asset types such as private equity, hedge fund investments, commodities, insurance risk securities and, ultimately, CDO equities.

CDO equities are perceived to have a lower correlation when compared with the traditional asset classes of which they are made. This is not surprising since the CDO cashflow structure hedges the equity investment against short-term liquidity or technical fluctuations in the value of the collateral.

Indeed, the combination of non-generic collateral and active management should result in a low correlation between CDO equity returns and returns on benchmark asset classes, such as public equity, investment-grade corporate liabilities and government debt. Low long-term horizon return correlations, along with high expected returns, should lead asset investors such as insurance companies, pension plans, endowments and foundations to consider investment in CDO equity as an effective diversification strategy and "alternative investment" bucket in the portfolios of long-term horizon investments.

The problem is that historical data on CDO equity returns is unavailable because the market is relatively new and remains a very private one. Olberg *et al* (2001) looked at how to measure the correlation of CDO equities. Their route was to look at the underlying collateral markets as a starting point for thinking about correlations between returns on CDO equities and returns in other asset classes. In their analysis they took the Merrill Lynch Single B Index as the proxy of the CDO equities to measure correlations with other market indices.

Table 7 shows the historical annualised monthly return averages, standard deviations and correlations for the Merrill Lynch Single B Index, the Lehman Brothers Government Index, the Lehman Brothers Credit Index, the S&P 500 Index and the Russell 2000 Index.

As expected, the high-yield Merrill Lynch Single B Index returns display the highest correlation with the small-cap Russell 2000 Index and lowest correlation with the Lehman Brothers Government Index.

Table 7 is useful for fund managers who wish to invest in government bonds and do not want to lose the appreciation given by investing in equities. They are interested in seeing how the CDO equity would diversify their portfolio.

Using the data of Table 7, we have formed three different portfolios: LB Governments and ML single B; LB Governments and S&P; and ML single B and S&P. In Figure 11 we have prepared the efficient frontiers of these portfolios. The first name in each of the three portfolios has an initial weight of 100%. Subsequently, the

Table 7 Historical (December 1989 to December 2000) asset class return statistics and correlations (from Olberg *et al* (2001))

Historical (12/89–12/00) asset class return statistics					
	ML single B	**LB Govt**	**LB credit**	**S&P 500**	**Russell 2000**
Average (%)	9.3	7.62	8.21	15.48	12.85
Standard deviation (%)	21.48	14.17	16.26	47.98	63.64
Correlations					
	ML single B	**LB Govt**	**LB Credit**	**S&P 500**	**Russell 2000**
ML single B	1.00	0.31	0.47	0.49	0.57
LB Govt	0.31	1.00	0.95	0.34	0.15
LB Credit	0.47	0.95	1.00	0.43	0.26
S&P 500	0.49	0.34	0.43	1.00	0.69
Russell 2000	0.57	0.15	0.26	0.69	1.00

Figure 11 Three efficient frontiers: ML single B–LB governments; ML single B–S&P; and S&P–LB governments

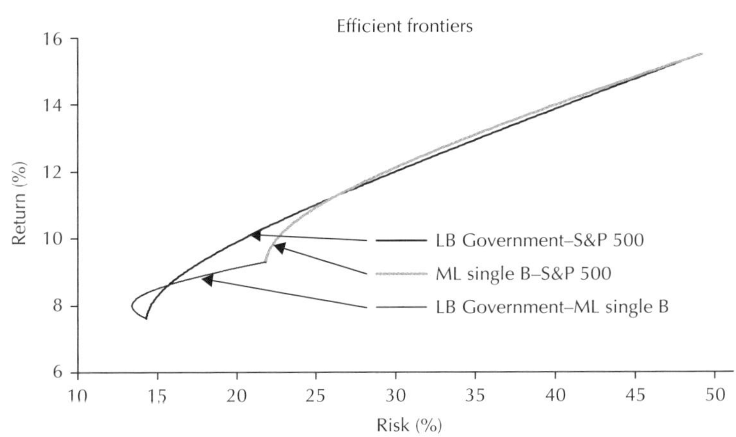

portfolio weights change, the first name weight moves from 100% to 0%, whereas the second name weight moves from 0% to 100%.

We can see that below a risk (standard deviation) of 15.8%, the fund manager would better diversify by combining government bonds with CDO equities (ML single B) rather than combining government bonds with equities (S&P 500).[21]

From Figure 11, we can make a further point: it is never good to combine equities with CDO equities.

THE MOODY'S DIVERSITY SCORE AND THE TABLE OF IDEALISED CUMULATIVE LOSSES

The ratings are important features of the CDO market. They summarise the view that one, two or all three of the main international rating agencies (Moody's, S&P and Fitch) have ratings not only on the credit quality of the collateral portfolio, but also on the quality of the CDO structure (principal waterfall, interest waterfall, par value tests, interest coverage, excess spread diversion etc).

Moody's (Cifuentes and O'Connor 1996; Cifuentes and Wilcox 1998; Tabe 2002), S&P (2002) and Fitch (2003) have their own methodologies to assess the credit risk in a collateral portfolio. For a comparison of the three rating methodologies, we recommend Zhu *et al* (2003). In the following, we review three aspects of Moody's methodology: the table of idealised cumulative losses, the binomial expansion technique (BET) and the diversity score.

Moody's methodology is based on the concept of expected losses, which reflects the amount that the CDO notes investors may lose up to the point when the CDO note matures. The approach Moody's takes is to calculate, at a given rating category, the level of subordination below a certain note, so that the expected cumulative losses of the note are the same as the benchmark of expected cumulative losses associated with that rating category. The benchmarks of expected cumulative losses are also known as the "table of idealised cumulative losses" and are shown in Table 8. These are cumulative losses based on the historical performances of rated bonds. The data includes actual credit default experiences of corporate bonds and asset-backed securities. The cumulative losses are calculated as frequencies of issuer losses over the total number of rated issuers. The issuers are then characterised by rating classes and maturities. For example, a loss probability of 2.035% means that if we were to hold the totality of bonds rated as Baa3, we would make a loss of 2.035% over a period of six years. The consequence is that for each level of expected cumulative losses and maturity, there is an associated

Table 8 Moody's idealised cumulative expected losses (from Cifuentes and O'Connor (1996))

	Year									
%	1	2	3	4	5	6	7	8	9	10
Aaa	0.000	0.000	0.000	0.001	0.002	0.002	0.003	0.004	0.005	0.006
Aa1	0.000	0.002	0.006	0.012	0.017	0.023	0.030	0.037	0.045	0.055
Aa2	0.001	0.004	0.004	0.026	0.037	0.049	0.061	0.074	0.090	0.110
Aa3	0.002	0.010	0.032	0.056	0.078	0.101	0.125	0.150	0.180	0.220
A1	0.003	0.020	0.064	0.104	0.144	0.182	0.223	0.264	0.315	0.385
A2	0.006	0.039	0.122	0.190	0.257	0.321	0.391	0.456	0.540	0.660
A3	0.021	0.083	0.198	0.297	0.402	0.501	0.611	0.715	0.836	0.990
Baa1	0.050	0.154	0.308	0.457	0.605	0.754	0.919	1.085	1.249	1.430
Baa2	0.094	0.259	0.457	0.660	0.869	1.084	1.326	1.568	1.782	1.980
Baa3	0.231	0.578	0.941	1.309	1.678	3.035	3.382	2.734	3.064	3.355
Ba1	0.488	1.111	1.722	2.310	2.904	3.438	3.883	4.340	4.780	5.170
Ba2	0.858	1.909	2.849	3.740	4.626	5.374	5.885	6.413	6.958	7.425
Ba3	1.546	3.030	4.329	5.385	6.523	7.419	8.041	8.641	9.191	9.713
B1	2.574	4.609	6.369	7.618	8.866	9.840	10.522	11.127	11.682	12.210
B2	3.938	6.419	8.553	9.972	11.391	12.458	13.206	13.833	14.421	14.960
B3	6.391	9.136	11.567	13.222	14.878	16.060	17.050	17.909	18.421	19.195
Caa	14.300	17.875	21.450	24.134	26.813	28.600	30.388	32.174	33.963	35.750

rating category or, in other words, the bond rating depends on its maturity and its expected loss.

Moody's sometimes refers to the table of idealised cumulative expected default rates (Tabe, 2002), which is prepared from Table 8, after adjusting the losses for a constant recovery rate, R, of 45%.

To aggregate the single creditor loss into the losses of the collateral portfolio, Moody's uses the BET.

The BET is based on the following assumptions: (a) the probability that one particular credit of the collateral portfolio defaults is independent of the probability that any other credit in the same portfolio defaults; and (b) all credits have the same size, maturity, probability of default, p, and loss, l, in the case of a default.

The consequence of such assumptions is that the probability of a loss of $X = nl$, with $n \leq D$, can be calculated with the binomial distribution

$$\Pr[X = nl] = \binom{D}{n} p^n (1-p)^{D-n} \quad \textbf{(23)}$$

where D is the diversity score of the collateral portfolio, as explained below.

To be able to use the BET, any portfolio of credits (bonds, loans, etc) must be conveniently approximated with a number of *homogeneous* credits D. The diversity score reduces the actual portfolio of collateral credits with correlated default probabilities to a *homogenous* portfolio of credits D with uncorrelated default probabilities.

Moody's defines the diversity score of a given collateral portfolio as the number of bonds D in an idealised comparison portfolio formed by matching the first two moments of the loss distribution of the original and comparison portfolios. A detailed explanation of alternative diversity score method calculations is given in Cifuentes *et al* (1999), whereas applications are discussed in Schorin and Weinreich (1998) and Duffie and Garleanu (1999).

These attempts have succeeded in bridging the gap of knowledge amongst practitioners on one side and Moody's on the other. However, as Schönbucher (2003) highlighted, the Moody's BET is not a formal portfolio default model, is inaccurate and is unsuitable for pricing. In addition, Moody's has never been generous in disclosing how the diversity score is calculated and updated and,

Table 9 Fitch and S&P confidence levels for rating CDO notes (AAA to B) as calculated by the author

	AAA (%)	AA (%)	A (%)	BBB (%)	BB (%)	B (%)
Fitch confidence levels	99.62	98.98	97.86	94.52	84.04	68.70
S&P confidence levels	99.95	99.55	97.87	90.94	47.54	33.09
S&P stressing factors	120	111	102	93	81	72
S&P pre stressing factor confidence levels	99.05	99.05	97.87	95.25	83.95	74.71

more importantly, how it has approximated the default behaviour of real portfolios of creditors, especially during the 2002 and 2003 that were years with very high defaults. In spite of these observations, the diversity score has become a market standard for communicating the degree of diversification of a portfolio.

An alternative approach is taken by S&P (2002) and Fitch (2003),[22] which use default probabilities to find the CDO note ratings. Perraudin and Peretyatkin (2003) discussed the differences between expected loss and default probability based ratings for all asset-backed securities (to which CDOs belong). They showed that thick notes (such as senior notes rated AAA) tend to have superior ratings if the expected loss approach is taken. They found this to be consistent with the view that Moody's enjoys greater market share for rating senior notes, while S&P and Fitch obtain a larger share for rating mezzanine notes.

We also note that the S&P and Fitch models do not arrive at an *idealised* construction of defaults, but rather build a distribution of aggregate default rates for the collateral portfolio. From the distribution, they apply different confidence levels for different ratings, and calculate the credit enhancements, firstly without and ultimately with recoveries.

In Table 9 we have extracted the rating confidence levels that S&P and Fitch use for rating CDO notes, together with the S&P stressing factors.

1 Most recently, CDO technology has been extended to emerging market debts, structured finance securities, commercial real-estate-linked debt, distressed assets, and last to arrive, private equity funds.

2 For the list of these securities, see Deacon (2003) and updates from press releases of the Bank of International Settlements at www.bis.org.

3 In a synthetic CDO the credit risk is synthetically transferred from the originating bank to capital markets, *via* Credit Default Swap.

4 The role of the CDO manager is discussed later.

5 Statistics regarding the recovery rates for CDO have been published in Standard and Poor's (S&P) (20 February 2004a) Recovery Rates for Credits in Global Synthetic CDOs Q4 2003, whereas the statistics of corporate defaults have been published in, S&P (February 2004b) Corporate Defaults in 2003 Recede from Recent Highs. Both reports can be found at www.standardandpoors.com.

6 Excess spread is the difference between the interests earned from the collateral assets and the expenses and the interests paid to the notes. We will look at the excess spread in the next section.

7 Subordination is the prioritisation of investor claims, and is defined in the next section.

8 Jobst (2002) showed how to use active credit portfolio management to remove credit risk from the bank balance sheet.

9 For a detailed analysis of how to create an arbitrage CDO, see Goodman (2001).

10 The triggers are all defined in the offering circular of the CDO transaction.

11 See Moody's (22 March 2002) Collateralised Debt Obligations Indices: January 2002 for a report on par value tests on current CDOs in USA and Europe. For example, for arbitrage cashflow CDOs, the senior note average par value OC test was equal to 126.33% in January 2002, whereas the senior note average interest rate coverage was, during the same period, 226.15%.

12 For an exhaustive explanation of the SPV laws, regulations, tax and accounting, see Deacon (2003).

13 At the time of writing, the new Basel regulation on capital charges before and after securitisation was under negotiation. An update can be found in the Basel Committee on Banking Supervision, Charges to the Securitisation Framework (30 January 2004), at www.bis.org.

14 For the current rules on regulatory capital charges before and after securitisaton, see the Basel Committee on Banking Supervision, Charges to the Securitisation Framework (30 January 2004).

15 This is an exemplified opportunity cost for regulatory capital relief. A full calculation would normally include rating agency costs, lawyer structuring fees and underwriting costs, and would take into account the amortising profile of the notes.

16 Swiss Bank brought Glacier Finance 1997-1 and 1997-2 to market in late 1997. Swiss Bank transferred the credit risk to the SPV, *via* a portfolio of credit linked notes.

17 This means that if an investor wishes to purchase the full equity piece, they will have to pay an amount equal to the equity piece face value (£2 in Figure 6).

18 The "term" is used to differentiate the term *securitisation* where the SPV liabilities are bonds, from *conduit* where the SPV liabilities are commercial papers.

19 See Moody's (22 March 2002) Collateralised Debt Obligations Indices: January 2002 for a report on excess spreads, average lives and other statistics on CDOs in USA and Europe.

20 Here we refer to the right of the equity investors to liquidate the collateral portfolio and use the proceeds to pay down the notes and interests due.

21 At 15.8%, the split between government bonds and ML single B is 40–60%.

22 S&P uses the CDO Evaluator to simulate correlated default times, with a one-step period Monte Carlo simulation. Fitch uses the Vector CDO model, a Merton-based model, where the aggregated distribution of correlated default times is calculated with a multi step Monte Carlo simulation.

REFERENCES

Basel Committee on Banking Supervision, 2004, "Charges to the Securitisation Framework", URL: http://www.bis.org, 30 January.

Cifuentes, A., and G. O'Connor, 1996, "The Binomial Expansion Method Applied to CBO/CLO Analysis", URL: http://www.moodys.com.

Cifuentes, A., and C. Wilcox, 1998, "The Double Binomial Method and its Application to a Special Case of CBO Structures", URL: http://www.moodys.com.

Cifuentes, A., I. Efrat, J. Gluck, and E. Murphy, 1999, "Buying and Selling Credit Risk: A Perspective on Credit-Linked Obligations", *Credit Derivatives,* pp. 112–23 (London: Risk Books).

Deacon, J., 2003, *Global Securitisation and CDOs* (New York: Wiley).

Duffie, D., and N. Garleanu, 1999, "Risk and Valuation of Collateralized Debt Obligations", *Financial Analysis Journal,* **57,** pp. 41–62.

Fitch, 2003, "The Vector CDO Model", URL: http://www.fitchratings.com.

Goodman, L., 2001, in Fabozzi and Goodman (eds), *Investing in Collateralized Debt Obligation,* Chapter 8.

Jobst, A., 2002, "Collateralised Loan Obligations", Centre for Financial Studies Working Paper.

Moody's, 2002, "Collateralised Debt Obligations Indices: January 2002", URL: http://www.moodys.com, 22 March.

Olberg, E., M. Nartey, H. Takata, and S. Shah, 2001, "Asset Management CDO Equity", *Risk Magazine,* April.

Perraudin, W., and V. Peretyatkin, 2002, "Securitisation-Sub-Group of the Basel Committee", Bank of England, Working Paper.

Perraudin, W., and V. Peretyatkin, 2003, "Expected Loss and Probability of Default Approaches to Rating Collateralised Debt Obligations and the Scope for Rating Shopping", *Credit Risk* (London: Risk Books).

Standard and Poor's, 2002, "CDO Evaluator Version 2.2", URL: http://www.standard-andpoors.com.

Standard and Poor's, 2004a, "Recovery Rates for Credits in Global Synthetic CDOs Q4 2003", URL: http://www.standardandpoors.com, 20 February.

Standard and Poor's, 2004b, "Corporate Defaults in 2003 Recede from Recent Highs", URL: http://www.standardandpoors.com, February.

Tabe, H., 2002, "Moody's Approach to Rating *i*th-to-default Basket Credit-linked Notes", URL: http://www.moodys.com.

Schönbucher, P., 2003, *Credit Derivatives Pricing Model* (New York: Wiley).

Schorin, C., and S. Weinreich, 1998, "Collateralized Debt Obligation", Morgan Stanley Dean Witter, Working Paper.

Schorin, C., and S. Weinreich, 2001, in Fabozzi and Goodman (eds), *Investing in Collateralized Debt Obligation.*

Wenbo, Z., D. Yan, D. Castro and S. McGarvey, 2003, "CDO Rating Methodologies Review", Merill Lynch, Working Paper.

Yvonne, F., and J. Gluck, 1998, "Moody's Approach to Rating Market-Value CDO", Moody's Investors Service, p. 12, URL: http://www.moodys.com.

9

Asymptotic Model of Economic Capital for Securitisations

Michael Pykhtin

KeyCorp

Securitisations have become a major tool of funding and risk management for banks. However, while several portfolio credit risk models for loan and bond portfolios were developed in the banking industry in the second half of the 1990s, assessing portfolio credit risk associated with securitisation tranches lagged far behind.[1] For example, a common approach to allocating economic capital to rated securitisation tranches was to assign the same capital as that of a bond with the same rating. However, even a crude analysis can show the inconsistency of this approach. Loss on a bond comes from default of a single borrower, while loss on a tranche comes from defaults of many borrowers in the underlying pool. Therefore, the proportion of the systematic risk must be much higher for a tranche than for a bond, and one cannot use the same sensitivity of loss for the systematic factors, eg, asset correlation, as one would use for bonds. Another fundamental distinction between tranches and bonds is the degree of dependence between default and loss given default (LGD) drivers. In the case of bonds, this dependence is relatively weak and assumed to be non-existent in most industry models.[2] In the case of tranches, both default and LGD of a tranche are driven by the same variable – the loss in the underlying pool. Thus, portfolio credit risk models developed for loan and bond portfolios are not directly applicable to securitisation tranches. A dedicated model is necessary to adequately describe portfolio credit risk associated with securitisations.

The need of a portfolio model of credit risk associated with securitisation tranches became more urgent with the development of the New Basel Capital Accord (known as Basel II). Since the inception of the current Basel Accord (now known as Basel I) in 1988, banks have learned to use inconsistencies in the old Accord to reduce regulatory capital requirements without reducing the actual economic risk they are taking. To discourage such practice, known as regulatory arbitrage, it was necessary to develop a simple analytical model that would adequately describe the economic risk of securitisations.

Two such models have been developed recently, one by Pykhtin and Dev (2002b; 2003) and the other by Gordy and Jones (2003). Both models are consistent with the asymptotic single risk factor (ASRF) framework – the foundation of the internal ratings based (IRB) approach in Basel II – as they consider a tranche being held in an asymptotically fine-grained portfolio driven by a single systematic risk factor. Both models found their application in the Basel II rules for securitisations (see paragraphs 538–643 in Basel Committee (2004)): the ratings based approach (RBA) was calibrated by Peretyatkin and Perraudin (2003) (a version of which is reproduced as a chapter of this volume) to Pykhtin and Dev's model and to a more general multi-period Monte Carlo model, while the supervisory formula approach (SFA) is based on Gordy and Jones' model. Even though the RBA and the SFA were calibrated to different models, this does not necessarily lead to inconsistency between the two approaches, as was shown by Gordy (2003b). He was able to map the parameters of one model to the parameters of the other so that the resulting capital requirements were similar. The relation between the tranche rating and its quantitative characteristics, which is necessary for calibration of the RBA, is discussed in Peretyatkin and Perraudin (2002).

In another chapter of this volume, Michael Gordy discusses the underpinnings of Gordy and Jones' model. In this chapter, we will focus exclusively on Pykhtin and Dev's model in its most general form.

ASYMPTOTIC SINGLE RISK FACTOR FRAMEWORK

Our task is to calculate expected loss (EL) and economic capital (EC) at some confidence level q associated with a securitisation tranche at a one-year time horizon. EC is usually defined for the entire portfolio under consideration as the qth percentile of the portfolio loss distribution (ie, a level of loss such that portfolio loss does not exceed it with probability q). Then, this portfolio EC is allocated to individual assets according to certain rules.[3] The asset's EC obtained in this way can be interpreted as the asset's contribution to the portfolio risk. Generally, while asset EL depends only on the characteristics of the asset itself, its contributory EC additionally depends on properties of the portfolio where the asset is held. Gordy (2003a) has shown that the only case when the asset EC is independent of the portfolio composition is when (a) the portfolio is infinitely fine-grained (ie, its largest exposure represents a negligible fraction of its total exposure) and (b) the portfolio losses are driven by a single systematic risk factor. Under these conditions, the portfolio EC equals its EL conditional on the systematic risk factor being equal to its qth ($(1-q)$th) percentile when the loss is an increasing (decreasing) function. Due to the linearity of the expectation operator, contributory EC of an asset is nothing but the EL on this asset conditional on the appropriate value of the systematic risk factor. We will use this ASRF framework in building our model.

We assume that a securitisation tranche is held in an infinitely fine-grained portfolio of assets. The tranche notional represents a negligible fraction of the total portfolio exposure, so that the portfolio remains infinitely fine-grained after inclusion of the tranche. The losses in the portfolio are driven by a single systematic risk factor Z having standard normal distribution. We will interpret this systematic factor as the state of the economy: higher values of Z corresponding to a strong economy and lower values corresponding to a weak economy. This interpretation makes portfolio EL conditional on Z a decreasing function of Z. Under the ASRF assumptions, Gordy's arguments are applicable to any asset, including securitisation tranches. Therefore, if we denote the stochastic one-year loss on a tranche by U, the tranche EC is

$$EC_q = E[U|Z = z_{1-q}] \tag{1}$$

where $z_{1-q} = N^{-1}(1-q)$ is the $(1-q)th$ percentile of the standard normal distribution.

TRANCHES AND POOLS

Any meaningful analysis of credit risk associated with a securitisation tranche must be based on the distribution of losses in the underlying pool of assets. Loss on a tranche is uniquely determined by the loss in the underlying pool via contractual distribution of payouts, known as cashflow waterfall. The structure of this waterfall can be quite complicated, depending on timings of pool defaults and recoveries as well as principal and interest payments. To take into account all this complexity, one needs to simulate pool cash flows dynamically and then apply the waterfall to generate losses on a tranche.[4] To make the model analytically tractable, we will simplify the structure of the waterfall and consider only losses of principal over fixed time period.

We assume that securitisation is defined on an underlying pool of assets, whose loss rate, L, at the one-year time horizon is distributed according to some probability density function $f(\cdot)$. We will denote the probability that the portfolio loss rate will exceed level l by $G(l)$. There is an obvious relation between these two functions: $f = -\mathrm{d}G/\mathrm{d}l$. The complementary distribution function is related to the more conventional distribution function $F(l) \equiv \Pr[L \leq l]$ *via* $G(l) = 1 - F(l)$ and is a non-increasing function of the pool loss rate defined on the interval [0, 1]. Since the loss cannot exceed the pool notional, the relation $G(1) = 0$ always holds. The value of the complementary distribution function at $l = 0$ is determined by the probability of exactly zero loss in the pool: $G(0) = 1 - \Pr[L = 0]$. For credit pools, this probability is always positive and $G(0) < 1$ because, strictly speaking, there is always a finite probability of no defaults in the pool. The probability of zero loss vanishes in the limit of an infinitely fine-grained pool, for which we have $G(0) = 1$.

A tranche under consideration is characterised by the lower bound (protection level) s and the upper bound $t \geq s$. The notional amount (thickness) is given by $t - s$. Both s and t are defined per unit of the pool notional and can take values between zero and one. This tranche experiences no losses if $L \leq s$, and absorbs pool losses up to the maximum given by $t - s$ when $L > s$. Formally, the loss on the tranche can be written as

$$U(s,t) = \int_s^t \mathrm{d}l\, 1_{\{L>l\}} \tag{2}$$

where $1_{\{\cdot\}}$ denotes the indicator function.

Equation (2) can be interpreted as follows. The tranche under consideration can be viewed as an infinite set of infinitesimally thin tranches (ITTs). An ITT characterised by the protection level l and notional dl experiences zero loss if $L \leq l$ and loss equal to dl if $L > l$. This interpretation is often helpful because an ITT is a much simpler object than a tranche of a finite thickness. In many respects, an ITT behaves like a loan with principal of dl, probability of default (PD) of $G(l)$ and deterministic LGD of 100%.

Expected loss

EL for the tranche is obtained by taking the expectation of Equation (2)

$$\mathrm{EL}(s,t) \equiv E[U(s,t)] = \int_{s}^{t} \mathrm{d}l\; G(l) \tag{3}$$

The linearity of the expectation operator ensures that the ITT intuition is preserved in Equation (3): the EL of a tranche is the sum of the ELs of the ITTs composing that tranche. The analogy between ITTs and loans can be easily seen: the EL of an ITT has the same form as the EL of a loan (the product of principal, PD and expected LGD).

Cases where the integral in Equation (3) can be evaluated in closed form are rare. However, numerical integration can often be avoided by a simple transformation of Equation (3). First, let us note that, according to Equation (3), the EL of any tranche can be written as the difference between ELs of two senior tranches:

$$\mathrm{EL}(s,t) = \mathrm{EL}(s,1) - \mathrm{EL}(t,1) \tag{4}$$

Let us now integrate Equation (3) for a senior tranche with protection level v by parts

$$\mathrm{EL}(v,1) = lG(l)\big|_{v}^{1} + \int_{v}^{1} \mathrm{d}l\, l\, f(l)$$

The first term in this expression vanishes at the upper limit because the pool loss cannot exceed the principal and, therefore, $G(1) = 0$ must always hold. The second term is the product of the pool EL conditional on the event $L > v$ and the probability of this event. Therefore, we can write the senior tranche EL as

$$\mathrm{EL}(v, 1) = G(v)\left(E[L \mid L > v] - v\right) \tag{5}$$

Equations (4) and (5) can be a useful alternative to Equation (3) if we can obtain a closed-form expression relating $G(v)$ and the expected shortfall $E[L \mid L > v]$.

It is straightforward to establish the equality of the total EL for all tranches in a given securitisation to the pool EL. Indeed, according to Equation (3), the total EL for all tranches equals EL(0, 1). Substituting $v = 0$ into Equation (5), we obtain

$$\mathrm{EL}(0, 1) = E[L]$$

regardless of the value of $G(0)$.

Economic capital

According to Equation (1), EC is given by the EL on the tranche in question conditional on the systematic factor being equal to its $(1 - q)$th percentile. By taking the expectation of Equation (2) conditionally on event $Z = z_{1-q}$, we obtain the tranche EC as

$$\mathrm{EC}_q(s, t) = E[U(s, t) \mid Z = z_{1-q}] = \int_s^t \mathrm{d}l\, G(l \mid z_{1-q}) \tag{6}$$

where $G(l \mid z) \equiv \Pr[L > l \mid Z = z]$ is the complementary distribution of loss in the underlying pool conditional on the realisation of the systematic factor. Equation (6) has the same form as Equation (3): the tranche EC is the sum of the ECs of the ITTs composing that tranche. The only difference between the ITT EC and EL is conditioning of the pool loss distribution on $Z = z_{1-q}$. In particular, we can write the tranche EC as the difference between ECs of two senior tranches,

$$\mathrm{EC}_q(s, t) = \mathrm{EC}_q(s, 1) - \mathrm{EC}_q(t, 1) \tag{7}$$

and obtain the EC for a senior tranche in the form

$$\mathrm{EC}_q(v, 1) = G(v \mid z_{1-q})\left(E[L \mid \{L > v\} \,\&\, \{Z = z_{1-q}\}] - v\right) \tag{8}$$

by repeating the derivation of Equation (5) with conditioning on $Z = z_{1-q}$.

Similarly to the case of EL, the total EC for all tranches equals $EC_q(0, 1)$ as follows trivially from Equation (6). Substituting $v = 0$ into Equation (8), we obtain

$$EC_q(0,1) = E[L \mid Z = z_{1-q}]$$

regardless of the value of $G(0 \mid z_{1-q})$. Thus, the EC for all tranches equals the EC of the underlying pool.

While Equations (3)–(5) that we derived for tranche EL are self-contained and can be calculated for any distribution of pool loss, their analogues for tranche EC (Equations (6)–(8)) additionally require specification of the relationship between the pool loss and systematic factor Z.

GLOBAL AND LOCAL SYSTEMATIC FACTORS

Very often, assets combined in a pool have more in common than assets in a well-diversified portfolio. For example, the assets in the pool may belong to the same industry. In such cases, correlations between the assets in the pool would on average be higher than the correlations implied by their common dependence on the global systematic risk factor. To describe this effect, we assume that losses in the pool are driven by a local systematic risk factor, appropriate for a given pool. While the global systematic risk factor Z can be interpreted as the state of the global economy, the local systematic factor, which we will denote by Y, describes the state of the industry (or other common property) for the assets in the pool. We assume that Y has standard normal distribution and that it is linearly related to Z:

$$Y = \rho_{YZ} Z + \sqrt{1 - \rho_{YZ}^2}\,\varepsilon \qquad \textbf{(9)}$$

where ρ_{YZ} is the correlation between the risk factors and ε is a standard normal variable independent of Z. We assume that higher values of Y correspond to stronger industry and smaller pool losses, which means $\rho_{YZ} > 0$ for cyclical industries. In a multi-factor portfolio model, Y would be called a composite factor and ε an industry-specific factor.

INFINITESIMALLY THIN TRANCHES DEFINED ON FINE-GRAINED POOLS

There is a large class of securitisations based on fine-grained underlying pools. Asset backed securities (ABSs) defined on retail pools (eg, auto loans) typically belong to this class. It turns out that the analysis greatly simplifies in such cases due to the fact that most of the idiosyncratic risk is diversified away in a fine-grained portfolio. For retail pools, one can safely assume that all idiosyncratic risk is completely diversified away and replace the original loss distribution by a much simpler limiting loss distribution of the infinitely fine-grained portfolio. When the pool loss is driven by a single systematic factor (Y in our case), one can even relate the EL and EC for ITTs (which are the integrands in Equations (3) and (6)) without making any specific assumptions about the nature of the pool loss distribution.

The limiting loss is given by the EL conditional on the systematic risk factor Y, as can be shown by applying the law of large numbers conditionally on Y (see Gordy (2003a) for details). Therefore, the pool limiting loss L^∞ is a deterministic monotonically decreasing function $L^\infty = \hat{l}(Y) \equiv E[L \mid Y]$ of the systematic factor. The maximum of this function, which we will denote as $l_{\max}$, is achieved in the limit $y \to -\infty$, while its minimum of zero is achieved as $y \to \infty$. We can invert this function to obtain the systematic factor as a function of loss: $Y = \hat{y}(L^\infty)$, defined in the interval $0 < l < l_{\max}$. Since event $L^\infty > l$ is equivalent to event $Y < y$ (assuming that l lies in the interval) and Y has standard normal distribution, the complementary loss distribution can be written as

$$G(l) = \begin{cases} N[\hat{y}(l)] & \text{if } 0 < l < l_{\max} \\ 0 & \text{if } l \geq l_{\max} \end{cases} \tag{10}$$

where $N(\cdot)$ denotes the standard normal distribution function. The probability of loss exceeding any $l \geq l_{\max}$ is, of course, zero.

Following similar logic and using Equation (9), we can obtain the conditional complementary distribution function for the portfolio loss, $G(l \mid z)$. Let us now condition losses on the event $Z = z$. Similarly to the unconditional case, conditional event $L^\infty > l \mid Z = z$ is equivalent to conditional event $Y < y \mid Z = z$ for all $0 < l < l_{\max}$. Equation (9) allows us to express this event as

$\varepsilon < (y - \rho_{YZ}z)/\sqrt{1-\rho^2_{YZ}}$. By applying the inverse of the standard normal distribution function to Equation (10), we obtain the relation $y = N^{-1}[G(l)]$, where $N^{-1}(\cdot)$ is the inverse to the normal cumulative distribution function. Since the "industry-specific" factor ε has standard normal distribution, we can write $G(l \mid z)$ as

$$G(l|z) = N\left(\frac{N^{-1}[G(l)] - \rho_{YZ}z}{\sqrt{1-\rho_{YZ}^2}}\right) \tag{11}$$

which has the form of the conditional default probability derived by Vasicek (1987). Although we have obtained Equation (11) for the case $0 < l < l_{\max}$, it also holds (formally) when $l \geq l_{\max}$ so that we do not need to consider the latter case separately. Thus, for a fine-grained pool and normally distributed systematic risk factors, the conditional and unconditional complementary distributions of losses (which are also the EC and EL of an ITT, respectively) are related by the Vasicek formula regardless of the nature of the pool loss distribution.

VASICEK MODEL FOR THE UNDERLYING POOL

From now on we assume that the pool underlying the securitisation consists of loans to M distinct borrowers. To avoid cumbersome notation, we assume that each borrower has exactly one loan with principal A_i. We also define the weight of a loan in the pool as the ratio of its principal to the total principal of the pool, $w_i = A_i/\Sigma_{j=1}^{M} A_j$. Losses in the pool occur due to borrowers' defaults which are described by the Vasicek model. Borrower i will default within one year with probability p_i. Default happens when a continuous ability-to-pay variable X_i describing financial well-being of borrower i at the horizon falls below a threshold. This ability-to-pay variable has standard normal distribution and can be interpreted as the standardised log-return on the borrower's assets. The default threshold for borrower i is given by $N^{-1}(p_i)$. The asset return variables depend linearly on the local systematic risk factor Y as

$$X_i = a_i Y + \sqrt{1-a_i^2}\,\xi_i \tag{12}$$

where a_i is a factor loading determining the sensitivity of borrower i to the local systematic factor and variable ξ_i has standard normal distribution. Variable ξ_i describes the idiosyncratic component of the asset return and is independent across borrowers. Asset correlation between borrower i and borrower j in the pool equals $a_i a_j$.

If borrower i defaults, the amount of loss is determined by its LGD stochastic variable Q_i with expectation μ_i and standard deviation σ_i. We assume that these LGD variables are independent between themselves as well as from all the other variables in the model. The pool loss rate, defined as the ratio of the pool loss to the total exposure of the pool, is

$$L = \sum_{i=1}^{M} w_i Q_i 1_{\left\{X_i \le N^{-1}(p_i)\right\}} \tag{13}$$

One can always convert Equation (13) and all the results derived below from relative units to currency units simply by replacing weights $\{w_i\}$ with exposures $\{A_i\}$ everywhere.

TRANCHES DEFINED ON FINE-GRAINED POOLS OF LOANS

Let us now consider a securitisation defined on a fine-grained pool of loans described by the Vasicek model. The limiting loss rate $L^{\infty} = \hat{l}(Y)$ can be obtained by taking the expectation of Equation (13) conditional on Y:

$$\hat{l}(Y) \equiv E[L \mid Y] = \sum_{i=1}^{M} w_i \mu_i p_i^{a_i \mid Y}(Y) \tag{14}$$

where

$$p_i^{a_i \mid Y}(y) = N\left(\frac{N^{-1}(p_i) - a_i y}{\sqrt{1 - a_i^2}}\right) \tag{15}$$

is the probability of default by borrower i conditional on $Y = y$.

The limiting loss does not depend on the distribution of the LGD variables around their expectations $\{\mu_i\}$ and Equation (14) holds for any LGD distribution. Maximum possible loss $l_{\max}$ is trivially obtained from Equation (14) as

$$l_{\max} = \lim_{y \to -\infty} \hat{l}(y) = \sum_{i=1}^{M} w_i \mu_i \tag{16}$$

Complementary loss distribution

As we have seen, calculation of tranche EL or EC is ultimately tied to the complementary loss distribution $G(l)$. As we have shown for fine-grained pools in general, the function $G(l)$ is simply related (by Equation (10)) to function $\hat{y}(l)$ which maps realisations of the limiting loss L^{∞} to realisations of the systematic factor Y (it is the inverse of $\hat{l}(y)$). Unfortunately, the inversion of Equation (14) is possible in closed form only for pools homogeneous in PD and local factor loading, and calculation of $G(l)$ for non-homogeneous pools has to be done numerically. Since the first derivative of $\hat{l}(y)$ is available in closed form

$$\hat{l}'(y) = -\sum_{i=1}^{M} w_i \mu_i \frac{a_i}{\sqrt{1-a_i^2}} n\left(\frac{N^{-1}(p_i) - a_i y}{\sqrt{1-a_i^2}}\right)$$

the fast-converging Newton–Raphson method can be used to solve $\hat{l}(y) = l$ for y. Function $n(\cdot)$ denotes the standard normal density.

For homogeneous pools (the ones with loans having the same PD $\bar{p}$, factor loading $\bar{a}$, expected LGD $\bar{\mu}$ and standard deviation of LGD $\bar{\sigma}$), the complementary loss distribution can be obtained in closed form. The limiting loss rate for the homogeneous pool is given by

$$\bar{l}(Y) = \bar{\mu} N\left(\frac{N^{-1}(\bar{p}) - \bar{a}Y}{\sqrt{1-\bar{a}^2}}\right) \tag{17}$$

which can be easily inverted to obtain

$$\bar{y}(l) = \frac{N^{-1}(\bar{p}) - \sqrt{1-\bar{a}^2}\, N^{-1}(l/\bar{\mu})}{\bar{a}}$$

Substituting this into Equation (10) and taking into account the fact that $l_{\max} = \mu$ in the homogeneous case, we obtain the Vasicek distribution (see Vasicek 1991, 2002) for fine-grained homogeneous pools:

$$\bar{G}(l) = \begin{cases} N\left[\dfrac{N^{-1}(\bar{p}) - \sqrt{1-\bar{a}^2}\, N^{-1}(l/\bar{\mu})}{\bar{a}}\right] & \text{if } 0 < l < \bar{\mu} \\ 0 & \text{if } l \geq \bar{\mu} \end{cases} \tag{18}$$

For a general non-homogeneous pool, it is possible to construct a comparable homogeneous portfolio (CHP) whose loss distribution closely resembles the one of the original non-homogeneous pool. The complementary loss distribution of the CHP, $\bar{G}(l)$, can be used either as a good closed-form approximation to $\bar{G}(l)$ or as an excellent initial guess for the Newton–Raphson method. In Panel 1 below, we show how to construct the CHP in the more general context of coarse-grained pools.

Expected loss

To calculate EL for a tranche, we need to integrate the complementary loss distribution $G(l)$ between the lower and upper bounds of the tranche according to Equation (3). Since $G(l)$ has to be obtained numerically, the integral in Equation (3) presents a problem. However, we can avoid evaluating the integral in Equation (3) by using Equations (4) and (5) instead. We will be able to use them if we can calculate the expected shortfall $E[L \mid L > v]$ that appears in Equation (5).

If the lower bound of the senior tranche v is above $l_{\max}$, the loss on the tranche is zero. Therefore, the loss on a senior tranche with $v < l_{max}$ is equivalent to the loss on a mezzanine tranche with the same lower bound v, but the upper bound equal to $l_{\max}$. Thus, it suffices to consider only the case $v < l_{\max}$. As we have seen above for fine-grained pools, event $L > v$ is equivalent to event $Y < \hat{y}(v) = N^{-1}[G(v)]$. Therefore, the expected shortfall can be written as

$$E[L^{\infty} \mid L^{\infty} > v] = E\left[\hat{l}\,(Y) \,\middle|\, Y < N^{-1}[G(v)]\right]$$

Now we will substitute $\hat{l}(Y)$ from Equation (14), write the conditional expectation in explicit form as an integral and evaluate this integral to obtain

$$\begin{aligned} E[L^{\infty} \mid L^{\infty} > v] &= \sum_{i=1}^{M} w_i \mu_i \frac{1}{G(v)} \int_{-\infty}^{N^{-1}[G(v)]} \mathrm{d}y\, n(y) N\left(\frac{N^{-1}(p_i) - a_i y}{\sqrt{1-a_i^2}}\right) \\ &= \frac{1}{G(v)} \sum_{i=1}^{M} w_i \mu_i N_2\left(N^{-1}(p_i), N^{-1}[G(v)]; a_i\right) \end{aligned}$$

where $n(\cdot)$ is the standard normal density and $N_2(\cdot, \cdot; a)$ denotes the bivariate standard normal distribution function with the correlation parameter a.[5] This distribution function appears here as the probability that borrower i defaults and the pool loss rate exceeds level v. Substituting this result into Equation (5), we obtain the senior tranche EL as

$$\mathrm{EL}(v,1)=\sum_{i=1}^{M} w_i\mu_i N_2\left(N^{-1}(p_i), N^{-1}[G(v)]; a_i\right)-vG(v) \tag{19}$$

The EL for an arbitrary tranche can be obtained by using Equation (19) with Equation (4).

Economic capital

EC can be calculated as the integral of the ITT capital $G(l \mid z_{1-q})$ between the tranche bounds according to Equation (6). However, this method is not convenient because it requires numerical evaluation of the integral. This situation is very similar to the one we had for EL, and we will proceed in exactly the same way. To avoid the numerical integration, we will calculate the EC of a tranche as the difference between the ECs of two senior tranches according to Equation (7). EC for a senior tranche is given by Equation (8), which requires evaluation of the conditional complementary loss distribution $G(v \mid z)$ and the conditional expected shortfall $E[L \mid \{L > v\} \;\&\; \{Z = z\}]$. As we have shown in Equation (11), $G(v \mid z)$ is related to $G(v)$ by the Vasicek formula for arbitrary fine-grained pools if the systematic risk factors are normally distributed. The conditional expected shortfall can be computed as follows.

Similarly to the EL case, we can write the expected shortfall that appears in Equation (8) as

$$\begin{aligned} E[L^{\infty} \mid \{L^{\infty}>v\}\,\&\,\{Z=z\}] &= E\left[\hat{l}(Y) \,\middle|\, \{Y<N^{-1}[G(v)]\}\,\&\,\{Z=z\}\right] \\ &= \sum_{i=1}^{M} w_i\mu_i \Pr\left[X_i \le N^{-1}(p_i) \,\middle|\, \{Y<N^{-1}[G(v)]\}\,\&\,\{Z=z\}\right] \end{aligned} \tag{20}$$

The conditioning on event $Z = z$ presents an extra difficulty here in comparison with the EL case. Let us substitute the relation between the global and local risk factors given by Equation (9) into Equation (12):

$$X_i = a_i\rho_{YZ}Z + a_i\sqrt{1-\rho_{YZ}^2}\,\varepsilon + \sqrt{1-a_i^2}\,\xi_i$$

$$= a_i \rho_{YZ} Z + \sqrt{1-(a_i \rho_{YZ})^2}\,\eta_i$$

Here we have defined a new standard normal variable η_i which is a linear combination of the "industry-specific" factor ε and the idiosyncratic component of the ith borrower's asset return

$$\eta_i = b_i \varepsilon + \sqrt{1-b_i^2}\,\xi_i$$

where b_i is the correlation between η_i and ε is given by

$$b_i = a_i \sqrt{\frac{1-\rho_{YZ}^2}{1-(a_i \rho_{YZ})^2}} \tag{21}$$

It is interesting to note that, conditionally on $Z = z$, η_i is the standardised asset return, ε is the systematic factor driving pool loss and b_i is the factor loading. The probability of default conditional on $Z = z$ is given by

$$p_i^{r_i|Z}(z) = N\left(\frac{N^{-1}(p_i) - r_i z}{\sqrt{1-r_i^2}}\right) \tag{22}$$

where

$$r_i \equiv a_i \rho_{YZ} \tag{23}$$

is the sensitivity of the asset return to the global factor Z. The conditional asset correlation between distinct borrowers i and j is given by $b_i b_j$.

Now we can incorporate the conditioning on $Z = z$ into the expressions defining the conditional default probability in Equation (20) and rewrite Equation (20) as

$$\begin{aligned} &E[L^\infty | \{L^\infty > v\} \,\&\, \{Z=z\}] \\ &= \sum_{i=1}^{M} w_i \mu_i \Pr\left[\eta_i \le N^{-1}[p_i^{r_i|Z}(z)] \,\middle|\, \varepsilon < N^{-1}[G(v|z)]\right] \\ &= \sum_{i=1}^{M} w_i \mu_i \frac{\Pr\left[\{\eta_i \le N^{-1}[p_i^{r_i|Z}(z)]\} \,\&\, \{\varepsilon < N^{-1}[G(v|z)]\}\right]}{\Pr\left[\varepsilon < N^{-1}[G(v|z)]\right]} \end{aligned} \tag{24}$$

The second equality in Equation (24) relies on the definition of conditional probability. Since ε and η_i are standard normal variables with correlation b_i, the probability in the numerator of the right-hand side of Equation (24) is given by the standard bivariate normal distribution function

$$\Pr\left[\{\eta_i \le N^{-1}[p_i^{r_i|Z}(z)]\} \,\&\, \{\varepsilon < N^{-1}[G(v|z)]\}\right] = N_2\left(N^{-1}[p_i^{r_i|Z}(z)], N^{-1}[G(v|z)]; b_i\right)$$

Now we can substitute the conditional EL given by Equation (24) into Equation (8) to obtain the EC for a senior tranche:

$$\mathrm{EC}_q(v,1) = \sum_{i=1}^{M} w_i \mu_i N_2\left(N^{-1}[p_i^{r_i|Z}(z_{1-q})], N^{-1}[G(v|z_{1-q})]; b_i\right) - vG(v|z_{1-q}) \qquad \textbf{(25)}$$

where the conditional complementary distribution function $G(v\,|\,z_{1-q})$ is related to the unconditional one $G(v)$ by Equation (11). Economic capital for an arbitrary tranche can be obtained by using Equation (25) with Equation (7). Thus we have avoided the numerical integration in calculating EL and EC for tranches defined on fine-grained pools.

Examples

Now we will examine how the EC of different tranches depends on the correlation between the local and global systematic risk factors ρ_{YZ}. We will show this dependence for a homogeneous, asymptotically fine-grained pool of loans with PD $\bar{p} = 0.5\%$ and expected LGD $\bar{\mu} = 40\%$. The confidence level in this and all other examples in the remainder of this chapter will be set at $q = 99.9\%$ in accordance with the Basel II IRB requirements.

When we vary ρ_{YZ}, we cannot keep both the local factor loading $\bar{a}$ and the global factor loading $\bar{r}$ fixed, as they are related by Equation (23). If we fix $\bar{a}$, we are fixing the risk of the pool on a stand-alone basis and allowing the contributory risk of the pool (ie, when the pool is viewed as part of the large portfolio) to vary with ρ_{YZ}. If, on the other hand, we fix $\bar{r}$, we are fixing the pool contributory risk and allowing the pool stand-alone risk to vary with

ρ_{YZ}. Quantitatively, these risks can be described as ECs assigned to the pool either on the stand-alone basis, K_{SA}, or on the contributory basis, K_C. As we have discussed above, since the large portfolio is infinitely fine grained and driven by a single systematic risk factor Z, the contributory EC of any asset in the portfolio is given by its EL conditional on $Z = z_{1-q}$. For a homogeneous pool of loans this amounts to

$$K_C = \bar{\mu}\bar{p}^{\bar{r}|Z}(z_{1-q})$$

The pool itself is also infinitely fine grained, so therefore the pool stand-alone EC is given by the pool EL conditional on $Y = y_{1-q}$:

$$K_{SA} = \bar{\mu}\bar{p}^{\bar{a}|Y}(y_{1-q})$$

A very informative way of analysing the risk of various tranches that can be defined on a pool is to plot the ITT capital $G(l \mid z_{1-q})$ as a function of the credit protection level l. The economic capital for a tranche with a lower bound s and an upper bound t is given by the area under the curve between s and t. The total area under the curve, representing the EC for all tranches, equals K_C. Figure 1 shows such plots of the ITT capital for several values of ρ_{YZ}.

In the examples shown in Figure 1(a), we fix the local factor loading $\bar{a}$ at value 0.6 (ie, the local asset correlation is 0.36) and allow the sensitivity of borrowers' asset returns $\bar{r}$ o the global factor Z to change along with ρ_{YZ}. The stand-alone EC is $K_{SA} = 7.34\%$ in this case. When $\rho_{YZ} = 1$, local and global factors coincide and, conditionally on Z, the pool loss $L^\infty = \hat{l}(Y)$ is deterministic. Therefore, the ITT capital, which is given by $\Pr[L^\infty > l \mid Z = z_{1-q}]$, equals one for loss levels below the pool EC and zero above the pool EC. The contributory and stand-alone ECs are equal in this case. As ρ_{YZ} declines, so do $\bar{r}$ and K_C (and, therefore, the total area under the curve), while K_{SA} remains fixed at 7.34%. Since we measure tranche EC on the contributory basis, the total EC for all tranches in a securitisation decreases with ρ_{YZ}. At the same time, as ρ_{YZ} declines, the pool loss conditional on $Z = z_{1-q}$ becomes uncertain (as the weight of the "industry-specific" component ε becomes non-zero). This causes the remaining total risk in the pool to be redistributed from more junior to more senior tranches.

Figure 1 ITT capital for a homogeneous infinitely fine-grained pool of loans (PD $\bar{p}=0.5\%$)

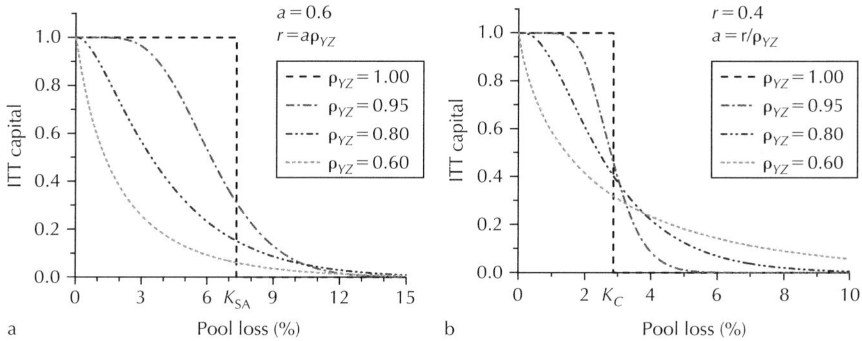

In the examples shown in Figure 1(b), we fix $\bar{r}$ at value 0.4 (ie, the global asset correlation is 0.16) and allow $\bar{a}$ to change along with ρ_{YZ}. When $\rho_{YZ} = 1$, the contributory and stand-alone ECs are equal to 2.88%. As ρ_{YZ} declines, both $\bar{a}$ and K_{SA} increase, while K_C remains fixed at 2.88%. Now the total contributory risk of a securitisation remains the same and the only effect of a decrease in ρ_{YZ} is redistribution of risk from more junior to more senior tranches.

TRANCHES DEFINED ON COARSE-GRAINED POOLS OF LOANS

While the use of the limiting loss distribution is appropriate for securitisations based on fine-grained pools (such as retail ABSs), it cannot be used for securitisations based on coarse-grained pools (such as CDOs). Unfortunately, the general coarse-grained case is not analytically tractable. To make it tractable, we will replace the original non-homogeneous pool with the CHP mentioned in the context of fine-grained pools above.

The idea of replacing a non-homogeneous credit portfolio with a CHP was introduced by Gordy (2003a), where he used it to study granularity adjustment. He showed how to construct a CHP using a moment matching technique for an extended version of the CreditRisk+ model. In Panel 1, we use his methodology to construct the CHP for the Vasicek model with independent LGDs. By constructing the CHP we mean finding its parameters (PD $\bar{p}$, factor loading $\bar{a}$, expected LGD $\bar{\mu}$, standard deviation of LGD $\bar{\sigma}$ and effective number of loans $\bar{M}$) from the parameters of the original pool.

PANEL 1 COMPARABLE HOMOGENEOUS PORTFOLIO

We are given a non-homogeneous portfolio with M loans, loan i having weight w_i in the portfolio, probability of default p_i, factor loading a_i, expected LGD μ_i and standard deviation of LGD σ_i. The loss rate of this portfolio, L, can be written as

$$L = \sum_{i=1}^{M} w_i Q_i 1_{\{x_i \le N^{-1}(p_i)\}}$$

Since the distribution of L is not available, we want to construct a CHP of $\bar{M}$ loans, all of them having the same weight $\bar{w} = 1/\bar{M}$, probability of default $\bar{p}$, factor loading $\bar{a}$, expected LGD $\bar{\mu}$ and standard deviation of LGD $\bar{\sigma}$. We want to choose these parameters in such a way that the CHP loss distribution matches the loss distribution of the original portfolio as close as possible. The loss rate of this portfolio, $\bar{L}$, can be written as

$$\bar{L} = \frac{1}{\bar{M}} \sum_{i=1}^{\bar{M}} \bar{Q}_i 1_{\{\bar{X}_i \le N^{-1}(\bar{p})\}}$$

The distribution of $\bar{L}$ is known and given by Equation (32).

The five parameters ($\bar{M}$, $\bar{p}$, $\bar{a}$, $\bar{\mu}$, $\bar{\sigma}$) of the CHP can be chosen by matching moments of the two loss distributions. A variety of matching rules can be used, but we will follow the simple and intuitive rules used by Gordy (2003a) for construction of the CHP in the context of the CreditRisk+ model.

The first rule equates the expected exposure-weighted default rates and determines the effective probability of default for the CHP:

$$\bar{p} = \sum_{i=1}^{M} w_i p_i \tag{I}$$

The second rule equates expected portfolio losses and determines the effective expected LGD:

$$\bar{\mu} = \frac{1}{\bar{p}} \sum_{i=1}^{M} w_i p_i \mu_i \tag{II}$$

The remaining three rules equate contributions of different sources of risk to loss variance. The contributions of the systematic risk to loss variance are

$$\operatorname{Var}\left[E[L \mid Y]\right] = \sum_{i=1}^{M} \sum_{j=1}^{M} w_i w_j \mu_i \mu_j \left(N_2\left[N^{-1}(p_i), N^{-1}(p_j); a_i a_j\right] - p_i p_j\right)$$

for the original portfolio and

$$\mathrm{Var}\left[E[\bar{L}\mid Y]\right]=\bar{\mu}^2\left(N_2\left[N^{-1}(\bar{p}),N^{-1}(\bar{p});\bar{a}^2\right]-\bar{p}^2\right)$$

for the CHP. Equating them, we obtain the third rule

$$N_2\left[N^{-1}(\bar{p}),N^{-1}(\bar{p});\bar{a}^2\right]=\frac{1}{\bar{\mu}^2}\sum_{i=1}^{M}\sum_{j=1}^{M}w_iw_j\mu_i\mu_jN_2\left[N^{-1}(p_i),N^{-1}(p_j),a_ia_j\right] \quad \textbf{(III)}$$

This rule implicitly determines the effective factor loading $\bar{a}$, which can be found by the Newton–Raphson method.

The contributions of the idiosyncratic risk to loss variance are

$$E\left[\mathrm{Var}[L\mid Y]\right]=\sum_{i=1}^{M}w_i^2\left[\mu_i^2\left(p_i-N_2\left[N^{-1}(p_i),N^{-1}(p_i);a_i^2\right]\right)+\sigma_i^2p_i\right]$$

for the original portfolio and

$$E\left[\mathrm{Var}[\bar{L}\mid Y]\right]=\frac{1}{\bar{M}}\left[\bar{\mu}^2\left(\bar{p}-N_2\left[N^{-1}(\bar{p}),N^{-1}(\bar{p});\bar{a}^2\right]\right)+\bar{\sigma}^2\bar{p}\right]$$

for the CHP. The first terms in these expressions (proportional to μ^2) represent the contribution of the idiosyncratic default risk, while the second terms (proportional to σ^2) represent the contribution of the idiosyncratic recovery risk. Equating them separately, we obtain the fourth rule that determines the effective number of loans,

$$\bar{M}=\frac{\bar{\mu}^2\left(\bar{p}-N_2\left[N^{-1}(\bar{p}),N^{-1}(\bar{p});\bar{a}^2\right]\right)}{\sum_{i=1}^{M}w_i^2\mu_i^2\left(p_i-N_2\left[N^{-1}(p_i),N^{-1}(p_i);a_i^2\right.\right.} \quad \textbf{(IV)}$$

and the fifth rule which determines the effective LGD variance,

$$\bar{\sigma}^2=\frac{\bar{M}}{\bar{p}}\sum_{i=1}^{M}w_i^2\sigma_i^2p_i \quad \textbf{(V)}$$

Thus we have determined all five parameters for the CHP.

The loss rate for the CHP is

$$\bar{L}=\frac{1}{\bar{M}}\sum_{i=1}^{\bar{M}}\bar{Q}_i1_{\left\{X_i\le N^{-1}(\bar{p})\right\}} \quad \textbf{(26)}$$

While it was not necessary to make an assumption on the LGD distribution for the fine-grained case, we have to make such an assumption now. We will assume that the LGD variable for each "effective" borrower i in the CHP is normally distributed with standard deviation $\bar{\sigma}$. This assumption has one great advantage over all other LGD distributions: it allows for analytical tractability of the non-asymptotic case. One might argue that the assumption of the normality of the LGDs is not very intuitive because it allows for values outside of the [0, 1] interval. However, if the LGDs are independent (as we have assumed from the beginning), the CHP loss distribution depends primarily on the first two moments of the LGD distribution, $\bar{\mu}$ and $\bar{\sigma}$. Higher moments become important only for extremely coarse-grained pools.

This observation can be explained by the central limit theorem. Conditionally on realisation m of the number of defaults in the CHP D, the loss rate is

$$\bar{L} \mid \{D = m\} = \frac{1}{\bar{M}} \sum_{i=1}^{m} \bar{Q}_i$$

According to the central limit theorem, this conditional loss variable becomes normally distributed with mean $\bar{\mu}m/\bar{M}$ and standard deviation $\bar{\sigma}\sqrt{m}/\bar{M}$ in the limit of large m, regardless of the distribution of $\bar{Q}_i$. Even for relatively small values of m, the sensitivity of $\bar{L} \mid \{D = m\}$ to the higher moments of $\bar{Q}_i$ quickly reduces with m. Since higher values of unconditional losses are associated with more defaults, the sensitivity of the unconditional loss distribution to the higher moments of $\bar{Q}_i$ decreases as one moves further into the tail. Thus, for a reasonably accurate description of the loss distribution to the right of $\bar{\mu}/\bar{M}$ (loss value roughly corresponding to a single default), we can safely assume a normal distribution of $\bar{Q}_i$.

Complementary loss distribution

We will follow Pykhtin and Dev (2002a) in deriving the complementary loss distribution of the CHP. To take advantage of the conditional independence of defaults, we will start by expressing $\bar{G}(l)$ as the expectation of the conditional (on the local systematic factor Y) complementary loss distribution

$$\bar{G}(l) = \int_{-\infty}^{\infty} \mathrm{d}y\, n(y) \Pr[\bar{L} > l \mid Y = y] \tag{27}$$

Since the pool is homogeneous, its total loss will depend only on the total number of defaults and it will not depend on what particular loans defaulted. Thus, the next logical step is to condition the CHP loss further on the number of defaulted loans D,

$$\bar{G}(l) = \int_{-\infty}^{\infty} \mathrm{d}y\, n(y) \sum_{m=0}^{M} \Pr[\bar{L} > l \mid \{Y = y\} \& \{D = m\}] \Pr[D = m \mid Y = y] \qquad \textbf{(28)}$$

where m runs through all possible realisations of D.

Conditionally on realisation of Y, the defaults are independent, and D has binomial distribution

$$\Pr[D = m \mid Y = y] = P_m^{\bar{M}}\left[\bar{p}^{\bar{a}|Y}(y)\right] \qquad \textbf{(29)}$$

with the elementary event probability equal to the probability of default in the CHP conditional on the event $Y = y$. The binomial probability of m successes out of M independent trials with the elementary event probability p is given by

$$P_m^M(p) = \binom{M}{m} p^m (1-p)^{M-m}$$

If we condition the CHP loss rate on the number of defaults $D = m$, Equation (26) will transform to

$$\bar{L} \mid \{D = m\} = \frac{1}{\bar{M}} \sum_{i=1}^{m} Q_i = \frac{m}{\bar{M}} \left(\bar{\mu} + \frac{\bar{\sigma}}{\sqrt{m}} \zeta \right)$$

where the sum is taken over m defaulted loans and ζ is a standard normal variable (the sum of m independent normal variables is also a normal variable). Conditioning on $Y = y$ is redundant here because LGD variables $\{Q_i\}$ are independent of Y. Now we can use the fact that the loss conditional on the number of defaults depends only on a single standard normal variable and obtain

$$\Pr[\bar{L} > l \mid \{Y = y\} \& \{D = m\}] = \Pr\left[\frac{m}{\bar{M}} \left(\bar{\mu} + \frac{\bar{\sigma}}{\sqrt{m}} \zeta \right) > l \right] = N\left[x_m(l)\right] \qquad \textbf{(30)}$$

where we have defined

$$x_m(l) = \frac{\bar{\mu} - \left(l\bar{M}/m\right)}{\left(\bar{\sigma}/\sqrt{m}\right)} \tag{31}$$

Substituting Equations (29) and (30) into Equation (28), we obtain the unconditional complementary loss distribution

$$\bar{G}(l) = \int_{-\infty}^{\infty} \mathrm{d}y \; n(y) \sum_{m=0}^{\bar{M}} P_m^{\bar{M}}\left[\bar{p}^{\bar{a}|Y}(y)\right] N\left[x_m(l)\right] \tag{32}$$

Expected loss

EL for the tranche can be found by substitution of Equation (32) into Equation (3). Integration over loss level l can be performed analytically by changing the integrating variable from l to x_m according to Equation (31) and using the relation $\int \mathrm{d}t\, N(t) = tN(t) + n(t)$. The integration results in

$$\mathrm{EL}(s,t) = \int_{-\infty}^{\infty} \mathrm{d}y \; n(y) \sum_{m=0}^{\bar{M}} P_m^{\bar{M}}\left[\bar{p}^{\bar{a}|Y}(y)\right]\left[h_m(s) - h_m(t)\right] \tag{33}$$

with $h_m(l)$ defined as

$$h_m(v) = \frac{m}{\bar{M}} \frac{\bar{\sigma}}{\sqrt{m}} \left(x_m(l) N\left[x_m(l)\right] + n\left[x_m(l)\right]\right) \tag{34}$$

The right-hand side of Equation (33) (as well as that of Equation (32)) can be easily evaluated numerically. Since the standard normal density $n(y)$ goes to zero very fast, infinite limits in the integral can be safely replaced by finite ones.[6] After approximating the integral by a discrete sum, the calculation reduces to evaluation of a double sum, which can be quickly performed even on a mid-level PC.[7] The problem of large binomial coefficients and small powers of the conditional default probability for large M can easily be avoided by computing binomial probabilities $P_m^M(p)$ recursively according to

$$P_m^M(p) = \frac{M - m + 1}{m} \frac{p}{1-p} P_{m-1}^M(p)$$

This is computationally costless since a sum over m is computed anyway.

Conditional complementary loss distribution

To calculate the EC for a tranche, we need to know the complementary loss distribution of the CHP conditional on event $Z = z_{1-q}$. The simple Vasicek formula that we derived for fine-grained pools (Equation (11)) is no longer applicable, and we need to derive a new relation for $\bar{G}(l \mid z_{1-q})$. This derivation can be done similarly to the derivation of $\bar{G}(l)$ above. Let us modify Equation (28) to include conditioning on $Z = z$:

$$\bar{G}(l|z) = \int_{-\infty}^{\infty} d\varepsilon\, n(\varepsilon) \sum_{m=0}^{M} \Pr[\bar{L} > l \mid \{Y = y\} \& \{D = m\} \& \{Z = z\}] \times \Pr[D = m \mid \{Y = y\} \& \{Z = z\}] \quad (35)$$

Since the integral now represents the expectation conditional on $Z = z$, the integration is done with respect to the "industry-specific" factor ε.

The conditional probability that there are exactly m defaults will still be binomial,

$$\Pr[D = m \mid \{Y = y\} \& \{Z = z\}] = P_m^{\bar{M}}\left[\bar{p}^{\bar{b}|\varepsilon}(z, \varepsilon)\right] \quad (36)$$

but with the elementary event probability being the PD conditional on both $Y = y$ and $Z = z$. Taking into account the relation between Y and Z given by Equation (9), we can express this conditional PD as a function of Z and ε:

$$\bar{p}^{\bar{b}|\varepsilon}(z, \varepsilon) = \frac{N^{-1}[\bar{p}^{\bar{r}|Z}(z)] - \bar{b}\varepsilon}{\sqrt{1 - \bar{b}^2}} \quad (37)$$

where $\bar{b}$ is the conditional on $Z = z$ correlation between the asset return X_i and the local factor Y. It is related to the unconditional correlation $\bar{a}$ *via* Equation (21).

The conditional probability of loss exceeding level l in Equation (35) is not affected by the extra conditioning on $Z = z$. Once we condition this probability on the number of defaults, the extra conditioning on either the local or global systematic factors becomes redundant because LGD variables are independent of either of them. Therefore, this probability is still given by Equation (30). Substituting Equations (30) and (36) into Equation (35), we obtain the conditional complementary loss distribution

$$\bar{G}(l \mid z) = \int_{-\infty}^{\infty} d\varepsilon\, n(\varepsilon) \sum_{m=0}^{M} P_m^{\bar{M}}\left[\bar{p}^{\bar{b}|\varepsilon}(z, \varepsilon)\right] N\left[x_m(l)\right] \tag{38}$$

Economic capital

The EC for a tranche is obtained by integrating $\bar{G}(l \mid z_{1-q})$ given by Equation (38) according to Equation (6). The only l-dependent part in Equation (38) is $N[x_m(l)]$, the same as in the unconditional complementary loss distribution. Thus, we have already done the integration in deriving Equation (33) and can write tranche EC as

$$EC_q(s, t) = \int_{-\infty}^{\infty} d\varepsilon\, n(\varepsilon) \sum_{m=0}^{M} P_m^{\bar{M}}\left[\bar{p}^{\bar{b}|\varepsilon}(z_{1-q}, \varepsilon)\right]\left[h_m(s) - h_m(t)\right] \tag{39}$$

where $h_m(l)$ is defined according to Equation (34). The right-hand side of Equation (39) can be evaluated in exactly the same way as the EL in Equation (33).

Examples

Now we will look at how tranche EC depends upon the granularity of the pool, pool credit quality and correlation between the local and global systematic factors. Figure 2 shows the ITT capital at $q = 99.9\%$ for homogeneous pools of $\bar{M}$ speculative grade ($\bar{p} = 5.0\%$) loans at two choices of the correlation between the risk factors: (a) $\rho_{YZ} = 0.95$ and (b) $\rho_{YZ} = 0.80$. The global factor loading is kept fixed at $\bar{r} = 0.40$ (corresponding to the global asset correlation of 0.16). The expected LGD for all pools is $\bar{\mu} = 40\%$, and the standard deviation of LGD is $\bar{\sigma} = 20\%$. The pool contributory EC is $K_C = 13.1\%$. Different curves correspond to different values of $\bar{M}$.

The main observation from Figure 2 is that reducing the effective number of loans in the pool reduces the risk of junior tranches and increases the risk of senior tranches. This behaviour is very intuitive: lack of diversification in any portfolio leads to increasing risk of very high losses. The crossover region, where the dependence of

Figure 2 ITT capital for homogeneous pools of speculative grade loans (PD $\bar{p} = 5.0\%$)

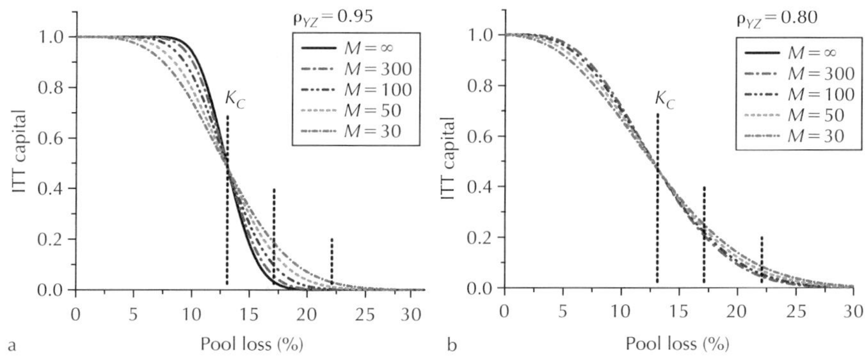

the ITT capital upon $\bar{M}$ changes its sign, is remarkably small and well defined. The transition happens in a very small vicinity of the pool contributory EC K_C.[8] This rule holds for a very wide range of model parameters, and breaks down only for very coarse-grained pools with low PD, as we will see below.

Reducing the level of correlation between the local and global risk factors reduces the sensitivity of tranche EC to $\bar{M}$, as can be seen from comparison of Figures 2(a) and 2(b). An alternative way of describing this effect is that more fine-grained pools are more sensitive to changes in ρ_{YZ}. At the intuitive level, this can be explained as follows. Conditionally on $Z = z_{1-q}$, more fine-grained pools have less uncertainty in the loss rate at given ρ_{YZ}. Therefore, they should be more sensitive to further increase in the pool loss uncertainty resulting from decreasing ρ_{YZ}.

To show these effects quantitatively for tranches of finite size, we have defined a securitisation based on each of the pools. There are four tranches in this securitisation: the first loss piece absorbing pool losses up to $K_C = 13.1\%$; two mezzanine tranches with notionals 4% (more junior) and 5% (more senior) of the pool notional; and the senior tranche taking losses above 22.1%. The tranche bounds are shown in Figure 2. Table 1 shows the EC for these tranches as a fraction of tranche notional for each of the pools.

Figure 3 shows the ITT capital for investment-grade pools with the PD $\bar{p} = 0.05\%$. All other pool parameters are the same as in the

Table 1 Tranche capital for homogeneous pools of speculative grade loans (PD $\bar{p}$ = 5.0%)

Tranche (%)	M = ∞ (%)	M = 300 (%)	M = 100 (%)	M = 50 (%)	M = 30 (%)
		ρ_{YZ} = 0.95			
0–13.1	93.7	92.6	90.8	88.6	86.3
13.1–17.1	20.0	22.7	26.3	29.5	32.1
17.1–22.1	0.57	1.27	3.02	5.79	9.08
22.1–100	0.00	0.00	0.00	0.02	0.08
		ρ_{YZ} = 0.8			
0–13.1	85.4	84.9	84.0	82.7	81.1
13.1–17.1	32.6	33.0	33.6	34.4	35.3
17.1–22.1	10.6	11.2	12.4	13.9	15.7
22.1–100	0.11	0.13	0.18	0.26	0.37

Figure 3 ITT capital for homogeneous pools of investment-grade loans (PD $\bar{p}$ = 0.05%)

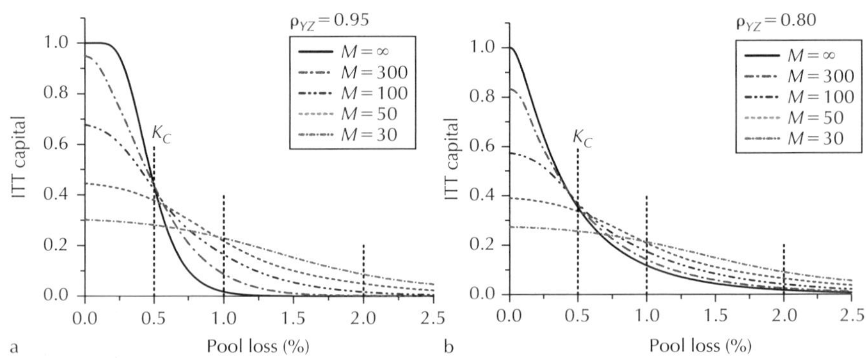

speculative-grade example above. The contributory capital is K_C = 0.50% for all pools. Most of the observations we have made for the speculative grade case apply here as well: the main effect of reducing the number of loans $\bar{M}$ in the pool amounts to redistribution of risk from more junior to more senior tranches. However, the magnitude of this effect is much larger than in the speculative-grade case.

This larger magnitude can easily be understood if we recall that the value of the ITT capital at zero is the probability of non-zero loss in the pool, conditional on $Z = z_{1-q}$. In the speculative-grade examples above, the PD was so high that, conditionally on $Z = z_{0.1\%}$, the probability of no defaults in the pool (and, therefore, zero pool loss) was negligible even for pools with $\bar{M}$ as low as 30. This is why all the curves in Figure 2 start at ITT capital equal to one when pool loss is zero. In contrast, the PD of the investment-grade pools is low enough that the probability of no defaults is significant even when it is conditioned on $Z = z_{0.1\%}$ and $\bar{M}$ is as high as 300. The smaller is $\bar{M}$, the larger is the conditional probability of no defaults, and the lower is ITT capital at zero loss. Therefore, the dependence of the ITT capital at low pool loss levels upon the number of loans in the pool must be much stronger for investment-grade pools than for speculative-grade pools. Since the total contributory risk of a pool does not depend on $\bar{M}$ (graphically, the total area under each curve must equal K_C), the reduction of risk at low loss levels must be compensated by the equal increase of risk at high loss levels.

We have also defined a sample securitisation for the investment-grade case. The first-loss piece absorbs losses up to $K_C = 0.50\%$, the junior and the senior mezzanine tranches take losses between 0.50% and 1.00% and between 1.00% and 2.00%, respectively, and the senior tranche takes losses above 2.00%. The tranche bounds are shown in Figure 3. Table 2 shows the EC for these tranches as a fraction of tranche notional for each of our investment-grade pools.

Table 2 Tranche capital for homogeneous pools of investment grade loans (PD $\bar{p} = 0.05\%$)

Tranche (%)	M = ∞ (%)	M = 300 (%)	M = 100 (%)	M = 50 (%)	M = 30 (%)
		$\rho_{YZ} = 0.95$			
0 – 0.5	85.2	72.9	58.3	42.0	29.3
0.5 – 1.0	14.3	22.7	27.3	30.0	25.7
1.0 – 2.0	0.24	2.14	6.60	11.1	15.4
2.0 – 100	0.00	0.00	0.01	0.03	0.07
		$\rho_{YZ} = 0.8$			
0 – 0.5	66.3	60.1	49.9	37.0	26.7
0.5 – 1.0	21.1	23.4	25.6	27.4	23.7
1.0 – 2.0	5.13	6.59	9.14	11.9	14.9
2.0 – 100	0.01	0.02	0.03	0.06	0.10

CONCLUDING REMARKS

In this chapter, we have given a detailed analysis of Pykhtin and Dev's model of credit risk for securitisation tranches. The model belongs to the asymptotic single risk factor framework as it views the securitisation tranche as part of an infinitely fine-grained portfolio of assets driven by a single "global" systematic risk factor. Typically, assets in the collateral pool underlying the securitisation have more in common between themselves (eg, they belong to the same industry) than with the assets outside the pool that make up the portfolio. Therefore, one would expect higher correlations across these assets than correlations between these assets and other assets in the portfolio. The model accommodates this situation by assuming that losses in the collateral pool are driven by another, "local", risk factor. This local risk factor is strongly, but not perfectly, correlated with the global one and is analogous to an industry risk factor in multi-factor portfolio models.

This model is rigorous enough to produce reliable estimates of EL and EC for securitisation tranches at a fixed time horizon, even though it simplifies the structure of the cashflow waterfall. The payoff from this simplification is that the model does not require Monte Carlo simulations. All calculations can be done analytically or semi-analytically (with some parts done numerically) in a fraction of a second and are free from Monte Carlo noise.

1 Examples include Risk Metrics' CreditMetrics, KMV's PortfolioManager, CSFB's CreditRisk+. See Bluhm *et al* (2002) for an excellent review of portfolio credit risk models.
2 Models that incorporate this dependence have appeared recently in the literature. See, for example, Frye (2000) and Pykhtin (2003).
3 See, for example, Bluhm *et al* (2002).
4 See Duffie and Gârleanu (2001) for a rigorous dynamic modeling framework for CDOs.
5 Relation $\int_{-\infty}^{z} dy\, n(y) N\left([x - ay]/\sqrt{1-a^2}\right) = N_2(x, z; a)$ can be verified by differentiating $N_2(x, z; a)$ with respect to z. Algorithms for evaluation of the bivariate normal distribution function are discussed in great detail in Vasicek (1998).
6 Integrating from –6 to 6 is enough for most practical purposes.
7 For a portfolio of 1,000 loans, typical computation time on a Pentium-III 733 MHz PC is just a few hundredths of a second.
8 Visually, it appears that all the curves in Figure 2 cross at one point when $l = K_C$. Strictly speaking, this is not the case.

REFERENCES

Basel Committee on Banking Supervision, 2004, "International Convergence of Capital Measurement and Capital Standards", A Revised Framework, June.

Bluhm, C., L. Overbeck, and, C. Wagner, 2002, *An Introduction to Credit Risk Modeling* (Chapman & Hall/CRC).

Duffie, D., and N. Gârleanu, 2001, "Risk and Valuation of Collateralized Debt Obligations", Working Paper, September.

Frye, J., 2000, "Collateral Damage", *Risk*, pp. 91–4, April.

Gordy, M., 2003a, "A Risk-Factor Model Foundation for Ratings-Based Bank Capital Rules", *Journal of Financial Intermediation,* **12(3)**, pp. 199–232.

Gordy, M., 2003b, "Reconciling Two Approaches to Setting Capital for Securitizations", Working Paper, October.

Gordy, M., and D. Jones, 2003, "Random Tranches", *Risk*, pp. 78–83, March.

Peretyatkin, V., and W. Perraudin, 2002, "Expected Loss and Probability of Default Approaches to Rating Collateralised Debt Obligations and the Scope for 'Ratings Shopping'", in Michael K. Ong (ed), *Credit Ratings: Methodologies, Rationale and Default Risk* (London: Risk Books).

Peretyatkin, V., and W. Perraudin, 2003, "Capital for Asset-backed Securities", Working Paper, February.

Pykhtin, M., and A. Dev, 2002a, "Analytical Approach to Credit Risk Modelling", *Risk*, pp. S26–S32, March.

Pykhtin, M., and A. Dev, 2002b, "Credit Risk in Asset Securitisations: Analytical Model", *Risk*, pp. S16–S20, May.

Pykhtin, M., and A. Dev, 2003, "Coarse-grained CDOs", *Risk*, pp. 113–6, January.

Pykhtin, M., 2003, "Unexpected Recovery Risk", *Risk*, pp. 74–8, August.

Vasicek, O., 1987, "Probability of Loss on Loan Portfolio", KMV Corporation.

Vasicek, O., 1991, "Limiting Loan Loss Probability Distribution", KMV Corporation.

Vasicek, O., 1998, "A Series Expansion for the Bivariate Normal Integral", *Journal of Computational Finance*, **1(4)**, pp. 5–10.

Vasicek, O., 2002, "Loan Portfolio Value", *Risk*, pp. 160–2, December.

10

*A Comparative Analysis of CDO Risk Models**

Tom Dewyspelaere, João B.C. Garcia; Olivier Renault

Dexia Group; Standard & Poor's

In this chapter, we analyse three techniques designed to assess the risk of collateralised debt obligations (CDOs). We describe their basic setup and then apply them to a realistic CDO structure in order to compare default probabilities and expected losses. We then perform a large number of scenarios using Standard & Poor's Portfolio Risk Tracker, and evaluate how changes in interest rates, recoveries, correlations etc, affect the default likelihood of the tranches, as well as their values-at-risk (VAR).

A REVIEW OF THE METHODS

This section is dedicated to a brief introduction to the three models that we use to compute CDO risk statistics. In order to remain concise, we only outline the various techniques but the interested reader may refer to the references listed at the end of the chapter for further details. The three techniques are the Gaussian copula method, the Binomial expansion technique (BET), and Portfolio Risk Tracker (PRT).

The Gaussian copula method

In the copula approach, default times for the entities in the underlying portfolio are simulated jointly. The joint distribution of

*The views expressed herein are those of the authors but not necessarily those of Dexia Group or Standard & Poor's. We thank Arnaud de Servigny, Ronny Langendries, Robert Lamb, Luc Léonard, Stéphanie Tetu and William Perraudin for their technical expertise and comments.

default times must obey two requirements: (a) it must recover the marginal distribution of default probabilities for each name in the underlying portfolio; (b) it must recover the default correlation for the underlying collateral.

In this chapter we use the copula function approach to generate correlated default times that follow the marginal distributions of the underlying collateral entities. We refer to Nelsen (1999) for a formal description of copulas, to Frees and Valdez (1998) for a survey article and to Li (1999) and Garcia *et al* (2003) for the use of normal copulas in pricing baskets of credit derivatives.

Consider that the collateral of the CDO is composed of M underlying names and that $P_1(t_1), P_2(t_2), \ldots, P_M(t_M)$ are the marginal distributions of default times for each entity. A copula function C is a function from $(0,1)^M$ in $(0,1)$ such that

$$C(P_1(t_1), P_2(t_2), \ldots, P_M(t_M)) = P(t_1, t_2, t_3, \ldots, t_M) \tag{1}$$

where P is the joint distribution function of default times. Under some standard technical conditions (eg, continuity of the marginals) it can be proved that any multivariate distribution can be written in the form of a copula function (Sklar 1996).

A common market practice is to use the multivariate normal copula that is defined as:

$$C(x_1, x_2, ..., x_M) = N_M(N^{-1}(x_1), N^{-1}(x_2), \ldots, N^{-1}(x_M), \Sigma)$$

where N^{-1} is the inverse of the univariate standard normal distribution and N_M is the multivariate normal distribution with correlation matrix function Σ.

In this chapter, in order to produce comparable results, the correlation matrix is calculated from the input parameters used in Portfolio Risk Tracker (see below). The marginal default probabilities are obtained from Standard & Poor's, based on the ratings of the collateral.

Once the defaults are determined the cashflows are passed through the waterfall and the algorithm is similar to that discussed in the BET approach below.

The Binomial expansion technique

The BET methodology is based on the concept of *diversity score* (DS) and it is an application of the binomial formula from probability theory to a simplified version of the portfolio. We refer to Cifuentes and O'Connor (1996) for a first reference on BET and to Garcia *et al* (2004) for a more detailed description and tests of the parameters on the BET algorithm. The idea behind the methodology is to map the portfolio of heterogeneous correlated securities with distinct probabilities of defaults into a portfolio of homogeneous independent securities (the idealised portfolio) each having the same probability of default.

The first step is the calculation of the DS of the collateral portfolio[1] (CP). The goal of the DS measure is to redefine the pool of correlated heterogeneous assets into a pool of fewer independent homogeneous assets. Thus, it is assumed that a portfolio of M correlated and non-homogeneous bonds has the same risk as a portfolio consisting of $DS < M$ uncorrelated and identical assets.

Diversification is measured on two levels. First, it is measured at the issuer level by dividing every issuer's exposure by the average issuer exposure and capping the resulting ratio to 1. This gives the equivalent unit score (EUS) per issuer. The more issuers with exposures that are larger than the average (high issuer concentration), the lower will be the average EUS of the issuers. Second, diversification is measured at the industry level by summing initially all EUS of all issuers in a certain industry (the so-called *aggregate industry equivalent unit score* (AIEUS) and then scaling down the AIEUS into an industry diversity score whereby the bigger AIEUS are scaled down more (eg, if AIEUS(industry i) = 1 then DS(industry i) = 1, if AIEUS(industry j) = 20 then DS(industry j) = 5). The DS of the pool is equal to the sum of all industry DS.

The second step consists of determining the expected cashflows from the collateral for each possible number of homogeneous bonds defaulting. The following assumptions are made.

a) *Principal payments from the collateral.* All homogeneous bonds have the same maturity derived from the weighted average life (WAL) of the portfolio. Alternatively, one can take into account the expected principal redemption schedule of the portfolio.

b) *Interest payments from the collateral.* All homogeneous bonds have the same coupon, equal to the weighted average coupon (WAC) of the portfolio.

c) *Recovery rate (WAR).* A standard approach uses one predetermined rate[2] (eg, 35%). Alternatively, one can use a recovery rate that takes into account the types of exposures (secured, unsecured, subordinate, bonds or loans, etc) of every portfolio.

Assume that N_T is the total notional of the collateral portfolio. The notional involved in the case of j defaults is given by

$$D_j = \frac{N_T}{DS} \cdot j \tag{3}$$

and the loss on D_j is given by

$$\text{Loss}_j = D_j \cdot (1 - \text{WAR}) \tag{4}$$

d) *Distribution of losses through time.* A standard approach assumes six default patterns:

i) 50 10 10 10 10 10
ii) 10 50 10 10 10 10
...
vi) 10 10 10 10 10 50

In each scenario one distributes the losses across 6 years. In (i) 50% of the losses occur in the first year and 10% in the remaining years. In (ii), 10% of the losses occur in the first year, 50% in the second and 10% in the remaining, and analogously for (iii) up to (vi). With the scenarios above one can determine the amount left in the collateral.

In the third step one goes through the waterfall determining the amounts received by each note holder. In order to account for interest rate risk a common market practice is to make parallel shifts on the levels of the yield curve.

In the fourth step one uses the weighted average rating factor (WARF) and the WAL of the CP to determine the probability of default p of one idealised bond[3]. With this probability and the binomial formula one can calculate the probability of each of the collateral cashflow scenario's generated in step 2 (0 up to DS idealised bonds defaulting). The probability of n (where $n \leq DS$) defaults (P_n) is given by

$$P_n = \binom{DS}{n} p^n \cdot (1-p)^{DS-n} \quad \mathbf{(5)}$$

The probability of default p is often adjusted by a stress factor γ (that will depend on the target rating).

Finally one calculates the loss distribution using the probability of each scenario with its respective loss. This can be used to compute default probabilities for the tranches, as well as expected losses.

The Portfolio Risk Tracker (PRT) model

PRT is Standard & Poor's credit risk portfolio model. This model is designed to compute risk statistics (expected loss, value at risk, expected shortfall, etc) on portfolios that can include a wide variety of assets, such as bonds and loans, swaps, equities, guarantees, credit default swaps and CDOs. The treatment of CDOs is novel in that it involves the joint simulation of assets on the balance sheet of the bank, as well as in the pools backing the various CDOs that the bank may have invested in.

PRT performs a full simulation of the assets in the CDO pool, including the simulation of their ratings, marked-to-model prices and recoveries in default. The model then applies the waterfall structure of the deal and distributes the cashflows in the specified order of priority. The full cashflow modelling enables users to assess the correlation between assets on the balance sheet and CDO tranches that may be backed by the same bonds. It also provides correlation measures for CDO tranches. A more detailed explanation of the model is provided in Perraudin and Renault (2004), but we just recall the basics of the modelling approach here.

The algorithms used by PRT differ depending on the calculation horizon θ chosen by the user. If the calculation horizon is equal to or longer than the maturity T of the CDO, Algorithm A is used, while if it is shorter ($\theta < T$), PRT relies on the more elaborate Algorithm B.

Algorithm A: Assessing the risk of the CDO to maturity

PRT is a dynamic ratings-based model, in which latent random variables drive the credit worthiness of obligors (see de Servigny and Renault (2004) for a survey of credit risk portfolio models). The ratings of the bonds in the CDO pool are simulated until the maturity of the deal, according to the migration probabilities supplied by the user and the assumption of correlation implicit in industry and country factor loadings.

At each annual time step, PRT checks for failures in tests (interest coverage (I/C) or overcollateralisation (O/C) tests) and triggers early amortisation accordingly. At each intermediary time step, the model assesses whether cashflows are sufficient to pay the promised interest on the notes. If not, interest is deferred to the next time period. Any residual cashflow after full service of the notes is reinvested in a reserve account at the riskless rate. After the reinvestment period, the principals on maturing bonds are used to amortise the tranches, starting with the most senior.

At the maturity of the deal, the final interest payment is paid as well as the remaining principal. If the proceeds from selling bonds and liquidating the reserve account exceed the debt service, the surplus goes to the holders of the equity tranche of the CDO. Losses on the various tranches can then be computed by looking at the difference between promised payments and actually received cashflows.

Algorithm B: Looking at shorter calculation horizons

When the calculation horizon is shorter than the maturity of the CDO, one has to rely on another approach in order to take into account the following fact. Changes in the value of CDO tranches between time 0 and θ should not only reflect losses that arose before or at θ, but also expected losses between θ and T.

In order to achieve this, PRT proceeds in two steps. In the first step, the model calculates numerical pricing functions that relate the price of a given CDO tranche to the distribution of ratings in the CDO pool at θ. In the second step these pricing functions are inserted into the main Monte Carlo simulation engine.

Step 1: evaluating pricing functions. The first step starts with a simulation until maturity T, in exactly the same way as in Algorithm A. The performance of a given tranche at time T is then linked to the behaviour of a random variable z. If z is positive, the tranche does not default and pays the discounted contractual value V. If z is negative, it does default and pays YV, with $0 \leq Y < 1$.

The expected discounted payoff on the tranche is then estimated as

$$\text{Tranche value at } \theta = \left(E\left(Y1_{z<0}\right) + E\left(1_{z>0}\right)\right)V$$
$$= E\left(Y1_{z<0} \middle| z<0\right)P(z<0)V + VP(z>0)$$

with the probability of default being estimated using a logit model:

$$P(z<0) = \frac{\exp(\beta' X)}{\exp(\beta' X)+1}$$

while the "recovery rate" is derived from a regression[4]:

$$E\left(Y \,|\, z<0, X\right) = \gamma' X$$

The explanatory variables X used in the regression include the fractions of the value of the underlying pool that are accounted for by specific ratings, "AAA" to "CCC". This modelling approach is similar to that proposed by Longstaff and Schwartz (2001) in an option pricing context.

In summary, the first step of the algorithm evaluates pricing functions for all tranches at time θ, conditional on the distribution of ratings at that time.

Step 2: Main Monte Carlo run. Once the numerical pricing functions have been evaluated, PRT starts the main simulation run, which includes all CDO tranches and other assets held in the bank's portfolio. Then the calculation procedure is as follows.

1. Ratings for all assets (on- and off-balance-sheet) are simulated until the chosen horizon θ.
2. Marked-to-model pricing of all assets is performed, conditional on the simulated ratings, interest rates, spreads, etc. The pricing of the CDO tranches is obtained using the numerical pricing functions obtained in Step 1 and the realisations of the distribution of the ratings in the pool.
3. Values-at-risk and other risk statistics at the portfolio and exposure levels can then be computed across the simulations.

For all the scenarios described below, we performed 300,000 Monte Carlo runs. It takes between 1 and 3 minutes on a standard PC, depending on θ.

THE CDO STRUCTURE

In the next section, we apply the various methodologies for risk analysis described above to a realistic CDO structure under various scenarios. The CDO comprises four tranches, two of which pay a fixed coupon while the other two pay a coupon indexed on Libor. More details on the structure are provided in Table 1.

In our simulations, we assume that the reinvestment period is two years and there are no management fees. In order to make our example realistic, we used a real CDO pool to back up the structure. All bonds in the pool have been issued by US or Canadian companies and they span 18 of the 24 GICS[5] industry groups. The

Table 1 CDO structure: (a) liabilities and (b) assets

(a)

	Par amount ($)	Coupon	I/C	O/C	Maturity
Tranche 1 (most senior)	85,000,000	3.5%	1.4	1.2	6 years
Tranche 2	60,000,000	4%	1.3	1.1	6 years
Tranche 3	35,000,000	Libor + 3%			6 years
Tranche 4 ("equity")	14,000,000	Libor + 5%			6 years
Total	194,000,000				

(b)

	Par amount ($)	Number of bonds	Average rate (%)	Recovery coupon (%)	Average maturity
AAA	1,403,920	2	10.0	35	3.0 years
AA	0	0	–	–	–
A	0	0	–	–	–
BBB	8,500,000	6	8.6	35	4.2 years
BB	32,245,000	16	8.2	35	4.0 years
B	103,729,000	33	9.5	35	4.0 years
CCC	45,666,359	13	9.7	35	5.5 years
Total	191,544,279	70	9.2	35	4.3 years

pool consists primarily of seasoned bonds with high coupons, high default probabilities and relatively short remaining times to maturity (about four years).

The deal follows a simple waterfall structure in which, at each time period, the cash generated by the pool is used to service the coupons and principals promised on the notes. Any unpaid interest is accrued until the next period, while any extra cash generated by the pool above the promised payments is invested in a reserve account at the riskless rate. During the reinvestment period (first two years of the deal), the principals of maturing bonds and the amounts recovered on defaulted securities are reinvested, while these proceeds are used to amortise the notes after the reinvestment period (last four years). A tranche is considered as defaulting if it misses any promised interest or principal payment.

SCENARIOS AND RESULTS

The purpose of this section is to analyse the impact of changes in inputs on the riskiness of the various tranches. More precisely, we evaluate how changes in correlations, interest rates, recovery rates and time horizon affect risk statistics, such as probabilities of default (PD), expected losses (EL) or VARs. These changes are all defined with respect to the base case scenario, described in the previous section.

Base case scenario

Table 2 provides results on the base case scenario for the three approaches reviewed above. The PDs are broadly similar for both the PRT and copula approach but the BET probabilities are

Table 2 Results on base case scenario

	Gauss. copula PD (%)	BET PD (%)	PRT	
			PD (%)	EL (%)
Tranche 1	0.90	0.00	0.14	0.011
Tranche 2	15.9	0.20	13.54	3.91
Tranche 3	91.20	29.44	47.67	30.55

PD: Probability of Default, EL: Expected Loss as % of par. (includes losses on interest, so EL can exceed 100% of par.)

markedly lower. EL measures are not comparable in the three approaches and are therefore only reported for PRT.

Mapping the PDs to a rating scale, the tranches would be approximately AAA, BB and B- rated, using the PRT model.

The base case scenario will be our benchmark for analysing the changes in PD and EL, when one changes some of the assumptions regarding recoveries, interest rates, correlations and time horizon.

Impact of correlations

CDO tranches can be seen as options on the pool of underlying bonds. Therefore, their performance is affected crucially by correlations across these bonds. In PRT, default correlations are driven by the sensitivities of the various obligors to country and industry factors and by the share of risk that is systematic (ie, factor driven) rather than idiosyncratic (firm specific). In the base case scenario, it was assumed that the idiosyncratic term accounted for 80% of obligor risk. This is in line with the assumptions in the Basel II guidelines for a wide variety of assets.

Table 3 contrasts probabilities of default obtained for the top three tranches, when correlations vary. The results are strikingly different, depending on the position of the tranche in the capital structure. For senior tranches (1 and 2), which are the most default remote, an increase in correlation (decrease in idiosyncratic parameter) means primarily that the likelihood of extreme numbers of defaults in the pool increases. Therefore, the probabilities of default of these two tranches increase sharply as the idiosyncratic parameter decreases.

For tranche 3, an increase in correlation implies that both very bad events (large number of defaults in the pool) and very good events (few defaults in the pool) become more likely. Tranche 3 occupies a medium/low position in the capital structure and

Table 3 Impact (%) of idiosyncratic term on tranche PD

	60%	70%	80% (base)	90%	100%
Tranche 1	1.31	0.61	0.14	0.00	0.00
Tranche 2	20.26	17.51	13.54	7.31	0.11
Tranche 3	46.57	47.04	47.67	48.74	51.07

shows a low sensitivity to changes in correlations because changes in correlations have offsetting effects. One can observe small increases in default probabilities when the correlation decreases, implying that the "good events" impact dominates the "bad events" impact.

We have not computed results for tranche 4, but would expect correlation increases to be associated with sharp falls in default probability of that tranche, as it will default most of the time, unless a cluster of survivals is recorded. These clusters are more likely when correlations are high.

Impact of recovery rates

Recovery rates in the pool also play an important role in determining the performance of the CDO tranches, especially for our chosen structure, which has low credit quality collateral. In PRT, recovery rates are assumed to follow a beta distribution with user-defined mean and standard deviation. When the standard deviation is set to zero, the distribution collapses to a point mass and recoveries are constant.

The results of the scenarios we ran on the CDO are displayed in Table 4. The first four scenarios assume a constant recovery rate for all defaulted bonds in the pool. These recovery rates are respectively 0% (complete loss), 25%, 35% (base case scenario) and 45%. The fifth scenario introduces volatility in recovery rates. The mean is equal to that of the base case but the standard deviation is set to 20%. Therefore, differences in default probabilities between the "Vol 20%" scenario and the base scenario are attributable to loss-given-default (LGD)[6] volatility.

Finally, the last scenario incorporates correlation between the PD and the LGD. Aggregate default rates (PD) and LGD have been shown to be correlated, in particular when looking at trading price

Table 4 Impact (%) of recovery rates on tranche PD

	0%	25%	35% (base)	45%	Vol 20%	PD/LGD corr
Tranche 1	7.20	0.82	0.14	0.01	0.18	0.34
Tranche 2	46.00	22.86	13.54	5.88	13.83	14.54
Tranche 3	75.92	58.25	47.67	34.61	47.67	47.19

measures of recoveries (see Altman *et al* 2003). In PRT, the user has the option to introduce correlation between these two key drivers of credit risk. The intuition behind the correlation is that, in a bad year, a large number of defaults are observed. This triggers an excess supply of liquidated assets, which depresses the value of recoveries.

By linking recoveries to the same factors that drive the default process, PRT achieves two things. First, it enables one to replicate the correlation discussed above. Second, it makes recovery risk systematic. Therefore, there will be years in which average recovery rates will be high and others where they will be lower. The latter will tend to coincide with the years where a large number of defaults are observed. The impact can be substantial on credit VAR, in particular at high confidence levels. PRT is designed so that recoveries are more correlated for companies belonging to the same industry and country.

The results of the first four scenarios reported in Table 5 are quite straightforward. The higher the recovery rate, the lower the probability of default of all tranches. Scenarios 5 and 6 deserve a bit more attention. In Scenario 5, the mean recovery rate is 35% and the standard deviation is 20%. The randomness of recovery rates is associated with a slight increase in default probabilities for the top two tranches. While the increase in default probabilities is intuitive (the randomness of recoveries make extreme events more likely), its size may appear small. This is due to the independence assumption of recovery rates. Default in senior tranches will occur when a large number of defaults in the pool are recorded. Given that recovery rates are independently simulated, the average recovery rate on all

Table 5 Impact (%) of interest rates on tranche PD (the first figure) and EL (the second figure)

	IR −1%	Base IR	IR +1%	IR +2%	Stochastic IR
Tranche 1	0.13	0.14	0.16	0.19	0.15
	0.010	0.011	0.013	0.016	0.012
Tranche 2	13.73	13.54	13.40	13.31	13.30
	3.90	3.91	3.94	3.99	3.82
Tranche 3	48.67	47.67	46.75	45.91	46.90
	30.87	30.55	30.31	30.15	29.94

defaulted bonds will tend to remain close to the 35% mean, with good recoveries providing compensation for bad recoveries. Therefore, the impact on default probabilities remains limited.

The independence assumption is lifted in scenario 6. Recovery rates still have a mean of 35% and a volatility of 20%, but they are now linked to the systematic factors that drive the default process (countries and industries). Thus, there will be more occurrences of large numbers of defaults and poor recoveries, and of small numbers of losses and good recoveries, than in the independent case. The impact on tranche default probability is quite dramatic. Compared to the base case scenario, the PD of tranche 1 more than doubles, while that of tranche 2 also increases significantly. However, the PD of tranche 3 falls slightly.

The explanation for this is similar to that provided in the above section on correlations. Tranche 3 occupies a relatively low position in the capital structure. Increasing the probability of extreme events in the pool (both good and bad events) has offsetting effects with the impact of "good events" slightly dominating the impact of "bad events".

Impact of interest rates

Changes in interest rates can have a significant impact on the performance of tranches, as they affect both the interest payable on the notes, as well as the price at which reinvestment can be made. We consider both parallel shifts to the yield curve and a full simulation of interest rates using PRT's built-in stochastic interest rate model.[7]

Looking at Table 5, the impact of interest rate changes appears limited. Overall, interest rate increases are detrimental to holders of tranche 1 and beneficial to holders of tranche 3, while they have mixed effects on tranche 2 (lower default probability but higher expected loss).

The main conclusion of Table 5 is that interest rates, on this structure, have a very limited impact, compared to correlations or recovery rates in particular. Using a copula approach, rather than PRT, similar results are obtained in terms of the magnitude of the changes.

Time horizon

As described in the second section, PRT is equipped with pricing functions, which enable users to look at risks over shorter horizons

Figure 1 Tranche 1 VAR (90%) as a percentage of mean value

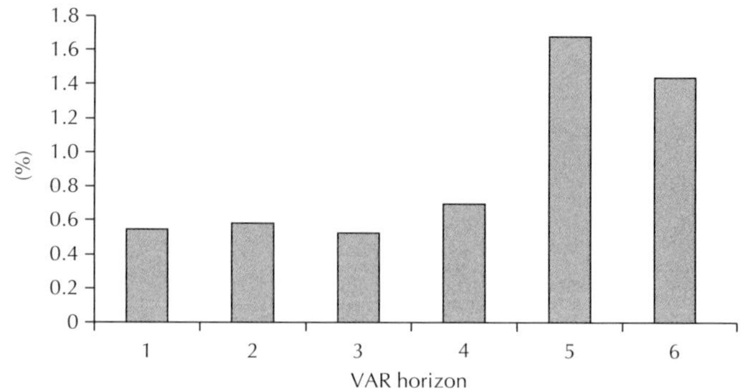

Figure 2 Tranche 2 VAR (90%) as a percentage of mean value

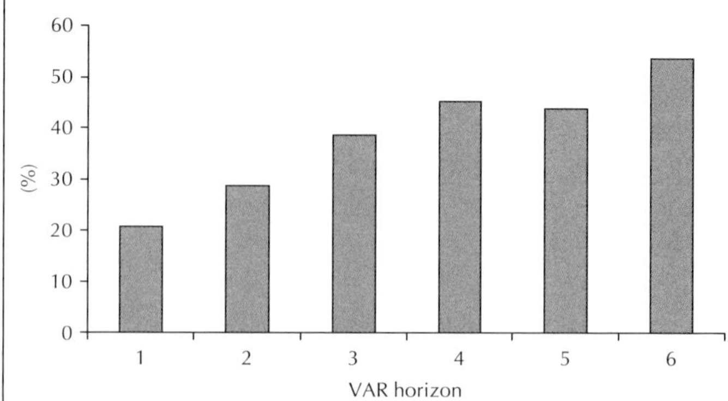

than the final maturity of the deal. In Figures 1 and 2, we display VARs of the top two tranches for holding horizons of one to six years, using the parameters of the base case. These VARs are scaled by the mean value of each tranche for comparative purposes. Note that the VARs reported below are quantiles of losses defined as deviations from expected value. Therefore, although a tranche may not default, it may generate a loss because of amortisation and other changes in its value.

The 99% VAR corresponds to the amount of loss on the tranche that will be exceeded 1% of the time. Obviously the loss levels are significantly higher for tranche 2 than for tranche 1. The pattern of losses is also very different. While losses build up progressively from year to year for tranche 2, they remain extremely low for tranche 1 until year 4 and then suddenly increase. This can be explained by the distribution of losses in the underlying pool. The first few losses hit the equity tranche and tranche 3, while the next losses start affecting tranche 2. It is only when a sufficiently large number of defaults are recorded that tranche 1 may experience large losses. This usually does not happen before year 5.

CONCLUDING REMARKS

In this chapter, we have reviewed three methods of CDO risk analysis: the Gaussian copula approach; the BET approach; and the CDO model embedded in PRT. Using a CDO structure, we performed a comparative analysis of the various factors impacting on PDs and ELs on CDO tranches, including changes in interest rates, recovery rates and correlations. Interest rates appear to have little impact on CDO risk compared to the other two drivers. The differences in default probabilities across scenarios highlight the importance of stress testing assumptions and of having a flexible model so as to allow for easy changes in the parameters. Our initial results show that systematic risk in recovery rates may have a significant impact on PDs. This has often been overlooked and would deserve further research.

1 The DS algorithm described and used in this chapter is the one that, from our experience, is the most widespread. There exists another Diversity Score algorithm that takes into account correlation, face value and default probability (based on rating and maturity). We refer the reader to Cifuents et al (1998) for more details on the alternative calculation method.
2 This approach uses issue ratings (as opposed to issuer ratings) for determining default probabilities and in doing so different recovery levels for assets with different seniorities are already taken into account.
3 This is done by using a table which maps rating factors to default probabilities (see García et al (2003)).
4 This specification does not preclude negative values or values above unity. Again, a logistic transformation could be employed but that is usually not necessary in practice.
5 See http://www.standardandpoors.com/gics for more details on this industry classification system.
6 LGD: Loss Given Default = 1 − recovery rate.
7 The interest rate model implemented in PRT is a Libor Market Model (see, eg, Musiela and Rutkowski (1998)).

REFERENCES

Altman, E., B. Brady, A. Resti, and A. Sironi, 2003, "The Link between Default and Recovery Rates: Theory, Empirical Evidence and Implications", Working Paper, NYU.

Cifuents, A., I. Efrat, J. Gluck, and E. Murphy, 1998, "Buying and Selling Credit Risk: A Perspective on Credit-linked Obligations", in *Credit Derivatives: Applications for Risk Management, Investment and Portfolio Optimisation*, pp. 105–16 (London: Risk Books).

Cifuentes, A., and G. O'Connor, 1996, "The Binomial Expansion Method Applied to CBO/CLO Analysis", Moody's Special Report.

De Servigny, A., and O. Renault, 2004, *Measuring and Managing Credit Risk* (McGraw-Hill).

Frees, E., and E. Valdez, 1998, "Understanding Relationships Using Copulas", *North American Actuarial Journal*, **2**, pp. 1–25.

Garcia, J., T. Dewyspelaere, and L. Leonard, 2004, "On Rating CDO's Using the BET Technique", Working Paper, Dexia Group.

Garcia, J., G. Gielens, L. Leonard, and T. Van Gestel, 2003, "On the Pricing of Baskets Using Gaussian Copula: A Market Test", Working Paper, Dexia Group.

Li, D., 1999, "The Valuation of the *i*th-to-Default Basket Credit Derivatives", Working Paper, RiskMetrics Group.

Longstaff, F., and E. Schwartz, 2001, "Valuing American Options by Simulation: A Simple Least-squares Approach", *Review of Financial Studies*, **14**, pp. 113–47.

Musiela, M., and M. Rutkowski, 1998, *Martingale Methods in Financial Modelling* (Springer).

Nelsen, R., 1999, "An Introduction to Copulas", in *Lecture Notes in Statistics*, **139** (Springer).

Perraudin, W., and O. Renault, 2004, *Standard & Poor's Portfolio Risk Tracker Technical Document* (Standard & Poor's).

Sklar, A., 1996, "Random Variables, Distribution Functions, and Copulas – A Personal Look Backward and Forward", In: L. Rüschendorf, B. Schweizer, and M. D. Taylor (eds), *Distributions with Fixed Marginals and Related Topics*, pp. 1–14, Lecture Notes-Monograph Series, Vol 28, Hayward, California: Institute of Mathematical Statistics.

11

Patterns of Risk Diversification in a Securitisation

Jeroen de Smet, Viktor Tchistiakov

ING Group

Since the first publication of the Basel II proposals on the treatment of credit risk for securitisations, discussion among professionals regarding the quantification of the risk embedded in these structures has become very intensive. One of the results of this broad discussion has been the broad acceptance of the concept that underpins the proposal, namely that capital should be based on a measure of the amount of systematic risk in a securitisation in addition to other risk drivers. The systematic risk is the risk that cannot be eliminated by diversification.

The Basel Committee on Bank Supervision (2003) proposed a framework for quantifying the regulatory capital requirements for securitisations. The different sets of calibrated quantifications available within this framework are based on the premise that the systematic risk increases when the rating of a tranche improves. The rating of a tranche improves with an increasing amount of first loss protection and an improvement of the credit quality of the underlying assets in the securitised pool. The model used for this quantification is described in Pykhtin and Dev (2002a,b 2003). Gordy and Jones (2002) also discuss a capital allocation framework for securitisations.

Many financial institutions use their own internal economic capital (EC) model for credit risk to measure and manage the risk in their portfolios. These models reflect the institutions' perceptions of credit risk based on their internal risk standards. Using such a model, an institution builds its own view on the amount of risk to which it feels it is exposed. In general, the EC methodologies and parameterisations employed by institutions differ from the modelling framework employed by regulators as well as those used by external rating agencies.

Next to an EC estimation methodology, an EC allocation over the different assets or sub-portfolios is also needed. An EC allocation methodology widely used by institutions is based on the concept of unexpected loss contribution (ULC), also referred to as volatility allocation (Ong, 1999). If one defines the unexpected loss (UL) of an exposure as the square root of the variance, ie, the standard deviation or volatility, of credit losses on that exposure, the ULC is the fraction of the UL that is not diversified when this exposure is added to the overall portfolio. Alternatively, the ULC may be defined as the increase in the total portfolio volatility that occurs when an exposure is added to the portfolio. The ULC divided by the volatility of the exposure is usually referred to as the retained risk (RR). This ratio is usually referred to as the retained risk (RR). EC is then calculated by multiplying the ULC by a constant capital multiple (CM) that depends on the portfolio. It is worth noting that the industry is partly moving towards an expected shortfall (ES) allocation approach, which is beyond the scope of this work (Kalkbrener *et al*, 2004).

One may contrast this and other approaches, widely used in the industry, with that taken by regulators. Making comparisons is complicated by confusing differences in the terminology employed by regulators and by many industry analysts. In the Basel II proposals, UL is used to denote the value-at-risk of a portfolio minus the expected losses (ELs) on that portfolio. The capital charges under Basel II are parameterised based on the marginal increase in unexpected loss so defined.

The industry ULC approach and the approach taken by the bank regulator (Basel II) are related to some extent. If the capital multiplier in the ULC approach is chosen so that the sum of the individual capital charges equals the total portfolio value at risk (VAR) minus the expected loss, then the two approaches are the same given that individual exposure credit losses are joint normally distributed. When these assumptions are not met, one may expect the two approaches to yield somewhat different results, however.

This chapter explores the implications of using the ULC approach. Although this approach can be used for benchmarking the Basel II proposals for securitisations, it is not meant as an alternative for this regulatory framework. The reason for studying it is to examine the implications of an approach widely used by many financial institutions. Since most institutions make a clear distinction between a generic regulatory capital (RC) standard and an internal EC view, there is room for an alternative formulation that is consistent with one type of EC model that reflects the financial institutions individual preferences. Moreover, one financial institution might face different regulatory frameworks. Therefore, it is preferred to have an institution specific EC methodology for internal risk management purposes. If properly defined, this would also reflect the institutions specific portfolio characteristics. In addition, some experts would state that there is a need for such alternative formulations to reduce model risk.

The approach presented here fits into a ULC framework and it is used to demonstrate the fundamental difference in the credit risk diversification characteristics of a securitisation when compared to those of a regular loan or bond. We also demonstrate within the ULC framework that some patterns are not necessarily so strict as often perceived. We show that within this framework the amount of diversification of a higher quality tranche is not necessarily less than that of a lower quality tranche of the same pool of securitised assets. In addition, we elaborate on the joint default probability of a regular asset with a securitised tranche and compare this with the joint default probability for two regular assets.

It is shown that tranches derived from a pool of securitised assets have a much greater variety in their risk behaviour than regular assets in terms of diversification, loss distribution and default properties. In a portfolio context, they cannot be treated in the same way as regular assets. Our framework demonstrates that the general view of an increasing systematic amount of risk with increasing level of subordination of the tranche needs more refinement.

ANALYTIC ULC METHODOLOGY

To study the amount of diversification benefit of a tranche with a given level of subordination and width taken from a pool of securitised assets, one needs to know the loss distribution of both the reference portfolio and the pool. We employ for this purpose the analytic Vasicek distribution for credit losses on a portfolio under the assumption that the portfolio and the pool are homogeneous infinitesimally fine-grained (Vasicek, 1987), which is a single factor formulation. Using these loss distributions, we shall derive the ULC of a specific tranche by calculating loss correlations.

In the following, $\varphi(x)$ is the normal probability density and $N(x)$ is the cumulative standard normal probability distribution, which is defined as

$$N(x_0) = \int_{-\infty}^{x_0} \varphi(x)\mathrm{d}x \tag{1}$$

and $N^{-1}(x_0)$ is its inverse. Furthermore, the subscripts p, s, and t denote the *portfolio*, *securitised pool* and a *tranche* of the securitised pool, respectively.

Portfolio

The correlation of the portfolio with a systematic factor x is ρ_p and the same single systematic factor correlation ρ_s, probability of default p_s, and loss given default LGD_s. The expected value of the losses in this portfolio, ie, the EL, is then given by

$$\mathrm{EL}_p \equiv E(L_p) = \int_{-\infty}^{\infty} L_p(x)\varphi(x)\mathrm{d}x \tag{2}$$

where

$$L_p(x) = \mathrm{LGD}_p N\left(\frac{N^{-1}(p_p) - \sqrt{\rho_p}\,x}{\sqrt{1-\rho_p}}\right) \tag{3}$$

Here, the LGD_p is the loss given default (LGD). A deterministic LGD is assumed, whereas commonly a stochastic LGD is applied. The UL is defined as the volatility of the losses that is found through the variance of the portfolio σ_p^2:

$$\mathrm{UL}_p^2 \equiv \sigma_p^2 = \int_{-\infty}^{\infty} L_p^2(x)\varphi(x)\mathrm{d}x - \mathrm{EL}_p^2 \tag{4}$$

Securitised asset pool

Given is a homogeneous pool of assets in a securitisation structure with the same single systematic factor correlation, probability of default and LGD ρ_s, p_s and LGD_s, respectively. Substituting these in Equations (2)–(4) gives expressions for EL_s, L_s and UL_s^2 for this pool of assets.

Tranche characteristics

The EL of a tranche EL_t that starts at its lower bound l_l and that is capped at its upper bound l_u is given by

$$EL_t = \int_{-\infty}^{\infty} L_t(l_l, l_u, x)\varphi(x)\mathrm{d}x \tag{5}$$

where

$$L_t(l_l, l_u, x) = \max\left[0, \min\left[l_u - l_l, L_s(x) - l_l\right]\right] \tag{6}$$

and $L_s(x)$ is the asset pool equivalent of Equation (3). The UL_t is defined by the variance

$$UL_t^2 \equiv \sigma_t^2 = \int_{-\infty}^{\infty} L_t(l_l, l_u, x)^2 \varphi(x)\mathrm{d}x - EL_t^2 \tag{7}$$

The probability of default of a tranche p_t is given by

$$p_t = 1 - N\left(\frac{1}{\sqrt{\rho_s}}\left[\sqrt{1-\rho_s}N^{-1}(l_l) - N^{-1}(p_s)\right]\right) \tag{8}$$

and defined as the probability that the tranche is hit by the accumulated losses in the pool.

Tranche–portfolio relations

The covariance σ_{tp}^2 between the tranche and the portfolio is given by

$$\sigma_{tp}^2 = \int_{-\infty}^{\infty} L_p(x)L_t(l_l, l_u, x)\varphi(x)\mathrm{d}x \tag{9}$$

and finally we have for the single factor loss correlation between the tranche and the portfolio

$$\rho_{tp} = \frac{\sigma_{tp}^2 - EL_t EL_p}{\sigma_p \sigma_t} \tag{10}$$

This is the relation used to determine the ULC of the tranche when it is added to the much larger portfolio, ie, the reference portfolio. The methodology can also be used when the pool is extracted from the portfolio. Note that substitution of all the above given expressions that define the modelled portfolio characteristics reveal that the LGD_p is of no influence to the tranche–portfolio correlation. This is a result of the homogeneous portfolio assumption. Although this same assumption is also applied to the pool, the LGD_s is of influence to the loss correlation. This is due to the tranching, where a tranche is characterised by loss levels and these are directly related to the LGD_s.

The ULC_t is given by

$$ULC_t = \frac{\sigma_t^2 + \sigma_p(\sigma_t \rho_{tp})}{\sigma_p} \qquad \textbf{(11)}$$

It can be assumed that the size of one tranche is in general much smaller than the reference portfolio itself. This assumption is in general realistic and we find that the ULC_t can thus be very accurately approximated by

$$ULC_t \approx \sigma_t \rho_{tp} \qquad \textbf{(12)}$$

since $\sigma_p \gg \sigma_t$.

The RR is defined as the percentage of risk, ie, UL, that is not eliminated due to portfolio diversification. Expression (12) yields

$$RR_t \approx \rho_{tp} \qquad \textbf{(13)}$$

The EC amount of the tranche is now given by

$$EC_t = UL_t \cdot RR_t \cdot CM = ULC_t \cdot CM \qquad \textbf{(14)}$$

where CM is the capital multiple, ie, the number of times the CW volatility of the reference portfolio (UL_p) to reach the institution's confidence level C_l. This C_l is determined by the institution and, together with the properties of the portfolio of this institution, the CM is determined to reach the set of VAR. With a set of parameters for this reference portfolio we can extract the CM from Equations

(2)–(4) that are applicable to this reference portfolio. The loss at C_l is given by $L_p(N^{-1}(C_l))$ and thus

$$\begin{aligned} \mathrm{CM} &= \frac{L_B(N^{-1}(C_l)) - \mathrm{EL}_p}{\mathrm{UL}_p} \\ &= \left(\mathrm{LGD}_p \cdot N\left[\frac{N^{-1}(p_p)}{\sqrt{1-\rho_p}} + N^{-1}(C_l)\sqrt{\frac{\rho_p}{1-\rho_p}} \right] - \mathrm{EL}_p \right) \mathrm{UL}_p^{-1} \end{aligned} \quad \mathbf{(15)}$$

This completes a set of equations that can be used to approximate the risk contribution of an actual tranche when it is added to a reference portfolio. To find the percentage of EC relative to the tranche size we have to divide the amount found by Equation (14) by the tranche size.

We have used this formulation for some actual transactions where the reference portfolio was the Basel II "super-portfolio" and have derived corresponding risk weights (RWs). A comparison between these alternative RWs and the Basel II RWs for this limited set of real transactions revealed that the method gives similar values and patterns (Batchvarov *et al*, 2004). We will not elaborate on this particular application. One of the major difficulties is dealing in a consistent way with the ratings that rating agencies attach to securitisations. Furthermore, to make a fair comparison with the proposals contained in the new Basel II accord, it is necessary to study the universe or a representation of the universe of securitisations. Such a data set was not available to us.

LOSS CORRELATION BETWEEN TRANCHE AND REFERENCE PORTFOLIO

We elaborate on several examples, which illustrate the theoretical results derived so far. First, a definition of a representative reference portfolio is given by setting

$$\rho_p = 0.2, \quad p_p = 0.007 \quad \mathrm{LGD}_p = 1$$

The LGD_p value is not representative, but it was demonstrated that this is not relevant in the present context. We add to this reference portfolio a tranche that is obtained from three different homogeneous pools of assets that possess the following stand-alone asset characteristics:

$$\begin{array}{llll} \text{A} & \rho_s = 0.15, & p_s = 0.050 & \text{LGD}_s = 1 \\ \text{B} & \rho_s = 0.25, & p_s = 0.015 & \text{LGD}_s = 1 \\ \text{C} & \rho_s = 0.35, & p_s = 0.005 & \text{LGD}_s = 1 \end{array}$$

We study three rather arbitrary tranching schemes for securitised tranches that are derived from asset Pool A. Figure 1 shows the loss correlation for each tranche scheme. Schemes 1 and 2 have a tranching of 2%, 6%, 92% and 4%, 6%, 90%, respectively. Scheme 1 is plotted with thick lines and filled diamonds, whereas scheme 2 is presented by the less thick line marked with open squares. These schemes show a rapid increase in loss correlation for increasing levels of subordination, which normally correspond to lower levels of EL and probability of default and therefore to higher ratings. This is a rather typical pattern found in many actual transactions and illustrates that, when the ratings improve, the amount of RR also increases, and therefore highly rated tranches have a relatively low diversification benefit and they are therefore relatively risky in a portfolio context. Scheme 3 is plotted with thin lines marked with filled circles and illustrates that this general pattern depends on the precise positioning and size, ie, attachment and detachment points, of the tranches. This 5%, 15%, 80% scheme shows that the mezzanine tranche has a higher loss correlation of than the senior tranche.

Table 1 shows the quantifications that correspond to Figure 1. The figures for ELs, ULs, and ULCs are given as a percentage of their corresponding tranche exposures. The EL decreases with increasing level of subordination for all schemes. In Schemes 1 and 2 the UL first increases and than drops to very low levels. Comparison of the ULC pattern with the UL pattern for Scheme 3 tells us that when the stand-alone risk in terms of UL percentage decreases with increasing level of subordination, the ULC does not necessarily follow the same pattern due to diversification effects. Scheme 1 follows a rather general accepted pattern of decreasing stand-alone and diversified risk. However, note that the amount of diversification for the senior tranche is negligible.

In practice, tranches tend to grow in size when the subordination level increases. The EL or the probability of default are the dominant

Figure 1 Three different tranching schemes based on pool A. The beginning and length of the line indicate the attachment point, ie, level of subordination, and the tranche width up to its detachment point. Lines of identical thicknesses marked with identical symbols correspond to one tranching scheme. Vertical positioning represents the loss correlation of the tranche with the reference portfolio

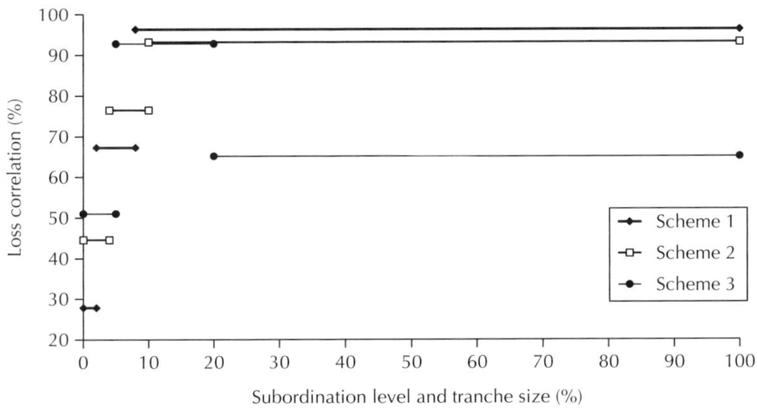

metrics of risk to determine the rating. The loss correlation with the reference portfolio is not part of this rating process, and in general will not be part of that process, but it is worth considering this aspect for securitisations in the context of credit portfolio management for a financial institution. The general pattern of decreasing diversification possibilities with improved ratings is true. However, the above examples demonstrate that this might stem from the traditional choice of tranching in combination with a rather generic external rating based, ie, probability of default or EL based, approach, to securitisations. When alternative tranching schemes are considered, this general pattern does not necessarily hold in its most general form.

To understand the phenomenon of a senior tranche possessing a lower loss correlation than the mezzanine tranche, we change the way of presenting the loss correlation over the pool losses. For Pools A to C we apply a sweep of the tranche over the full pool size. We take a tranche width of size 1% and move it from subordination level 0% to 99% in steps of 1%. Figure 2(a) shows the loss correlation patterns as a function of the level of subordination. The loss correlations first increase to a maximum value and subsequently drop to very low levels. Compare Scheme 3 from Figure 1 with the

Table 1 Quantification of tranching schemes for pool A

Pool A	Tranche	Attachement point (%)	Detachment point (%)	Tranche size (%)	EL %	UL %	Loss correlation (%)	ULC %	p_t %
Scheme1	junior	0	2	2	89	22	28	6	100
	mezzanine	2	8	6	40	39	67	26	74
	senior	8	100	92	0.9	2.8	96	2.7	18
Scheme 2	junior	0	4	4	74	31	45	14	100
	mezzanine	4	10	6	25	36	76	28	47
	senior	10	100	90	0.6	2.3	93	2.2	12
Scheme 3	junior	0	5	5	68	32	51	16	100
	mezzanine	5	20	15	10	21	93	19	37
	senior	20	100	80	0.07	0.9	65	0.6	1.2

Figure 2 (a) As Figure 1, but now for a sweep of a thin tranches over the three different pools. Tranche thickness is 1% and loss correlation is plotted at the attachment points of the tranches. (b) As (a) but also for a 5% tranche thickness and one result for a 25% tranche thickness, plotted as a function of the tranche's default probability on a logarithmic scale

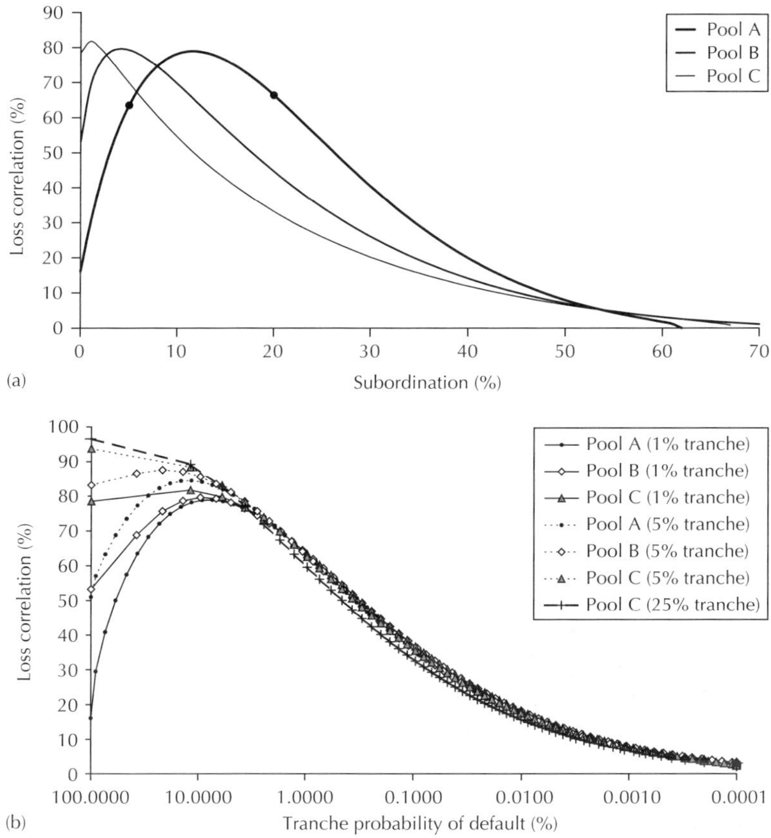

thick line that corresponds to this Pool A. The transition points between the tranches are marked with filled circles at 5% and 20%. It is obvious that the mezzanine tranche is positioned in the high loss correlation area, whereas the junior tranche benefits from the low loss correlation at the lower subordination levels. The senior tranche is not influenced by the peak in the loss correlation positioned around the 12% level of subordination.

Figure 2(b) shows the same sweeps as Figure 2(a) for the 1% tranche thickness, but now as a function of the probability of default of the tranche on a logarithmic scale. These results are represented by the solid lines. In addition, the dashed lines represent the results for sweeps with a 5% tranche thickness. For Pool C the sweep with a tranche width of 25% is shown. The relation between loss correlation and default probability of the tranche for decreasing probabilities, ie, higher levels of subordination, is approximately identical for these different pools. The impact of thicker tranches is not very significant. Only in the lower quality region of the pool are large differences in loss correlation found.

Figures 3(a) and 3(b) are complementary to Figure 2(a) and show the EL, UL and ULC of the tranche sweep over Pool A. Figure 3(a) shows the relations as a function of the level of subordination, whereas Figure 3(b) gives these relations as a function of the tranche's probability of default on a logarithmic scale. Obviously, the EL decreases whereas the UL and ULC show a peak.

When we compare the behaviour of a tranche with a regular exposure that possesses the same probability of default as the considered tranche, we have to take into account the loss dynamics of the pool versus the loss dynamics of a single exposure. For a single exposure the LGD normally is a stochastic variable rather than a deterministic value. As a first approximation it is fair to state that this LGD distribution is independent of the probability of default and the size of the exposure. For a tranche, however, the LGD distribution is both dependent on the attachment point and the size of the tranche. The attachment point determines the probability of default and the loss probability distribution over the rest of the tranche determines the LGD distribution of the tranche. Therefore the LGD of a tranche depends on its probability of default and its exposure at risk (EAD). The loss correlation between a tranche and a portfolio does show a relation with the probability of default of the tranche that is not extremely sensitive to the pool characteristics for the higher levels of subordination.

Our framework can be used in an EC modelling environment that is based on a ULC approach. We feel that it is important to emphasise the possibilities of the patterns found. It is possible to position a tranche such that it possesses a minimal loss correlation and therefore contains a higher diversification potential than tranches that are determined according to a more common tranching scheme for the same structure. These patterns found within this

Figure 3 (a) As Figure 2 for pool A only. Instead of the loss correlation the levels of EL and UL (Contribution) are plotted. (b) As (a) but as a function of the tranche's default probability on a logarithmic scale

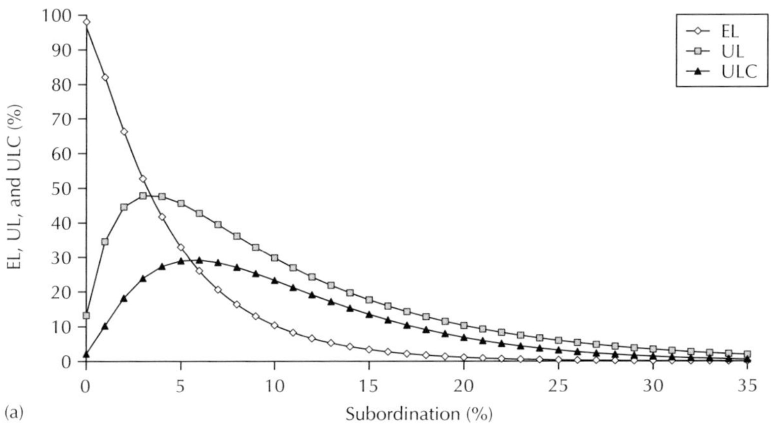

(a)

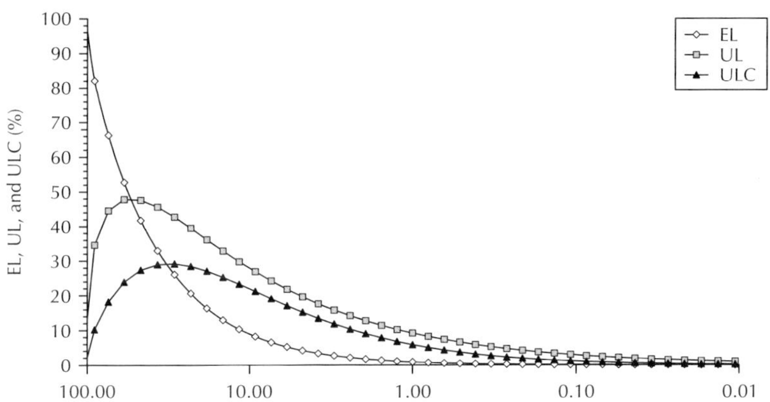

(b)

formulation are related to the general loss dynamics of a credit portfolio.

JOINT DEFAULT PROBABILITY BETWEEN A TRANCHE AND A REGULAR ASSET

Many institutions have credit risky exposures through securitisations. Typically, these exposures form part of a larger portfolio consisting of other types of exposures, such as bonds and loans that contain credit risk. Very often the general EC model employed for measurement and management of a portfolio or a portfolio segment is build around exposures that behave in a less complicated fashion on an individual basis than do securitised exposures. It is important to take the special behaviour of securitised products into account when the EC consumption of such a structure is determined in a portfolio context.

The previous sections have described the single factor framework to determine the risk diversification of a securitisation when such an exposure is added or removed from a reference portfolio. To illustrate that the default behaviour of a securitised tranche in a portfolio context differs from other more straightforward exposures, we will determine p_{jdp} between a securitised tranche and a regular exposure, eg, a bond or loan. We will compare this with the p_{jdp} between two regular exposures.

The previous sections have already demonstrated that the LGD_t and the p_t of a tranche cannot be seen as the equivalent of the LGD and p of a regular exposure. Here, we will focus on the difference caused by the default characteristics only. The differences found indicate that a significant error is made when a securitisation is treated as a normal exposure in a credit risk portfolio model. Financial institutions should recognise this special risk behaviour of securitisations.

The p_{jdp} can be determined numerically through the definition of indicator functions for a regular exposure i_{r1} and a securitised exposure i_s. This first regular exposure is denoted by a subscript $r1$. The actual p_{jdp} can be determined through a numerical solution of the following expression:

$$p_{jdp}^{ind} \equiv \int_{-\infty}^{\infty}\int_{-\infty}^{\infty} i_s(x)i_{r1}(x,y)\varphi(x)\varphi(y)\mathrm{d}y\mathrm{d}x \tag{16}$$

where

$$i_s(x) = \begin{cases} 1, & \text{when } l(x) \geq l_l \\ 0, & \text{when } l(x) < l_l \end{cases} \tag{17}$$

with

$$l(x) = N\left(\frac{N^{-1}(p_s) - x\sqrt{\rho_s}}{\sqrt{1-\rho_s}}\right) \tag{18}$$

for the securitised tranche. The above definition of the actual joint default probability, ie, Equation (16), corresponds to the simultaneous default of a regular asset and an infinitesimally thin tranche with the given attachment point. It can also be interpreted as the loss covariance between a regular exposure and an infinitesimally thin tranche.

For the regular exposure we have

$$i_{r1}(x, y) = \begin{cases} 1, & \text{when } \operatorname{dd}(x, y) \leq N(p_{r1}) \\ 0, & \text{when } \operatorname{dd}(x, y) > N(p_{r1}) \end{cases} \tag{19}$$

with

$$\operatorname{dd}(x, y) = x\sqrt{\rho_{r1}} + y\sqrt{1-\rho_{r1}} \tag{20}$$

Here x is the systematic factor and y is the idiosyncratic factor of the model, which are assumed to be independent and normally distributed.

Denote a second regular asset by a subscript $r2$. When we have these two regular assets we can determine the p_{jdp} through the bivariate normal distribution, which is the classical approach, for which we have ultimately the one-dimensional expression

$$p_{jdp}^{biv}(p_{r1}, p_{r2}, \rho) = \int_{-\infty}^{N^{-1}(p_{r1})} N\left(\frac{N^{-1}(p_{r2}) - \sqrt{\rho}x}{\sqrt{1-\rho}}\right)\varphi(x)\mathrm{d}x \tag{21}$$

For two regular assets that follow a default behaviour depending directly on the normal behaviour of the systematic factor x, the asset correlation in Equation (21) is given by

$$\rho = \sqrt{\rho_{r1}\rho_{r2}} \tag{22}$$

We will compare the numerical results for the joint default probability between a tranche and a normal asset with the value we find from the classical formulation. This demonstrates that there exists a mismatch in terms of p_{jdp} when a tranche of a securitisation is added to the portfolio credit risk model and is treated as a regular exposure.

SEMI-ANALYTICAL RESULTS FOR THE JOINT DEFAULT PROBABILITY

Within the framework of assumptions, the p_{jdp} of a tranche derived from a homogeneous pool of assets and a regular asset possessing the same characteristics as these pooled assets follows the bivariate relation as given in Equation (21). Figure 4(a) shows the decreasing p_{jdp} as a function of the level of subordination for different

Figure 4 (a) Joint default probabilities as a function of a tranche's level of subordination for three different parameter settings of the pooled assets and the regular asset. See the legend for the values used for the parameters. (b) Probabilities of default as a function of the tranche's level of subordination corresponding to (a)

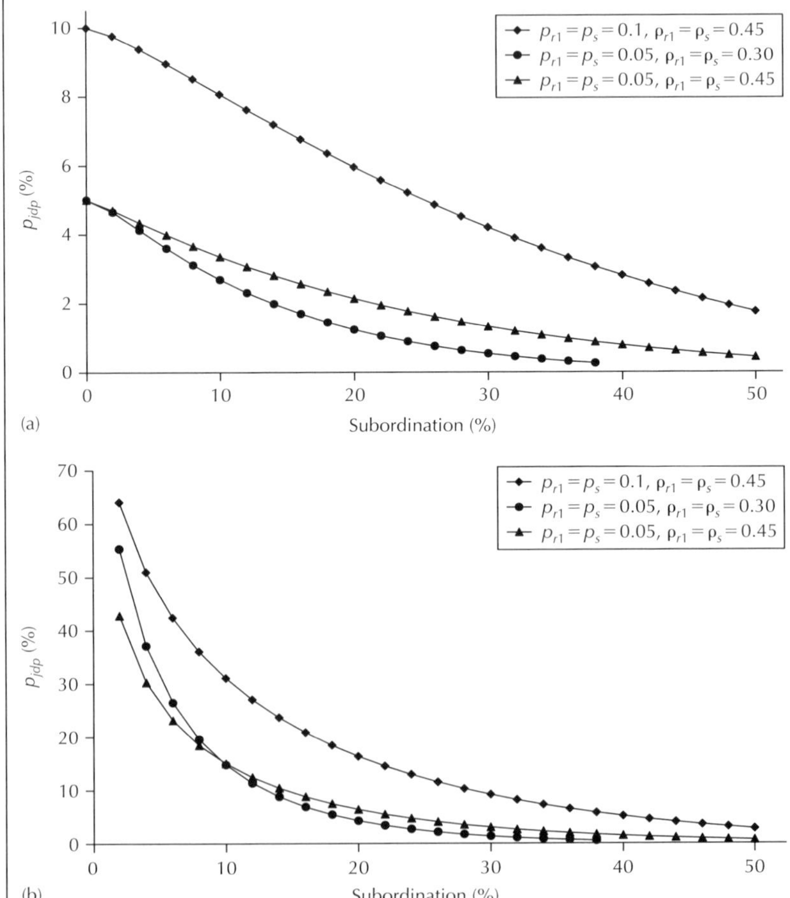

homogenous pools and a regular asset with the same probability of default and correlation. The figure legend shows the values used for the risk parameters. Figure 4(b) gives the corresponding p_t. The two cases with $p_s = p_{r1} = 5\%$ obviously start at the same level of $p_{jdp} = 0.05$. The low correlation pool shown with filled circles, however, has a faster decreasing p_{jdp} due to the faster decreasing default probability of the tranche p_t. There is no difference found between the p_{jdp} determined by the indicator definition or the bivariate definition. Apparently, a tranche behaves as a regular asset in terms of default behaviour in the cases where the pooled assets and the regular asset are identical in terms of the two major risk drivers ρ and p. Nevertheless, the loss correlation behaviour is still very tranche specific due to the different LGD characteristics. Even in this exceptional case of a homogeneous pool combined with a regular asset identical to the assets in the pool, the LGD has to be treated differently in a portfolio modelling approach.

The situation changes when we determine the p_{jdp} between a tranche of a homogeneous pool and a regular asset with different risk drivers. In these cases we find a difference between the actual values given in Equation 16 and the bivariate formulation given in Equation 21. We first discuss three cases where the normal asset has a higher correlation with the single market factor than the assets in the pool. These cases are referred to as Models A to C. Then we discuss Models D and E for which the reverse is true. The models have the following risk drivers for the pooled assets and the normal asset:

$$
\begin{array}{lllll}
\text{Model A} & \rho_{r1} = 0.60, & p_{r1} = 0.007, & \rho_s = 0.25, & p_s = 0.03 \\
\text{Model B} & \rho_{r1} = 0.40, & p_{r1} = 0.05, & \rho_s = 0.15, & p_s = 0.07 \\
\text{Model C} & \rho_{r1} = 0.60, & p_{r1} = 0.02, & \rho_s = 0.15, & p_s = 0.05 \\
\text{Model D} & \rho_{r1} = 0.20, & p_{r1} = 0.05, & \rho_s = 0.50, & p_s = 0.02 \\
\text{Model E} & \rho_{r1} = 0.20, & p_{r1} = 0.02, & \rho_s = 0.50, & p_s = 0.05
\end{array}
$$

Figure 5 shows the p_{jdp} for the indicator and bivariate formulations as a function of increasing level of subordination. Each curve starts at the level p_{r1} for a 0% level of subordination. With increasing level of subordination the actual p_{jdp} determined by the indicator formulation (Equation (16)) is systematically larger than the bivariate expression (Equation (21)). For low levels of subordination

Figure 5 Actual joint default probability of a tranche and a regular asset compared with the bivariate value found for the same cases. These are the mismatches found for the three situations where the regular asset has a higher systematic risk than the individual pooled assets

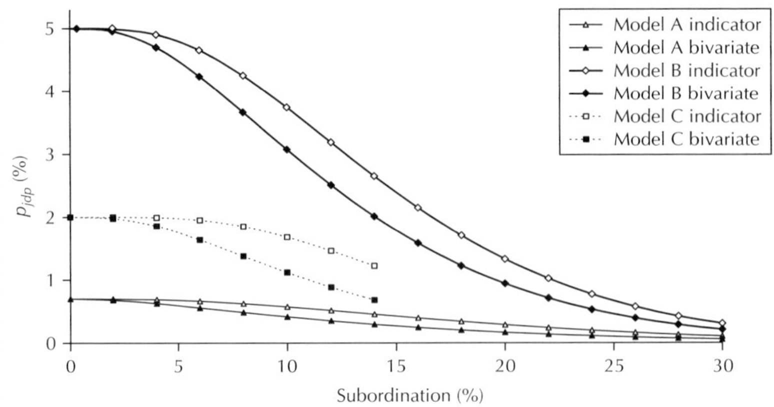

the p_{jdp} only moderately deviates from the maximum value. Although the curves seem to converge with an increasing level of subordination, the relative difference increases up to the level of 30% subordination as shown.

Figures 6(a) and 6(b) show the results for Models D and E, respectively. These models correspond to the case where the pooled assets have a higher asset correlation than the regular exposure. In this case the p_{jdp} quickly drops from its maximum value to a much lower value. This is driven by the correlations that influence the tranche default probability. Furthermore, the actual p_{jdp} determined by the indicator formulation is systematically lower than the bivariate expression.

The reason for the different values found for the actual p_{jdp} and the bivariate expression is obviously caused by the difference in the underlying default process. For a regular exposure this is driven by normally distributed random variables x and y. For a tranche the normally-distributed driver is first transformed to a non-normal distribution on which the default behaviour of the tranche depends. Only in the very specific case where the pooled assets are identical to the regular asset is the default behaviour correctly described by the bivariate formulation.

Table 2 Bivariate equivalent correlations for the actual p_{jdp}, ie, based on the indicator-function formulation as given in Equation (16)

Model	ρ_s	ρ_{r1}	$\rho = (\rho_{r1}\rho_{r2})^{1/2}$	ρ_{eq}
A	0.25	0.60	0.39	0.60
B	0.15	0.40	0.25	0.40
C	0.15	0.60	0.30	0.60
D	0.50	0.20	0.32	0.20
E	0.50	0.20	0.32	0.20

Figure 6 (a) As Figure 5 but for the case where the regular asset has a lower systematic risk than the individual pooled assets. (b) As (a) but for different parameters

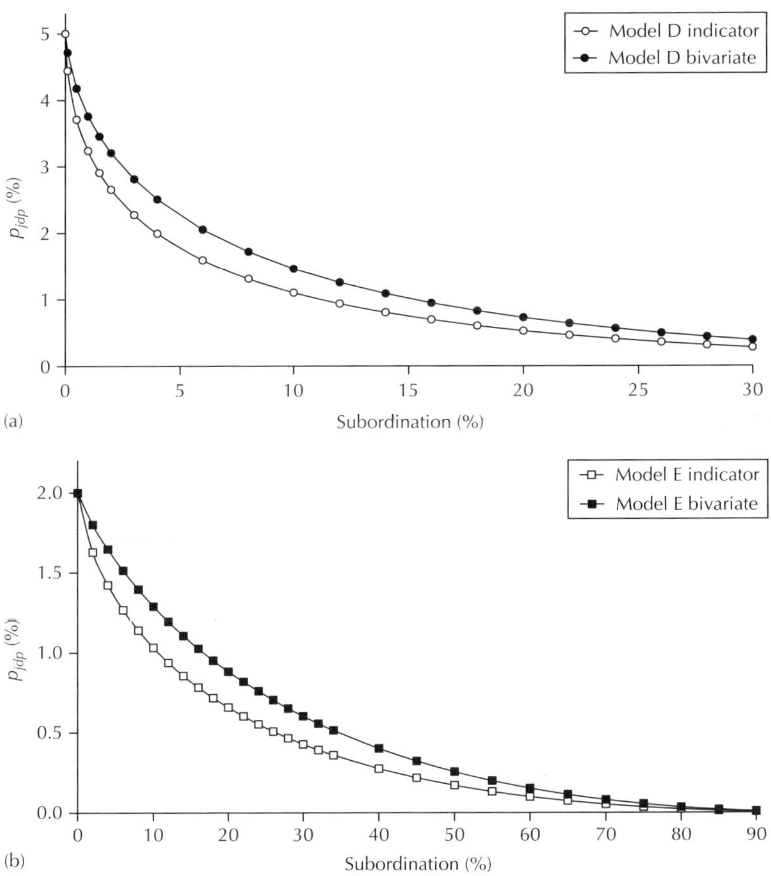

PANEL 1

From Equation (18) it follows that $l(x) \geqslant l$, is equivalent to

$$x \geq \frac{\sqrt{1-\rho_s} N^{-1}(l_l) - N^{-1}(p_s)}{\sqrt{\rho_s}}$$

given that $\rho_s > 0$. Thus the integration with respect to x of the indicator function reduces to the integration of the constant l on the interval $(-\infty, \bar{x})$, where

$$\bar{x} = \frac{\sqrt{1-\rho_s} N^{-1}(l_l) - N^{-1}(p_s)}{\sqrt{\rho_s}}$$

Equations (19) and (20) imply that the integration with respect to y of the indicator function reduces to the integration of the constant l on the interval, where $(-\infty, \bar{y}(x))$

$$\bar{y}(x) = \frac{N^{-1}(p_{r1}) - x\sqrt{\rho_{r1}}}{\sqrt{1-\rho_{r1}}}$$

Thus Equation (16) reads

$$p_{jdp}^{ind} = \int_{-\infty}^{\bar{x}} \int_{-\infty}^{\bar{y}(x)} \varphi(x)\varphi(y)\mathrm{d}y\mathrm{d}x = \int_{-\infty}^{\bar{x}} \varphi(x) \int_{-\infty}^{\bar{y}(x)} \varphi(y)\mathrm{d}y\mathrm{d}x = \int_{-\infty}^{\bar{x}} \varphi(x) N(\bar{y}(x))\,\mathrm{d}x \quad \textbf{(1a)}$$

We note that $N(\bar{y}(x))$ is the tranche default probaility (see Equation 18). Equation (1a) is in fact the same as the expression for p_{jdp} of two regular loans with the corresponding default probabilities $N(\bar{y}(x))$ and p_{r1} and the asset correlation ρ_{r1} (compare Equation (1a) with Equation 21). This proves the results presented in Table 1 that adding a tranche to a portfolio is equivalent from the p_{jdp} point of view to adding a regular loan that has the same asset correlation as all other loans in the portfolio. The asset correlation in the securitisation pool only affects the tranche's probability of default given an attachment point.

BIVARIATE EQUIVALENT CORRELATION

We can conclude from the above results for the p_{jdp} that there is a systematic pattern in the difference between the actual (Equation 16) and the bivariate (Equation 21) approach. The results for a normal asset and a tranche derived from a pool of identical assets (Figures 4(a) and 4(b)) suggest that the bivariate assumption is not incorrect for this situation. When the assets are not identical, however, we have seen that the actual p_{jdp} systematically deviates from the bivariate approach. We will now follow a slightly different method that might seem arbitrary at first sight. Given the actual p_{jdp} from the indicator formulation, we can search for the equivalent correlation ρ_{eq} in the bivariate formulation that gives the numerically determined actual p_{jdp}.

We use a bisection algorithm to determine the values for ρ_{eq}. Table 2 shows the results for Models A to E. The equivalent correlation turns out to be independent of the level of subordination of the tranche and equals the asset correlation of the regular asset in the reference portfolio. In Panel 1 this result is analytically derived. Since assets in the reference portfolio possess characteristics that reflect a wide range of levels of systematic risk, it is not straightforward to take advantage of this behaviour.

CONCLUDING REMARKS

The ULC modelling framework presented here can be used to examine how much the credit risk in a tranche is diversified when it is added to a portfolio. Of course, the assumptions adopted in our stylised framework are not necessarily valid. For example, not all securitisation pools are accurately approximated by homogeneously and infinitely fine-grained pools. Furthermore, the data needed to implement this approach is not always available. Often, only a public rating is available. Specifics of the pool and of the structure, eg, credit enhancement, complicate the quantification of diversification even further.

Depending on the EC model that a bank employs, the single factor formulation may limit the applicability of the approach described here. When the EC model uses a multi-factor correlation model, it might be possible to reduce it to a single factor equivalent for the special purpose of estimating the diversification of a securitisation. First extensions of the model to a more general correlation framework and incorporation of more refined definitions of the reference portfolio have facilitated the modelling of more realistic pools and portfolios. Such extensions have yielded identical patterns as observed and described here. Other extensions would include migration patterns, granularity adjustments (Vasicek, 2002) and default timing effects. Also other capital methodologies should be investigated to confine model risk.

Despite the fact that the described approach might contain limitations for some practical purposes, it provides a useful way of analysing the quantitative phenomena of diversification patterns in credit portfolios containing tranches of structured products. Using it, we have demonstrated that the potential amount of diversification embedded in tranches does not necessarily decrease with an increasing level of subordination. It is a combination of the default probability and loss distribution over the tranche that ultimately fixes the diversification benefit of an in- or divestment. The difference in credit risk characteristics affects the joint default probability and this should be accounted for in a credit risk portfolio model.

REFERENCES

Basel Committee on Bank Supervision, 2003, "Third Consultative Paper: First Pillar (IV Credit Risk – Securitisation Framework", Bank for International Settlements, pp. 99–120, April.

Batchvarov, A., D. Picone, P.-P. Hoogbruin, J. de Smet and V. Tchistiakov, 2004, "An Empirical Test of Basel Risk Weights Applied to Securitisation", *Structured Products* (London: Risk Books).

Gordy, M., and D. Jones, 2002, "Capital Allocation for Securitizations with Uncertainty in Loss Prioritization", Federal Reserve Board.

Kalkbrener, M., H. Lotter, and L. Overbeck, 2004, "Sensible and Efficient Capital Allocation for Credit Portfolios", *Risk*, pp. S19–S24, January.

Ong, M., 1999, *Internal Credit Risk Models; Capital Allocation and Performance Measurement* (London: Risk Books).

Pykhtin, M., and A. Dev, 2002a, "Analytical Approach to Credit Risk Modelling", *Risk*, pp. S26–S32, March.

Pykhtin, M., and A. Dev, 2002b, "Credit Risk in Asset Securitisations: Analytical Model", *Risk*, pp. S16–20, May.

Pykhtin, M., and A. Dev, 2003, "Coarse-grained CDOs", *Risk*, pp. 113–16, January.

Vasicek, O., 1987, "Probability of Loss on Loan Portfolio", KMV Corporation.

Vasicek, O., 2002, "Loan Portfolio Value", *Risk*, pp. 160–162, December.

12

How Risky are Structured Exposures Compared with Corporate Bonds?

William Perraudin; Astrid Van Landschoot

Imperial College and Bank of England;
National Bank of Belgium

Understanding the relative risks one faces when investing in different sectors of credit markets will always be important for market participants and regulators alike. However, the debate about capital initiated by the Basel Committee's recently published proposals on regulatory capital make this issue especially topical (see Basel Committee on Banking Supervision (2004)).

In brief, the Committee's proposals involve requiring each bank to hold capital to cover its banking book credit exposures largely based on the rating of these exposures.[1] For bonds and loans, the ratings for most banks will be internally generated based on systems approved by supervisors. For structured products, the ratings will mostly be agency ratings provided by the major international rating agencies.

Whether internal or external, the rating for an exposure is based on its expected loss or default probability. These aspects of an exposure are not the same as the exposure's unexpected loss, which is generally thought to be an appropriate basis for setting capital. However, experience suggests that, for reasonably homogeneous categories of assets, one may expect to find a stable relationship between expected loss and default probabilities and hence ratings on the one hand and unexpected loss and hence capital on the other hand.

Under the current Basel proposals, very different capital charges are envisaged for bonds and loans than for securitisation exposures such as holdings of tranches of collateralised debt obligations (CDOs) or asset-backed securities (ABS). In general, the capital charges for securitisation exposures are considerably greater than similarly rated bonds or loans (bonds or loans with the same expected losses or default probabilities). For some industry practitioners, this has been controversial.

This chapter investigates the relative risks involved in investing in bonds and in tranches of securitisations by examining secondary market returns on these securities.

We begin by investigating return volatility, value-at-risk (VAR) and expected shortfall (ES)[2] for investments in individual structured products and bonds that have the same agency rating. The relative risks associated with investing in individual assets depend on the portfolio within which they are held, however. Volatilities on individual assets are uninformative on the incremental risks that exposures contribute to portfolios.

Indeed, one might expect, *a priori*, that returns on structured exposures will be less volatile than returns on the underlying exposures in their pools as they represent claims to derivatives written on diversified pools of assets and hence are not much affected by idiosyncratic risks. On the other hand, structured exposures could contribute significantly to risk when held in a wider portfolio, as the risks they contain are largely factor or systematic risks that, in many cases, will be closely positively correlated with shocks to overall portfolio value.

To investigate the factor risk in bonds versus that in structured exposures, we also look at the volatility, VAR and ES of broad indices. Individual exposures may have highly volatile returns but the index may be quite stable if the return volatility is idiosyncratic. By looking at index return statistics, we are able to filter out much of the idiosyncratic risk.

Furthermore, we examine the betas of individual exposures calculated against the indices for their respective market returns.[3] The use of a beta as a measure of incremental risk is suggested by the role betas play in asset pricing theory. Under the assumptions of the Capital Asset Pricing model, beta is a sufficient statistic for the incremental risk that a security contributes to a wider portfolio.

When asset returns are normally distributed, the beta is also closely related to the marginal value of risk of an exposure, ie, the amount by which investing in an additional unit of the investment in question boosts the total portfolio VAR.

The data we employ in our study consist of secondary market time series returns on the constituent bonds and structured exposures in the Merrill Lynch ABS master index and the Merrill Lynch corporate bond index. We restrict attention in both cases to the fixed rate, US$-denominated bonds and ABS tranches in these indices.

Despite the practical importance of this topic, there has been relatively little academic investigation of diversification in defaultable debt markets. Pedrosa and Roll (1998) studied the distribution of factors driving changes in credit spreads. Varotto (2000) looked at whether credit risk reduction can be better achieved by diversifying across industry or country.

DATA

The data we employ consist of weekly observations of returns on individual US ABS exposures and US corporate bonds in the period January 1997 to December 2003. The ABS exposures in question are those included in the US ABS master index (fixed rate) constructed by Merrill Lynch. The US corporate bonds are those included in the US corporate bond master index constructed by Merrill Lynch. We restrict attention to US$-denominated tranches and bonds.

For each tranche or corporate bond, we obtained a monthly rating series, the type, the maturity, and the coupon rate. Merrill Lynch distinguishes between ABS exposures with six different types of underlying collateral: (i) home equity loans (HEL), (ii) credit cards (Cards), (iii) automobile (Auto), (iv) manufactured housing (MH), (v) utilities (Util), and (vi) miscellaneous (Misc). Table 1 provides the different collateral types and a definition of the corresponding structured exposure. Corporate bonds are divided into three types according to the nature of the issuer: (i) financials (Fin), (ii) industrials (Ind), and (iii) utilities (Util).

The Merrill Lynch ABS and corporate bond indices only include investment grade assets. When we condition on ratings, we distinguish between AAA, AA, A, and BBB rated assets. If we only

Table 1 Definitions of different ABS types

Types of collateral	Definition of ABS
Home equity loans	Securitisation of home equity lines of credit. The latter are revolving lines of credit secured (collateralised) by homes.
Credit cards	Securitisation of retail credit card receivables (both bankcard and proprietary credit card receivables).
Automobile loans	Securitisation of retail automobile loans including auto warehouse loans, automobile leases, and automobile loans.
Manufactured housing	Securitisation of factory-built or pre-fabricated homes (includes mobile homes). Manufactured homes are the only homes with a national building code.
Utility	A structured security backed by various forms of mutual fund related revenues such as gas or electricity receivables.

looked at returns on securities while they were part of the Merrill Lynch indices, this would induce a survivorship bias in that large negative returns associated with periods in which the security was downgraded and ceased to be investment grade would be omitted from our dataset. However, our approach is to condition on the rating that a security has on January 1st in any given calendar year and then to track the subsequent returns on that security even if the security falls out of the index.

This approach does not entirely eliminate survivorship bias as it is typically the case that securities, on average, become less liquid when their rating falls below investment grade levels. In this case, the security is less likely to be quoted and hence time series returns are less likely to be available. Nevertheless, one may expect this survivorship bias to be less serious than that which we avoid by our approach.

To estimate the statistics of returns such as volatilities, we require that at least 25 weekly returns are available in a given year. Figure 1 shows the availability of bonds and ABS tranches satisfying our criterion of 25 weekly returns year by year for different ratings (AAA, AA, A, and BBB) and, in the case of ABS tranches, for different collateral types (HEL, Cards, Auto, MH, Util, and Misc).

The histograms show that the distribution by rating of the bond and ABS samples are very different in that there are very few AAA

Figure 1 Numbers of bonds and ABS tranches with 25 weekly returns in a year: (A) numbers of bonds by rating; (B) numbers of ABS tranches by rating

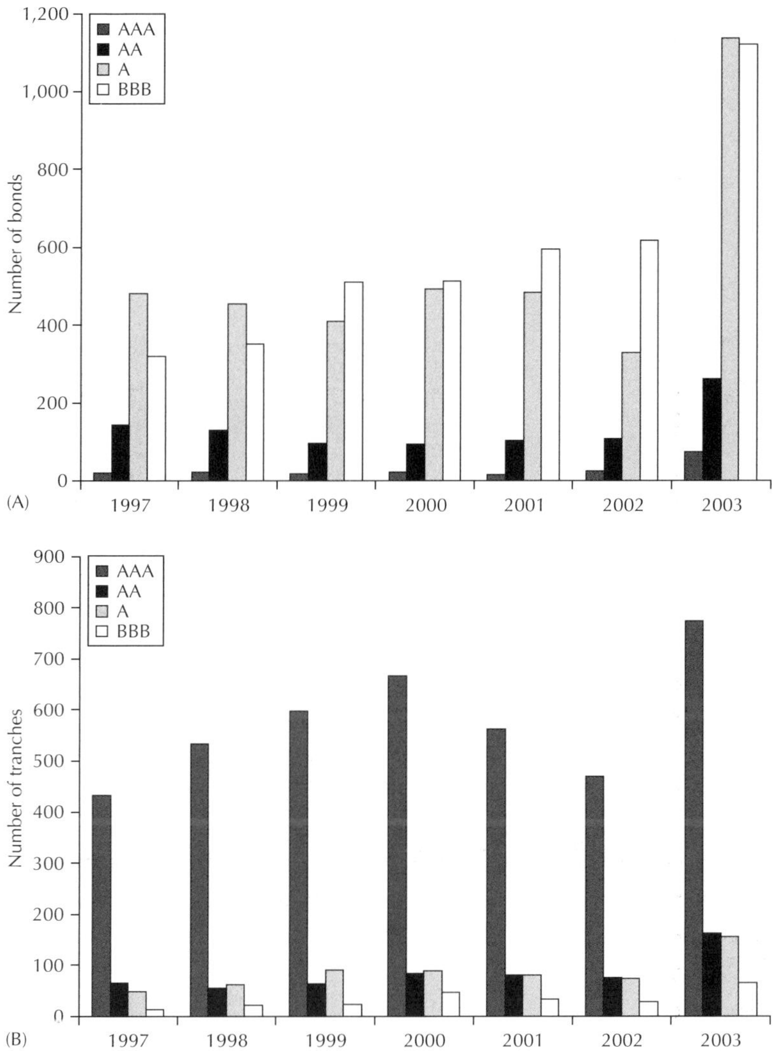

and AA bonds whereas a large fraction of the ABS tranches are in these highest rating categories. Equally, there are comparatively few BBB ABS tranches while a large fraction of the bonds in the sample are rated BBB.

Figure 1 Numbers of bonds and ABS tranches with 25 weekly returns in a year: (C) numbers of ABS tranches by colleteral type

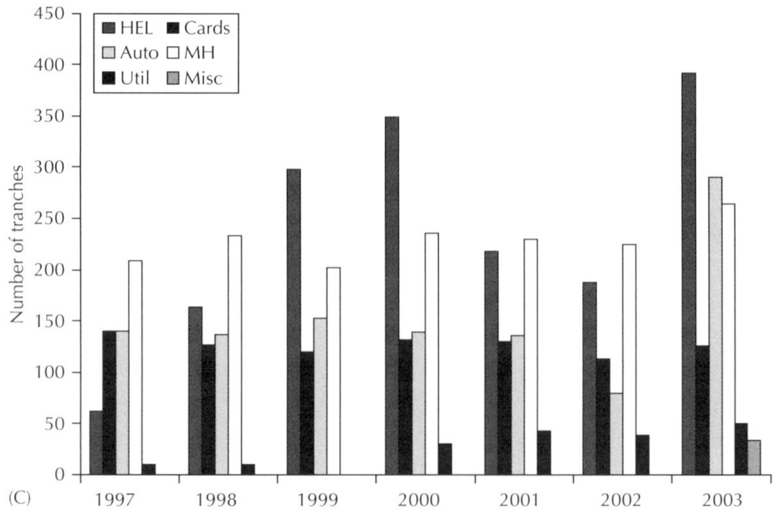

The number of bonds and ABS tranches in our sample has tended to increase over time although not exponentially. The largest increase in the number of securities occurred in the last year of our sample for bonds. Among ABS tranches, those with home equity loans, utility receivables and miscellaneous increased most over the sample period although in the case of the latter two categories this was from a very low base. The number of tranches with manufactured housing and credit card collateral was fairly consistent over the sample period.

One should stress that the number of securities in the sample is not directly indicative of the size of the market in the categories included. Rather it indicates the size of the liquid market that Merrill Lynch decided to include in its indices. The results described are therefore primarily useful for the reader in interpreting the results we obtained on the risk measures described below.

Table 2 shows the average maturities of corporate bonds and ABS tranches in our sample. The table indicates that, for our sample at least, the average maturities for ABS tranches for different rating categories are greater than for similarly rated corporate bonds. This is no longer true if one restricts attention to ABS tranches with credit card or auto loan collateral. Manufactured

Table 2 Average maturity for bonds and ABS

		AAA	AA	A	BBB		
Bonds	mean	11.53	7.53	10.68	13.35		
	min	1.31	1.19	1.05	1.24		
	max	68.06	43.75	90.49	90.50		
ABS tranches	mean	16.20	22.97	12.17	22.81		
	min	1.01	1.25	1.67	5.97		
	max	37.64	33.71	30.24	33.51		
		HEL	**Cards**	**Auto**	**MH**	**Util**	**Misc**
ABS tranches	mean	22.70	5.58	3.47	26.45	8.15	10.34
	min	4.61	1.39	1.06	6.97	2.05	1.50
	max	37.52	11.77	9.93	31.99	18.00	29.25

Note: Figures are presented in years.

housing and home equity loan ABS tranches have very long average maturities. It is likely that our sample contains a higher proportion of relatively newly issued securities, which are more likely to be liquid "on-the-run" issues. This is particularly true in the case of ABS tranches since this market expanded considerably through our sample period.

EMPIRICAL RESULTS

Individual exposures

For each tranche and corporate bond return series, we estimated the mean, volatility, skewness and kurtosis of the annualised weekly returns for each of the years in our sample, ie, 1997–2003. The averages of these statistics across individual securities are reported in panels A–D of Table 3.

The returns are calculated as changes in the natural logarithm of "clean prices", ie, prices adjusted upwards to allow for accrued interest. To express these values on an annual basis, we multiply average weekly returns by 52. Similarly, volatilities calculated from weekly data are multiplied by the square root of 52. Skewness and kurtosis coefficients are dimensionless and hence do not require transformation.

The mean returns reported in panel A of Table 3 should be seen as indicators of how the market performed in these years and not

Table 3 Summary statistics of annualised weekly returns by rating category

	1997	1998	1999	2000	2001	2002	2003	Total
Panel A: Average annualised weekly returns								
Part 1: Corporate bonds								
AAA	3.33	1.77	−8.09	2.14	2.9	3.76	−1.27	**0.65**
AA	3.65	1.44	−5.97	3.24	2.92	2.01	−1.75	**0.79**
A	2.84	0.93	−8.87	1.82	2.71	3.31	−0.29	**0.35**
BBB	5.27	−0.9	−9.1	2.22	2.15	2.7	3.64	**0.85**
Part 2: ABS								
AAA	0.58	−0.06	−2.08	2.46	1.88	0.1	−0.92	**0.28**
AA	1.88	−0.87	−3.2	2.41	1.92	−3.44	−4.3	**−0.80**
A	0.44	−0.32	−2.91	2.73	2.77	−3.19	−9.88	**−1.48**
BBB	2.32	−4.1	−6.4	2.86	2.95	−25.41	−43.8	**−10.23**
Panel B: Volatility of annualised weekly returns								
Part 1: Corporate bonds								
AAA	3.98	5.28	4.8	5.18	4.33	5.12	12.59	**5.90**
AA	3.7	4.68	4.11	2.65	3.26	3.86	11.08	**4.76**
A	4.62	5.78	5.97	4.69	5.82	7.6	12.61	**6.73**
BBB	5.76	8.11	7.35	7.12	8.69	11.22	9.21	**8.21**
Part 2: ABS								
AAA	1.67	2.25	2.16	2.36	3.06	2.57	2.44	**2.36**
AA	2.79	3.51	4.22	4.34	4.6	8.52	12.61	**5.80**
A	1.83	3.59	3.98	3.55	4.03	6.11	15.04	**5.45**
BBB	3.72	5.51	15.83	10.86	4.56	27.64	40.05	**15.45**
Panel C: Skewness of annualised weekly returns								
Part 1: Corporate bonds								
AAA	0.11	−0.38	0.06	−0.69	−0.19	−0.2	−0.12	**−0.20**
AA	0.12	−0.15	0.12	−0.22	0.1	0.06	−0.04	**0.00**
A	0.05	−0.35	0.08	−0.46	−0.23	−0.39	−0.06	**−0.19**
BBB	0.08	−0.75	−0.01	−0.55	−0.61	−0.29	−0.07	**−0.31**
Part 2: ABS								
AAA	−0.08	0.64	0.2	−0.04	0	0.01	−0.16	**0.08**
AA	0.06	−0.03	0.11	−0.45	−0.66	−1.54	−0.21	**−0.39**
A	0.02	0.06	−0.36	−0.19	−0.42	−0.6	−0.54	**−0.29**
BBB	0.23	−0.74	−1.81	0.31	−0.27	−1.68	−1.86	**−0.83**
Panel D: Kurtosis of annualised weekly returns								
Part 1: Corporate bonds								
AAA	3.41	4.83	2.98	5.84	4.93	4.58	4.53	**4.44**
AA	3.38	4.49	3.07	3.94	4.91	4.15	4.71	**4.09**
A	3.49	5	3.27	4.4	4.91	6.3	4.38	**4.54**
BBB	3.12	5.36	4.29	5.39	5.48	6.38	4.97	**5.00**
Part 2: ABS								
AAA	4.42	6.95	5.04	4.82	6.35	5.58	5.66	**5.55**
AA	3.98	6.83	4.67	4.68	6.39	12.27	10.58	**7.06**
A	4.82	5.72	6.12	5.13	5.94	7.01	9.09	**6.26**
BBB	3.28	5.16	14.38	17.39	5.69	15.81	16	**11.10**

Note: For each bond and ABS, we calculate four statistics: average, standard deviation, skewness, and kurtosis of annualised weekly returns. The table presents the average of each statistic by rating. Figures are presented in percentages.

as estimates of equilibrium expected returns. To estimate the latter, much longer time series would be required. The table shows significant year-to-year volatility in bonds, while in the ABS market a period of modest gains and losses was followed by a distinct deterioration at the end of the sample period.

The volatilities reported in panel B of Table 3 exhibit a similar pattern with low volatilities in the earlier years particularly for ABS tranches with a sharp rise in volatilities at the end of the sample period. For ABS tranches, the increase in volatility for the lower credit quality tranches in 2002 and 2003 is spectacular.

Comparing the average volatilities across the whole sample period for bonds and ABS tranches for given rating categories, the results suggest that the volatility of A and AA grade ABS tranches resembled that on bonds, while AAA and BBB ABS tranches had lower and higher return volatilities respectively, than similarly rated bonds. As stressed in the introduction, this does not of itself imply that, for example, AAA ABS tranches are less risky than AAA-rated bonds, as the former may have greater factor correlation that will boost the risk of holding a wider portfolio.

Panels C and D of Table 3 contain estimates of skewness and kurtosis coefficients for bond and ABS tranche returns. These suggest that while there is some variation in the relative skewness of bond and ABS tranche returns, ABS tranche returns are fatter tailed than bond returns for all rating categories, except AAA.

Table 4 contains sample statistics similar to those in Table 3, but broken down by issuer type (for bonds) and collateral type (for ABS tranches) rather than by rating. The results show that while the sample distribution of bond returns varies relatively little across issuer type, ABS tranche return sample distributions have exhibited very pronounced differences across collateral categories. Specifically, the volatility of returns for tranches with auto loan collateral has been low, while that for tranches with manufactured housing collateral have, at the end of the sample period, been exceedingly high.

Interestingly, the kurtosis of returns on ABS tranches has been similar for different collateral types and consistently higher than that for bond returns of different issuer types.

Figure 2 and 3 shows time series plots of annualised volatilities of weekly ABS and bond returns over the sample period by using a moving window of one year. Figure 2 rather dramatically

Table 4 Summary statistics for annualised weekly returns by issuer/collateral type

	1997	1998	1999	2000	2001	2002	2003	Total
Panel A: Average annualised weekly returns								
Part 1: Corporate bonds								
Fin	2.23	0.73	−6.01	1.2	3.01	2.27	−0.35	**0.44**
Ind	4.43	−0.05	−9.24	2.25	2.37	3.2	1.63	**0.66**
Util	3.42	2.1	−9.57	3.65	1.59	1.26	4.33	**0.97**
Part 2: ABS								
HEL	0.63	−0.35	−2.01	3.01	2.35	0.49	−1.2	**0.42**
Cards	0.46	0.4	−2.8	2.63	2.5	1.48	−1.58	**0.44**
Auto	−0.04	0.21	−1.16	0.99	1.2	−1.76	−1.37	**−0.28**
MH	1.57	−0.91	−3.67	2.31	1.56	−6.41	−17.43	**−3.28**
Util	−0.03	0.24	–	4.37	4.14	4.34	−0.75	**2.05**
Misc	–	–	–	–	–	–	−2.89	**−2.89**
Panel B: Volatility of annualised weekly returns								
Part 1: Corporate bonds								
Fin	3.42	4.89	4.68	3.73	3.52	4.89	11.43	**5.22**
Ind	5.25	7.09	7.01	6.25	8.03	10.29	10.84	**7.82**
Util	5.68	6.28	5.53	5.63	7.68	11.38	10.38	**7.51**
Part 2: ABS								
HEL	1.92	2.22	3.38	3.45	2.84	2.04	2.92	**2.68**
Cards	1.86	2.64	2.17	2.38	3.54	2.08	2.13	**2.40**
Auto	0.82	1.08	1.03	1.03	1.46	0.78	1.42	**1.09**
MH	2.57	3.69	4.22	4.31	4.64	9.98	25.55	**7.85**
Util	1.01	1.53	–	2.84	5.18	4.13	4.4	**3.18**
Misc	–	–	–	–	–	–	3.1	**3.10**
Panel C: Skewness of annualised weekly returns								
Part 1: Corporate bonds								
Fin	0.1	−0.25	0.01	−0.34	0	−0.04	−0.02	**−0.08**
Ind	0.06	−0.54	0.04	−0.53	−0.49	−0.3	−0.09	**−0.26**
Util	0.08	−0.6	0.11	−0.46	−0.61	−0.52	0	**−0.29**
Part 2: ABS								
HEL	−0.07	0.83	0.26	0.12	−0.07	0.2	−0.28	**0.14**
Cards	0.04	0.56	−0.04	−0.07	−0.17	−0.21	−0.16	**−0.01**
Auto	−0.19	0.65	0.02	−0.08	0.81	0.67	−0.12	**0.25**
MH	0	0.11	−0.13	−0.37	−0.66	−1.3	−0.75	**−0.44**
Util	−0.05	0.71	–	0.06	−0.43	0.38	0.11	**0.13**
Misc	–	–	–	–	–	–	−0.16	**−0.16**
Panel D: Kurtosis of annualised weekly returns								
Part 1: Corporate bonds								
Fin	3.34	5.27	3.52	4.07	5.05	5.33	4.52	**4.44**
Ind	3.24	5	3.92	5.11	5.28	6.11	4.66	**4.76**
Util	3.98	4.95	2.83	4.61	4.8	7.5	5.38	**4.86**

Table 4 *(continued)*

	1997	1998	1999	2000	2001	2002	2003	Total
Part 2: ABS								
HEL	4.96	7.5	5.62	5.88	5.71	5.63	6.64	**5.99**
Cards	4.52	6.36	4.68	5.11	6.84	4.82	4.48	**5.26**
Auto	4.68	6.99	5.41	5.41	7.92	5.18	5.88	**5.92**
MH	4	6.36	5.54	5.53	5.8	9.97	11.8	**7.00**
Util	4.92	6.02	–	3.48	4.9	6.23	5.2	**5.13**
Misc	–	–	–	–	–	–	8.67	**8.67**

Note: Home equity loans (HEL), credit cards (Cards), automobile (Auto), manufactured housing (MH), utilities (Util) and miscellaneous (Misc).
For each bond and ABS, we calculate four statistics: average, standard deviation, skewness, and kurtosis of annualised weekly returns. The table presents the average of each statistic by issuer/collateral type. Figures are presented in percentages.

illustrates the fact that the bond volatilities behave similarly for bonds of different rating categories (although they are generally higher for lower rating grades). In contrast, ABS tranche return volatilities are very different for different rating categories, with lower ratings grades being very much riskier.

It also seems to be true that ABS tranche return volatilities experience regime changes in stress periods. At the end of the sample period, ABS return volatilities for all rating categories except AAA increase dramatically. The plots show the extent to which this increase is caused by deterioration in the credit standing of tranches with manufactured housing collateral. Leaving aside this sector, the increases in ABS volatilities at the end of the sample period are quite small (see Figure 3).

To understand what happened to the manufactured housing sector during our sample period, one may consult sources such as Davidson *et al* (2003). This suggests that industry fundamentals in this sector were under considerable stress. Symptoms included excess dealer inventory, deterioration of delinquencies continued retail consolidation and rising repossessions. Overall, the deterioration in the general economy and a spike in the jobless rate caused a decline in the credit performance of securitised manufactured housing transactions. The market was further undercut by sales of repossessed units so that by the start of 2001 annualised manufactured housing shipments had dropped to their lowest level since 1991. A vicious circle arose in which the drop in prices further discouraged new purchases.

Figure 2 Average annualised weekly volatility of individual exposures by rating: (A) bonds and (B) ABS tranches

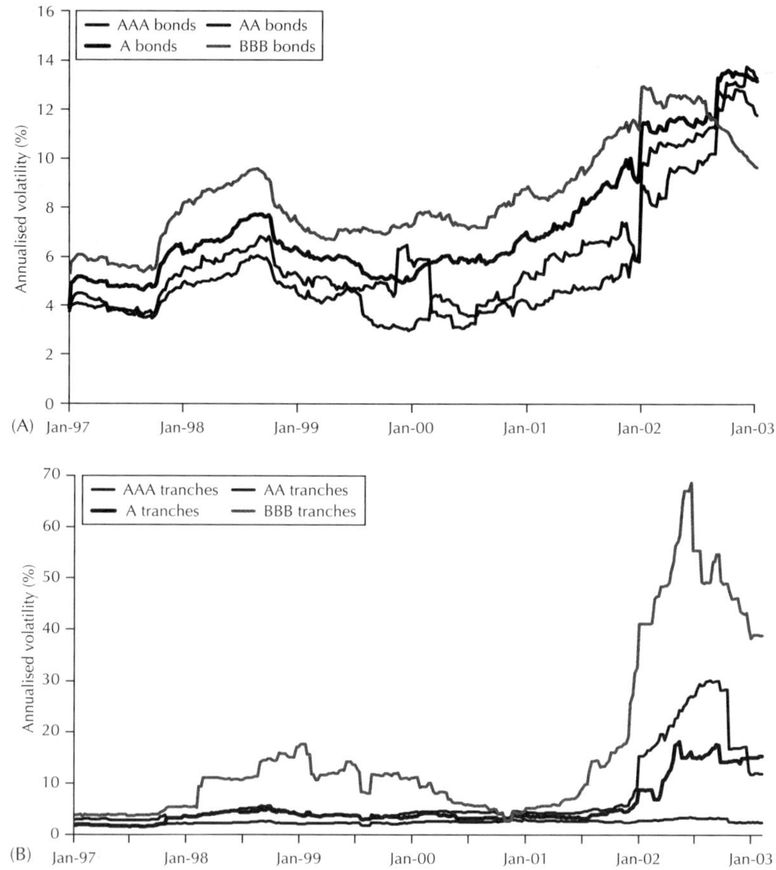

Tables 5 and 6 report panel regressions of individual security volatilities on rating dummies, issuer/collateral type dummies, maturity in years and annual time dummies for bonds and for ABS tranches. To be more precise, we estimate the following random effects model

$$\sigma_{it} = \mu + \lambda_t + \beta' x_{it} + \alpha_i + u_{it}$$

Here μ is the constant term and λ denotes the year dummies. σ denotes annualised volatility of weekly returns over a period of one year. Our dataset consists of weekly data, which means that we use a moving window of one year to estimate volatilities.

Table 5 Regression results for weekly corporate bond return volatilities

	(1)	(2)	(3)	(4)	(5)
ct	**8.67**	**8.73**	**3.78**	**2.92**	1.23
	(0.00)	(0.00)	(0.00)	(0.00)	(0.06)
AA	−1.20			−0.28	−0.27
	(0.08)			(0.65)	(0.65)
A	−0.18			0.30	0.54
	(0.78)			(0.61)	(0.33)
BBB	0.62			0.80	0.54
	(0.35)			(0.18)	(0.34)
Fin		−0.41		**1.30**	0.66
		(0.36)		(0.00)	(0.08)
Ind		0.16		−0.07	−0.04
		(0.71)		(0.84)	(0.90)
Maturity			**0.34**	**0.34**	**0.32**
			(0.00)	(0.00)	(0.00)
Dum98					**1.27**
					(0.00)
Dum99					0.33
					(0.12)
Dum00					−0.01
					(0.95)
Dum01					**1.45**
					(0.00)
Dum02					**3.22**
					(0.00)
Dum03					**3.71**
					(0.00)
Adj R^2	1.1%	0.6%	22.1%	22.3%	29.3%
BP LM test	756.1	766.5	301.2	299.4	244.6
(*p*-value)	0.00	0.00	0.00	0.00	0.00

Note: The dependent variable is the annualised volatility of weekly corporate bond returns. The random effects model is used for the analysis. BP LM denotes the Breusch–Pagan Lagrange Multiplier test for random effects. *p*-values are given between brackets. Coefficients that are significant at a 5% level are bold.

x includes rating and type dummies and maturity in years. For ABS, we include five collateral type dummies (HEL, Cards, Auto, MH, Util) and for corporate bonds, we include two issuer type dummies (Fin and Ind). Our data set includes ABS and corporate bonds that are considered a random sample from some larger populations. It is therefore appropriate to use a random effects model. We assume that the random variables α and u are normally distributed.

Table 6 Regression results for weekly corporate ABS return volatilities

	(1)	(2)	(3)	(4)	(5)
ct	**2.26**	3.16	−0.57	−2.99	**−5.67**
	0.00	0.08	0.08	0.09	0.00
AA	**3.62**			**1.76**	**1.00**
	0.00			0.00	0.04
A	**4.92**			**4.83**	**4.59**
	0.00			0.00	0.00
BBB	**19.73**			**16.76**	**16.48**
	0.00			0.00	0.00
HEL		−0.29		−1.94	2.10
		0.87		0.26	0.23
Cards		−0.76		1.45	**4.02**
		0.68		0.40	0.02
Auto		−2.01		1.38	3.21
		0.27		0.43	0.06
MH		**5.43**		1.67	**6.51**
		0.00		0.34	0.00
Util		0.75		**3.65**	**5.91**
		0.70		0.05	0.00
Maturity			**0.23**	**0.25**	**0.15**
			0.00	0.00	0.00
Dum98					0.51
					0.35
Dum99					0.75
					0.16
Dum00					0.27
					0.61
Dum01					0.19
					0.73
Dum02					**1.54**
					0.01
Dum03					**4.56**
					0.00
Adj R^2	12.8%	6.9%	5.5%	18.5%	20.5%
BP LM test	82.0	63.0	75.3	25.1	31.0
(*p*-value)	0.00	0.00	0.00	0.00	0.00

Note: The dependent variable is the annualised weekly volatility of weekly ABS returns. The random effects model is used for the analysis. BP LM test is the Breusch–Pagan Lagrange Multiplier test for random effects. *p*-values are given between brackets. Coefficients that are significant at a 5% level are bold. Home equity loans (HEL), credit cards (Cards), automobile (Auto), manufactured housing (MH), utilities (Util).

Figure 3 Average annualised weekly volatility of individual exposures by sector: (A) bonds and (B) ABS tranches

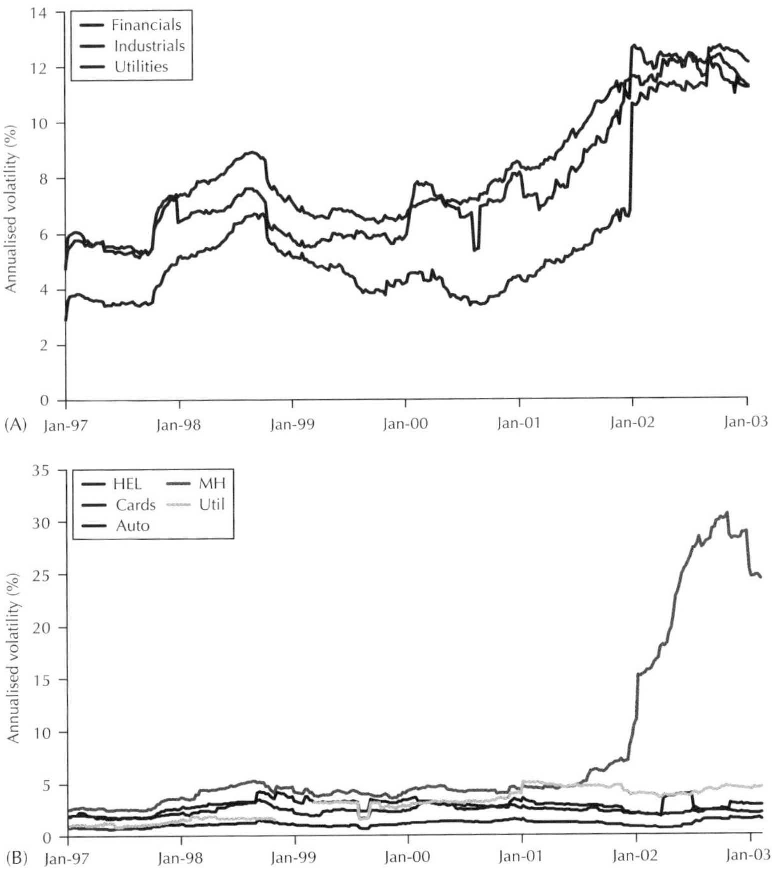

The bond regression results in Table 5 suggest that there is a consistent maturity effect and that volatilities for bonds issued by financials appear significantly higher, but the only other significant differences between volatilities are associated with the year in which the volatility is measured. In particular, rating does not play a significant role. These results suggest that the primary drivers for volatility in this market are factors that do not depend on expected loss or default probability such as liquidity and possible risk premiums.

In contrast, the volatilities of ABS tranche returns have a range of strongly significant explanatory variables in the regression results reported in Table 6. Rating and sector play big roles. (To some degree, these may appear more significant than they actually are as interaction effects could be omitted between date and sector.) The lower rating categories are much more volatile and tranches with collateral made up of manufactured housing, utility and credit card receivables have the highest volatilities. Maturity is also a significant influence on ABS return volatility although not as large in magnitude as the maturity effect in bond volatilities.

For each corporate bond and tranche return series, we estimated the value-at-risk (VAR) and expected shortfall (ES) for each year in our sample, ie, 1997–2003. The confidence level for both risk measures is 5% (ie, the VAR is the loss that will be exceeded on 5% of occasions). The averages of the VAR and ES across individual securities are reported in Table 7. The results reinforce some of the conclusions of the analysis of volatilities presented above. For AAA grades, ABS returns are less risky than bond returns. As one moves down the investment grade categories to BBB, the ABS tranche returns appear substantially riskier. The ES measure that is very sensitive to outliers makes the ABS exposures appear particularly risky in that the AA as well as the BBB categories have much higher ES than the equivalent bond categories. Meanwhile, for the A-grade categories the risk is roughly the same by this measure.

Portfolios of exposures

As mentioned in the introduction, the measures of risk most relevant for calculating appropriate levels of economic or regulatory capital are those that reflect the contribution that individual exposures make to fluctuations in the value of a wider portfolio within which they are held. One can examine such contributions to volatility by considering the distribution of returns on indices of individual securities in which idiosyncratic volatility has been diversified away to a large extent. Alternatively, one may look at individual security measures of incremental risk such as the beta of a security return with the return on a market index.

Table 8 contains results similar to those contained in Table 7, but for returns on indices of corporate bonds and ABS tranches. The indices are equally weighted indices created by the authors, sorting securities into rating categories according to the rating observed at the start of each calendar year. The qualitative picture that emerges

Table 7 Average value-at-risk (VAR) and expected shortfall (ES) for individual exposures

	1997	1998	1999	2000	2001	2002	2003	Total
Panel A: Average VAR								
Part 1: Corporate bonds								
AAA	49.46	68.22	64.76	49.65	67.03	74.75	168.46	**77.48**
AA	44.04	64.30	55.11	31.16	41.85	46.50	140.16	**60.45**
A	56.92	75.26	76.43	61.66	78.61	88.74	163.40	**85.86**
BBB	67.74	110.09	92.12	96.32	113.7	140.89	108.42	**104.18**
Part 2: ABS								
AAA	19.01	27.24	25.54	24.84	39.88	30.77	29.94	**28.17**
AA	29.82	42.42	49.15	46.69	60.48	80.53	151.35	**65.78**
A	20.56	46.67	43.94	32.62	55.05	78.51	194.21	**67.37**
BBB	39.16	86.16	127.69	83.54	63.97	291.02	506.71	**171.18**
Panel B: ES								
Part 1: Corporate bonds								
AAA	55.56	91.85	71.10	85.18	75.73	84.33	202.11	**95.12**
AA	48.93	78.86	62.37	38.78	50.64	55.86	174.91	**72.91**
A	64.87	99.75	90.48	80.00	97.00	125.20	197.45	**107.82**
BBB	75.12	149.86	114.63	126.37	150.32	190.89	137.73	**134.99**
Part 2: ABS								
AAA	23.72	34.92	33.33	32.26	51.38	44.32	40.90	**37.26**
AA	35.46	61.65	63.99	67.14	81.01	171.67	237.08	**102.57**
A	25.54	62.50	64.12	51.92	68.05	132.26	312.92	**102.47**
BBB	46.88	105.64	306.95	164.44	77.92	604.35	906.18	**316.05**

Note: For each bond and ABS, we calculate the value-at-risk and expected shortfall of annualised weekly returns. The table presents the average of each statistic by rating. Figures are presented in percentages.

from the table resembles that suggested by the individual security results in Table 7. Again, the BBB-rated ABS tranches are much riskier than the BBB-rated corporate bonds. The contrast is especially apparent when one looks at the ES measure. AAA-rated bonds are riskier than AAA-rated ABS tranches. AA- and A-rated bonds are broadly as risky as similarly rated ABS tranches.

We argued in the introduction that betas with respect to a market index (defined as covariances between individual security returns and the index return divided by the variance of the index return) may provide some insight into the contribution of single securities to the total risk faced by an investor who holds the index portfolio. Tables 9 and 10 report the average betas of individual exposure returns on an aggregate investment in an equally

Table 8 Value-at-risk (VAR) and expected shortfall (ES) for indices

	1997	1998	1999	2000	2001	2002	2003	Total
Panel A: VAR								
Part 1: Corporate bonds								
AAA	47.13	77.31	50.96	50.13	52.82	51.34	68.92	**56.94**
AA	40.00	64.00	54.63	27.84	37.12	33.71	60.54	**45.41**
A	46.72	77.21	66.03	44.87	60.30	55.19	69.71	**60.00**
BBB	60.98	97.81	74.50	58.82	79.92	47.74	81.22	**71.57**
Part 2: ABS								
AAA	16.10	31.07	19.35	18.38	34.51	20.82	20.85	**23.01**
AA	29.64	41.19	41.95	37.48	52.05	75.24	66.26	**49.12**
A	18.41	44.99	34.65	28.57	48.91	51.13	76.66	**43.33**
BBB	30.09	82.43	66.29	48.17	48.43	153.02	212.34	**91.54**
Panel B: ES								
Part 1: Corporate bonds								
AAA	51.37	94.04	63.26	65.91	73.88	59.99	70.98	**68.49**
AA	43.84	73.43	57.29	33.83	56.11	42.40	64.43	**53.05**
A	52.37	98.37	80.91	55.24	80.64	67.96	78.25	**73.39**
BBB	66.46	130.16	79.03	79.23	105.83	68.14	88.52	**88.20**
Part 2: ABS								
AAA	20.42	31.91	21.16	23.37	45.00	29.63	27.47	**28.42**
AA	31.55	54.97	47.62	52.55	68.02	87.84	97.17	**62.82**
A	23.09	56.37	50.50	33.50	62.43	69.66	109.16	**57.82**
BBB	37.17	94.61	169.88	72.68	56.82	313.16	414.76	**165.58**

Note: The table presents the value-at-risk and expected shortfall of bond and ABS index returns by rating. Figures are annualised weekly returns and presented in percentages.

weighted index of the same exposures. (Note that this means that, in the case of ABS tranches for example, the beta is the covariance of a single ABS tranche return with the return on an equally weighted index of ABS tranche investments.)

Over all, the ABS tranches have higher betas with respect to an index of ABS tranche returns than bonds with respect to a bond index. Interestingly, the betas for ABS tranches decline sharply with the rating whereas the betas for bonds are fairly stable for different rating categories. This suggests that there are multiple factors driving ABS tranches and that they are particularly important for lower rating grades, whereas there are few common factors driving bond returns. It is also interesting to note that the levels of the average betas tend to decline over time for both bond and ABS securities.

Table 9 Average bond betas versus a bond index return

		1997	1998	1999	2000	2001	2002	2003	Total
All bonds									
Beta	Mean	0.92	0.83	0.82	0.67	0.73	0.47	0.36	**0.69**
	Stdev	0.5	0.5	0.59	0.46	0.46	0.38	0.5	
# regressions		916	914	978	1038	1043	763	2341	
AAA bonds									
Beta	Mean	1.08	1.00	0.89	0.77	1.09	0.74	0.21	**0.83**
	Stdev	0.48	0.59	0.37	0.49	0.55	0.38	0.24	
# regressions		20	21	16	18	12	11	64	
AA bonds									
Beta	Mean	1.13	1.12	1.35	1.06	1.17	0.75	0.22	**0.97**
	Stdev	0.59	0.61	0.85	0.45	0.48	0.54	0.25	
# regressions		130	120	83	77	63	29	233	
A bonds									
Beta	Mean	0.99	0.92	0.92	0.81	0.84	0.46	0.23	**0.74**
	Stdev	0.53	0.52	0.63	0.52	0.52	0.35	0.25	
# regressions		449	424	378	443	401	180	1006	
BBB bonds									
Beta	Mean	0.73	0.61	0.66	0.49	0.59	0.46	0.53	**0.58**
	Stdev	0.32	0.3	0.42	0.3	0.35	0.37	0.66	
# regressions		317	349	501	500	567	543	1038	

Note: For each bond, we estimate the beta versus a bond index return. The table presents the average and standard deviation of the betas by rating.

CONCLUDING REMARKS

This chapter has examined the risks involved in holding exposures to US$-denominated corporate bonds or tranches of ABS. The results suggest that the behaviour of returns in these two markets is very different in that, while bond volatilities and other risk measures behave in a reasonably consistent way over time and across sectors of the market, ABS tranche returns exhibit regime changes in which a particular sector deteriorates dramatically with substantial increases in risk over a relatively short period.

Our conclusions in this regard must be treated with caution as the regime change to which we allude occurs in a single sector, ABS with manufactured housing collateral, and once in our sample period. In effect, the volatilities we report should be seen as sample statistics revealing systematic patterns in the particular realisation of the last few years rather than reliable estimates of unconditional moments. Thus, for example, if the stress event driving our results

Table 10 Average ABS tranche betas versus an ABS tranche index return

		1997	1998	1999	2000	2001	2002	2003	Total
All tranches									
Beta	Mean	1.24	1.3	1	1.03	0.9	0.61	0.8	**0.98**
	Stdev	0.85	1.03	0.83	0.89	0.53	0.5	0.93	
# regressions		538	650	747	869	801	643	1036	
AAA tranches									
Beta	Mean	1.32	1.4	1.11	1.14	0.98	0.69	1.01	**1.09**
	Stdev	0.87	1.06	0.87	0.92	0.54	0.49	1.03	
# regressions		417	515	578	649	593	465	651	
AA tranches									
Beta	Mean	0.94	0.99	0.68	0.68	0.6	0.32	0.27	**0.64**
	Stdev	0.81	0.9	0.56	0.56	0.35	0.35	0.33	
# regressions		63	54	62	83	87	76	177	
A tranches									
Beta	Mean	1.14	1	0.66	1.01	0.87	0.61	0.77	**0.87**
	Stdev	0.52	0.74	0.46	0.78	0.51	0.53	0.69	
# regressions		44	60	86	89	87	73	142	
BBB tranches									
Beta	Mean	0.47	0.48	0.18	0.16	0.54	0.15	0.27	**0.32**
	Stdev	0.19	0.23	0.23	0.26	0.28	0.24	0.46	
# regressions		14	21	21	48	34	29	66	

Note: For each ABS tranche, we estimate the beta versus an ABS index return. The table presents the average and standard deviation of the betas by rating.

had been greater in magnitude, one might expect that returns on higher rated tranches would exhibit regime-change like behaviour.

However, it is fair to conclude from the results that we have reported that the operation of risks in the ABS market is very different from that in bonds. If we model ABS tranche returns in the reduced form way as we have done here, we must allow for regime shifts in which volatilities and other risk measures suddenly exhibit extreme behaviour. Future research should attempt to model risk in ABS tranches in a more structural way, explicitly allowing for the fact that they are generated non-linearly through shocks to highly levered claims written on pools of underlying assets. Within such a framework, one might hope to explain the dynamics of these markets without assuming regime changes.

1 For bonds and loans, the capital will be calculated by inputting default probabilities and loss given default (LGD) estimates and maturity into a formula. The regulatory capital for

structured exposures that possess agency ratings will be determined by consulting a simple look up table of charges for different rating grades. Distinction is made in this table between senior tranches, low granularity tranches and all other tranches.

2 The VAR for a return r over a given holding period and for a given confidence level α is defined implicitly by Probability($r < -\text{VAR}$) = α. The ES for r is defined by ES = E($r \mid r < -\text{VAR}$).

3 The beta of one return, r_1, against another, r_2, is defined as Covariance(r_1,r_2)/Variance(r_2).

REFERENCES

Basel Committee on Banking Supervision, 2004, "Basel II: International Convergence of Capital Measurement and Capital Standards: A Revised Framework", Basel Committee Publications No. 107, June.

Davidson, A., A. Sanders, L. Wolff, and A. Ching, 2003, "Securitization: Structuring and Investment Analysis", (New Jersey: John Wiley & Sons).

Pedrosa, M., and R. Roll, 1998, "Systematic Risk in Corporate Bond Credit Spreads", *Journal of Fixed Income*, **8(3)**, pp. 7–26, December.

Varotto, S., 2000, "Credit Risk Diversification and Bank Capital", Birkbeck College Mimeo, November.

Section 4

Basel II

13

Model Foundations for the Supervisory Formula Approach

Michael B. Gordy*

Federal Reserve Board

In its proposal for a New Basel Accord, the Basel Committee on Bank Supervision (2004, Part 2.IV) offers two methodologies for assigning regulatory capital charges to securitisation exposures under the internal ratings-based (IRB) approach. The ratings-based approach sets capital primarily as a function of an external rating, such as might be assigned by Moody's or Standard & Poor's, and is to be employed whenever an external rating is available. As many securitisation exposures are not externally rated, the alternative supervisory formula approach (SFA) determines the required capital as a function of the characteristics of the collateral pool and contractual properties of the tranche. This chapter sets forth the theoretical foundation for the SFA provided by the "uncertainty in loss prioritisation" (ULP) model of Gordy and Jones (2003).

Regulatory application places important constraints on model design. To avoid the inconsistencies that presently make securitisation an instrument for regulatory arbitrage (see Jones, 2000), the securitisation model must be fully compatible with the model underpinning IRB capital charges on whole loans. Cost-effective application to a wide variety of securitisations and participating institutions dictates that the capital rule be parsimonious, in the sense of using minimal information on the contents of the

*The opinions expressed here are those of the author, and do not reflect the views of the Board of Governors or its staff. I thank Peter Carr, Enrico De Giorgi, Hemant Ishwaran, David Jones and Dilip Madan for helpful comments.

securitised pool and on the contractual design of the securitisation, as well as computationally tractable. The distribution of payouts to participants in a securitisation (often termed the cashflow "waterfall") can be quite complex and deal-specific, depending, for example, on the time profiles of the pool's defaults, recoveries, and principal and interest payments on the underlying loans. For regulatory capital purposes, it is not practical to attempt to account for the myriad of possible deal-specific attributes of the waterfall. The ULP model satisfies both of these constraints.

The model foundation for the IRB approach is a special case of the class of credit value-at-risk (VAR) models currently in widespread use. Economic capital is set to cover total mark-to-market credit losses over a one-year horizon with probability q.[1] It is assumed that the bank's credit portfolio is infinitely fine-grained in the sense that any single obligor represents a negligible share of the portfolio's total exposure, and that a single, common systematic risk factor drives all dependence across credit losses in the portfolio. The salient implication of this asymptotic single risk-factor (ASRF) framework is that the economic capital requirement for the portfolio equals the portfolio's expected loss conditional on the systematic risk factor taking a value equal to the qth percentile of its probability distribution. Given the linearity of the expectation operator, this result implies that economic capital for each instrument in the portfolio (whether that instrument is a whole loan or a tranche of a securitisation) is its own expected loss conditional on the qth percentile of the systematic risk factor, and thus is independent of the composition of the rest of its portfolio.[2] When applied to securitisations, the ASRF framework implies "capital neutrality" in the sense that the sum of the economic capital charges for the individual tranches of a securitisation equals the economic capital for the underlying collateral pool.

The ULP model imposes the ASRF assumptions on the bank's overall portfolio. Bearing in mind that an obligor may appear concurrently in multiple securitisation transactions and directly in the bank's own loan book, we assume that the bank's aggregated exposure to each obligor represented in the collateral pool is small relative to the bank's overall portfolio. The ULP model introduces a new source of risk specific to the securitisation transaction, and so we also require the bank's total exposure to each transaction (that is, summing across the tranches held by the bank) to be small relative to the bank's overall portfolio. To be clear, the model does not require that the bank's total holdings of securitisation instruments be a small share of its total portfolio. Most importantly, the collateral pool need not be infinitely fine-grained. Indeed, the ULP model can be applied to securitisations of pools ranging from a single loan to infinitely many loans.

To avoid dependence on the contractual details of the cashflow waterfall, it is necessary to take a stylised view of the allocation of pool credit losses across tranche investors. Pykhtin and Dev (2002, 2003) propose perhaps the simplest approach, which is to assume that losses in the pool are allocated deterministically according to a strict loss prioritisation (SLP) rule. Let ζ denote the credit enhancement level, defined as the sum of the par values of all more junior tranches, and let T denote the tranche's par value or thickness. In practice, both ζ and T are readily observable to market participants. Under the SLP rule, the tranche absorbs pool losses only in excess of ζ, up to a maximum of T. That is, if L denotes pool losses, then the loss for the tranche investor is $\min\{L, \zeta + T\} - \min\{L, \zeta\}$.

The ULP model generalises this simple rule by adding a stochastic element to the distribution of loss across tranche investors. The credit enhancement level determines ex-ante *expected* protection against losses in the pool, but the actual protection conferred by the prioritised waterfall is random and realised only at the horizon. This divergence from the strict prioritisation of economic credit losses over the analysis horizon can arise from at least two sources. First, few securitisations actually call for strict prioritisation of all cashflows, as subordinated tranches typically are entitled to some cash payouts prior to more senior investors being paid out in full. Second, even with strict prioritisation of cashflows over the life of a securitisation, the nominal credit enhancement level ζ generally understates the ability of more junior tranches to absorb economic losses to the extent that their contractual yield is higher than the rate of interest on the underlying loans in the pool.[3]

It should be emphasised that the model is *not* positing that there is operational or legal risk in the execution of securitisation contracts. The new source of uncertainty instead reflects the potential gap between the accounting representation of the tranche (ie, its position and thickness relative to other holders of principal) and its vulnerability to economic loss. The intuition draws from the long vein of econometrics literature on models with hidden parameters. The details of the contractual cashflow waterfall are material but unobservable parameters in the "true" model of the securitisation. From the perspective of the econometrician (in our case, the regulator), such parameters act as sources of random error that must be "integrated out" rather than ignored. Were one to have unimpeded access to all details of the securitisation contract, a "full information" model along the lines of Duffie and Garleanu (2001) would naturally be preferred.

We first develop the ULP model under very general assumptions similar to those in Gordy (2003). A general methodology for simplifying computation of capital charges is then set forth. The model specification is completed in the next section, where we impose the specific functional forms and distributional assumptions to which IRB capital charges are calibrated. This ensures full consistency between the IRB approach and the proposed treatment of securitisation exposures. We conclude with a discussion of regulatory application.

MODELLING UNCERTAINTY IN LOSS PRIORITISATION

We seek to assign an economic capital charge to a securitisation exposure held in an asymptotically fine-grained portfolio. As in the Basel II framework for the treatment of whole loans, total capital must be sufficient to cover portfolio credit loss up to some percentile q of the loss distribution.

Dependence between obligors in the economy arises due to a single systematic risk factor X. Conditional on X, losses on each loan in the bank's portfolio and in the securitised pool are independent. Let L be book-value (or "default-mode") loss incurred within the pool as a share of total pool exposure, and let $H_q(\cdot)$ be the cumulative distribution function (cdf) of L conditional on $X = x_q$, where x_q denotes the qth percentile of the distribution of X. We need make only very weak restrictions on the underlying model of portfolio risk. For example, we could make any of a wide variety of distributional assumptions on X and on recovery risk. The technical requirements are those set forth in Gordy (2003).

The collateral pool is securitised into a continuum of prioritised tranches, each of which is of infinitesimal thickness.[4]

Assume for the moment that losses are allocated deterministically in accordance with SLP, and let $K_{\text{slp}}(\zeta)$ be the cumulative capital charge (as a share of total pool exposure) on the junior-most share ζ of the structure. Under the ASRF assumptions, this is given by

$$\begin{aligned} K_{\text{slp}}(\zeta) &= E[\min\{\zeta, L\} \mid X = x_q] \\ &= \int_0^1 \min\{\zeta, \ell\}\, \mathrm{d}H_q(\ell) = \zeta - \int_0^\zeta H_q(\ell)\, \mathrm{d}\ell \end{aligned} \tag{1}$$

where the last equality follows from integration by parts. The marginal contribution to the cumulative capital function, or $K'_{\text{slp}}(\zeta)$, gives the capital charge per dollar of tranche notional value for the infinitesimally thin tranche at credit enhancement level ζ. If the bank holds the set of infinitesimal tranches from ζ to $\zeta + T$, then economic capital on the bank's position is $K_{\text{slp}}(\zeta + T) - K_{\text{slp}}(\zeta)$ per dollar of total pool exposure. Expressed as a percentage of the bank's exposure, capital is $(K_{\text{slp}}(\zeta + T) - K_{\text{slp}}(\zeta))/T$.

By construction, the sum of capital charges across all tranches is $K_{\text{slp}}(1)$. At $\zeta = 1$, we have

$$K_{\text{slp}}(1) = E[\min\{1, L\} \mid X = x_q] = E[L \mid x_q] = \mathcal{K}_{\text{pool}},$$

where $\mathcal{K}_{\text{pool}}$ denotes the capital the pool would require if held on balance sheet. Thus, securitisation does not alter the total capital that must be held against a pool of loans.

We now generalise this basic result to allow for uncertainty in loss prioritisation. Let $Z(\zeta)$ be the effective credit enhancement level associated with the nominal credit enhancement level ζ. Both ζ and Z are expressed as a share of total pool exposure, so $Z(\zeta)$ is a random process mapping $[0, 1]$ to $[0, 1]$. A natural choice for the specification of Z is the Dirichlet process with parameter τ.[5] Under this specification, we have $Z(0) = 0$ and $Z(1) = 1$ (with certainty), and the marginal distribution for $Z(\zeta)$ is $\text{Beta}(\tau\zeta, \tau(1 - \zeta))$. Intuitively, the assumption of a Dirichlet process allows the effective credit enhancement level $Z(\zeta)$ to "wiggle" around its expected value ζ while still pinning down the boundary values at $\zeta = 0$ and $\zeta = 1$. Parameter τ controls the variance of the process around its expected path. As $\tau \to \infty$, the wiggle room disappears and

Figure 1 Sample paths of the Dirichlet process

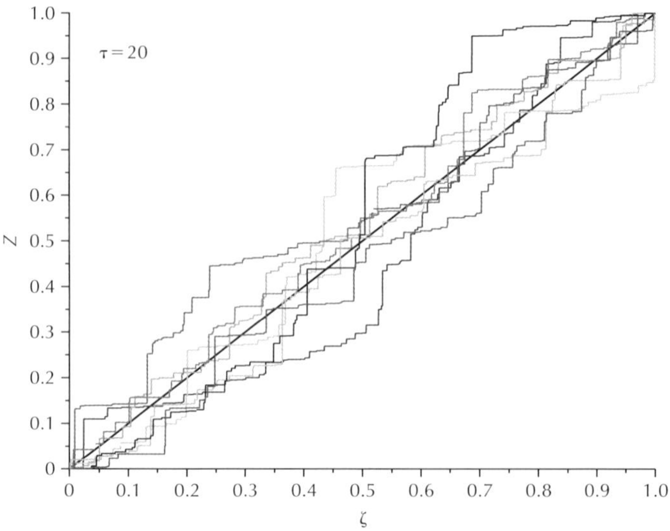

$|Z(\zeta) - \zeta| \to 0$, almost surely. Sample paths for $\tau = 20$ and $\tau = 400$ are shown in Figures 1 and 2, respectively.

When Z is independent of all other risks in the portfolio, the ASRF assumptions imply (as usual) that the appropriate capital charge for a tranche is its expected loss conditional on $X = x_q$.[6] The cumulative capital function is then

$$\begin{aligned} K(\zeta) &= E[\min\{Z(\zeta), L\} \mid X = x_q] \\ &= E[Z(\zeta)] - E\left[\int_0^{Z(\zeta)} H_q(\ell)\,\mathrm{d}\ell\right] \\ &= \zeta - \int_0^1 \frac{z^{\tau\zeta-1}(1-z)^{\tau(1-\zeta)-1}}{B(\tau\zeta, \tau(1-\zeta))}\,\mathrm{d}z \int_0^z H_q(\ell)\,\mathrm{d}\ell \\ &= \zeta - \int_0^1 (1 - B(z; \tau\zeta, \tau(1-\zeta)))H_q(z)\,\mathrm{d}z \end{aligned} \quad \textbf{(2)}$$

where the function $B(y;\, a,\, b)$ is the Beta(a, b) cdf evaluated at y.[7] Because $Z(1) = 1$ with certainty, we have $K(1) = \mathcal{K}_{\text{pool}}$ as under the SLP case. Thus, uncertainty in loss prioritisation does not alter the total required capital for the securitisation.

Figure 2 Sample paths of the Dirichlet process

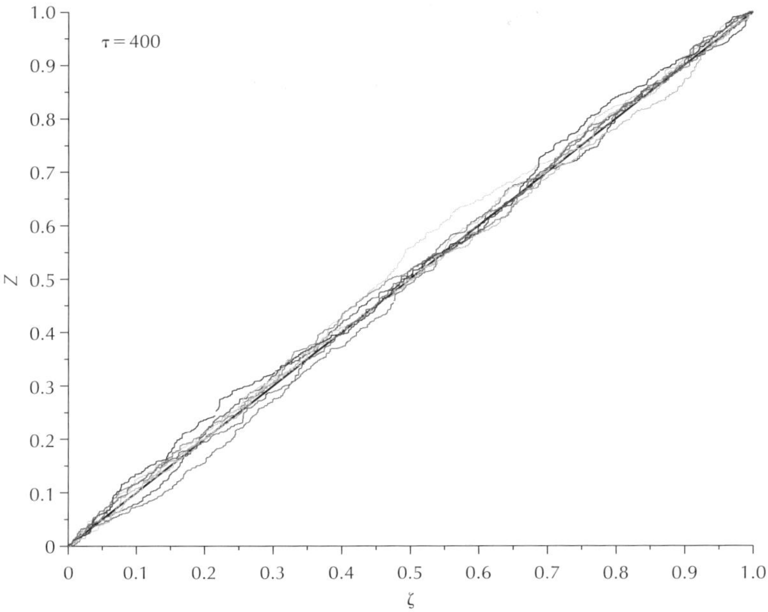

The uncertainty in loss prioritisation model embeds the SLP model as a limiting case. As $\tau \to \infty$, uncertainty in the division of risk vanishes, and the beta cdf for $Z(\zeta)$ converges to $\mathbb{1}_{\{z \geq \zeta\}}$. Thus,

$$\lim_{\tau \to \infty} K(\zeta) = \zeta - \int_0^1 (1 - \mathbb{1}_{\{z \geq \zeta\}}) H_q(z)\,\mathrm{d}z = \zeta - \int_0^{\zeta} H_q(z)\,\mathrm{d}z = K_{\mathrm{slp}}(\zeta)$$

As $\tau \to 0$, the contractual exposure shares become less and less informative of the actual division of risk. The limiting distribution for $Z(\zeta)$ is Bernoulli such that $Z(\zeta) = 1$ with probability ζ and $Z(\zeta) = 0$ with probability $1 - \zeta$. Thus,

$$\lim_{\tau \to 0} B(z; \tau\zeta, \tau(1-\zeta)) = 1 - \zeta, \quad \forall\, z \in (0, 1)$$

We substitute this result in Equation 2 to obtain

$$\lim_{\tau \to 0} K(\zeta) = \zeta - \int_0^1 \zeta H_q(z)\,\mathrm{d}z = \zeta \cdot E[L \mid x_q]$$

which implies a proportional sharing of $\mathcal{K}_{\text{pool}}$ across the tranches (ie, the tranches are treated as *pari passu*). Intermediate values of τ correspond to greater or lesser degrees of smoothing between these extremes.

If the collateral pool is itself asymptotically fine-grained, as is a reasonable characterisation of most retail securitisations, then Equation 2 has a simple analytic solution. In the asymptotic case, $H_q(z) = \mathbb{1}_{\{z \geq E[L \mid x_q]\}}$. Using the integral

$$\int B(y; a, b)\,\mathrm{d}y = y \cdot B(y; a, b) - \frac{a}{a+b} \cdot B(y; a+1, b) \quad (3)$$

we find

$$\begin{aligned} K(\zeta) = {} & \zeta \cdot B(E[L \mid x_q]; \tau\zeta + 1, \tau(1 - \zeta)) \\ & + E[L \mid x_q](1 - B(E[L \mid x_q]; \tau\zeta, \tau(1 - \zeta))). \end{aligned} \quad (4)$$

In the SLP case, any tranche of a securitisation of an asymptotically fine-grained pool that is senior to the $\mathcal{K}_{\text{pool}}$ threshold requires zero capital, and any tranche of such a securitisation that is strictly junior to the $\mathcal{K}_{\text{pool}}$ threshold requires dollar-for-dollar capital. In our generalised model, senior tranches always require some capital because of the possibility that the "realised" exposure of the senior tranches exceeds $1 - \mathcal{K}_{\text{pool}}$, and junior tranches require less than dollar-for-dollar capital because of the possibility that their realised exposure is less than $\mathcal{K}_{\text{pool}}$. Thus, the extended model unambiguously increases capital for tranches senior to $\mathcal{K}_{\text{pool}}$, and unambiguously reduces capital for tranches junior to $\mathcal{K}_{\text{pool}}$. For tranches that straddle this breakpoint, the effect is ambiguous but typically small.

For less fine-grained pools, uncertainty in loss prioritisation has a smaller effect. Figure 3 shows the effect of τ and n using the model specification imposed in the SFA. The case of $n = \infty$ is shown in the bottom panels. When $\tau = \infty$, marginal capital is dollar-for-dollar up to $\mathcal{K}_{\text{pool}}$ and then zero thereafter. Setting $\tau = 1000$ provides a modest degree of smoothing, and much lower values of τ a much greater degree of smoothing. For a collateral pool of $n = 128$ (middle row of panels), which might be representative of the most fine-grained CDO pools, undiversified idiosyncratic risk is sufficient to smooth away the cliff effect at $\mathcal{K}_{\text{pool}}$.[8] In this case, the capital and marginal capital curves for $\tau = 1000$ are indistinguishable from those of

Figure 3 Effect of τ on capital and marginal capital

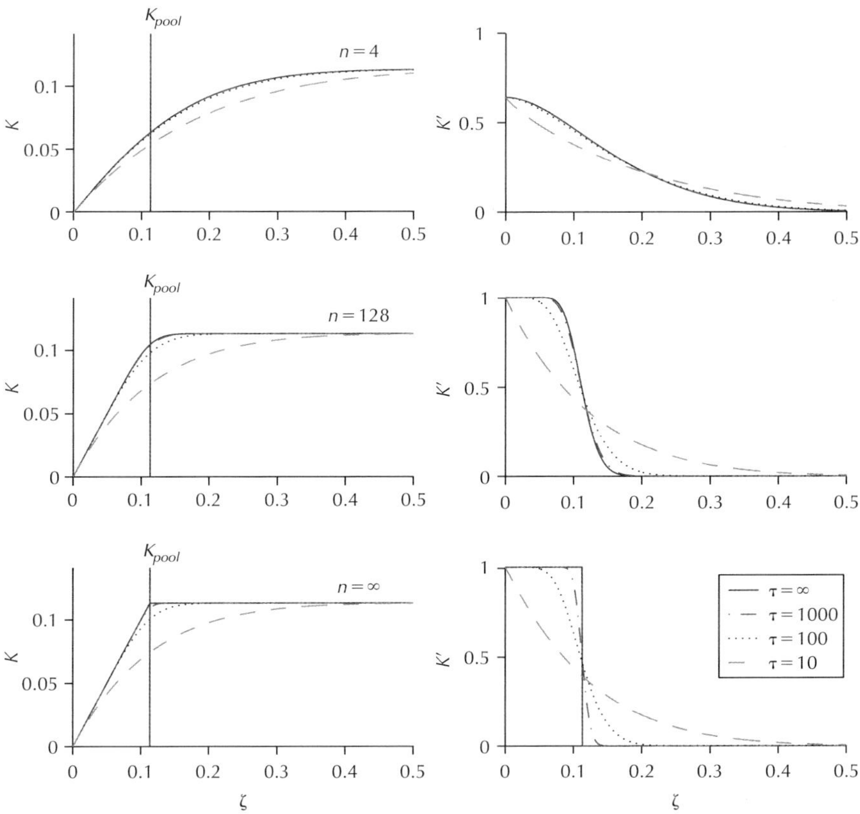

Note: Homogeneous collateral pools with default probability PD = 0.02, expected LGD = 0.5 and asset-correlation $\rho = 0.2$. We set VAR target quantile $q = 0.999$ and recovery risk parameter $\gamma = 0.25$.

$\tau = \infty$. Uncertainty in loss prioritisation has no material effect on capital unless τ is below, say, 100. When $n = 4$ (upper row of panels), idiosyncratic risk within the pool has a dominant effect on the distribution of losses across tranches, and τ must be extremely low (on the order of 10) for uncertainty in $Z(\zeta)$ to have any additional smoothing effect.

FITTING A SIMPLE FUNCTIONAL FORM

Unless we restrict ourselves to analysis of securitisations of asymptotically fine-grained pools, the pool's conditional loss distribution

$H_q(z)$ is likely to be analytically intractable, which would require that we use numerical integration or simulation to solve for $K(\zeta)$ in Equation 2.[9] For regulatory purposes, a simpler and more transparent functional solution is required, even if it comes at slight expense in precision.

We define the *fitting function* $F(\cdot)$ by

$$F(\zeta) = 1 - \frac{K'(\zeta)}{K'(0)} \tag{5}$$

This definition is useful because it exploits three known properties of the first derivative of $K(\zeta)$: $K'(\zeta)$ is non-increasing on the unit interval and we have $K'(0) \approx 1 - H_q(0)$ and $K'(1) = 0$.[10] From these properties, we see that $F(\zeta)$ is non-decreasing on the unit interval and that $F(0) = 0$ and $F(1) = 1$. Thus, F behaves like a cumulative distribution function for a random variable with support on the unit interval. Although this cdf is typically of intractable form, we might expect that it can be closely approximated by the cdf of a simple distribution such as the beta.

We parameterise F in terms of its mean (μ) and variance (σ^2). To attain the mean parameter, we rearrange Equation 5 as $K'(\zeta) = K'(0)(1 - F(\zeta))$, and integrate to get

$$K(\zeta) = K'(0)\int_0^{\zeta} (1 - F(y))\, dy$$

At $\zeta = 1$, we can integrate by parts to get

$$\int_0^1 F(y)\, dy = 1 - \int_0^1 y f(y)\, dy = 1 - \mu$$

which implies that

$$\mu = \frac{K(1)}{K'(0)} \approx \frac{E[L \mid x_q]}{1 - H_q(0)} \tag{6}$$

The variance of F is more challenging. By definition,

$$\sigma^2 = \int_0^1 y^2 f(y)\, dy - \mu^2 = \frac{-1}{K'(0)}\int_0^1 y^2 K''(y)\, dy - \mu^2$$

This integral does not have an analytical solution, but asymptotic expansion in $1/\tau$ provides an approximation for large τ. Gordy and Jones (2003) show that

$$\sigma^2 \approx \frac{1}{K'(0)}(V[L|x_q] + E[L|x_q]^2) - \mu^2 + \frac{1}{\tau}\frac{1}{K'(0)}(E[L|x_q](1 - E[L|x_q]) - V[L|x_q]). \quad (7)$$

The expression for σ^2 has been arranged to show that it naturally decomposes into two components. The first is the contribution of undiversified idiosyncratic risk in the collateral pool (ie, the impact of pool granularity), and equals the exact formula for σ^2 in the SLP case. The second is the contribution of ULP and is inversely proportional to τ.

The calculations simplify further in the special case of $n = \infty$, which includes most securitisations of retail pools. When $n = \infty$, $K'(0) = 1$ and $V[L|x_q] = 0$, so we have $\mu = E[L|x_q]$ and $\sigma^2 = (1/\tau) E[L|x_q](1 - E[L|x_q])$.

A COMPLETE SPECIFICATION

Thus far, we have not needed to specify a model for portfolio loss or to choose a cdf to assign to the fitting function. We complete the specification in order to arrive at the formulation seen in the SFA.

We assume that the collateral pool is homogeneous and that the conditional loss distribution H_q comes from a single-factor, default-mode model with conditionally idiosyncratic recovery risk (that is, LGDs are independent conditional on X). This implies that the number of defaults in a portfolio of n loans is distributed Binomial(p_q, n), where p_q is the conditional probability (given $X = x_q$) of default for a single loan in the pool. If LGD for a single default has a continuous distribution, then H_q is continuous on unit interval support, except that there is probability mass at $L = 0$. The probability of zero loss is the probability that every borrower performs, so $H_q(0) = (1 - p_q)^n$. If LGD has conditional mean *ELGD* and standard deviation *VLGD*, then the mean and variance of the conditional loss distribution are given by $E[L|x_q] = ELGD \cdot p_q$ and

$$V[L|x_q] = \frac{1}{n}(ELGD^2 p_q(1-p_q) + p_q VLGD^2) \quad \textbf{(8)}$$

To retain consistency with the IRB treatment of whole loans, we adopt the CreditMetrics model of obligor dependence and LGD volatility. That is, we assume that X has standard normal distribution and that the conditional probability of default is given by

$$p_q = \Phi\left(\frac{\Phi^{-1}(PD) + \Phi^{-1}(q)\sqrt{\rho}}{\sqrt{1-\rho}}\right)$$

where Φ is the standard normal cdf and ρ is the correlation in asset returns.[11] Loss rates given default are drawn as independent beta random variables. Following the convention in CreditMetrics and KMV Portfolio Manager, we assume the variance of loss given default is given by

$$VLGD^2 = \gamma \cdot ELGD \cdot (1 - ELGD) \quad \textbf{(9)}$$

where γ is a parameter in [0, 1]. Special cases include $\gamma = 0$, which corresponds to fixed LGD rates (no recovery risk), and $\gamma = 1$, which arises when LGD is distributed Bernoulli (ie, zero recovery with probability *ELGD*, full recovery otherwise).

A variety of two-parameter distributions for approximating the fitting function would lead to a closed-form solution for the capital function. The beta distribution is a natural choice given its unit interval support and thus has been adopted in the SFA.[12] Let θ be the precision of F defined by

$$\theta \equiv \frac{\mu(1-\mu)}{\sigma^2} - 1$$

The parameter θ measures the precision of F in the same manner as τ measures the precision of the distribution for $Z(\zeta)$.

To distinguish between the "true" fitting function, which is of intractable form, and the approximation based on the beta cdf, let $\hat{F}$ denote the approximation. Similarly, let $\hat{K}$ denote the approximation implied by $\hat{F}$ to the true K function. The solution to $\hat{K}(\zeta)$ is given by

$$\begin{aligned}\hat{K}(\zeta) &= \int_0^\zeta \hat{K}'(y)\,\mathrm{d}y = K'(0)\int_0^\zeta (1-\hat{F}(y))\,\mathrm{d}y \\ &= (1-H_q(0))\cdot(\zeta\cdot(1-B(\zeta;\theta\mu,\theta(1-\mu))) \\ &\quad + \mu\cdot B(\zeta;\theta\mu+1,\theta(1-\mu)))\end{aligned} \tag{10}$$

where the final equality follows using Equation 3. Note that, when $n = \infty$, we have $\theta = \tau - 1$ and $\hat{K}(\zeta)$ simplifies to

$$\begin{aligned}\hat{K}(\zeta) &= \zeta\cdot(1-B(\zeta;(\tau-1)\mathcal{K}_{\text{pool}},(\tau-1)(1-\mathcal{K}_{\text{pool}}))) \\ &\quad + \mathcal{K}_{\text{pool}}\cdot B(\zeta;(\tau-1)\mathcal{K}_{\text{pool}}+1,(\tau-1)(1-\mathcal{K}_{\text{pool}}))\text{.}\end{aligned} \tag{11}$$

Gordy and Jones (2003) examine the robustness of the fitted $\hat{K}(\zeta)$ to the "true" $K(\zeta)$ given by Equation 2, and find that the fitted $\hat{K}$ function performs extremely well nearly everywhere in the parameter space. The only exception arises when the pool is comprised of a *single* loan to an investment grade borrower with very low expected LGD and low asset-correlation. At least in the context of the proposed New Basel Accord, this circumstance cannot arise in practice.[13]

Consistency with the IRB treatment of whole loans implies that pool capital, $\mathcal{K}_{\text{pool}}$, is equal to the IRB capital charge for the pool. In the one-year, default-mode setting of the model, we have $\mathcal{K}_{\text{pool}} = \mathcal{K}_{\text{irb}} = ELGD \cdot p_q$. Some simplification in implementing the ULP model can be obtained by noting that parameters PD, ρ and q enter the calculations only via p_q, and that $p_q = \mathcal{K}_{\text{irb}}/ELGD$. Thus, a sufficient set of collateral pool parameters is n, $\mathcal{K}_{\text{irb}}$ and $ELGD$. As a practical matter, parameterisation of the ULP in terms of $\mathcal{K}_{\text{irb}}$ compensates for some of the limitations of the model's default-mode notion of credit loss.[14] Strictly speaking, the model assumes that the underlying assets are of one-year maturity. If the pool were of longer maturity, there would be no mechanism in the model for recognition of economic losses in the pool due to rating migrations short of default. Absence of arbitrage implies that economic losses in the pool must equal the sum of economic losses to the tranches.[15] Under the advanced IRB approach, capital charges for the underlying pool incorporate maturity effects, so parameterisation in terms of $\mathcal{K}_{irb}$ may be more robust than parameterisation in terms of PD and ρ.

APPLICATION TO REGULATORY CAPITAL TREATMENT

The SFA specifies capital for a tranche of credit enhancement level ζ and thickness T as $(S[\zeta + T] - S[\zeta])$ times the notional size of the collateral pool. The function $S[\zeta]$ has at its baseline the ULP $\hat{K}(\zeta)$ function of Equation 10, but imposes certain supervisory overrides on top. In addition to tranche parameters ζ and T, the bank is required to supply collateral pool parameters n, $\mathcal{K}_{irb}$ and $ELGD$. Supervisory values of model parameters $\tau = 1000$ and $\gamma = 0.25$ are imposed.[16]

From an operational perspective, the only significant challenge in implementing the ULP model lies in obtaining the pool characteristics n, $\mathcal{K}_{irb}$ and $ELGD$. As collateral pools are never truly homogeneous, the number of loans must be adjusted for concentration. For example, a pool with one US$100 million exposure and 99 US$1 million exposures has a loss distribution more akin to that of a homogeneous pool of three or four loans than one of 100 loans. The SFA specifies that the "effective" n be calculated as an inverse Herfindahl index of the exposure sizes in the pool. Gordy (2003, Section 4) shows that this specification can arise naturally in mapping from a heterogeneous portfolio to a comparable homogeneous portfolio. In some situations, investors may receive incomplete information on the distribution of exposure sizes in a pool, such as the share of the largest exposure and the cumulative share of the four largest exposures. The SFA provides a rule for estimating n from such information that is based on upper bounds for the Herfindahl index given one or two concentration ratios.

For an originator, obtaining the pool average $\mathcal{K}_{irb}$ and $ELGD$ poses no special burden because these would need to be estimated for regulatory capital if retained on balance sheet. Outside investors sometimes have more limited access to information on the collateral pool. However, it is reasonable to expect investors in unrated tranches to have sufficient information to estimate $\mathcal{K}_{irb}$. Otherwise, in the absence of a rating, it is difficult to see how an investor could perform due diligence. In most situations, $\mathcal{K}_{irb}$

for the pool would be calculated on a "bottom-up" basis from instrument-level *PD* and *ELGD* estimates, so the pool average *ELGD* would be straightforward to estimate at the same time. For certain asset classes such as purchased receivables, bottom-up estimation can pose a significant operational burden, so banks are permitted to use a "top-down" approach in which *PD* and *ELGD* are estimated at the pool level.[17] If the bank could obtain only historical loss rates for comparable pools, then the most conservative treatment consistent with the estimated expected loss (*EL*) for the pool is to set *ELGD* to 100% and *PD* to *EL*. $\mathcal{K}_{irb}$ is then calculated according to the corporate risk-weight function.

At least for the seniormost tranches, setting *ELGD* to 100% results in at least as high a capital charge as under any other *ELGD* assumption, so is "conservative" in the supervisory sense.[18] Holding fixed $\mathcal{K}_{irb}$, n and the supervisory ULP parameters (τ, γ), denote by $K(\zeta; \lambda)$ the $K(\zeta)$ function for $ELGD = \lambda$. In Panel 1, the following is proved.

Proposition 1. For all $\lambda < 1$, $K(\zeta; 1) \leq K(\zeta; \lambda)$.

Consider a senior tranche beginning at nominal credit enhancement level ζ and of thickness $1 - \zeta$. In the ULP model, capital for such a tranche is given by $K_{irb} - K(\zeta; \lambda)$ per dollar of total pool collateral. Proposition 1 implies that this capital charge is maximised when $\lambda = 1$.

The result applies to a collection of tranches as well. Say, for example, that supervisors were to impose $ELGD = 1$ on all tranches above some credit enhancement level ζ (eg, $\zeta = \mathcal{K}_{irb}$). Then Proposition 1 implies that total capital on tranches senior to ζ would be greater than under any alternative *ELGD* assumption. However, if we consider on its own a tranche other than the most senior, it is not possible to say whether the proposed treatment is the most conservative. The intuition is that changing *ELGD* redistributes capital across tranches, but this cannot change the total capital for the securitisation as a whole. If capital on the seniormost tranche increases, then capital on the juniormost tranche must be reduced. The effect on the intermediate tranches is ambiguous. As a practical matter, experience with the model suggests that assuming an *ELGD* of 100% should result in a

PANEL 1 PROOF OF PROPOSITION 1

The proof of Proposition 1 is an application of the theory of stochastic dominance. In order to make clear their dependence on the *ELGD* parameter, we write the pool loss as L_λ and its conditional cdf as $H_q(\ell;\lambda)$. Equation 2 implies that Proposition 1 holds if and only if

$$\int_0^1 (1-B(\ell;\tau\zeta,\tau(1-\zeta)))H_q(\ell;\lambda)\,d\ell \le \int_0^1 (1-B(\ell;\tau\zeta,\tau(1-\zeta)))H_q(\ell;1)\,d\ell \qquad \textbf{(1a)}$$

for all $\zeta \in [0, 1]$ and $\lambda < 1$. Define the function $\omega_\zeta(\ell)$ by

$$\omega_\zeta(\ell) = \int_0^\ell (1-B(t;\tau\zeta,\tau(1-\zeta)))\,dt$$

Using integration by parts, we find that Equation (1a) holds if and only if

$$\int_0^1 \omega_\zeta(\ell)h_q(\ell;\lambda)\,d\ell \ge \int_0^1 \omega_\zeta(\ell)h_q(\ell;1)\,d\ell$$

for all $\zeta \in [0, 1]$ and $\lambda < 1$. The function $h_q(\cdot;\lambda)$ is the conditional probability density function for L_λ, which allows us to write the necessary and sufficient condition as

$$E[\omega_\zeta(L_\lambda)\,|\,X = x_q] \ge E[\omega_\zeta(L_1)\,|\,X = x_q] \qquad \textbf{(1b)}$$

for all $\zeta \in [0, 1]$ and $\lambda < 1$.

Consider two variables Y_1 and Y_2 with cdfs F_1 and F_2, respectively. We say that F_1 is a mean-preserving spread of F_2 if $E[Y_1] = E[Y_2]$ and Y_2 second-order stochastic dominates Y_1 (written as $Y_2 \succ_2 Y_1$). The seminal result of Rothschild and Stiglitz (1970) on mean-preserving spreads is as follows.

Lemma 1. For positive random variables Y_1 and Y_2 with $E[Y_1] = E[Y_2]$, the following statements are equivalent:

- $Y_2 \succ_2 Y_1$;
- $Y_1 =^d Y_2 + \varepsilon$ *for some* ε *such that* $E[\varepsilon\,|\,Y_2] = 0$;
- $E[u(Y_2)] \ge E[u(Y_1)]$ *for all u increasing and concave; and*
- $\int_0^y (F_2(t) - F_1(t))\,dt \le 0$ *for all* $y \le 0$.

Because the beta cdf is bounded from above by 1 and increasing (at least weakly), the ω function is increasing and concave (at least weakly). Therefore, if $H_q(\cdot; 1)$ is a mean-preserving spread of $H_q(\cdot; \lambda)$, then the condition in Equation 1b follows immediately.

Let $U_\lambda(i)$ be the loss on loan i ($i = 1,\ldots, n$) in the pool for $ELGD = \lambda$. Conditional on $X = x_q$, we have $U_\lambda(i) \equiv D_i \cdot \mathrm{LGD}_i$ where D_i *is* a Bernoulli default indicator with $\Pr(D_i = 1 \mid x_q) = \mathcal{K}_{irb}/\lambda$ and LGD_i is a beta-distributed loss given default with mean λ and variance $\gamma\lambda(1 - \lambda)$. When *ELGD* equals 1, LGD_i is equal to 1 with certainty, so each U_1 is distributed Bernoulli with $\Pr(U_1(i) = 1 \mid x_q) = \mathcal{K}_{irb}$. For $\lambda < 1$, the U_λ have a mixed distribution. However, regardless of λ, we have $E[U_\lambda(i) \mid x_q] = \mathcal{K}_{irb}$. To show second-order stochastic dominance, we need the following "single-crossing" result.

Lemma 2. Let Y_1 and Y_2 be random variables on [0, 1] *with cdfs F_1 and F_2 and equal means. If there exists $y_0 > 0$ such that $F_1(y) \geq F_2(y)$ for $0 \leq y < y_0$ and $F_1(y) \leq F_2(y)$ for $y_0 \leq y \leq 1$ (and we do not have $F_1(y) = F_2(y)$ everywhere on at least one of these intervals), then $Y_2 \succ_2 Y_1$.*

The lemma is a corollary of Fishburn and Vickson (1978, Section 2.16).

In our application, $\Pr(U_1 \leq y \mid x_q) = 1 - \mathcal{K}_{irb}$ for all $y < 1$. For any $\lambda < 1$,

$$\Pr(U_\lambda = 0 \mid x_q) = 1 - \mathcal{K}_{irb}/\lambda < 1 - \mathcal{K}_{irb} = \Pr(U_1 = 0 \mid x_q)$$

Because the beta distribution is continuous, there must exist $\delta > 0$ such that for all $y \in (1 - \delta, 1)$,

$$\Pr(U_\lambda \leq y \mid x_q) > 1 - \mathcal{K}_{irb} = \Pr(U_1 \leq y \mid x_q)$$

Thus, the two distributions must cross at least once. They cannot cross more than once, because the conditional cdf for U_1 is flat and the conditional cdf for U_λ is strictly increasing. Therefore, the single-crossing condition of Lemma 2 is satisfied, so $U_\lambda(i) \succ_2 U_1(i)$ conditional on x_q for all loans i and for all $\lambda < 1$.

Our final lemma is as follows.

Lemma 3. Let $Y_j(i)$ for $i = 1, \ldots, n$ be iid draws from a distribution F_j on the positive real line. Let $M_j = (1/n)\Sigma_{i=1}^{n} Y_j(i)$ for $j = \{1, 2\}$, and let G_j denote the distribution of M_j. If F_1 is a mean-preserving spread of F_2, then G_1 is a mean-preserving spread of G_2.

Proof.[22] By Lemma 1, we have a sequence of variables ε_i such that $Y_1(i) =^d Y_2(i) + \varepsilon_i$ and $E[\varepsilon_i \mid Y_2(i)] = 0$. Therefore, we have $M_1 =^d M_2 + \varepsilon^*$ where $\varepsilon^* \equiv (1/n)\, \Sigma_{i=1}^{n} \varepsilon_i$. Because the $Y_j(i)$ are iid across i, the ε_i must be iid and independent of $Y_2(k)$ for all pairs (i, k). Therefore,

$$E[\varepsilon^* | M_2] = \frac{1}{n}\sum_{i=1}^{n} E[\varepsilon_i | Y_2] = 0$$

By Lemma 1, G_1 is a mean-preserving spread of G_2.

Conditional on $X = x_q$, the $U_\lambda(i)$ are independently and identically distributed. The pool loss is given as the mean of the $U_\lambda(i)$. Therefore, Lemma 3 implies directly that $H_q(\cdot; 1)$ is a mean-preserving spread of $H_q(\cdot; \lambda)$, which in turn implies that Proposition 1 holds.

conservative treatment for any highly-rated tranche with credit enhancement level above $\mathcal{K}_{\text{irb}}$. For lower mezzanine positions, however, assuming an *ELGD* of 100% may not be desirable from a supervisory viewpoint.

As noted in many industry comments on the Basel proposal, supervisory overrides in the SFA can add a substantial buffer of regulatory capital onto the baseline ULP capital function. The most important of these are a dollar-for-dollar capital requirement for tranches with $\zeta \leq \mathcal{K}_{\text{irb}}$ and a floor on capital of 56 basis points per dollar of notional tranche value. A full explanation for these overrides must consider supervisory concerns and objectives that are outside the context of the ULP model and thus beyond the scope of this chapter. Clearly, however, the overrides serve to limit exploitation of inadequacies in the model's stylised representation of a securitisation.

The ULP model assumes that the collateral pool contains only simple whole loans or bonds. In practice, it is not uncommon for securitised pools to include other asset types. In particular, the collateral pool may consist of tranches of other securitisations. Such resecuritisations are often termed "CDOs of CDOs", but the collateral may include a variety of structured finance instruments, such as asset-backed securities (ABS) and commercial mortgage-backed securities.[19] Pools of CDO tranches behave differently from pools of ordinary loans, and so formulaic implementation of the ULP model in a regulatory rule may be subject to manipulation.

To take a highly stylised example, consider a bank that wishes to securitise a large retail pool of loans. It could package these loans in two ways:

(a) an ordinary ABS in which tranches of the securitised pool are sold directly to investors; or
(b) a CDO of an ABS in which the securitised pool is sold off (as a single 100% tranche) to a CDO conduit, which in turn is broken into tranches for sale to investors.

These structures differ in legal form, but not in risk. That is, the nominal tranche $(\zeta, \zeta + T]$ of security (a) has the same return distribution as the comparable tranche of security (b). However, their treatment under the SFA would differ. For security (a), we would assign $n_a = \infty$ and $\mu_a = \mathcal{K}_{\text{irb}}$. For security (b), we would assign $n_b = 1$. With probability one, there will be at least one default in the underlying ABS retail pool, so the ABS security comprising the CDO collateral pool should be assigned a *PD* of 100% and *ELGD* equal to $\mathcal{K}_{\text{irb}}$.[20] This gives us $H_q(0) = 0$, so $\mu_b = \mathcal{K}_{\text{irb}}$. Because the ABS pool is infinitely fine-grained, the "true" conditional variance of loss ($\text{V}[L \mid x_q]$) for the security is zero. If this were recognised in the SFA, then $\sigma_b^2 = \sigma_a^2$, so $K_a(\zeta) = K_b(\zeta)$ for all ζ. However, for the sake of parsimony, the SFA hardwires the specification for conditional variance in Equation 9. This may be appropriate for a collateral pool of whole loans, but in this case implies that $\sigma_b^2 \gg \sigma_a^2$, which in turn implies that $K_a(\zeta) \geq K_b(\zeta)$ for all ζ. Thus, in the absence of the "dollar-for-dollar up to $\mathcal{K}_{\text{irb}}$" override, an originator could restructure (a) into (b) in order to reduce the burden of SFA capital for the junior tranches.

Restructuring can also be used to shift the burden of regulatory capital in the opposite direction. To take another stylised example, consider an originating bank with a collateral pool of ten loans. Say the bank were to divide each loan into 100 identical shares, and then gather together one share of each loan to form 100 identical collateral pools. Each pool is securitised, and in each case the originating bank retains an equity position large enough to absorb all material risk. If the 100 equity positions were gathered together for resecuritisation, the new pool would appear to have $n = 100$, but would in fact behave like a pool of ten loans.[21] The problem here is that the restructuring violates the ULP model's assumption of conditional independence in the collateral pool. In the absence of a capital floor in the SFA, the regulatory capital charge on senior tranches of the resecuritisation would be too low.

1 In this context, credit losses reflect valuation changes that result from credit quality migrations or defaults by obligors, but exclude valuation changes arising from general movements of interest rates and the market price of risk.

2 See Gordy (2003) for a derivation of this result under minimal restrictions on the portfolio and very general modelling assumptions.

3 Consider a homogeneous US$100 pool of 8% one-year loans. Suppose the most junior tranche has an initial value of US$20 and pays 20%, while the US$80 senior tranche pays 5%. From the perspective of the senior tranche, $\zeta = 20$ and $T = 80$. However, suppose that 22% of the loans default, implying a total cashflow available for distribution of US$84.24. In this case, the senior tranche would still be paid in full even though the pool's loss exceeds ζ. Excess spread accounts, which are often seen in securitisations of credit card receivables, create a similar effect.

4 Pykhtin and Dev (2002, 2003) appear to have been the first to use infinitesimally thin tranches as an analytical convenience in modelling securitisation.

5 More precisely, Z follows a Dirichlet process with parameter τU, where U is the uniform measure on $[0, 1]$. The Dirichlet process was introduced in the Bayesian literature by Ferguson (1973). It can arise as the limiting process for the Dirichlet distribution, which is a multivariate generalisation of the beta distribution (Ishwaran and Zarepour, 2002, Theorem 3). It has previously appeared in the finance literature in Chow (1998) and as the "gamma bridge" of Ribeiro and Webber (2003).

6 If securitisation instruments were to account jointly for a significant share of the bank's portfolio and if (conditional on $X = x_q$) the Z processes were not independent across those securitisations, then the risk in loss prioritisation would not be diversified away, and thus would demand capital of its own. Similar reasoning motivates the assumption that the bank's aggregate exposure to each obligor in the collateral pool constitutes a trivial share of the bank's portfolio.

7 The final expression is obtained using integration by parts of "$v \cdot du$", where the "du" part is the beta *pdf* and the "v" part is the integral over H_q.

8 Conversations with market participants suggest that few CDOs contain over 200 names. When corrected for concentration in exposure sizes as described later in this chapter, we would expect that "effective n" would typically be under 100.

9 Monte Carlo simulation of $K(\zeta)$ is straightforward but computationally intensive. Since $K(\zeta) = E[\min\{Z(\zeta), L\} \mid x_q]$, we need only draw a sample of paths $\{z_1(\zeta), \ldots, z_T(\zeta)\}$ for $Z(\zeta)$ and a sample of $\{\ell_1, \ldots, \ell_T\}$ for L (from the H_q distribution). $K(\zeta)$ is estimated by $(1/T)\, \Sigma\min\{z_i(\zeta), \ell_i\}$.

10 The exact derivative of $K(\zeta)$ at $\zeta = 0$ is intractable. For the limiting case of $\tau = \infty$, we have $K'_{\mathrm{slp}}(\zeta) = 1 - H_q(\zeta)$, so $K'_{\mathrm{slp}}(0) = 1 - H_q(0)$. One can show that $K'(0)$ converges to this limit at an exponential rate in τ, so the approximation works well for large τ. Moreover, as a practical matter, one finds that the fitted cumulative capital function $\hat{K}(\zeta)$ is relatively insensitive to errors in the $K'(0)$ input.

11 The CreditMetrics model is documented by Gupton *et al* (1997). For a derivation of p_q from this model, see Koyluoglu and Hickman (1998) or Gordy (2000). This same expression appeared earlier in Vasicek's (1991) analysis of the asymptotic loss distribution in KMV Portfolio Manager.

12 Note that this application of the beta cdf has nothing to do with the use of the beta as the distribution for $Z(\zeta)$ and the distribution for LGD.

13 For corporate borrowers, investment grade status implies high asset-correlation. Retail borrowers can have a lower asset-correlation, but securitisation of a single retail loan is prohibitively expensive, at least under current market practice.

14 Pykhtin and Dev's (2002, 2003) model suffers from the same limitations.

15 Much as a decline in the asset value of a firm will be spread among shareholders and bondholders, a decline in the value of the pool will not be allocated by strict prioritisation, but rather will be spread to some degree across all tranches.

16 Translation from the notation of this chapter to that of the Basel Committee on Bank Supervision (2004) is straightforward. The quantities $H_q(0)$, μ, σ^2 and θ map to the SFA quantities h, c, f and g, respectively. The expression for $V[L \mid x_q]$ in Equation 8 can be rearranged to equal the SFA ν parameter.

17 See Basel Committee on Bank Supervision (2004, Sections 365–367).

18 For retail pools, estimation of *ELGD* is unnecessary as it drops out of the capital formula. Given $\mathcal{K}_{\text{irb}}$, we need *ELGD* only to calculate the contribution of undiversified idiosyncratic risk to the variance of pool loss. As $n \to \infty$, such risk vanishes.

19 According to Ganapati and Tejwani (2002), the resecuritisation market surpassed US$45 billion in size by mid-2002 and constituted over one-fifth of the overall new issue volume of cashflow CDOs over the prior two years.

20 In order to avoid the use of internal models in estimating *ELGD*, the Basel Committee on Bank Supervision (2004, Paragraph 634) requires that securitisation exposures in the collateral pool be assigned *ELGD* of 100%. While this changes the calculations in this example, the qualitative result is the same.

21 Again, we are abstracting from the special rule for *ELGD* on securitisation exposure collateral noted in endnote 20.

22 We are grateful to E. De Giorgi for suggesting this proof.

REFERENCES

Basel Committee on Bank Supervision, 2004, "International Convergence of Capital Measurement and Capital Standards: A Revised Framework", Publication No 107, Bank for International Settlements, June.

Chow, W., 1998, "A Dirichlet Process Mixture Model of Overnight HIBOR", December.

Duffie, D., and N. Garleanu, 2001, "Risk and Valuation of Collateralized Debt Obligations", *Financial Analysts Journal*, **57(1)**, pp. 41–59.

Ferguson, T. S., 1973, "A Bayesian Analysis of Some Nonparametric Problems", *Annals of Statistics* **1(2)**, pp. 209–30.

Fishburn, P. C., and R. G. Vickson, 1978, "Theoretical Foundations of Stochastic Dominance", in *Stochastic Dominance* (Lexington Books).

Ganapati, S., and G. Tejwani, 2002, "Structured Credit Strategies: The Case for Structured Finance CDOs", Structured Credit Research, Lehman Brothers, July.

Gordy, M., and D. Jones, 2003, "Random Tranches", *Risk,* **16(3)**, pp. 78–83.

Gordy, M. B., 2000, "A Comparative Anatomy of Credit Risk Models", *Journal of Banking and Finance*, **24(1–2)**, pp. 119–49.

Gordy, M. B., 2003, "A Risk-Factor Model Foundation for Ratings-Based Bank Capital Rules", *Journal of Financial Intermediation*, **12(3)**, pp. 199–232.

Gupton, G. M., C. C. Finger, and M. Bhatia, 1997, *CreditMetrics – Technical Document* (J.P. Morgan & Co.).

Ishwaran, H., and M. Zarepour, 2002, "Dirichlet Prior Sieves in Finite Normal Mixtures", *Statistica Sinica*, **12**, pp. 941–63.

Jones, D., 2000, "Emerging problems with the Basel Capital Accord: Regulatory Capital Arbitrage and Related Issues", *Journal of Banking and Finance*, **24(1–2)**, pp. 35–58.

Koyluoglu, H. U., and A. Hickman, 1998, "Reconciliable Differences", *Risk*, **11(10)**, pp. 56–62.

Pykhtin, M., and A. Dev, 2002, "Credit Risk in Asset Securitisations: Analytical Model," *Risk*, **15(5)**, pp. S16–S20.

Pykhtin, M., and A. Dev, 2003, "Coarse-Grained CDOs", *Risk*, **16(1)**, pp. 113–16.

Ribeiro, C., and N. Webber, 2003, "Valuing Path Dependent Options in the Variance-Gamma Model by Monte Carlo with a Gamma Bridge", *Journal of Computational Finance*, **7(2)**, Winter.

Rothschild, M., and J. E. Stiglitz, 1970, "Increasing Risk I: A Definition", *Journal of Economic Theory*, **2(3)**, pp. 225–43.

Vasicek, O. A., 1991, "Limiting Loan Loss Probability Distribution", KMV Corporation, August.

14

*Capital for Structured Products**

Vladislav Peretyatkin; William Perraudin

Birkbeck College; Imperial College and Bank of England

Structured products are complex instruments, the payoffs on which depend on the performance of pools of correlated underlying assets that possess a tranche structure, ie, a set of rules that prescribe how cashflows on the underlying pool are split between the holders of several classes of claim of different seniorities.

This chapter describes a methodology for calculating ratings-based capital charges for structured products such as structured exposures. The *Portfolio Risk Tracker* model that we employ is a generalisation of industry-standard, ratings-based credit portfolio models.[1]

As a check of our approach, we exposit and implement a simple asymptotic model for calculating capital for structured exposures that was developed by Pykhtin and Dev (2002a) and (2002b). This asymptotic model is related to the one-factor models of Gordy (2003) and Gordy and Jones (2003). We show that when restricted to a one-year structured transaction of negligible size compared with the bank's wider portfolio and when parameterised consistently, *Portfolio Risk Tracker* yields the same capital requirements as the Pykhtin and Dev approach. Using *Portfolio Risk Tracker,* we show that one may calculate capital charges under more general and less stylised assumptions, for example, for longer maturity structures and for structures that are non-negligible compared to the bank's wider portfolio.

Employing both the Pykhtin–Dev model and *Portfolio Risk Tracker*, we provide an analysis of appropriate capital charges for

*This chapter was prepared for the Securitisation Sub-Group of the Basel Committee. Earlier drafts of this paper were entitled "Capital for Asset Backed Securities".

structured exposure tranches with different rating categories. The issues we examine are as follows.

1. *Global consistency*: how total capital implied by the current RBA for all the tranches in a structured exposure compares with the total economic capital implied by our models and with the capital structured exposure issuers would have to hold against the underlying pool under the current proposals if the exposures were held directly on balance sheet, ie, Kirb.
2. *Rating category-specific consistency*: how capital requirements for different rating categories like those proposed by the Basel Committee under the ratings based approach (RBA) compare with the charges implied by the model under different correlation assumptions.
3. *Granularity effects*: how capital charges vary as granularity decreases when the structured exposure is small or large compared with the wider bank portfolio.
4. *Sector effects*: how capital charges vary when the underlying asset pool is made up of exposures to different sectors, for example, credit card receivables, C&I loans or residential mortgages.
5. *Maturity effects*: how capital charges implied by the model vary for different maturities.

The structure of this chapter is as follows. The second and third sections describe the Pykhtin–Dev and *Portfolio Risk Tracker* approaches, respectively. The fourth section sets out the analysis of ratings-based structured exposure capital charges. The final section contains our concluding remarks.

ASYMPTOTIC MODELS

Building on derivations in an unpublished note by Vasicek (1991), Pykhtin and Dev (2002a) and (2002b) examine capital requirements for tranches in a structured product that comprises a negligible fraction of a larger bank portfolio.[2] Their approach generalises the single common factor approach that is the basis of the work of Gordy (2003) and Gordy and Jones (2003) by allowing for possibly imperfect correlation between (i) a common factor driving credit risk in the bank's wider portfolio and (ii) a common factor driving the credit quality of the exposures in the structured product pool.

Pykhtin and Dev suppose that the wider portfolio of the bank in question has a single risk factor and is diversified so that aggregate losses are a function simply of this common factor. In this case, one may show that the marginal VAR (at a confidence level of α) for a small additional exposure equals its expected loss, conditional on the common factor in the bank portfolio equalling its α quantile.

For very thin tranches in a structured exposure, the loss given default is 100% so the expected loss is simply the probability that losses exceed the protection level of the tranche. In this case, the marginal VAR on such a tranche is just the conditional expected loss, ie, the probability that losses exceed the tranches protection, conditional on the common factor in the bank portfolio equalling its α quantile.

To derive marginal VARs for thin tranches, it therefore suffices to calculate the distribution of total losses on the pool of exposures, conditional on the factor driving the bank portfolio equalling its α quantile.

Pykhtin and Dev use the results of Vasicek, who derives a simple closed formula for the distribution of aggregate losses on a credit portfolio. The modifications they make are: (i) to derive this distribution, conditional on a given level of losses on the wider bank portfolio; and (ii) to allow for random loss given default.

The basic assumptions of the Vasicek–Pykhtin–Dev approach are as follows. Suppose that the ith exposure in the structured exposure pool defaults over a single period of time, such as a year, if a normally distributed latent variable Z_i falls below zero. Assume that

$$Z_i = \sqrt{\rho}X + \sqrt{1-\rho}\varepsilon$$

where X is a common factor and ε is an independent exposure-specific error. Suppose that X is correlated with a single factor denoted as Y driving the wider bank portfolio in that

$$X = \sqrt{\rho_Y}Y + \sqrt{1-\rho_Y}\eta$$

Suppose that Y, ε and η are standard normal random variables so that X and Z_i are also standard normal random variables. Conditional on Y, X is then distributed as $N\left(\sqrt{\rho_Y}Y, 1-\rho_Y\right)$. Since, conditional on X, defaults by individual exposures in the structured product pool are independent, it follows (see Vasicek (1991)) that the probability of k defaults in a year out of n exposures conditional on Y is

$$P_k = \binom{n}{k} \int_{-\infty}^{\infty} \left(\Phi\left(\frac{1}{\sqrt{1-\rho}} \left[\Phi^{-1}(p) - \sqrt{\rho} u \right] \right) \right)^k \left(1 - \Phi\left(\frac{1}{\sqrt{1-\rho}} \left[\Phi^{-1}(p) - \sqrt{\rho} u \right] \right) \right)^{n-k} \mathrm{d}\Phi\left(\frac{u - \sqrt{\rho_Y} Y}{\sqrt{1-\rho_Y}} \right)$$

The cumulative probability that the percentage of losses on the pool does not exceed θ is then

$$F_n(\theta) = \sum_{k=0}^{[n\theta]} P_k$$

Using the substitution $s = \Phi\left(1/\sqrt{1-\rho}\left[\Phi^{-1}(p) - \sqrt{\rho u}\right]\right)$ yields

$$F_n(\theta) = \sum_{k=0}^{[n\theta]} \binom{n}{k} \int_0^1 s^k (1-s)^{n-k} \, \mathrm{d}W(s)$$

where

$$W(s) \equiv \Phi\left(\frac{1}{\sqrt{1-\rho_Y}} \left(\frac{1}{\sqrt{\rho}} \left(\sqrt{1-\rho}\Phi^{-1}(s) - \Phi^{-1}(p) \right) - \sqrt{\rho_Y} Y \right) \right)$$

When loss given default (LGD) is random, Pykhtin and Dev argue that it can be well approximated by independent, normally-distributed random variables with identical means μ and variances σ^2. In this case, the conditional distribution of losses becomes

$$\hat{F}_n(l) = \sum_{k=0}^{[n\theta]} \binom{n}{k} \int_0^1 s^k (1-s)^{n-k} \, \mathrm{d}W(s) \Phi\left(\frac{ln - \mu k}{\sigma\sqrt{k}} \right)$$

Capital charges appropriate for a very thin tranche with protection l are then simply

$$G_n(l) = 1 - \hat{F}_n(l)$$

When the portfolio for the structured exposure is highly granular, Vasicek shows that the distribution of losses simplifies. The conditional loss distribution that one obtains then implies that the capital charge function for a thin tranche with protection l is

$$G(l) = 1 - \Phi\left(\frac{1}{\sqrt{1-\rho_Y}}\left(\frac{1}{\sqrt{\rho}}\left(\sqrt{1-\rho}\Phi^{-1}(l/\mu) - \Phi^{-1}(p)\right) - \sqrt{\rho_Y}\Phi^{-1}(\alpha)\right)\right)$$

To obtain the marginal capital charge for a tranche with discrete thickness $t_2 - t_1$ and protection level t_1, one may simply use the fact that marginal VARs sum for different exposures. The capital for such a thick tranche is therefore just $\int_{t_1}^{t_2} G(l)\mathrm{d}l$, ie, the integral of $G(l)$ from t_1 to t_2.

In fact, the approximation used by Pykhtin and Dev that losses given default on different exposures are independent and normally distributed is unsatisfactory when the granularity is extremely low, as in this case the probability of a loss rate greater than unity or less than zero may be significant. In our implementation of the Pykhtin–Dev approach, we therefore employed both the approach described above and, as an alternative, a numerical solution in which independent beta-distributed LGDs were simulated by a Monte Carlo replication. For granularity levels of four or less, this approach yielded estimates that were somewhat different from those obtained with the standard Pykhtin–Dev model described above. As we shall see in the section "Checks of the methodology" below, the results with our beta-distributed recoveries are identical, apart from sampling error, to those obtained using the *Portfolio Risk Tracker* model under identical assumptions.

THE *PORTFOLIO RISK TRACKER* MODEL

Ratings-based models

To analyse portfolios including structured products, we used the ratings-based credit risk model, *Portfolio Risk Tracker*. As in standard, ratings-based credit portfolio models, in *Portfolio Risk Tracker* the ratings of different exposures are driven by realisations of normally-distributed latent variables. The correlations of these variables are taken to equal those of weighted averages of equity indices, where the weights are selected appropriately given the relative importance of different industries and countries for the obligor in question.

Portfolio Risk Tracker generalises standard one-period, ratings-based models in that it may be run for any horizon with intermediate cashflows (including recoveries in the event of default) being cumulated up to some terminal date. If the terminal date exceeds the maturity of the longest-dated exposure, the model yields hold-to-maturity risk measures for the portfolio that one is analysing.

Structured products within ratings-based models

Portfolio Risk Tracker has the feature that one may include investments in structured products as exposures within wider credit portfolios. The primary difficulty in achieving this is that in ratings-based models, for each Monte Carlo replication, one needs to value all exposures with maturities greater than the terminal horizon of the VAR calculation, conditional on the realised rating at that date. This is non-trivial for securities such as structured products, as they represent levered positions in portfolios of credit sensitive exposures and hence contain non-linearities comparable to those of option contracts. Unlike standard option contracts, however, structured products are too complex for one to deduce closed-form valuation expressions.

To solve this difficulty, *Portfolio Risk Tracker* employs a flexible but accurate approach to calculating the values of structured products. In brief, this consists of "pre-processing" the structured product exposures before one runs the main VAR Monte Carlo replication so as to obtain reduced form pricing expressions. These functions are then used in a second stage as the full model is simulated.

Structured product pre-processing

Here we describe the pre-processing approach in somewhat more detail. Suppose the initial date is 0 and the horizon for the VAR calculation is T. To pre-process a structured product, one conducts an initial Monte Carlo replication within *Portfolio Risk Tracker* using risk-adjusted rating transition matrices on the structured products alone and retaining in memory for each structured product tranche several thousand cashflow histories for different Monte Carlo replications. One then discounts the cashflow history after period T back to T and then, for each structured product tranche, one estimates a non-linear statistical model relating the mean of the discounted cashflows to statistics of the distribution of ratings in the structured product pool.

Since the simulations are performed using risk-adjusted transition matrices, the mean of these discounted future payoffs equals their market value at T. The statistical model gives the mean conditional on statistics of the ratings distribution of the underlying structured product pool, in other words a pricing function linking ratings statistics to value. For a given Monte Carlo replication, plugging structured product rating pool statistics into the estimated function, one obtains the conditional value of the structured product tranche. This approach resembles one independently developed by Longstaff and Schwartz (2001) in a recent paper on pricing American options by Monte Carlo replication.

Introducing different types of structured products in the *Portfolio Risk Tracker* model is straightforward, as the techniques employed for reduced form valuation are flexible. The structures examined in this chapter are a simplified version of those discussed by Duffie and Garleanu (2001). An arbitrary number of tranches may be accommodated, a reserve account is maintained for excess interest payments and precise rules are followed for the accruals in principal that arise if coupons are unpaid.

The statistical pricing model

We now consider in more detail the reduced form pricing approach employed within *Portfolio Risk Tracker*. The discounted payoffs on structured product tranches have the feature that for some discrete atom of probability, they yield the full contractual cashflow of the tranche, whereas if there is some default they yield somewhat less. We suppose that for a given tranche, if a random variable z is positive, the tranche pays the contractually agreed series of coupons, the value of which is V. However, if z is negative it defaults and the discounted cashflow equals a random variable y times the no-default price V. y is in effect like a recovery rate.

The expected discounted payoff Y on the tranche is then

$$
\begin{aligned}
E(Y) &= \big(E[y1(z<0)] + E[1(z>0)]\big)\,V \\
&= \big(E(y \mid z<0)\,\Pr(z<0) + \Pr(z>0)\big)\,V
\end{aligned}
$$

Here, $\Pr(\cdot)$ indicates a probability and $E(\cdot)$ is the expectations operator. We assume that

$$E\left(y \mid z<0, X\right)=\gamma' X \quad \text{and} \quad \Pr(z<0)=\frac{\exp\left(\beta' X\right)}{1+\exp\left(\beta' X\right)}$$

Our statistical modelling of discounted payoffs therefore consists of estimating a logit model (by non-linear Maximum Likelihood) that there is a default on the tranche in question and then estimating the recovery rate in the event of default as a linear regression. The explanatory variables we use in both the logit modelling and the regression consist of shares of the value of the underlying structured product pool in different rating categories.

Risk adjustments and pricing

As mentioned above, one may run *Portfolio Risk Tracker* either with actual rating transition matrices or with risk-adjusted transition matrices. The former approach is appropriate if one wishes to calculate quantities such as VARs or probabilities that a portfolio will default over some given horizon. The latter approach is appropriate if one wishes to price a cashflow.

The exercises involved in the risk analysis of structured products include both kinds of simulation as the calculations include VARs and pricing. The historical rating transition matrix we use in this study is a matrix for all obligors calculated by Standard and Poor's. To calculate a risk-adjusted transition matrix, we follow an approach similar to that of Kijima and Komoribayashi (1998) and Jarrow *et al* (1997). They employ benchmark spreads from the corporate bond market to deduce risk-adjusted transition probabilities by shifting probability weight so that bonds are correctly priced as discounted expected payoffs.

Both Jarrow–Lando–Turnbull and Kijima–Komoribayashi calculate risk-adjusted transition matrices that change over time and depend on prices of risk in a somewhat arbitrary manner. We prefer to assume that the risk-adjusted matrix is time homogeneous and calculate it from one-, three-, five- and seven-year maturity spreads. We have verified that this is a good approximation to the term structure of credit spreads with which we are working (namely the average Bloomberg credit spreads for US industrials over the 1991 to

2000 period) by calculating the risk–neutral spreads that would be implied by this transition matrix for medium and long maturities.

Marginal VAR calculations

The accuracy of the marginal VAR calculations within *Portfolio Risk Tracker* is increased by the application of Extreme Value Theory smoothing to the tails of the relevant distributions. The approach taken is to fit Pareto distributions to the 1% worst portfolio value outcomes with a view to improving estimates of the 0.1% VAR quantiles. Such a fitting is performed for the total portfolio and then successively to the portfolio less each individual exposure. The marginal VAR is then estimated by taking the difference between the 0.1% quantile of the smoothed total portfolio value tail distribution and the corresponding quantile when a given exposure is excluded from the portfolio.

Checks of the methodology

To check the approach, one may first examine whether it yields the correct mean price. To do this, we calculate the expected cashflow on tranches up to various different horizons plus the value of the structured product at that horizon. Given that we use risk–neutral transition probabilities and discount values consistently, when the calculation is carried out for a horizon equal to the structured product maturity, we obtain by this method the exact tranche value. If our model is working correctly, then the average discounted cashflows up to some horizon T plus the average discounted value of the tranche, as given by our pricing function, should be the same for any value of T less than or equal to the structured product maturity.

We find that for horizons significantly earlier than the structured product maturity and for reasonably senior tranches we obtain very small biases of the order of 10 basis points. For very junior tranches, the biases can be greater but are, in general, not more than 1%. For the equity tranche and for tranches that default more than 50% of the time, we use a simple regression without any logit modelling and find that this yields unbiased results.

As a further check of our pricing approach, we examined whether aspects of the distribution of values apart from the mean are correctly fitted. To achieve this, we constructed hedged positions that are long a portfolio of loans and short a position consisting of all the tranches of a structured product containing the same loans as in the first portfolio. If the calculations are accurate, there should be little volatility in the hedge position and the VARs for different quantiles of the hedged position payoff distribution should be very small. We found, in these calculations, that the VARs of the hedge position were around 5% of the VARs of the original portfolio of loans and that volatility was extremely small on the hedged position.

Comparison of the Pykhtin–Dev approach and *Portfolio Risk Tracker*

We adopt the following assumptions.

1. The VAR horizon is a year and the maturity of all the loans in the bank's portfolio and in the structured product pool is one year.
2. There is a single common factor in the structured product pool and another single common factor in the wider bank portfolio.
3. The structured product exposure is negligibly small compared with the wider bank portfolio.

Then, the Pykhtin–Dev model and *Portfolio Risk Tracker* should yield identical capital charges.

Figure 1 shows capital charges based on marginal VARs for tranches in a structured product. The wider bank portfolio and the structured product underlying pool within *Portfolio Risk Tracker* are assumed to consist of 500 BBB-rated loans and 4 BB-rated loans, respectively. The par value of the exposures in the structured product pool are assumed to equal 0.5% of the par value of the loans making up the wider bank portfolio. Parameters are chosen so that the latent variables for pairs of exposures in the bank portfolio have 20% correlations and likewise for pairs of loans in the structured product pool. The common risk factor in the bank portfolio and the common risk factor in the structured product pool are assumed to have a correlation of 60%. LGDs are taken to be independent and to have means of 45% and volatilities of 25%.

As may be seen from Figure 1, the capital charges implied by the two models are almost identical. The *Portfolio Risk Tracker* calculations are performed with 200,000 Monte Carlo replications so the slight discrepancies are attributable to sampling error.

Figure 1 Capital charges implied by Pykhtin–Dev and *Portfolio Risk Tracker* for thin tranche (4 BB-rated loans in pool). A modified version of the Pykhtin–Dev model for granular structured products was used which assumes beta-distributed rather than normally-distributed losses given default

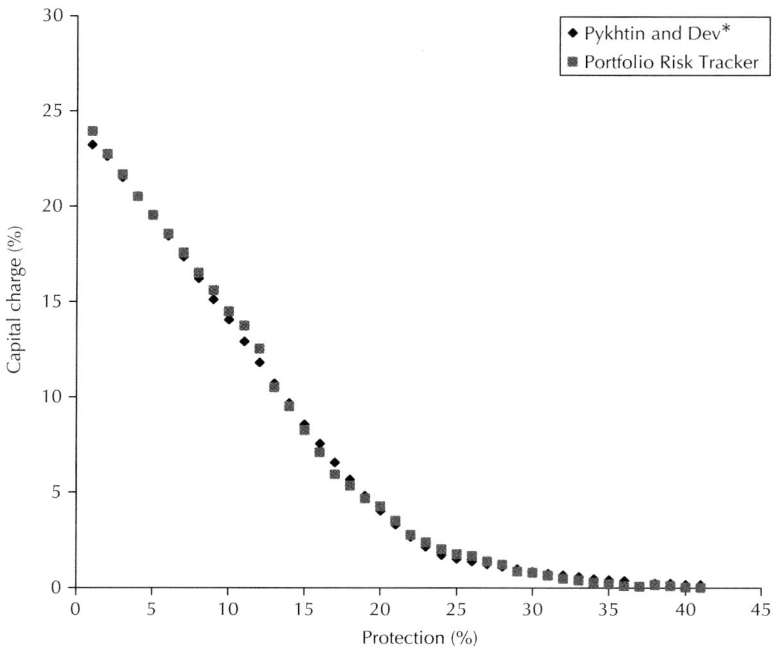

Rating-specific capital charges within *Portfolio Risk Tracker* and the Pykhtin–Dev models

For a given structure, one can calculate the marginal capital requirement for each tranche using either the *Portfolio Risk Tracker* or the Pykhtin–Dev model in a straightforward fashion. Inferring the correct capital charge for tranches that have a given rating is a somewhat more complicated issue. The approach we take is to calculate capital and expected losses for the tranches in a given structure and then to fit a curve through the observations of (capital, expected loss) pairs. Evaluating these curves at benchmark expected loss levels associated with different rating categories gives us capital charges for those rating categories.

The data generated from the Pykhtin–Dev model tends to be highly smooth so our curve-fitting approach is just linear interpolation. In some cases, the *Portfolio Risk Tracker* model data is noisier so we fit it to a function consisting of a weighted sum of power functions. The fitting is done using a weighted least-squares approach that attributes more weight to the high credit quality tranches for which the capital charges are less noisy. We systematically examined the data to ensure that the fits were accurate.

The benchmark expected loss levels associated with different rating categories are obtained by calculating the expected losses over different time periods of bonds with different initial ratings assuming: (i) a historical Standard and Poor's rating transition matrix; (ii) a recovery rate of 50%; and (iii) that the coupon rates on the bonds equal those implied by time series averages of Bloomberg yield data for different rating categories from 1991 to 2001.[3]

Note that we employ expected loss benchmarks to obtain ratings rather than the obvious alternative approach of default probability benchmarks. For very thin tranches, it makes no difference, as LGDs on very thin tranches are invariably 100%. However, for thick tranches a tranche may be less risky than a thin tranche with the same rating if the rating is based on default probabilities.

Peretyatkin and Perraudin (2002) discuss differences between expected-loss- and default-probability-based structured product ratings. As they show, thick senior tranches tend to have superior ratings if the expected loss approach is taken. This observation is consistent with the common view that Moody's (who employ an expected loss methodology) enjoy greater market share for senior thick tranches while Standard and Poor's and Fitch (who use default-probability-based rating techniques) obtain a relatively larger share of the thinner mezzanine tranches.

It is, in our view, better in capital calculations like those of this chapter to use an expected loss methodology since for thin tranches there is no difference and thick senior tranches (for which differences may exist) tend to be rated in the market following an expected-loss approach.

ANALYSIS OF CAPITAL FOR STRUCTURED PRODUCT TRANCHES

Comparative statics

We begin by looking at some key sensitivities of capital charge calculations to model assumptions. Figure 2 shows capital charges for

Figure 2 Thin tranche VARs under different factor correlation assumptions (64 B-rated loans)

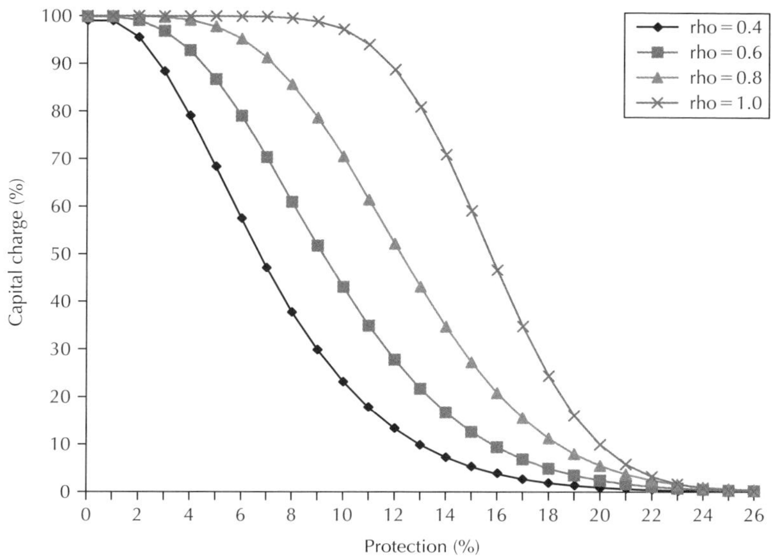

thin tranches plotted against protection for several structures, assuming different levels of correlation between the common factor driving the structured product pool and the common factor driving the wider bank portfolio. The structured product pool is assumed to comprise of 64 equal-sized, B-rated loans.

As is evident from Figure 2, the greater the correlation, the steeper is the capital charge curve. In the limit as the correlation tends to one and as the granularity of the portfolio approaches infinity, the capital curve approximates to a step function with a 100% weight for all levels of protection below the capital that the underlying structured product pool would attract if held on balance sheet, and 0% otherwise.

Decreasing the degree of correlation between the structured product pool and the wider bank portfolio factors smoothes out capital for investments in high-granularity structured products and is therefore comparable to the approach taken by Gordy and Jones (2003) in their work on the parameterisation of the Supervisory Formula Approach. Gordy and Jones achieve smoothing by supposing that the seniority of different tranches is random and then integrating over a suitable distribution for levels of protection.

It might be argued that the assumption of imperfect correlation between bank portfolio and structured product pool factors is inconsistent with the approach taken elsewhere in work on capital charges for loans for the Basel review. This is not necessarily the case, as one could suppose that loans in the structured product pool have less idiosyncratic risk than do loans in the broader bank portfolio. In this case, the pair-wise correlation of loans in the structured product pool and in the broader bank portfolio could be set equal to the correlation between pairs of loans in the broader bank portfolio. This would be both realistic (in that structured product pools will often be fairly concentrated in exposure type) and would yield total capital for the structured product pool if it were held on balance sheet equal to what one would obtain with perfect correlation.

Figure 3 shows capital charges for different granularities for a representative structured product with thin tranches based on an

Figure 3 Thin tranche capital charges for different granularities (BB-rated loans, 60% correlation)

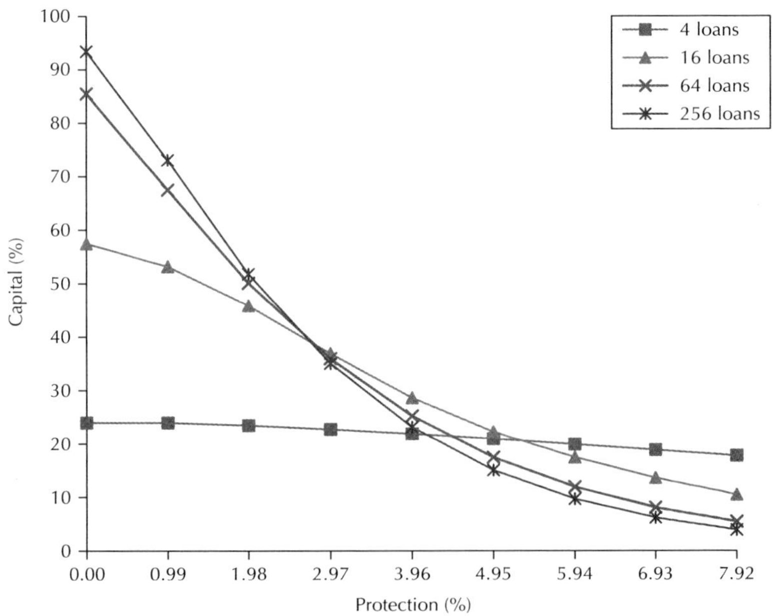

underlying pool of BB-rated loans. As expected, the capital curves become flatter as the granularity is reduced. The intuition is that capital charges equal the expected loss on a tranche, conditional on the bank's total losses being at their VAR quantile level. Lower granularity increases idiosyncratic risk and hence shifts expected losses from junior tranches (which, like conventional equity, resemble call options) to senior tranches (which, like conventional debt, resemble short positions in put options).

Global consistency

An important basic question one may wish to ask about ratings-based capital charges is how the implied levels of capital for a bank, if it held all the tranches, compare with what an originator would have to hold against the underlying pool of exposures if the latter were held on balance sheet.

Tables 1–3 show total capital for some representative structured product structures assuming different correlation levels for the bank portfolio and structured product pool factors and assuming different deduction rules. (Recall that under the current ratings-based approach (RBA) contained in the Basel Committee's proposals for structured exposure regulatory capital charges, tranches rated less than BB are subject to full deduction.)

To understand the entries in the tables, one may consider an example. The uppermost element in the column headed B+ in Table 1(a) is the sum of the capital for all the tranches in a structured product assuming that a 60% correlation and that exposures rated B+ and below are deducted.

Table 1(b) is a small subtable showing the total capital for all the tranches in the structured product: (i) based on capital charges derived from our model but with perfect correlation between risk factors; (ii) implied by the Basel Committee's October 2002 working paper[1] thick tranche RBA weights (see Table A1); (iii) implied by the October 2002 working paper thin tranche RBA weights (see Table A1); and (iv) implied by the QIS 3 formula if the loans were held on balance sheet and no maturity adjustment were made.

The numbers in the table show that, if the loans were held on balance sheet, they would be subject to a 7.2% charge. This figure is confirmed by the perfect-correlation case calculation using the

Table 1 (a) Capital for the entire structure under different deduction rule assumptions (256 BB-rated loans in the pool). (b) The total capital for all the tranches in the structured product

(a)

Factor correlation	No floor %	B− %	B %	B+ %	BB− %	BB %	BB+ %	BBB− %
0.6	3.15	3.69	4.09	4.76	5.33	5.95	6.83	7.28
0.7	3.93	4.24	4.53	5.06	5.56	6.12	6.93	7.36
0.8	4.85	4.97	5.14	5.50	5.88	6.35	7.07	7.47
0.9	5.93	5.95	5.99	6.15	6.36	6.68	7.25	7.59

Entries in the table are equal to the total capital implied by the model using different bank and structured exposure pool factor correlations and different deduction rules. A deduction rule of B+ implies that capital of 100% is imposed on any tranche rated B+ or below. The "No floor" column indicates deduction is not imposed for any rating category.

(b)

Perfect correlation model capital[1]	7.18%
Thick tranche RBA weights capital[2]	5.61%
Thin tranche RBA weights capital[3]	6.01%
QIS 3 whole loans capital[4]	7.20%

[1]Capital for entire structure if the structured exposure risk factor and main portfolio risk factor are perfectly correlated.
[2]Capital for entire structure using thick tranche RBA approach weights from October 2002 working paper.
[3]Capital for entire structure using thin tranche RBA approach weights from October 2002 working paper.
[4]Capital for loans using QIS 3 technical guidance formula assuming no maturity adjustment.

model. The capital implied by the RBA is somewhat lower, being 6.0% and 5.6% depending on whether the baseline charges or the concessionary weights for thick senior tranches are used. As one may see from the upper block of numbers, assuming a 90% correlation, deduction for BB+ and below would be needed if the correct model-based charges were used in order to replicate the 7.2% on-balance-sheet capital charge.

Tables 2 and 3 show total capital for structured products similar to that employed in Table 1 but with underlying pool quality of B-rated and BBB-rated loans, respectively. The results in Tables 2 and 3 confirm those in Table 1 in that on-balance-sheet capital is slightly higher than that implied by the RBA even without the concessionary treatment of thick senior tranches. Again, using the

Table 2 (a) Capital for the entire structure under different deduction rule assumptions (256 B-rated loans in the pool). (b) The total capital for all the tranches in the structured product

(a)

Factor correlation	No cap %	B− %	B %	B+ %	BB− %	BB %	BB+ %	BBB− %
0.6	8.68	9.68	10.44	11.59	12.34	13.37	12.34	14.92
0.7	10.03	10.54	11.07	11.99	12.64	13.56	12.64	15.02
0.8	11.50	11.68	11.96	12.57	13.07	13.84	13.07	15.14
0.9	13.11	13.12	13.19	13.44	13.71	14.24	13.71	15.30

(b)

Perfect correlation model capital[1]	14.83%
Thick tranche RBA weights capital[2]	12.57%
Thin tranche RBA weights capital[3]	12.93%
QIS 3 whole loans capital[4]	14.84%

See notes for Table 1(b).

Table 3 (a) Capital for the entire structure under different deduction rule assumptions (256 BBB-rated loans in the pool). (b) The total capital for all the tranches in the structured product.

(a)

Factor correlation	No cap %	B− %	B %	B+ %	BB− %	BB %	BB+ %	BBB− %
0.6	1.08	1.31	1.46	1.80	1.99	2.40	2.84	3.06
0.7	1.42	1.58	1.68	1.96	2.13	2.50	2.91	3.12
0.8	1.86	1.93	2.00	2.20	2.33	2.64	3.00	3.20
0.9	2.40	2.41	2.44	2.53	2.61	2.82	3.11	3.28

(b)

Perfect correlation model capital[1]	3.05%
Thick tranche RBA weights capital[2]	2.47%
Thin tranche RBA weights capital[3]	2.87%
QIS 3 whole loans capital[4]	3.31%

See notes for Table 1(b).

model-based capital charges and a correlation of 0.9, deduction must start at a higher level than B+ to yield total capital equal to the on-balance-sheet charge.

Rating category-specific consistency

The next issue we examine is the consistency of RBA capital charges from the Basel Committee's October 2002 working paper with those implied by the model for different individual rating categories. Table 4 looks at capital charges for tranches from a structured product with a highly granular underlying portfolio of 256-rated loans under different correlation assumptions.

The results in Table 4 show that the capital charges for the higher rating categories are justified if the correlation between the bank factor and the factor driving the structured product pool is around 60% (although in this case the capital charges on the BB− to BB+ grades in the RBA would perhaps be too high). If a higher correlation is assumed (which is necessary as we saw in the last section if the total capital under the RBA is to approximate to the total on-balance-sheet capital of the structured product pool), then the capital charges for most of the investment grade categories appear too low.

Granularity effects

Tables 5–7 show capital charges for different rating categories based on underlying structured product pool portfolios with different credit qualities and granularities. In each case, a curve is fitted to the data. In the lower part of the tables (labelled 5b, 6b, and 7b), the results for different credit qualities are averaged.

The results of Table 5 are calculated assuming that the structured product exposure is negligibly small compared with the wider bank portfolio. (The par value of the structured product pool exposures is 0.5% of the par value of the exposures in the wider bank portfolio.) Tables 6 and 7 contain results assuming that the structured product exposure is a larger fraction of the total par of the bank's portfolio (3% and 5%, respectively).

The results show that when the structured product pool is large relative to the wider bank portfolio, if granularity is low, tranches attract distinctly larger capital requirements than do otherwise comparable tranches of structured products with well-diversified

Table 4 Individual tranche capital charges for a highly granular pool of B-rated loans under different factor correlation assumptions

Factor correlation	AAA	AA+	AA	AA−	A+	A	A−	BBB+	BBB	BBB−	BB+	BB	BB−	B+	B	B−	CCC
0.6	0.59	0.98	1.30	1.50	1.70	1.90	3.58	4.96	7.06	7.71	10.07	17.11	23.15	32.88	54.28	60.28	77.05
0.7	0.87	1.47	1.98	2.29	2.61	2.92	5.60	7.76	11.02	12.02	15.61	25.81	34.03	46.34	69.47	75.03	88.29
0.8	1.12	1.99	2.75	3.22	3.70	4.18	8.41	11.84	16.97	18.51	23.97	38.62	49.37	63.72	84.77	88.68	95.95
0.9	1.08	2.12	3.16	3.85	4.54	5.24	12.06	17.85	26.48	29.01	37.80	58.72	71.35	84.49	96.03	97.23	98.72
RBA thin tranche[1]	0.96		1.20			1.60		4.00	6.00	8.00	20.00	34.00	52.00	1.00	1.00	1.00	1.00

[1]Based on capital charges from the Basel Committee on Banking Supervision (2002).

Table 5 (a) Capital charges for individual tranches assuming 60% factor correlation with main bank portfolio and thin tranche structure. (b) As per (a) showing average over all underlying pool qualities for each granularity

(a)

	Pool rating	AAA	AA+	AA	AA−	A+	A	A−	BBB+	BBB	BBB−	BB+	BB	BB−	B+	B	B−	CCC
1 loan	BBB	0.04	0.08	0.12	0.14	0.17	0.19	0.46	0.72	1.19	1.35	1.99	–	–	–	–	–	–
	BB	0.02	0.05	0.07	0.09	0.10	0.12	0.28	0.44	0.72	0.82	1.21	2.74	4.51	–	–	–	–
	B	0.01	0.03	0.04	0.05	0.06	0.06	0.16	0.24	0.40	0.45	0.67	1.52	2.50	4.66	13.44	17.47	–
	CCC	0.01	0.02	0.03	0.03	0.04	0.04	0.10	0.16	0.26	0.29	0.43	0.98	1.61	3.01	8.69	11.29	23.62
4 loans	BBB	0.13	0.24	0.31	0.34	0.36	0.39	0.66	0.92	1.37	1.52	2.13	4.47	7.14	–	–	–	–
	BB	0.10	0.17	0.24	0.29	0.33	0.37	0.80	1.21	1.75	1.87	2.28	3.75	5.38	8.85	22.18	–	–
	B	0.07	0.12	0.17	0.21	0.24	0.27	0.59	0.85	1.24	1.37	1.86	3.57	5.43	9.10	17.04	20.32	34.73
	CCC	0.03	0.06	0.09	0.11	0.13	0.15	0.35	0.55	0.87	0.97	1.38	2.81	4.35	7.47	17.29	20.98	35.83
16 loans	BBB	0.27	0.46	0.61	0.71	0.79	0.87	1.60	2.22	3.20	3.47	4.37	6.60	8.90	13.73	–	–	–
	BB	0.27	0.45	0.62	0.72	0.82	0.92	1.74	2.41	3.43	3.77	4.95	8.28	11.36	16.90	28.23	32.50	49.95
	B	0.20	0.36	0.49	0.58	0.66	0.74	1.48	2.11	3.05	3.37	4.48	7.94	11.14	16.66	31.37	36.10	51.90
	CCC	0.13	0.23	0.34	0.40	0.47	0.53	1.12	1.63	2.45	2.72	3.69	6.98	10.19	15.90	31.87	37.20	55.34
64 loans	BBB	0.51	0.82	1.10	1.25	1.40	1.55	2.85	3.86	5.39	5.92	7.42	12.31	15.80	22.96	34.86	40.31	60.74
	BB	0.51	0.83	1.10	1.28	1.45	1.60	3.01	4.13	5.81	6.35	8.25	13.84	18.59	26.17	44.03	48.65	64.23
	B	0.44	0.73	0.99	1.16	1.31	1.46	2.81	3.91	5.56	6.07	7.98	13.74	18.70	26.83	46.29	51.89	68.77
	CCC	0.32	0.57	0.79	0.93	1.07	1.20	2.39	3.39	4.96	5.48	7.32	13.04	18.17	26.79	47.02	53.12	71.03
256 loans	BBB	0.69	1.04	1.35	1.54	1.74	1.93	3.55	4.89	6.77	7.43	9.74	15.67	21.22	26.35	47.13	50.45	59.84
	BB	0.68	1.05	1.38	1.57	1.76	1.95	3.66	5.03	7.09	7.78	10.07	16.93	22.86	32.52	51.78	56.97	71.95
	B	0.65	1.01	1.33	1.53	1.72	1.90	3.59	4.96	7.04	7.72	10.05	17.01	23.00	32.69	54.37	59.95	77.07
	CCC	0.56	0.90	1.21	1.40	1.59	1.77	3.39	4.75	6.78	7.43	9.75	16.72	22.83	32.54	54.38	60.46	77.41

(b)

	AAA	AA+	AA	AA–	A+	A	A–	BBB+	BBB	BBB–	BB+	BB	BB–	B+	B	B–	CCC
1 loan	0.02	0.04	0.06	0.08	0.09	0.10	0.25	0.39	0.64	0.73	1.08	1.74	2.87	3.84	11.07	14.38	23.62
4 loans	0.08	0.15	0.20	0.23	0.27	0.30	0.60	0.88	1.31	1.43	1.91	3.65	5.57	8.47	18.84	20.65	35.28
16 loans	0.21	0.38	0.52	0.60	0.68	0.76	1.49	2.09	3.03	3.33	4.37	7.45	10.40	15.80	30.49	35.27	52.40
64 loans	0.45	0.74	1.00	1.15	1.31	1.45	2.77	3.82	5.43	5.96	7.74	13.23	17.81	25.69	43.05	48.49	66.19
256 loans	0.64	1.00	1.32	1.51	1.70	1.89	3.55	4.91	6.92	7.59	9.90	16.58	22.48	31.02	51.92	56.96	71.57

Table 6 (a) *Portfolio Risk Tracker* tranche capital charges for 1-year structure constituting 3% of main bank portfolio with average rating of BBB. (b) As per (a) showing average over all underlying pool qualities for each granularity

(a)

	Pool rating	AAA	AA+	AA	AA–	A+	A	A–	BBB+	BBB	BBB–	BB+	BB	BB–	B+	B	B–	CCC
1 loan	BBB	0.55	2.77	4.53	5.54	6.46	7.31	13.58	17.40	21.59	22.58	24.97	–	–	–	–	–	–
	BB	1.00	2.56	3.90	4.72	5.49	6.23	12.78	18.12	26.39	29.08	38.98	50.85	51.68	–	–	–	–
	B	1.01	1.96	2.79	3.31	3.81	4.28	8.72	12.54	18.74	20.82	28.70	39.53	47.23	57.12	72.15	74.82	–
	CCC	0.37	0.70	0.99	1.15	1.31	1.46	2.76	3.78	5.33	5.82	7.62	12.55	17.84	26.75	49.00	55.90	76.55
4 loans	BBB	0.36	0.52	0.66	0.74	0.82	0.90	1.59	2.17	3.12	3.44	4.64	8.40	11.65	–	–	–	–
	BB	0.46	0.85	1.17	1.35	1.52	1.68	2.93	3.79	4.95	5.28	6.39	8.64	11.33	16.58	33.70	–	–
	B	0.72	1.01	1.23	1.36	1.47	1.58	2.42	3.00	3.80	4.04	4.85	10.34	14.01	19.50	32.33	36.57	52.52
	CCC	0.34	0.39	0.44	0.47	0.51	0.55	1.07	1.67	2.82	3.24	4.97	9.86	14.27	21.19	37.67	42.84	59.82
16 loans	BBB	0.48	0.69	0.87	0.97	1.07	1.16	1.91	2.48	3.35	3.63	4.62	7.92	10.67	15.66	–	–	–
	BB	0.48	0.69	0.86	0.97	1.07	1.17	2.11	2.94	4.33	4.81	6.64	12.32	16.24	22.03	35.31	39.62	55.53
	B	0.39	0.72	1.01	1.18	1.34	1.49	2.85	3.96	5.69	6.25	8.34	14.15	18.69	25.67	41.70	46.62	62.61
	CCC	0.11	0.33	0.52	0.63	0.74	0.84	1.73	2.43	3.50	3.84	5.09	10.41	15.69	23.74	41.99	47.53	65.28
64 loans	BBB	0.63	1.03	1.35	1.54	1.72	1.89	3.28	4.33	5.88	6.36	8.07	13.16	16.71	22.16	36.09	41.15	–
	BB	0.60	1.23	1.74	2.04	2.31	2.56	4.57	5.98	7.87	8.42	10.23	16.39	21.03	28.30	45.24	50.42	66.73
	B	0.40	0.78	1.11	1.32	1.51	1.70	3.43	4.91	7.29	8.09	11.09	17.68	22.97	30.92	48.57	53.83	70.36
	CCC	0.70	1.27	1.74	2.01	2.27	2.51	4.50	6.00	8.15	8.82	11.18	19.11	26.42	36.73	57.11	62.64	78.64
256 loans	BBB	0.67	1.19	1.61	1.85	2.07	2.28	3.91	5.06	6.62	7.07	8.60	16.92	22.09	30.02	47.80	53.03	–
	BB	0.80	1.38	1.84	2.10	2.35	2.58	4.40	5.69	7.45	7.98	9.74	16.04	21.19	29.51	49.43	55.51	73.89
	B	0.95	1.53	1.99	2.26	2.51	2.74	4.66	6.08	8.11	8.73	10.93	19.57	26.23	35.81	55.50	61.01	77.43
	CCC	0.45	1.08	1.60	1.91	2.20	2.47	4.73	6.41	8.82	9.56	12.13	20.78	28.45	39.10	59.57	64.97	80.23

(b)

	AAA	AA+	AA	AA−	A+	A	A−	BBB+	BBB	BBB−	BB+	BB	BB−	B+	B	B−	CCC
1 loan	0.73	2.00	3.05	3.68	4.27	4.82	9.46	12.96	18.01	19.58	25.07	34.31	38.92	41.93	60.57	65.36	76.55
4 loans	0.47	0.69	0.87	0.98	1.08	1.18	2.00	2.66	3.67	4.00	5.21	9.31	12.81	19.09	34.56	39.70	56.17
16 loans	0.36	0.61	0.81	0.94	1.05	1.16	2.15	2.95	4.22	4.63	6.17	11.20	15.32	21.78	39.66	44.59	61.14
64 loans	0.58	1.08	1.49	1.73	1.95	2.16	3.95	5.30	7.30	7.92	10.14	16.58	21.78	29.53	46.75	52.01	71.91
256 loans	0.72	1.30	1.76	2.03	2.28	2.52	4.43	5.81	7.75	8.33	10.35	18.33	24.49	33.61	53.08	58.63	77.18

Table 7 (a) *Portfolio Risk Tracker* tranche capital charges for 1-year structure constituting 5% of main bank portfolio with average rating of BBB. (b) As per (a) showing average over all underlying pool qualities for each granularity

(a)

	Asset quality	AAA	AA+	AA	AA−	A+	A	A−	BBB+	BBB	BBB−	BB+	BB	BB−	B+	B	B−	CCC
1 loan	BBB	0.20	3.63	6.40	8.02	9.50	10.86	21.39	28.21	36.45	38.62	44.89	–	–	–	–	–	–
	BBB	1.53	3.77	5.70	6.88	7.99	9.05	18.49	26.19	38.13	42.01	56.32	84.20	89.88	–	–	–	–
	B	1.50	3.01	4.33	5.15	5.93	6.69	13.71	19.75	29.54	32.82	45.23	69.62	79.76	87.62	91.11	93.35	–
	CCC	0.58	1.57	2.42	2.93	3.42	3.88	7.92	11.16	16.10	17.68	23.47	33.75	42.26	53.92	75.20	80.37	92.77
4 loans	BBB	0.85	1.15	1.39	1.53	1.66	1.79	2.85	3.70	5.03	5.46	7.08	12.16	15.51	–	–	–	–
	BBB	1.08	1.95	2.63	3.02	3.37	3.69	6.12	7.67	9.52	10.01	11.41	14.83	18.87	26.15	44.41	–	–
	B	1.34	2.64	3.66	4.24	4.78	5.27	8.98	11.37	14.26	15.03	17.27	24.80	29.77	36.73	50.83	54.92	68.63
	CCC	0.56	1.78	2.76	3.34	3.87	4.36	8.28	10.96	14.48	15.48	18.69	25.30	31.03	39.30	56.33	61.12	75.40
16 loans	BBB	0.52	0.76	0.95	1.06	1.16	1.26	2.04	2.62	3.46	3.73	4.65	7.89	10.65	15.71	–	–	–
	BBB	0.56	1.00	1.36	1.57	1.77	1.96	3.56	4.80	6.64	7.22	9.32	14.94	18.84	24.52	37.40	41.62	57.76
	B	0.66	1.13	1.52	1.76	1.97	2.18	3.96	5.37	7.51	8.19	10.70	16.79	21.69	29.15	45.94	51.00	67.00
	CCC	0.34	0.68	0.97	1.14	1.30	1.46	2.76	3.77	5.27	5.74	7.44	13.99	19.96	28.77	47.74	53.27	70.41
64 loans	BBB	0.77	1.29	1.70	1.94	2.17	2.38	4.07	5.30	7.03	7.55	9.36	14.40	17.82	22.94	35.87	40.66	–
	BBB	0.74	1.40	1.93	2.24	2.53	2.80	4.97	6.54	8.71	9.36	11.58	18.04	23.01	30.66	48.02	53.21	69.21
	B	0.52	0.95	1.33	1.56	1.79	2.00	4.03	5.79	8.67	9.64	13.33	21.39	27.55	36.45	54.85	60.04	75.60
	CCC	0.75	1.38	1.91	2.22	2.52	2.80	5.20	7.09	9.94	10.85	14.15	23.13	30.99	41.82	62.25	67.54	82.22
256 loans	BBB	0.74	1.29	1.72	1.96	2.19	2.40	4.07	5.23	6.77	7.21	8.68	17.11	22.32	30.33	48.46	53.84	–
	BBB	0.89	1.60	2.15	2.47	2.77	3.04	5.15	6.58	8.43	8.96	10.64	17.92	23.37	31.99	52.09	58.11	76.12
	B	0.96	1.63	2.16	2.48	2.77	3.05	5.33	7.05	9.53	10.31	13.04	22.48	29.52	39.46	59.14	64.48	79.91
	CCC	0.60	1.30	1.87	2.21	2.53	2.82	5.27	7.09	9.69	10.48	13.25	22.97	31.04	42.13	62.94	68.30	83.07

(b)

	AAA	AA+	AA	AA−	A+	A	A−	BBB+	BBB	BBB−	BB+	BB	BB−	B+	B	B−	CCC
1 loan	0.95	3.00	4.71	5.74	6.71	7.62	15.38	21.33	30.06	32.78	42.48	62.52	70.63	70.77	83.15	86.86	92.77
4 loans	0.96	1.88	2.61	3.03	3.42	3.78	6.56	8.43	10.82	11.49	13.61	19.27	23.80	34.06	50.52	58.02	72.01
16 loans	0.52	0.89	1.20	1.38	1.55	1.71	3.08	4.14	5.72	6.22	8.03	13.40	17.79	24.54	43.69	48.63	65.06
64 loans	0.69	1.26	1.72	1.99	2.25	2.49	4.57	6.18	8.59	9.35	12.11	19.24	24.84	32.97	50.25	55.36	75.68
256 loans	0.80	1.45	1.98	2.28	2.56	2.83	4.96	6.49	8.61	9.24	11.41	20.12	26.56	35.98	55.66	61.18	79.70

pools. If the structured product is 5% of the bank portfolio, capital charges for 1-loan securitizations are several times higher than those for securitizations of well-diversified pools. On the other hand, when structured product pools are very small compared to the wider bank portfolio, capital charges for tranches of widely diversified pool structured products are systematically higher than for those of low-granularity structured products.

In fact, the granularity results shown in Tables 5–7 suggest that there is a significant size effect even leaving aside the granularity of the structured product pools in question. Comparing the model-based capital calculations we report for large structured product exposures with those for negligibly small structured product exposures, it is apparent that the latter have capital charges about a third to a half higher in many cases, even if one restricts attention to the high-granularity calculations.

Sector effects

To investigate the impact on capital charges of the sector from which the underlying assets are taken, we ran a series of simulations under different assumptions about asset correlation and loss given default. The sectors we looked at included: (i) credit card receivables; (ii) residential mortgages; (iii) other retail; (iv) small and medium enterprises (SME); and (v) commercial and industrial (C&I). The assumptions adopted coincided with the assumptions made in work completed as part of the parameterisation of the internal ratings based (IRB) approach on capital charges for whole loans from these sectors held on balance sheet.

The assumptions on asset correlation and loss given default are given in Table 8. The correlation assumption for residential mortgages was set relatively high in the work on the IRB in an attempt to

Table 8 Assumed asset correlation parameters and LGD

	C&I	Credit cards	Retail	MBS	SME
ρ_{BBB}	0.223	0.132	0.155	0.150	0.203
ρ_{BB}	0.181	0.086	0.114	0.150	0.161
ρ_{B}	0.124	0.024	0.034	0.150	0.104
ρ_{CCC}	0.120	0.020	0.020	0.150	0.100
LGD	0.45	0.8	0.75	0.25	0.45

proxy for their relatively long maturity. Rather than adjust this to more plausibly low levels, we preferred to maintain consistency with the IRB parameterisation work by adopting the same correlation.

The results of our simulations for underlying assets from different sectors are shown in Table 9. As usual, the rows correspond to different underlying pool credit qualities and the columns correspond to different ratings of individual tranches. All the calculations are performed assuming thin tranches and 60% correlation between the underlying pool common factor and the common factor driving the wider bank portfolio.

The consistent finding is that appropriate capital charges for retail exposures to structured product tranches with retail underlying pools are lower than for exposures to tranches with C&I or SME pools. Among structures with retail pools, those requiring highest capital are those with mortgage pools. These results reflect the different assumptions about correlations shown in Table 8. The differences between capital charges across retail and corporate underlying pools disappear for tranches with very low ratings (ie, sub BB−). However, they appear consistently for tranches with higher ratings and are most marked when the credit quality of the underlying pools is low.

Maturity effects

Table 10 shows capital charges by rating category generated using the *Portfolio Risk Tracker* model for several maturities. In each case, the maturities of the structured product and of the underlying pool of loans are assumed to be equal. The numbers shown in the table are obtained by fitting curves to capital calculations for three different underlying credit qualities (BBB, BB and B) and then averaging the capital charges for these three curves evaluated at the benchmark expected loss levels corresponding to the ratings.[j]

The results provide evidence of a clear maturity effect. Sampling errors in the Monte Carlo results mean the AAA and AA results are not monotonically increasing in maturity but for lower rating categories an obvious upward trend in capital charges is evident as maturity rises.

Even though maturity affects the appropriate capital charge for tranches with particular ratings, it is not obvious that the total

Table 9 Pykhtin–Dev-based tranche capital charges, assuming 60% correlation and thin tranche structure, for: (a) credit card receivables pool; (b) residential mortgages pool; (c) other retail pool; and (d) small and medium enterprises pool

(a)

	AAA	AA+	AA	AA−	A+	A	A−	BBB+	BBB	BBB−	BB+	BB	BB−	B+	B	B−	CCC
BBB	0.61	0.94	1.25	1.45	1.61	1.76	3.33	4.4	6.2	6.8	8.7	14.1	19.8	24.8	45.2	48.2	56.5
BB	0.60	0.93	1.24	1.41	1.59	1.77	3.30	4.5	6.5	7.1	9.0	15.1	20.9	28.9	48.3	54.2	69.8
B	0.38	0.65	0.88	1.03	1.18	1.32	2.51	3.4	4.9	5.5	7.0	12.1	16.8	24.1	43.1	48.0	65.3
CCC	0.16	0.32	0.46	0.53	0.60	0.67	1.39	2.1	3.4	3.8	5.5	12.3	17.9	26.2	46.1	51.8	69.7
Average	0.44	0.71	0.95	1.10	1.24	1.38	2.63	3.61	5.24	5.79	7.57	13.41	18.87	25.99	45.68	50.52	65.32

(b)

	AAA	AA+	AA	AA−	A+	A	A−	BBB+	BBB	BBB−	BB+	BB	BB−	B+	B	B−	CCC
BBB	0.48	0.81	1.15	1.35	1.44	1.52	2.42	3.3	4.9	5.4	7.6	11.2	11.9	13.5	20.1	23.1	37.5
BB	0.62	0.95	1.28	1.50	1.66	1.81	3.41	4.7	6.4	7.0	9.4	15.0	20.5	29.4	45.5	52.8	65.2
B	0.64	0.98	1.32	1.51	1.69	1.87	3.52	5.0	6.9	7.6	9.9	16.9	23.2	32.6	53.7	59.5	76.2
CCC	0.45	0.79	1.06	1.24	1.42	1.60	3.12	4.4	6.4	7.0	9.2	16.1	22.3	32.1	54.3	60.5	77.8
Average	0.54	0.88	1.21	1.40	1.55	1.70	3.12	4.35	6.14	6.77	9.03	14.78	19.47	26.92	43.39	48.99	64.17

(c)

	AAA	AA+	AA	AA−	A+	A	A−	BBB+	BBB	BBB−	BB+	BB	BB−	B+	B	B−	CCC
BBB	0.65	1.00	1.31	1.49	1.67	1.85	3.39	4.8	6.5	7.1	9.4	14.9	20.9	26.6	47.5	49.9	58.5
BB	0.65	1.01	1.32	1.52	1.71	1.89	3.50	4.8	6.9	7.5	9.7	16.4	21.8	30.7	50.6	57.3	72.8
B	0.46	0.77	1.02	1.19	1.36	1.50	2.86	3.9	5.6	6.1	8.0	13.7	18.5	26.7	46.5	51.8	68.9
CCC	0.20	0.34	0.48	0.58	0.67	0.77	1.76	2.7	4.5	5.1	7.4	13.0	17.9	26.0	45.5	51.7	69.8
Average	0.49	0.78	1.03	1.19	1.35	1.50	2.88	4.07	5.84	6.42	8.62	14.48	19.77	27.50	47.50	52.69	67.48

(d)

	AAA	AA+	AA	AA−	A+	A	A−	BBB+	BBB	BBB−	BB+	BB	BB−	B+	B	B−	CCC
BBB	0.68	1.04	1.35	1.53	1.72	1.90	3.49	4.9	6.7	7.3	9.3	15.4	19.6	28.8	39.9	42.3	54.0
BB	0.68	1.05	1.36	1.57	1.77	1.95	3.62	5.0	7.0	7.7	10.0	16.8	22.9	31.5	51.5	59.0	71.4
B	0.63	1.00	1.33	1.51	1.70	1.88	3.57	4.9	6.9	7.6	9.9	16.8	22.7	32.3	53.5	59.7	76.2
CCC	0.44	0.88	1.22	1.41	1.60	1.79	3.39	4.7	6.7	7.4	9.7	16.7	22.7	32.7	54.6	60.6	77.9
Average	0.61	0.99	1.31	1.51	1.70	1.88	3.51	4.88	6.86	7.50	9.73	16.43	21.97	31.33	49.87	55.42	69.88

Table 10 *Portfolio Risk Tracker* tranche capital charges for highly granular BB-rated small structures with different maturities

	AAA	AA+	AA	AA−	A−	A+	A+	BBB+	BBB	BBB−	BB+	BB	BB−	B+	B	B−	CCC
1 year	0.54	0.99	1.36	1.58	1.77	1.96	3.50	4.63	6.25	6.75	8.75	14.78	19.87	28.30	49.53	56.21	76.26
2 years	0.17	0.86	1.72	1.89	2.27	2.70	4.99	6.98	9.30	11.83	14.65	20.50	26.31	35.74	55.72	62.58	78.81
3 years	0.67	1.55	2.68	2.80	3.31	3.93	6.29	8.55	10.91	14.59	18.66	24.57	30.93	40.79	58.84	65.15	77.46
4 years	1.41	2.53	3.86	3.99	4.62	5.45	7.88	10.38	12.86	17.32	20.97	26.49	32.83	42.27	56.79	61.28	67.66
5 years	1.29	2.49	3.82	3.96	4.67	5.62	7.96	10.51	13.03	17.83	23.05	29.14	35.98	45.27	57.17	60.41	64.02

0.5 recovery rate was assumed.

Table 11 *Portfolio Risk Tracker* total capital charges for a BB-rated pool on and off balance sheet

Maturity	Whole loans IRB	Off balance sheet (RBA thin)	Off balance sheet (RBA thick)
1	8.0	5.8	5.4
2	9.1	8.2	7.9
3	10.2	10.4	10.1
4	11.3	13.2	12.9
5	12.4	15.7	15.5

capital for a structured transaction (ie, the sum of the capital for all the tranches if they are held by banks) will be inappropriate under the RBA if maturity is higher. The reason behind this is that raising the maturity of the structure and of the underlying assets may lead to a greater fraction of the tranches having lower ratings and hence being subject to the relatively high capital charges the RBA imposes for low-rated tranche exposures.

This point is confirmed by the results shown in Table 11. This compares total RBA capital for a structured transaction entirely held by banks with the capital that a bank would have to hold against the underlying loans under the IRB approach if the loans were held on balance sheet. As one may see, the total RBA capital rises substantially as maturity increases, reflecting the fact that the proportion of the deal subject to full deduction increases with maturity.

For the reader's convenience, Table 12 shows the capital charges in the October 2002 Basel proposal.[6] Information about the data inputs employed in our calculations is available from the authors upon request.

CONCLUDING REMARKS

This chapter has documented an approach one may use to calculate ratings based capital charges for exposures to structured product tranches. We have employed: (i) a simple analytical model, the Pykhtin–Dev model; and (ii) a more elaborate Monte Carlo model, *Portfolio Risk Tracker*. When *Portfolio Risk Tracker* is restricted to cases covered by the Pykhtin–Dev model, the two approaches yield identical results. The *Portfolio Risk Tracker* approach permits one to

Table 12 Tranche capital charges in October 2002 Basel proposals

External rating	Thin tranche capital charge (%)	Thick tranche capital charge (%)
AAA	0.96	0.56
AA+	1.2	0.8
AA	1.2	0.8
AA−	1.2	0.8
A+	1.6	1.6
A	1.6	1.6
A−	1.6	1.6
BBB+	4	4
BBB	6	6
BBB−	8	8
BB+	20	20
BB	34	34
BB−	52	52
Below B+ and unrated	Deduction	Deduction

analyse capital under a wider set of situations, for example, when the structured product is large or of maturity greater than one year. (It can also handle many real-world complications of structured products, such as collateral and interest coverage triggers, reinvestment periods and more or less aggressive reinvestment policies by collateral managers, but these features of the model are not employed in this study.)

We have focussed on: (i) the consistency of ratings-based capital weights with the capital that originators would have to hold if they maintained loans on balance sheet; (ii) on the consistency of the RBA weights proposed by the Basel Committee with model-based measurements of appropriate capital requirements under different assumptions; and (iii) on granularity and maturity effects.

We conclude that, for all except AAA tranches, the capital requirements for investment quality tranches are broadly consistent with the model-based capital charges under the assumption that the correlation between risk factors driving the structured exposure pool and the bank's wider portfolio are about 60%.

On granularity, we find that there is a case for an upward adjustment in capital for low-granularity structured products when the structured product exposure in question contributes a significant fraction of the credit risk of the bank involved. When the structured product exposure is negligibly small compared with the bank's wider portfolio, the high-granularity charges are a conservative estimate of what the true capital should be.

Considering the sectors of underlying assets, we find that tranches of structures with underlying pools of retail exposures generally merit less capital than tranches of structures with corporate (either SME or C&I) underlying exposures. This reflects the differences in the asset correlations of exposures coming from these different sectors.

On maturity, we find that longer maturity structures have consistently higher capital charges than one-year maturity structures. In some cases, the longer maturity leads to capital charges that are more than twice as high. However, when structures are of longer maturity, a greater fraction of the total par value of the deal tends to have a lower rating. The effective supervisory over-ride in the RBA by which B-rated tranches and below are deducted from capital means that total capital is significantly higher for long maturities. Hence, despite the lack of an explicit adjustment for maturity in the RBA, the total capital for longer maturity structures is therefore relatively conservative.

1 *Portfolio Risk Tracker* is Standard and Poor's credit portfolio model. The authors of this paper have worked with Standard and Poor's on the development of this model. The model permits one to calculate economic capital for investments in securitisation tranches held within larger portfolios of credit exposures and is hence well suited for analysing appropriate capital charges for structured products. *Portfolio Risk Tracker* is a registered trademark.

2 A related model was developed earlier by Lucas *et al* (2001).

3 The benchmark expected losses for several maturities are given in Table 11.

4 See Basel Committee on Banking Supervision (2002).

5 Of course, for a given rating category, the benchmark expected loss for the three-year case is distinctly higher than that for the one-year case.

6 The proposals have changed slightly since that date and may conceivably evolve in the future. Under the latest proposals (see Basel Committee on Banking Supervision (2004)), the base capital charges are AAA 0.96%, AA 1.2%, A+ 1.44%, A, 0.96%, A− 1.6%, BBB+ 2.8%, BBB 4.8%, BBB− 8%, BB+ 20%, BB 34%, BB− 52%, sub-BB deduction. Thick tranches no longer receive special treatment but the senior tranche in a structure has capital charges: AAA 0.56%, AA 0.64%, A+ 0.8%, A, 0.96%, A− 1.6%, BBB+ 2.8%, BBB 4.8% and base case charges for BBB− and below. If a structure has a low granularity pool, the capital charges are AAA 1.6%, AA 2.0%, A+ 2.8%, A 2.8%, A− 2.8% and base case charges for BBB+ and below.

REFERENCES

Basel Committee on Banking Supervision, 2004, "Basel II: International Convergence of Capital Measurement and Capital Standards: A Revised Framework", Basel Committee Publications No. 107, June.

Basel Committee on Banking Supervision, 2004, "Second Working Paper on the Treatment of Asset Securitisations", October.

Duffie, D., and N. Garleanu, 2001, "Risk and Valuation of Collateralized Debt Obligations", *Financial Analysts Journal,* **57**(1), pp. 41–59.

Gordy, M. B., 2003, "A Risk-Factor Model Foundation for Ratings-Based Bank Capital Rules", *Journal of Financial Intermediation,* **12**(3), pp. 199–232.

Gordy, M., and D. Jones, 2003, "Random Tranches", *Risk,* pp. 78–83, March.

Jarrow, R. A., D. Lando, and S. M. Turnbull, 1997, "A Markov Model for the Term Structure of Credit Spreads", *Review of Financial Studies,* **10**, pp. 481–523.

Kijima, M., and K. Komoribayashi, 1998, "A Markov Chain Model for Valuing Credit Risk Derivatives", *Journal of Derivatives,* **5**, pp. 97–108, Fall.

Longstaff, F., and E. Schwartz, 2001, "Valuing American Options by Simulation: A Simple Least Squares Approach", *Review of Financial Studies,* **14**, pp. 113–47.

Lucas, A., P. Klaassen, P. Spreij, and S. Straetmans, 2001, "An Analytic Approach to Credit Risk of Large Corporate Bond and Loan Portfolios", *Journal of Banking and Finance,* **25**(9), pp. 1635–64 (Erratum *Journal of Banking and Finance,* **26**(1), pp. 201–2).

Peretyatkin, V., and W. Perraudin, 2002, "Expected Loss and Probability of Default Approaches to Rating Collateralised Debt Obligations and the Scope for 'Ratings Shopping' ", in M. K. Ong (ed), *Credit Ratings: Methodologies, Rationale and Default Risk* pp. 495–506 (London: Risk Books).

Pykhtin, M., and A. Dev, 2002a, "Credit Risk in Asset Securitizations: Analytical Model", *Risk,* pp. S26–S32, March.

Pykhtin, M., and A. Dev, 2002b, "Credit Risk in Asset Securitizations: The Case of CDOs", *Risk,* pp. S16–S20, May.

Vasicek, O., 1991, Limiting Loan Loss Probability Distribution, KMV mimeo, August.

15

An Empirical Test of Basel Risk Weights Applied to Securitisation

Alexander Batchvarov; Domenico Picone; Peter-Paul Hoogbruin, Jeroen de Smet, Viktor Tchistiakov

Merrill Lynch; Royal Bank of Scotland; ING Group

In May 2003, BIS published the results of the Quantitative Impact Study 3 (QIS) as well as the Consultative Paper 2 (CP2). Both documents were expected by the securitisation industry in anticipation of resolution of some long-standing concerns the industry had with regards to the treatment of securitisation under the new Basel proposal. Unfortunately, CP2 not only did not put such concerns to rest, but actually exacerbated them. An issue of particular contention is the proposed risk weightings of securitised products under all approaches – standardised, ratings-based approach (RBA) and supervisory formula approach (SFA), and as a corollary – the calibration of the formulae used to derive such risk weightings. In the pronouncement of the Basel Committee press release, dated 10 October 2003, there is an indication on the need to simplify the treatment of asset securitisation, including the replacement SFA with a less complex approach, to change the overall treatment of expected versus unexpected credit losses, and to revisit the treatment of certain credit risk mitigation techniques. Given the extension of the

This chapter is a result of the work of the European Securitisation Forum (ESF) Quantitative Group on the treatment of securitisation under BIS capital measurements and standards guidelines. The authors would like to thank Tom Wilde, Member, ESF Quant Group and Director of Credit Susse Corporation, for his insightful comments, critiques and recommendations in the process of the preparation of this chapter. The views expressed in this chapter are of the authors only.

working period for the final BIS document until mid 2004, we certainly hoped that the time could be wisely used to address what we believed to be the inconsistencies and harshness in the treatment of securitisation. In order to better understand the positions of the regulator and the securitisation industry with regards to securitisation risk weightings, we embarked on a project to analyse real transactions in several asset classes, use industry models to assign risk weights to their tranches and compare those risk weights with the respective risk weights arrived at by using CP guidelines.

The publication of the BIS International Convergence of Capital Measurements and Capital Standards in June 2004 revealed very little changes in the capital treatment of securitisation compared to the draft versions available, when the work on this chapter started. Hence, the review and conclusions we present here remain valid and need to be addressed, so that the capital treatment of securitisation exposures is better aligned to the actual risks they represent, which we believe not to be fully the case at present.

STUDY SET UP

For the purpose of the empirical work, we collected publicly available data on 15 European transactions, covering the following types of assets: (a) Residential Mortgages – 3 RMBS; (b) Retail Revolving Exposures/Credit Cards – 6 credit card ABS; (c) Other Retail/Auto Loans – 6 auto loan ABS. We also relied on publicly available information regarding losses, recoveries and yield spreads with regards to the above asset classes, as well as on deal specific structural and performance information. The choice of the above asset classes was meant to reflect their prevalence on the securitisation market, the wealth of available data, as well as the retail nature of the exposures, as opposed to corporate exposures, which we understand have been used to calibrate securitisation exposures' risk weights.

We calculated the Risk Weights using four different models and formulae:

A *Proprietary model*, developed by European commercial banks for usage by the European securitisation forum (ESF) quantitative group.

B *Perraudin & Peretyatkin or Pyhktin & Dev models* as the former is widely used by banks' risk management department and the former was used as a basis for the development of the RBA approach and risk weights.

Both A and B are single factor models and we apply them, as we understand such an approach has been adopted by the regulators and to the extent that we have information as to how they have been used by them. We used single factor models, even though some banks may be in possession of more complex and precise multi-factor models.

C *SFA* as proposed under CP2. In our SFA calculations we deliberately eliminated the floor in order to establish the real risk weights determined by the formulae. By eliminating the floor we meant to exclude one of the more apparent regulatory over rides in establishing SFA risk weights. In addition, by comparing the actual risk weights, computed by the models, with the floor, we could determine its appropriateness.

D *RBA* prescribed risk weights for the respective deal tranches, as stipulated by CP2.

In our study, we calculated risk weights for each of the tranches of the selected transactions using all four model approaches and presented the results together for comparison purposes. We carried out the calculations twice: by including and excluding excess spread in each transaction. The reason for such distinction is our belief that: (1) excess spread plays an important part in the securitisation deal and acts as the first layer of protection to bondholders as opposed to the retained "equity piece", which acts as a second layer of protection; (2) excess spread levels and the role it plays, differs significantly by asset class; and (3) it is not fully taken into consideration either in the rating process or in regulatory approaches, as we understand them. In order to maintain a conservative bias, however, we have assumed quantities of excess spread that are significantly lower than the actual excess spread levels of the transactions in question.

Finally, we have worked on the premise that regulatory capital is sized for a one year period in line with assumptions for other types of exposures, rather than for the life of the securitisation exposure. However, we note that credit enhancement and related expected losses for different securitisation exposures are sized by the rating agencies for the life of the respective securitisation transaction.

DESCRIPTION OF THE MODELS

We first present a very brief general outline of the major differences between Model A and B. Figures 1 and 2 present the assumed relations between the assets in the bank portfolio and the securitised pool of assets for both models. Both models are driven by a systematic factor X. In Model A this is sufficient to derive a capital percentage for a tranche. In Model B another systematic factor Y is introduced which in turn is related to X. In Model B a capital percentage follows in a conditional expectation approach, whereas in Model A this additional condition is not needed. The following sections give a comprehensive description of the mathematical derivation and contain the values of the applied parameters.

Industry proprietary model

We have used a proprietary single factor model and applied it to the same sample transactions. The proprietary model was formulated

Figure 1 Scheme of correlation structure for Model A: ρ_s and ρ_p are prescribed

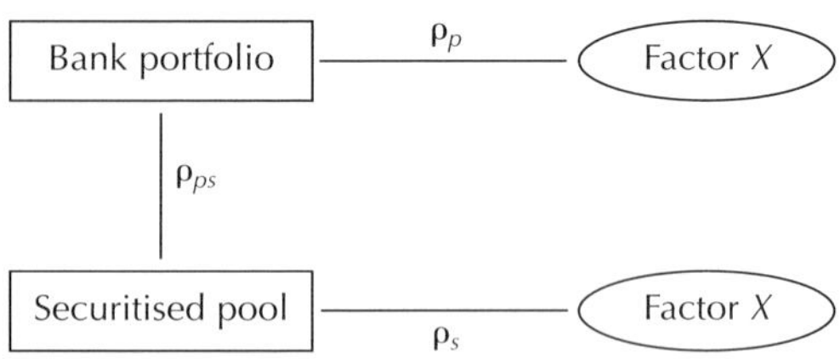

Figure 2 Scheme of correlation structure for Model B: ρ_Y and ρ are prescribed

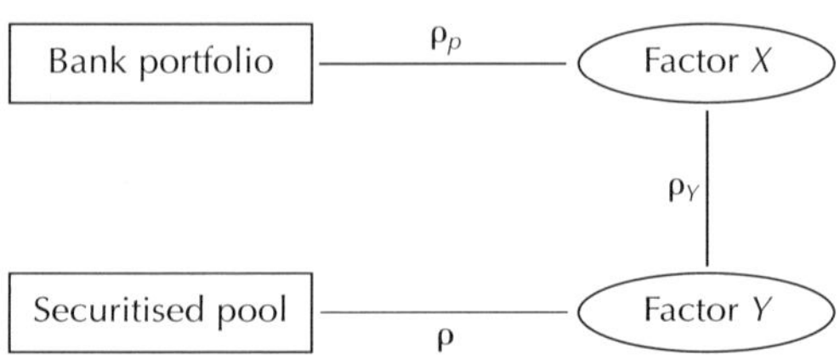

exclusively for this study. The correlation of a tranche from this pool with the Basel super-portfolio was determined in order to find the Unexpected Loss Contribution of this tranche. After multiplication by the Capital Multiple that follows from the superportfolio parameterisation, and after addition of the Expected Loss part of the tranche, an Economic Capital figure follows and the equivalent risk weighting can be derived.

Introduction

We can use the analytic Vasicek distribution for the credit loss distribution when we assume a homogeneous infinitesimally fine-grained portfolio (see Risk, 2002). In the following, $f(x)$ is the normal distribution and $N(x)$ is the cumulative standard for normal distribution defined as

$$N(x) = \int_{-\infty}^{x} \phi(x_0)\,\mathrm{d}x \tag{1}$$

and $N^{-1}(x)$ is its inverse. In the following, the subscripts p, s, and t denote the *portfolio*, *securitised pool*, and a *tranche* of the securitised pool, respectively.

Portfolio

Like in model B, the asset or loss correlation of the portfolio with a single factor X is ρ_p, and the individual assets can cause a loss with a probability of default p_p. The Expected Loss EL_p is then given by

$$\mathrm{EL}_p = \int_{-\infty}^{\infty} L_p(x)\phi(x)\,\mathrm{d}x \tag{2}$$

where

$$L_p(x) = \mathrm{LGD}_p N\left(\frac{N^{-1}(p_p) - \sqrt{\rho_p}\,x}{\sqrt{1-\rho_p}}\right) \tag{3}$$

Here, the LGD_p is the Loss Given Default. The variance of the portfolio σ_p^2 is given by

$$\sigma_p^2 = \int_{-\infty}^{\infty} L_p^2(x)\phi(x)\,\mathrm{d}x - \mathrm{EL}_p^2 \tag{4}$$

Securitised asset pool

Given is a homogeneous pool of assets in a securitisation structure with single factor loss correlation, probability of default, and loss given default ρ_s, p_s, and LGD_s, respectively. Substituting these in Equations (2) to (4) gives expressions EL_s, L_s and σ_s^2.

Tranche characteristics

The Expected Loss EL_t for a tranche starting at its lower bound l_l and capped at its upper bound l_u we find

$$EL_t = \int_{-\infty}^{\infty} L_t(l_l, l_u, x)\phi(x)\,dx \tag{5}$$

where

$$L_t(l_l, l_u, x) = \max[0, \min[l_u - l_l, L_s(x) - l_l]] \tag{6}$$

and $L_s(x)$ is the asset pool equivalent of Equation (3). The variance is given by

$$\sigma_t^2 = \int_{-\infty}^{\infty} L_t(l_l, l_u, x)^2 \phi(x)\,dx - EL_t^2 \tag{7}$$

The probability of default of a tranche p_t is

$$p_t = 1 - N\left(\frac{1}{\sqrt{\rho_S}}\left[\sqrt{1-\rho_s}\,N^{-1}(l_l) - N^{-1}(p_s)\right]\right) \tag{8}$$

Tranche – Portfolio relations

The covariance σ_{tp}^2 between the tranche and the portfolio is given by

$$\sigma_{tp}^2 = \int_{-\infty}^{\infty} L_p L_t(l_l, l_u, x)\phi(x)\,dx \tag{9}$$

and finally we have for the single factor loss correlation between the tranche and the portfolio

$$\rho_{tp} = \frac{\sigma_{tp}^2 - EL_t EL_p}{\sigma_p \sigma_t} \tag{10}$$

This is the relation which is needed to determine the Economic Capital (EC) of the tranche when it is added to the much larger portfolio, ie, the superportfolio (see the following section). Note that substitution of all expressions available for the portfolio reveals that the LGD_p is of no influence to the tranche-portfolio correlation. Furthermore, the methodology can also be used when the pool is extracted from the portfolio. Normally, the EC amount of the tranche is given by

$$\text{EC}_t = \text{UL}_t \text{RR}_t \text{CM}_{C_t} = \text{ULC}_t \text{CM}_{C_t} \tag{11}$$

where RR_t is the Retained Risk of the tranche, the UL_t is the stand-alone Unexpected Loss of the tranche, ie, the standard deviation of the losses of the tranche σ_t, and the ULC_t is the Unexpected Loss Contribution. This expression has to be corrected for purposes of this study later. The Capital Multiple CM_{C_t} is a constant that depends on the applied confidence level C_l. The ULC_t is given by

$$\text{ULC}_t = \frac{\sigma_t^2 + \sigma_p(\sigma_t \rho_{tp})}{\sigma_p}$$

The Basel II "superportfolio"

Basel assumes an overall reference portfolio. This "superportfolio" is denoted by subscript B. We set the following "superportfolio" characteristics

$$\begin{aligned} \rho_p &= \rho_B = 0.2 \\ p_p &= p_B = 0.007 \\ \text{LGD}_p &= \text{LGD}_B = 0.50 \end{aligned} \tag{12}$$

and the confidence level C_l for which capital has to be allocated is $C_l = 0.995$. With these parameters, we can extract the CM from Equation (11) that is applicable to this superportfolio and thus the EC_B for which the loss at C_l is given by $L_B(C_l)$:

$$\begin{aligned} \text{CM}_B &= \frac{L_B(C_l) - \text{EL}_B}{\text{UL}_B} \\ &= \left(\text{LGD}_p N\left[\frac{N^{-1}(p_B)}{\sqrt{1-\rho_B}} + N^{-1}(C_l)\sqrt{\frac{\rho_B}{1-\rho}} \right] - \text{EL}_B \right) \text{UL}_B^{-1} \\ &= 5.5924 \end{aligned} \tag{13}$$

The definition of Basel regulatory capital incorporates the EL part of an exposure. Therefore, we have to adapt Equation (11) for the EL_t contribution:

$$EC_{B_t} = CM_B ULC_{B_t} + EL_t \quad (14)$$

where subscripts B_t refer to the tranche characteristics with respect to the Basel II superportfolio. A Basel Risk Weight RW_t is then given by

$$RW_t = \frac{EC_{B_t}}{0.08(l_u - l_b)} \quad (15)$$

Perraudin & Peretyakin and Pyhktin & Dev models

We understand that Perraudin and Peretyatkin have used a model similar to Pykhtin and Dev's model (2002) to derive the floor of 56 bps and other risk weights.[1] As we have had limited access to information and description of the Perraudin and Peretyatkin work, in order to determine which assumptions they have used in their model, we have attempted to recalculate the floor risk weight using the Pyhtkin and Dev model.

The Pykhtin and Dev model

In our exposition, we have assumed infinite granularity throughout. We have updated this section to allow for different pairwise asset correlations between assets in the pool and in the bank portfolio. This reflects example calculations (in Tables 2 and 3) in which the correlation in the pool is set equal to the IRB correlation function for the pool asset class.

Bank portfolio. The IRB model is assumed to be driven by a single systematic factor X. Correlations to the factor are labelled as ρ_p. We will reserve the more usual ρ for the correlation parameter in the pool underlying the securitisation, as this is the correlation that appears in the IRB approach. This ρ is equivalent to the ρ_s used in model A. Thus, each obligor A in the bank portfolio has asset process

$$Z_A = \rho_p^{1/2} X + (1-\rho_p)^{1/2} \varepsilon_A \quad (16)$$

where ε_A is specific behaviour of A and is independent of the systematic factor, ie, everything else.

Securitised asset pool. IRB model is again assumed to be driven by a systematic factor, Y, having a correlation of $\sqrt{\rho_Y}$, with X (ρ_Y will be taken to be 60%). We can write, as holds for any pair of standard normal variables

$$Y = \rho_Y^{1/2} X + (1-\rho_Y)^{1/2} \eta \quad \textbf{(17)}$$

where η is independent of X and Y. In the securitisation pool the systematic factor is Y, and the equation analogous to (16) for the securitisation pool is

$$Z_B = \rho^{1/2} Y + (1-\rho)^{1/2} \varepsilon_B \quad \textbf{(18)}$$

where we have used Y instead of X as systematic factor, and ρ for the asset correlation relevant to the pool asset class. If the pool asset class is retail, then one might argue that ρ should take on the values set by the IRB approach for retail. It happens that only ρ, and not ρ_p enters the capital Equation (30), so there is no need to worry about the composition of the rest of the bank's portfolio except in terms of the parameter ρ_Y, which describes the correlation between the two pools of assets.

By substituting (17) into (18) we have, for an asset in the securitised asset pool

$$Z_B = \rho^{1/2} \rho_Y^{1/2} X + \rho^{1/2} (1-\rho_Y)^{1/2} \eta + (1-\rho)^{1/2} \varepsilon_B \quad \textbf{(19)}$$

where X, η and ε_A ε_B are pairwise independent.

The correlation between an asset price in the bank portfolio and one in the securitisation pool is, from (19) and (16):

$$\text{corr}(Z_A, Z_B) = \rho_p^{1/2} \rho^{1/2} \rho_Y^{1/2} \quad \textbf{(20)}$$

For model A it is possible to derive a similar correlation.

Formula for capital. Choose a confidence level q = 99.9%. Then by the conditional expectation theorem, the capital for any tranche held by the securitisation of the pool is given by

$$\text{Capital} = E(L \text{ from tranche} \mid X = X_q) \tag{21}$$

If F and f are the cumulative and marginal density functions of losses from a pool of assets, then the expected loss, $E(L)$, for a tranche from l_l to l_u is

$$E(L) = \int_{l_l}^{l_u} (x - l_l)\phi(x)\,dx + (l_u - l_l)\int_{l_u}^{1} \phi(x)\,dx \tag{22}$$

Integration by parts gives the alternate.

$$E(L) = \int_{l_l}^{l_u} 1 - F(x)\,dx = \int_{l_l}^{l_u} G(x)\,dx \tag{23a}$$

and the expected loss per unit of tranche, $E(\tilde{L})$ is

$$E(\tilde{L}) = \frac{1}{l_u - l_l}\int_{l_l}^{l_u} G(x)\,dx \tag{23b}$$

where $G = 1 - F$ is the marginal capital rate, which Pyhktin and Dev call the "complementary distribution function". In particular, if we condition on $X = X_q$ then (23b) gives the % capital requirement for the tranche consistent with the IRB approach in general.

To calculate (21) using (23a,b), we need the cumulative density of losses in the pool, but this must be conditional on $X = X_q$, to arrive at that loss at the confidence level of 99.9%. Using (19) we have

$$\begin{aligned} &P(Z_B \le N^{-1}(p_B) \mid X = X_q) \\ &= P\left(\varepsilon_B \le \frac{N^{-1}(p_s) - \rho^{1/2}\rho_Y^{1/2} - \rho^{1/2}(1-\rho_Y)^{1/2}\eta}{(1-\rho)^{1/2}}\right) \end{aligned} \tag{24}$$

ie, default probabilities in the pool conditional on $X = X_q$ are given by:

$$P(\eta) = N\left(\frac{N^{-1}(p_s) - \rho^{1/2}\rho_Y^{1/2}X_q - \rho^{1/2}(1-\rho_\gamma)^{1/2}\eta}{(1-\rho)^{1/2}}\right) \tag{25}$$

With given LGD_s in the loss of x corresponds to the conditional default rate of x/LGD_s, so

$$F(x) = P(P(\eta) \le x/\text{LGD}_s)$$
$$= P\left(N\left(\frac{N^{-1}(p_s) - \rho^{1/2}\rho_Y^{1/2}X_q - \rho_Y^{1/2}(1-\rho_Y)^{1/2}\eta}{(1-\rho)^{1/2}} \right) \le x/\text{LGD}_S \right) \quad (26)$$

which since η is unit normal, gives

$$F(x) = N\left(\frac{(1-\rho)^{1/2} N^{-1}(x/\text{LGD}_s) - N^{-1}(p_s) + \rho^{1/2}\rho_Y^{1/2}X_q}{\rho^{1/2}(1-\rho_Y)^{1/2}} \right) \quad (27)$$

The marginal rate is therefore

$$G(x) = 1 - N\left(\frac{(1-\rho)^{1/2} N^{-1}(x/\text{LGD}_s) - N^{-1}(p_s) + \rho^{1/2}\rho_Y{}^{1/2}X_q}{\rho^{1/2}(1-\rho_Y)^{1/2}} \right) \quad (28)$$

We understand this is the function arrived at by Perraudin and Peretyatkin.

Deriving RBA risk weights. As Perraudin and Peretyatkin mention, the formula (28) is not in itself sufficient to derive RBA risk weights, since they must come from the rating and not from characteristics of the underlying pool. Furthermore, we do not know the details of the model that Perraudin and Peretyatkin used to arrive at the final risk weights.

In our calibration exercise, we use the formulae above to calculate the floor of a AAA tranche with different credit supports, and com pare our results with the 56 bps that BIS CP2 uses for the calibration.

Our calibration exercise is based on the PD of 1 bp and LGD of 50%, we understand have been used, and it is applied to the AAA tranche only.

Step 1. If we look at the tranche unconditionally, then it is just an ordinary Merton portfolio with dependence given by (17), so the expected loss of a tranche, unconditional on X, $E(L_{\text{Unconditional}})$, can also be calculated, and is given by

$$E(L_{\text{Unconditional}}) = \int_{l_l}^{l_u} G_1(x)\,\mathrm{d}x \tag{29}$$

where

$$G_1(x) = 1 - N\left(\frac{(1-\rho)^{1/2}N^{-1}(x/\text{LGD}_s) - N^{-1}(p_s)}{\rho^{1/2}}\right) \tag{30}$$

Step 2. Assume a 1 bp p_t, ie, the PD of tranche, and an LGD_t of 50%, hence, the $E(L_{\text{Unconditional}})$ for a AAA rated tranche is 0.5 bp of the tranche notional.

Therefore, we can write (29) for a AAA rated tranche, with the $E(L_{\text{Unconditional}})$ set to 0.5 bps:

$$\frac{1}{1-l_l}\int_{l_l}^{1} G_1(x)\,\mathrm{d}x = 0.00005 \tag{31}$$

For a given choice of l_l, this condition determines the only free parameter which is the pool PD (p_s), *via* Equation (30).

Finally, we plug this value of p_s into Equation (29b) to get the capital % for the tranche.

Step 3. Repeat for various possible values of a realistic range say 5–20%. Provided the capital obtained is not extremely sensitive to l_l (since the risk weight does not depend on l_l), then some midpoint of the resulting capital numbers can be taken as the RBA risk weight.

Recalculation results. We tried the method (Steps 1–3) with the following results. Table 1: Calibration Results, with 50% LGD, $\rho = 20\%$, $\rho_Y = 60\%$, $q = 99.9\%$.

Conclusion and comments

1. Our results above are in broad agreement with Perraudin and Peretyatkin's. We have obtained about 65–75 bp where the authors have 56 bp.
2. We have not made any inappropriate, in our judgement, or undisclosed assumptions. We have assumed with regards to the

simulation of the Perraudin and Peretyatkin model and we have made assumptions only on the basis of clear information available to us.

3. However, a key piece of data on which the calculation depends is an assumed 1 bp "PD" for the AAA tranche or more particularly the corresponding 0.5 bp EL. This 0.5 bp seems to be arbitrary, not supported by underlying data – the "true" figure at this level is surely subject to much uncertainty. This criticism, by its nature, does not necessarily apply to the lower ratings.
4. An alternative, and in our opinion, better approach, that would not challenge the model or the correlation parameters, would be to proceed from direct evidence about PD in the underlying pool of assets rather than backing it out from the 0.5 bp EL. The unconditional EL, instead of being equal to an assumed 0.5 bp, would be an output parameter of the model. Such ELs being certainly very small, should be regarded as unobservable, there would be no question of any direct comparison of EL with experience. For example, we can ask what range of pool qualities, expressed in terms of PD, is needed in a pool of corporate assets to allow an 85% tranche to be rated AAA.
5. It seems possible that the backed out pool PD (p_s) is too high (see Table 1, row 2) relative to the actual pool characteristics which we suggest using as the inputs in note (4) above. In that case, the method described at (4) would give lower risk weights. In case 4, the PDs correspond to speculative grade ratings, where we have assumed that a 95% tranche of a BB pool could get a AAA rating, which in our experience is very unlikely. If so, Table 1 could be recalculated with realistic pool

Table 1 Spread reserve account

Three month average excess spread (%)	Reserve fund target (%)
4.5	0.0
4.0–4.5	1.5
3.5–4.0	2.0
3.0–3.5	3.0
3.0	4.0

Source: S&P

PD's for a more robust calibration of the floor risk weight in particular.

6. A natural extension of points 4 and 5, would be to extend the calibration exercise to different types of asset classes, ie, mortgages, credit cards, consumer loans, etc, and using real transaction data, in order to link the *unconditional* PD and EL to real capital structures.

SFA

These are established under Basel II CP2. In the SFA formulation used here the floor is deliberately removed from the original Basel II expression.

RBA

These are established under Basel II CP2.

MODELLING ASSUMPTIONS

In order to calculate the risk weights for different securitised tranches, a number of quantitative inputs need to be calculated. Below we describe the assumptions that we have made to arrive at the respective inputs.

Calculation of Kirb

Kirb for credit cards (revolving retail)

In calculating the Kirb, we have empirically checked that the revolving retail pools generate enough income to offset 75% of expected losses (ie, Future Margin Income $>2 \times$ Sigma of Charge-Offs).

Excess spread, reserve account and trapping

Excess Spread is generally defined as finance charge collections minus note interest, servicing fees, and charge-offs allocated to the respective note. It is the first layer of protection for note respective note. A portion of the excess spread is deposited into a Spread/Reserve Account and regulated by the terms of an agreement. Typically, the transaction agreements require a target reserve balance based on the current level of excess spread – this is known as a trapping mechanism: should the excess spread fall below certain level, it must be "trapped" in order to accumulate a defined level of reserve account. Deposits of excess spread cash in the reserve account are isolated legally from the originator and are available first to service amounts owing to the investor.

Credit cards (revolving retail). Credit card securitisations have ample amounts of excess spread and the mechanisms for its utilisation are common and widely used. An indicative example of a trapping mechanism is set up in Table 1.

Should the 3-month average excess spread (after covering charge-offs) drop below 3.5%, excess spread is trapped into the Spread/Reserve Account until the Spread/Reserve Account reaches 2.0%. In the model we produced, we assumed that the excess spread is between 3% and 4% pa, and thus, it is trapped into a reserve account until the Spread/Reserve reaches 2.5%. We believe 2.5% is a very conservative assumption, given that the excess spread in the credit card transactions in question varies in a range of between 6% and 12%.[2] We also verified that the excess spread of 2.5% is sufficient to cover the Kirb condition that allows offsetting 75% of expected losses in the following manner: Future Margin Income > [2 × Sigma of Charge-Offs + 2.5%].

Auto loans (other retail). In the five auto loan transactions, subject to our review, the Spread/Reserve Accounts are built up with excess spread during the revolving period (3 years in each deal considered) and are assumed to reach their maximum targets (3.5–5%) in a few months from the closing data. The minimum excess spread (after the Spread/Reserve Accounts are built) recognised by the rating agencies varies between 2% and 3%. For auto loan transaction number 2, information on the excess spread was not available. Auto loan transactions number 1 and 3 have also a trapping mechanism that captures excess spreads in case the delinquency or default rate triggers are hit. In those cases the trapping mechanism redirects the excess spread to the Spread/Reserve Account until the latter reaches 6%. As with credit cards, amounts are isolated legally and available first to investors in the auto-loan securitisation tranches. In our exercises we have used excess spread of 1%. We believe this to be a very conservative assumption given the experience of excess spread generated in auto loan transactions in Europe.

Residential MBS (Mortgages). The two MBS transactions benefit from two types of Reserve Funds:

- First Reserve Funds, which are partially funded at the closing date, and built up to the required amounts within few months from excess spread;
- Second Reserve Funds, which compensates for the loss of spread. In case spread reduces below a certain threshold (MBS transaction number 2 below 1.05%, MBS transaction number 3 below 0.95%), they will build up according to a trapping mechanism.

In general, measuring the impact of excess spread in a MBS transaction, in order to give the correct benefit to the Second Reserve Fund, is difficult. Excess spread varies according to prepayments, loan substitution and the collateral mix. The presence of the trapping mechanism avoids the decline of excess spread below a prudent level without replenishing Second Reserve Fund. All factors considered, we believe that we gave a conservative benefit to the excess spread by allowing 0.50% pa.

Losses

Losses in RMBS. Moody's estimates that the projected lifetime loss in a pool of UK residential mortgages with an average life of 8 years has a mean of 1.14% with a standard deviation of 1.24%.[3] The worst ever vintage, that of origination year 1989, experienced a lifetime loss of 4.5%. The average severity rate is estimated to be 24%, and the worst, again for 1989 vintage, at 45%. For a pool with the above loss characteristics, triple-A credit enhancement levels is estimated at 10.3% by Moody's. The three MBS transactions used in our empirical study are all UK originated and have an AAA enhancement level in the range of 9–12%. Therefore they are very close to Moody's results. Hence, we have used the following inputs in the MBS calculation: PD rate pa = 0.59% (1.14%/8/LGD) and LGD = 24%.

Losses in retail revolving/credit cards. The PD rate pa was derived from the transaction charge-offs published in Moody's deal Performance Overviews. An LGD of 75% was used in line with the assumptions for retail exposures, made by the regulators.

Losses in other retail/auto loans. Default statistics show that the cumulative default rate in a pool of European auto loans has a mean of 3.4% with an Average Life of 6 years. As result, we have used the following inputs in all Other Retail calculations: PD rate pa = 0.57% = 3.4%/6 and LGD = 75%.

Modifying the deals' capital structure to account for excess spread

The Excess Spread and the Reserve Account were treated as the unrated tranche of the securitisation. To arrive to the new capital structure, expressed in percentages, the Excess Spread and the Reserve Account were multiplied by the collateral size at the closing date of the transaction and added to the same collateral. The new collateral was used as the denominator for calculating the new percentages of the rated and unrated tranche (Excess Spread and Spread/Reserve Account).

For example, the Auto Loan transaction number 1 had a collateral with the value of €511 million at the closing date. The initial deal capital structure is the following: 96% of Aaa note, 4% of A2 note, 3.25% as the maximum of initial balance of the Reserve Account, and 1.0% as Excess Spread. The modified capital structure is: Aaa 92.08%, A2 3.84% and 4.08% as unrated. In those examples, where the Excess Spread is excluded, only the Reserve Account is treated as the unrated tranche.

RESULTS AND OBSERVATIONS

The numerical results of this empirical study are presented in Tables 2 and 3:

- The Table 2 is called *Summary without Excess Spread*, where the Risk Weights are calculated without the use of the Excess Spread that the transaction is expected to generate.
- The Table 3 is called *Summary with Excess Spread*, where we have used a conservative portion of the Excess Spread to offset losses.

A review of the tables' results suggests the following observations:

1. The alternative methodology, based on a proprietary model, produces results that closely replicate the results of the Pyhktin–Dev and Perraudin–Peretyakin models'.

Table 2 ESF Quant Group – Summary of transactions: ESF Quant Group, RBA, SFA and P–P (without excess spread benefit or trapping mechanisms)

Type		**Other Retail**					
Transaction		Auto Loan 1	Auto Loan 2	Auto Loan 3	Auto Loan 4	Auto Loan 5	Auto Loan 6
Pool PD		0.57%	0.57%	0.57%	0.57%	0.57%	2.78%
Pool LGD		75%	75%	75%	75%	75%	30%
Pool Maturity		5	5	5	5	5	5
Risk Weights							
Corporate (TO > 50)		14.04%	14.04%	14.04%	14.04%	14.04%	9.18%
Residential Mortgages (para 288)		5.53%	5.53%	5.53%	5.53%	5.53%	6.54%
Qualifying revolving exposures (para 289)		3.08%	3.08%	3.08%	3.08%	3.08%	2.25%
Other retail (para 301)		5.28%	5.28%	5.28%	5.28%	5.28%	4.06%
Correlations							
Corporate (TO > 50)		21.04%	21.04%	21.04%	21.04%	21.04%	14.99%
Residential Mortgages (para 288)		15.00%	15.00%	15.00%	15.00%	15.00%	15.00%
Qualifying revolving exposures (para 289)		8.78%	8.78%	8.78%	8.78%	8.78%	4.24%
Other retail (para 291)		14.30%	14.30%	14.30%	14.30%	14.30%	7.67%
N (or –1 indicates retail treatment)		−1	−1	−1	−1	−1	−1
K_IRB		**5.28%**	**5.28%**	**5.28%**	**5.28%**	**5.28%**	**4.06%**
Correlation in pool		**14.30%**	**14.30%**	**14.30%**	**14.30%**	**14.30%**	**7.67%**
Tranche structure							
Aaa	AAA	**92.98%**	**92.75%**	**92.98%**	**90.38%**	**90.48%**	**91.84%**
Aa3	AA−	0.00%	0.00%	0.00%	0.00%	0.00%	0.00%
A1	A+	0.00%	0.00%	0.00%	**5.77%**	**4.76%**	**5.34%**
A2	A	**3.87%**	**3.86%**	**3.87%**	0.00%	0.00%	0.00%
Baa1	BBB	0.00%	0.00%	0.00%	0.00%	0.00%	0.00%
Baa2	BBB−	0.00%	0.00%	0.00%	0.00%	0.00%	0.00%
Unrated	Unrated	**3.15%**	**3.38%**	**3.15%**	**3.85%**	**4.76%**	**2.82%**
		100.00%	**100.00%**	**100.00%**	**100.00%**	**100.00%**	**100.00%**
Perraudin – Peretyatkin or Pyhktin – Dev formula							
Aaa	AAA	*1.12%*	*0.97%*	*1.12%*	*0.20%*	*0.21%*	*0.00%*
Aa3	AA−	0.00%	0.00%	0.00%	0.00%	0.00%	0.00%
A1	A+	0.00%	0.00%	0.00%	*111.43%*	*74.71%*	*112.87%*
A2	A	*233.66%*	*204.51%*	*233.66%*	0.00%	0.00%	0.00%
Baa1	BBB	0.00%	0.00%	0.00%	0.00%	0.00%	0.00%
Baa2	BBB−	0.00%	0.00%	0.00%	0.00%	0.00%	0.00%
Unrated	Unrated	*1014.92%*	*982.35%*	*1014.92%*	*918.69%*	*802.51%*	*1126.46%*
P-P Expected Loss (BP)		*0.05*	*0.04*	*0.05*	*0.01*	*0.01*	*0.00*
ESF Quant Group ULC model							
Aaa	AAA	*0.34%*	*0.30%*	*0.30%*	*0.13%*	*0.14%*	*0.00%*
Aa3	AA−	0.00%	0.00%	0.00%	0.00%	0.00%	0.00%
A1	A+	0.00%	0.00%	0.00%	*57.51%*	*38.31%*	*61.86%*
A2	A	*83.97%*	*72.52%*	*76.32%*	0.00%	0.00%	0.00%
Baa1	BBB	0.00%	0.00%	0.00%	0.00%	0.00%	0.00%
Baa2	BBB−	0.00%	0.00%	0.00%	0.00%	0.00%	0.00%
Unrated	Unrated	*1250.00%*	*1208.30%*	*1272.59%*	*1092.27%*	*914.71%*	*12150.00%*

Revolving Retail					Residential Mortgages		
Credit Cards 1	Credit Cards 2	Credit Cards 3	Credit Cards 4	Credit Cards 5	MBS 1	MBS 2	MBS 3
6.67%	4.00%	6.67%	4.23%	4.00%	0.59%	0.59%	0.59%
75%	75%	75%	75%	75%	24%	24%	24%
1	1	1	1	1	1	1	1
24.76%	19.18%	24.76%	19.68%	19.18%	2.58%	2.58%	2.58%
27.81%	20.55%	27.81%	21.25%	20.55%	1.83%	1.83%	1.83%
7.3968%	6.15%	7.40%	6.24%	6.15%	1.01%	1.01%	1.01%
12.96%	11.13%	12.96%	11.29%	11.13%	1.73%	1.73%	1.73%
12.43%	13.62%	12.43%	13.45%	13.62%	20.92%	20.92%	20.92%
15.00%	15.00%	15.00%	15.00%	15.00%	15.00%	15.00%	15.00%
2.3205%	3.22%	2.32%	3.09%	3.22%	8.69%	8.69%	8.69%
3.45%	5.70%	3.45%	5.42%	5.70%	14.19%	14.19%	14.19%
−1	−1	−1	−1	−1	−1	−1	−1
7.3968%	**6.15%**	**7.40%**	**6.24%**	**6.15%**	**1.83%**	**1.83%**	**1.83%**
2.32%	**3.22%**	**2.32%**	**3.09%**	**3.22%**	**15.00%**	**15.00%**	**15.00%**
90.00%	**87.00%**	**88.00%**	**88.00%**	**84.00%**	**89.95%**	**90.14%**	**88.20%**
0.00%	0.00%	0.00%	0.00%	0.00%	**3.94%**	**3.35%**	**2.93%**
5.00%	**5.00%**	**5.00%**	**4.00%**	**7.00%**	0.00%	0.00%	**3.22%**
0.00%	0.00%	0.00%	0.00%	0.00%	**1.48%**	**5.03%**	0.00%
5.00%	**8.00%**	**7.00%**	**8.00%**	**9.00%**	0.00%	0.00%	0.00%
0.00%	0.00%	0.00%	0.00%	0.00%	**3.25%**	0.00%	**3.22%**
0.00%	0.00%	0.00%	0.00%	0.00%	**1.38%**	**1.48%**	**2.44%**
100.00%	**100.00%**	**100.00%**	**100.00%**	**100.00%**	**100.00%**	**100.00%**	**100.00%**
7.02%	*0.00%*	*0.90%*	*0.02%*	*0.00%*	*0.00%*	*0.00%*	*0.00%*
0.00%	0.00%	0.00%	0.00%	0.00%	*0.00%*	*0.00%*	*0.00%*
1025.40%	*47.53%*	*617.02%*	*73.94%*	*10.97%*	0.00%	0.00%	*0.02%*
0.00%	0.00%	0.00%	0.00%	0.00%	*0.26%*	*36.10%*	0.00%
1249.99%	*1043.22%*	*1246.91%*	*1069.73%*	*946.20%*	0.00%	0.00%	0.00%
0.00%	0.00%	0.00%	0.00%	0.00%	*65.43%*	0.00%	*9.40%*
0.00%	0.00%	0.00%	0.00%	0.00%	*896.23%*	*858.85%*	*583.18%*
0.53	*0.00*	*0.04*	*0.00*	*0.00*	*0.00*	*0.00*	*0.00*
15.32%	*0.00%*	*0.36%*	*0.02%*	*0.00%*	*0.00%*	*0.00%*	*0.00%*
0.00%	0.00%	0.00%	0.00%	0.00%	*0.00%*	*0.00%*	*0.00%*
1250.00%	*24.05%*	*552.51%*	*37.71%*	*5.87%*	0.00%	0.00%	*0.01%*
0.00%	0.00%	0.00%	0.00%	0.00%	*0.29%*	*17.70%*	0.00%
1250.00%	*1250.00%*	*1250.00%*	*1250.00%*	*1208.74%*	0.00%	0.00%	0.00%
0.00%	0.00%	0.00%	0.00%	0.00%	*32.68%*	0.00%	*5.34%*
0.00%	0.00%	0.00%	0.00%	0.00%	*1043.00%*	*984.58%*	*626.65%*

Table 2 (Continued)

Supervisory Formula: Floor set to zero							
Aaa	AAA	*0.05%*	*0.02%*	*0.05%*	*0.00%*	*0.00%*	*0.00%*
Aa3	AA−	0.00%	0.00%	0.00%	0.00%	0.00%	0.00%
A1	A+	0.00%	0.00%	0.00%	*400.88%*	*245.30%*	*373.13%*
A2	A	*821.23%*	*748.16%*	*821.23%*	0.00%	0.00%	0.00%
Baa1	BBB	0.00%	0.00%	0.00%	0.00%	0.00%	0.00%
Baa2	BBB−	0.00%	0.00%	0.00%	0.00%	0.00%	0.00%
Unrated	Unrated	*1250.00%*	*1250.00%*	*1250.00%*	*1250.00%*	*1250.00%*	*1250.00%*
RBA							
Aaa	AAA	*7.00%*	*7.00%*	*7.00%*	*7.00%*	*7.00%*	*7.00%*
Aa3	AA−	0.00%	0.00%	0.00%	0.00%	0.00%	0.00%
A1	A+	0.00%	0.00%	0.00%	*325.00%*	*153.00%*	*306.00%*
A2	A	*696.00%*	*624.00%*	*696.00%*	0.00%	0.00%	0.00%
Baa1	BBB	0.00%	0.00%	0.00%	0.00%	0.00%	0.00%
Baa2	BBB−	0.00%	0.00%	0.00%	0.00%	0.00%	0.00%
Unrated	Unrated	*1250.00%*	*1250.00%*	*1250.00%*	*1250.00%*	*1250.00%*	*1250.00%*

2. Risk weights for all triple-A tranches are uniformly very low and well below the floor set up in the SFA formula, which itself produces very low risk weights for those tranches, once the floor is excluded. We note that even when excluding excess spread, risk weights for credit card and mortgage securitisation are well below the floor of 0.56%.
3. The risk weights for mezzanine tranches vary within a very wide range for all asset classes considered, except for mortgage securitisations. It appears that small differences in structures and assumptions could lead to widely divergent risk weights for that part of the ABS capital structure. We particularly note that the risk weights for the mezzanine tranches of RMBS are well below those for other asset classes as well as below those proposed by the regulators.
4. We note the discrepancy in risk weights produced by the SFA on one hand, compared to the results of our industry models on the other – they are somewhat similar for RMBS, much higher for auto loan ABS and divergent for credit card ABS.
5. The unrated tranches in the different asset classes (before inclusion of excess spread) command a wide range of risk weights, often well below the existing requirement for deduction from capital. This suggests that yet another regulatory override, that of deduction of equity tranches, may be devoid of full justification.

0.01%	0.00%	0.00%	0.00%	0.00%	0.00%	0.00%	0.00%
0.00%	0.00%	0.00%	0.00%	0.00%	0.00%	0.00%	0.00%
729.00%	0.98%	229.18%	1.74%	0.02%	0.00%	0.00%	0.00%
0.00%	0.00%	0.00%	0.00%	0.00%	0.00%	141.17%	0.00%
1250.00%	1032.17%	1250.00%	1047.42%	1002.00%	0.00%	0.00%	0.00%
0.00%	0.00%	0.00%	0.00%	0.00%	256.82%	0.00%	8.08%
0.00%	0.00%	0.00%	0.00%	0.00%	1250.00%	1250.00%	1038.58%

7.00%	7.00%	7.00%	7.00%	7.00%	7.00%	7.00%	7.00%
0.00%	0.00%	0.00%	0.00%	0.00%	15.00%	15.00%	15.00%
610.00%	20.00%	118.00%	20.00%	20.00%	0.00%	0.00%	20.00%
0.00%	0.00%	0.00%	0.00%	0.00%	20.00%	106.00%	0.00%
1250.00%	972.00%	1250.00%	1250.00%	947.00%	0.00%	0.00%	0.00%
0.00%	0.00%	0.00%	0.00%	0.00%	100.00%	0.00%	75.00%
0.00%	0.00%	0.00%	0.00%	0.00%	1250.00%	1250.00%	1250.00%

6. The inclusion of excess spread as an unrated tranche leads to significant reduction in risk weights for the mezzanine pieces of all asset classes.
7. It is also surprising to see that credit cards experience PD's between 4–6.7% and correlation of 2–3.2%, while the MBS have PD's of 0.6% and reach a correlation of 15%. From our experience, the average borrower first defaults on his credit card payments, and only as a last option defaults on his mortgage payment. In credit cards the correlation, as suggested by the regulators, is a function of the assumed PD, that is, a lower PD would produce a higher correlation number. In this view, credit card obligors with higher PD's default in a more idiosyncratic fashion than low PD obligors. For example, low-income obligors are affected less by an economic downturn, and more by personal factors. Therefore, their defaults are less systemic and more idiosyncratic. In the context of EC models, this is the same thing as using lower correlation for credit card pools with higher PD.

   On the other hand, RMBS (all with much lower PD than credit cards) face a constant 15% correlation, and do not benefit from the same principle applied above to credit cards. We used the same correlation function used for non-revolving pools (auto loans), and found a further reduction of Risk Weights (as calculated with the Pyhktin–Dev and Perraudin–Peretyakin models)

Table 3 ESF Quant Group – Summary of transactions: ESF Quant Group, RBA, SFA and P – P (with excess spread benefit and trapping mechanisms)

Type		**Other Retail**					
Transaction		Auto Loan 1	Auto Loan 2	Auto Loan 3	Auto Loan 4	Auto Loan 5	Auto Loan 6
Pool PD		0.57%	0.57%	0.57%	0.57%	0.57%	2.78%
Pool LGD		75%	75%	75%	75%	75%	30%
Pool Maturity		5	5	5	5	5	5
Risk Weights							
Corporate (TO > 50)		14.04%	14.04%	14.04%	14.04%	14.04%	9.18%
Residential Mortgages (para 288)		5.53%	5.53%	5.53%	5.53%	5.53%	6.54%
Qualifying revolving exposures (para 289)		3.08%	3.08%	3.08%	3.08%	3.08%	2.25%
Other retail (para 301)		5.28%	5.28%	5.28%	5.28%	5.28%	4.06%
Correlations							
Corporate (TO > 50)		21.04%	21.04%	21.04%	21.04%	21.04%	14.99%
Residential Mortgages (para 288)		15.00%	15.00%	15.00%	15.00%	15.00%	15.00%
Qualifying revolving exposures (para 289)		8.78%	8.78%	8.78%	8.78%	8.78%	4.24%
Other retail (para 291)		14.30%	14.30%	14.30%	14.30%	14.30%	7.67%
N (or –1 indicates retail treatment)		–1	–1	–1	–1	–1	–1
K_IRB		**5.28%**	**5.28%**	**5.28%**	**5.28%**	**5.28%**	**4.06%**
Correlation in pool		**14.30%**	**14.30%**	**14.30%**	**14.30%**	**14.30%**	**7.67%**
Tranche structure							
Aaa	AAA	**92.09%**	**91.87%**	**92.09%**	**89.52%**	**89.62%**	**90.95%**
Aa3	AA–	0.00%	0.00%	0.00%	0.00%	0.00%	0.00%
A1	A+	0.00%	0.00%	0.00%	**5.71%**	**4.72%**	**5.29%**
A2	A	**3.84%**	**3.83%**	**3.84%**	0.00%	0.00%	0.00%
Baa1	BBB	0.00%	0.00%	0.00%	0.00%	0.00%	0.00%
Baa2	BBB–	0.00%	0.00%	0.00%	0.00%	0.00%	0.00%
Unrated	Unrated	**4.07%**	**4.30%**	**4.07%**	**4.77%**	**5.66%**	**3.75%**
		100.000%	**100.000%**	**100.000%**	**100.000%**	**100.000%**	**100.000%**
Perraudin – Peretyatkin or Pyhktin – Dev formula							
Aaa	AAA	*0.62%*	*0.54%*	*0.62%*	*0.11%*	*0.12%*	*0.00%*
Aa3	AA–	0.00%	0.00%	0.00%	0.00%	0.00%	0.00%
A1	A+	0.00%	0.00%	0.00%	*63.58%*	*42.42%*	*34.24%*
A2	A	*135.99%*	*118.50%*	*135.99%*	0.00%	0.00%	0.00%
Baa1	BBB	0.00%	0.00%	0.00%	0.00%	0.00%	0.00%
Baa2	BBB–	0.00%	0.00%	0.00%	0.00%	0.00%	0.00%
Unrated	Unrated	*888.46%*	*858.93%*	*888.46%*	*801.91%*	*704.78%*	*958.03%*
P-P Expected Loss (BP)		*0.03*	*0.02*	*0.03*	*0.01*	*0.01*	*0.00*
ESF Quant Group ULC model							
Aaa	AAA	*0.34%*	*0.30%*	*0.34%*	*0.08%*	*0.09%*	*0.00%*
Aa3	AA–	0.00%	0.00%	0.00%	0.00%	0.00%	0.00%
A1	A+	0.00%	0.00%	0.00%	*32.64%*	*22.37%*	*17.21%*
A2	A	*69.81%*	*60.47%*	*69.81%*	0.00%	0.00%	0.00%
Baa1	BBB	0.00%	0.00%	0.00%	0.00%	0.00%	0.00%
Baa2	BBB–	0.00%	0.00%	0.00%	0.00%	0.00%	0.00%
Unrated	Unrated	*1044.20%*	*997.67%*	*1044.20%*	*913.04%*	*783.67%*	*1233.77%*

	Revolving Retail					Residential Mortgages		
	Credit Cards 1	Credit Cards 2	Credit Cards 3	Credit Cards 4	Credit Cards 5	MBS 1	MBS 2	MBS 3
	6.67%	4.00%	6.67%	4.23%	4.00%	0.59%	0.59%	0.59%
	75%	75%	75%	75%	75%	24%	24%	24%
	1	1	1	1	1	1	1	1
	24.76%	19.18%	24.76%	19.68%	19.18%	2.58%	2.58%	2.58%
	27.81%	20.55%	27.81%	21.25%	20.55%	1.83%	1.83%	1.83%
	7.3968%	6.15%	7.40%	6.24%	6.15%	1.01 %	1.01%	1.01%
	12.96%	11.13%	12.96%	11.29%	11.13%	1.73%	1.73%	1.73%
	12.43%	13.62%	12.43%	13.45%	13.62%	20.92%	20.92%	20.92%
	15.00%	15.00%	15.00%	15.00%	15.00%	15.00%	15.00%	15.00%
	2.3205%	3.22%	2.32%	3.09%	3.22%	8.69%	8.69%	8.69%
	3.45%	5.70%	3.45%	5.42%	5.70%	14.19%	14.19%	14.19%
	−1	−1	−1	−1	−1	−1	−1	−1
	7.3968%	**6.15%**	**7.40%**	**6.24%**	**6.15%**	**1.83%**	**1.83%**	**1.83%**
	2.32%	**3.22%**	**2.32%**	**3.09%**	**3.22%**	**15.00%**	**15.00%**	**15.00%**
	87.80%	**84.88%**	**85.85%**	**85.85%**	**81.95%**	**89.51%**	**89.70%**	**87.77%**
	0.00%	0.00%	0.00%	0.00%	0.00%	**3.92%**	**3.34%**	**2.91%**
	4.88%	**4.88%**	**4.88%**	**3.90%**	**6.83%**	0.00%	0.00%	**3.20%**
	0.00%	0.00%	0.00%	0.00%	0.00%	**1.47%**	**5.00%**	0.00%
	4.88%	**7.80%**	**6.83%**	**7.80%**	**8.78%**	0.00%	0.00%	0.00%
	0.00%	0.00%	0.00%	0.00%	0.00%	**3.24%**	0.00%	**3.20%**
	2.44%	**2.44%**	**2.44%**	**2.45%**	**2.44%**	**1.86%**	**1.96%**	**2.92%**
	100.000%	**100.000%**	**100.000%**	**100.000%**	**100.000%**	**100.000%**	**100.000%**	**100.000%**
	0.70%	0.00%	0.04%	0.00%	0.00%	0.00%	0.00%	0.00%
	0.00%	0.00%	0.00%	0.00%	0.00%	0.00%	0.00%	0.00%
	556.86%	3.01%	183.05%	4.93%	0.51%	0.00%	0.00%	0.01%
	0.00%	0.00%	0.00%	0.00%	0.00%	0.10%	15.17%	0.00%
	1241.31%	707.83%	1160.84%	740.97%	630.82%	0.00%	0.00%	0.00%
	0.00%	0.00%	0.00%	0.00%	0.00%	27.67%	0.00%	3.78%
	1250.00%	1250.00%	1250.00%	1250.00%	1250.00%	731.28%	701.89%	494.99%
	0.03	0.00	0.00	0.00	0.00	0.00	0.00	0.00
	0.28%	0.00%	0.03%	0.00%	0.00%	0.00%	0.00%	0.00%
	0.00%	0.00%	0.00%	0.00%	0.00%	0.00%	0.00%	0.00%
	461.32%	2.03%	101.58%	3.23%	0.43%	0.00%	0.00%	0.01%
	0.00%	0.00%	0.00%	0.00%	0.00%	0.11%	7.70%	0.00%
	1250.00%	937.40%	1250.00%	994.39%	833.56%	0.00%	0.00%	0.00%
	0.00%	0.00%	0.00%	0.00%	0.00%	14.05%	0.00%	5.28%
	1250.00%	1250.00%	1250.00%	1250.00%	1250.00%	806.74%	769.25%	554.20%

Table 3 (Continued)

Supervisory Formula: Floor set to zero							
Aaa	AAA	*0.00%*	*0.00%*	*0.00%*	*0.00%*	*0.00%*	*0.00%*
Aa3	AA−	0.00%	0.00%	0.00%	0.00%	0.00%	0.00%
A1	A+	0.00%	0.00%	0.00%	*203.34%*	*44.66%*	*155.88%*
A2	A	*528.18%*	*455.25%*	*528.18%*	0.00%	0.00%	0.00%
Baa1	BBB	0.00%	0.00%	0.00%	0.00%	0.00%	0.00%
Baa2	BBB−	0.00%	0.00%	0.00%	0.00%	0.00%	0.00%
Unrated	Unrated	*1250.00%*	*1250.00%*	*1250.00%*	*1250.00%*	*1220.79%*	*1250.00%*
RBA							
Aaa	AAA	*7.00%*	*7.00%*	*7.00%*	*7.00%*	*7.00%*	*7.00%*
Aa3	AA−	0.00%	0.00%	0.00%	0.00%	0.00%	0.00%
A1	A+	0.00%	0.00%	0.00%	*131.00%*	*20.00%*	*91.00%*
A2	A	*405.00%*	*332.00%*	*405.00%*	0.00%	0.00%	0.00%
Baa1	BBB	0.00%	0.00%	0.00%	0.00%	0.00%	0.00%
Baa2	BBB−	0.00%	0.00%	0.00%	0.00%	0.00%	0.00%
Unrated	Unrated	*1250.00%*	*1250.00%*	*1250.00%*	*1250.00%*	*1250.00%*	*1250.00%*

for mezzanine and unrated pieces. We believe that lower correlations should be used for the MBS transaction in line with industry practices.

8. Comparing the results calculated with the two industry models in transactions with the same asset type and a very similar capital structure, we are uncomfortable with the wide difference among the calculated risk weights, particularly in the credit card sector.

CONCLUDING REMARKS

Against the background of these results and observations, although we fully understand the limitations of the sample, we believe several key ideas need to be explored further:

1. *There is a need for a proper, risk sensitive calibration of the respective models in order to better reflect the differences in asset classes and avoid the over-charging of senior tranches.* Such sensitivity and calibration can be achieved by differentiating among asset classes and we suggest the particular securitisation exposure categories to include: (a) retail revolving exposures (often containing a large excess spread component flowing back to the originator, and consisting of a highly granular consumer portfolio); (b) non-revolving retail exposures such as auto loans; and (c) residential mortgages (typically secured and also less granular than auto

0.00%	0.00%	0.00%	0.00%	0.00%	0.00%	0.00%	0.00%
0.00%	0.00%	0.00%	0.00%	0.00%	0.00%	0.00%	0.00%
152.85%	0.00%	1.73%	0.00%	0.00%	0.00%	0.00%	0.00%
0.00%	0.00%	0.00%	0.00%	0.00%	0.00%	31.73%	0.00%
1250.00%	668.24%	1001.09%	682.83%	593.65%	0.00%	0.00%	0.00%
0.00%	0.00%	0.00%	0.00%	0.00%	73.31%	0.00%	0.96%
1250.00%	1250.00%	1250.00%	1250.00%	1250.00%	1248.18%	1224.73%	876.57%

7.00%	7.00%	7.00%	7.00%	7.00%	7.00%	7.00%	7.00%
0.00%	0.00%	0.00%	0.00%	0.00%	15.00%	15.00%	15.00%
40.00%	20.00%	20.00%	20.00%	20.00%	0.00%	0.00%	20.00%
0.00%	0.00%	0.00%	0.00%	0.00%	20.00%	20.00%	0.00%
1250.00%	620.00%	921.00%	1250.00%	636.00%	0.00%	0.00%	0.00%
0.00%	0.00%	0.00%	0.00%	0.00%	75.00%	0.00%	75.00%
1250.00%	1250.00%	1250.00%	1250.00%	1250.00%	1250.00%	1250.00%	1250.00%

loans or consumer loans, but more granular than corporate exposures); (d) corporate obligations (as mentioned before calibration of current securitisation risk weights are based on pools of corporate obligations); (e) commercial real estate (while a corporate obligation, it is secured and subject to intra-sector diversification).

2. *Elimination or significant reduction of the floor in the SFA should be considered, as well as the possibility of introducing different floors, if necessary, for different asset classes.* That should be further supported by a significant reduction of risk weights for senior tranches, in view of the modelling results and historical experience.
3. *Further analysis of excess spread should be performed in order for it to be better integrated as a risk mitigant in the securitisation structures, especially given the different roles excess spread can play in different transactions and among asset classes.* While CP3 expressly stated the function of future margin income (FMI) for qualifying revolving retail exposures on the bank's balance sheet, such treatment is not accorded for FMI for other retail assets. Additionally, we believe that an approach applying a 75% haircut and two times the standard deviation of the expected loss rate is overly conservative. Furthermore, the credit given for FMI does not capture the need to take into account the mitigating effect of excess spread for any asset class in a legal framework of a securitisation. Excess spread and unfunded spread/reserve accounts should

be taken into account in certain circumstances based on conservative assumptions.

4. *Additional work needs to be done to address the variations in risk weightings allocated to the mezzanine tranches within and among asset classes.* While we understand the reasons behind the assumption of infinitely thin tranches as a basis for calibration of risk weights for securitisation exposures, we are concerned that such assumption leads to overcharge for senior tranches and high degree of volatility in risk weights for mezzanine tranches. In practice definition of thinness is somewhat subjective and should not be applied only to securitisation but also to corporate and other exposures where there is tranching of the overall obligation.
5. *Additional analysis should be performed to size regulatory capital for "equity" tranches.* There appears to be significant variation in the appropriate risk weights for equity tranches among asset classes and better understanding the role of excess spread puts them in a second, rather than first, loss position. The required deduction from capital is a major contributing factor to lack of capital neutrality in case of securitisation of bank assets.

1 In Risk, 2002.

2 We have collected, from several credit card transactions launched in the European market, data covering a period of 3 years – such data is readily available as credit card indices published by the rating agencies.

3 Performance of the Residential Mortgages 1985–2000, Sep. 2, 2002, Nicholas Lindstrom, Moody's Investors Service.

Index